Elsie at Ebb Tide

Emerging from the Undertow

of Alzheimer's

Elsie at Ebb Tide:
Emerging from the Undertow of Alzheimer's

© 2013 by Bella Barbara Erakko

All Rights Reserved

Except for brief quotations in articles or reviews, no part of this book may be reproduced or transmitted in any form or by any means, electronic or mechanical, or by any information and retrieval system, without prior written permission from the author. For contact information:

www.ElsieAtEbbTide.com

Cover Design: Elsie Watercolor by Brenda Beck Fischer

Cover Concept: Joan Atkins, Caroll Williams, and Pamela York Taylor; Graphic Design by J Barry Wright

Editor: Carolyn Males
Copy Editing: Deb Nichols

Type Font: PoynterGothicText

Dedicated to my mother
who went so unwillingly
into Alzheimer's
yet taught me so much about love
and the eternal dance
between body and spirit

And to every soul
who enters into this strange portal
that pushes past mind
and memory.

Introduction

Elsie Julia Elizabeth Norlund Nurmi
Dancing up Front ... into Life

Introduction

Elsie Nurmi died on Friday, October 13, 2000—enough into the new millennium to firmly plant her feet and say, "I made it" but not long enough to make much of a dent. She was, frankly, demented, one in a long family line of those stricken with Alzheimer's.

I feel, in some ways, those last years were the best for both of us. We had more fun; we laughed more. She resisted the disease with aplomb, insisting she never be told she had it. As her memory faded, she knew enough to ask me to get her a new brain. "Can't you find a doctor for that, Barbara?"

She also knew enough to hurtle her cold fury at me, when I moved her from Florida to Maryland where I could supervise her care, icily telling me, "I *never* used the word 'love' with you. I don't really like you."

I watched her life peel away, like an onion. First to go were the names of friends and her how-to-do-it knowledge. Sandra and I, her two daughters, dropped off the memory tree soon after like overripe fruit. The memory of Herby, her deceased husband, languished for a while, then it too was gone. Last to go and most slowly was the memory of her job and her name.

Elsie Julia Elizabeth Norlund Nurmi, Protocol Officer, U.S. Department of State.

She led American delegations overseas using presidential aircraft. She attended coronations, private audiences with the pope, and met queens. When heads of state visited the United States, she coordinated hotels, food, and travel. In such heady circumstances, what surprised her most were the funny human moments such as handing first lady Lady Bird Johnson a bouquet of flowerless stems.

But then her memory slipped. Was she *in* the motorcade when Kennedy died? In the car behind him? She told everyone who saw the personally signed presidential photos that she was part of history. Only she couldn't quite remember which part. But then it no longer mattered. She forgot it all.

As she forgot *this* world, she began to see into another world. She caught up with old friends visiting from the other side. Strangely, only the deceased paid social calls in this between-land. She'd point them out, frustrated that we couldn't see them.

These forays seemed nice, like postcards from the future, a future we all will encounter one day. Sometimes she brought back important information. One afternoon she told us her brother had died, saying, "I can't stop him. He won't listen to me." The next day, we heard the same news by telephone.

Of course, over time her words began to go to garble-land. Eventually, we had only sweet phrases like "Thank you." "Yes." "No." And "NOOOO!"

~ ~ ~

Elsie's journey into forgetfulness began in Florida with misplaced scissors, lost staplers, forgotten names. Her memory loss took a great leap forward when she traveled to Finland, land of the Midnight Sun. She suddenly didn't know what Finland was, where it was, or how to flush a toilet.

After she collapsed in a doctor's office from dehydration, Elsie finally entered assisted care in the Finnish-American Rest Home, eating *nisua* bread and drinking strong coffee.

The next stamp on her "passport" was to a Maryland facility dedicated to Alzheimer's residents. Although it received a national award as an architectural jewel for the memory impaired, I soon learned the jewel's setting was tarnished. Residents mistakenly entered wrong rooms and battled one another for ownership. Seeing her terrified and losing weight, I moved her into a supervised three-bedroom home. There, a year later, she fell and broke her hip.

When the surgeon advised me she probably had less than a year to live, I transformed my house into a nursing facility, moving myself to a guest bedroom upstairs and relocating my office into a walk-in closet. My mother was coming home.

~ ~ ~

As the thirteen-year-long disease progressed, I began to observe something remarkable happening. Mom became more honest. No longer able to be polite, her ☐eses and noes came from all that was left of her—an unvarnished unadorned soul.

As I sat by her side talking to her as though she were entirely aware, I felt she *was* entirely there—and aware. I conversed with her *spirit*, knowing that it was immutable and simply trapped in a diseased body. Eventually, in the last year of her life when anyone might believe nothing of Elsie remained, I believed *all* of Elsie remained. I was convinced that telepathic modes of communication existed. How else could she know her brother died 24 hours before we did?

We only had to find a way to connect.

Having worked with Kenna, a friend and medical intuitive with over 20 years experience in energy healing techniques, I saw no reason why she couldn't telepathically communicate with my mother. Certainly, I told myself, I'd recognize whether or not an authentic connection occurred. Mom would give me clear clues. Thus began a series of conversations that not only spanned the last nine months of Mom's life but also continued after she passed over.

~ ~ ~

It's been years since Mom died. During that time, friends often asked me to write my story about Mom. I wasn't sure the world needed another book about Alzheimer's, but I also realized ... *this book would be different.*

I instinctively believed my mother's *spirit* remained entirely intact—just blocked by the disease—and I sought *different* ways of communicating with her. It proved beneficial to my mother who was frightened by what was happening, and to my sister and me because we felt a way still existed for us to connect.

As the disease ravaged her body, I saw and felt a pure soul emerging. Quite remarkable, it seemed as shocking in some respects as a caterpillar melting down to liquid in a cocoon only to emerge as a butterfly. The last time I saw her, she gripped my arms and stared at me fiercely. Rather than "lights out," as we commonly say of those with advanced Alzheimer's, I saw a *transcendent light on.*

I'd never received a gaze from "the other side." It shook me to my core and left me in unquenchable awe. I realized something quite remarkable lay buried beneath the rubble of this disease. One could almost *see* body turn into spirit.

~ ~ ~

Elsie at Ebb Tide; Emerging from the Undertow of Alzheimer's is written in many voices: Normal Elsie. Elsie with Alzheimer's. Elsie via the medical intuitive Kenna (we kept word-for-word transcripts of every communication). Elsie through her children, Sandra's and my memories. And why not ask *Elsie* to help write the book? After all, Kenna could still connect with her.

I felt Mom would have valuable information. Specifically I had two questions: First, what would she want to say about her experience with Alzheimer's now that she was on the other side and several years had passed? Second, what would she want caregivers to know?

I decided that not only Kenna, but four psychics with established reputations should be asked to interview Mom for the purposes of this book.

~ ~ ~

Having made that decision, I struggled with how to present Elsie—all of the Elsies. I recalled what happened when the bestseller *Million Broken Pieces* got promoted as nonfiction only to be discredited for having some fictionalized episodes.

I could hardly call this book nonfiction because all I really had were fragments of memories verbally told or extracted from her terse diary entries such as, "We went to school in a covered wagon, and it rolled over. The girl next to me was screaming and I told her to SHUT UP."

Being Elsie's daughter via nature *and* nurture, I decided to simply step into Elsie's shoes—allowing the reader to be with her waking up, hating the cold (true), having breakfast in a wood-stove-heated kitchen (true), and then getting into the covered wagon. Fictionalized reality.

Obviously, readers have to decide how much of Elsie's otherworldly stories are valid according to their worldview. But one thing you can count on as real: My story. What I felt about having a mother get Alzheimer's. How I coped. What I did.

As my friends watched their parents succumb, they often commented, "You really helped me to look at things so differently."

I never saw Alzheimer's as a "dread disease." I always saw Elsie as whole and intact, present and real. I talked to her that way. I felt as though her true complete self hovered in and around this diseased body—listening, watching, enjoying, not quite ready to say good-bye.

I knew, as did my sister Sandra, that when she decided to go, it would be fast. Kenna accompanied her telepathically when the crisis came and Mom was being transported by ambulance to the hospital. In pain and realizing life had little more to offer her except more pain, she told Kenna, "No wonder people die. To get some rest!"

And an hour later, poof! She was gone. Passport expired.

Who's Who?

Every Alzheimer's book I've reviewed deals with the story chronologically. But the actual experience of the person suffering dementia is anything but orderly. Instinctively I wanted the reader to have a controlled *experience* of Alzheimer's.

One winter day I sat on my sofa leafing through one of Mom's diaries. She assiduously recorded daily events, mostly shopping bargains, visits with friends, and her social calendar. It was a sleepy afternoon. After a while, I fell into a sort of silent reverie, staring peacefully at the glowing flames in my fireplace. With my mind quieted, inspiration unexpectedly struck with the words: *Write the book as though it were a calendar but without the years*.

I jumped up, pacing back and forth. Perhaps Mom could become revealed through vignettes written about different times in her life. On any given day, she could be elder Elsie, child Elsie, career Elsie, confused Elsie. After all, our healthy memories work this way. Even in the course of a few minutes, our minds move from past to future to present. We are not so unlike people with early Alzheimer's except that when asked, we can provide the time and place.

I quickly realized, however, that the progression of the disease itself must move chronologically through the pages so that we see her falter, need assistance, then succumb to full-blown care. One could not see Elsie bedridden one day, and then on the next see her merely being forgetful. Otherwise, Elsie's life and personality—coherent and incoherent—emerge as though from an artist's brush, stroke by stroke, until her story is complete.

Because I chose this approach, I occasionally had to move events to earlier or later months than they actually occurred. For example, President Johnson's trip to the Philippines occurred in November, but I placed it in September so it would be presented before the end of Mom's life, not after.

~ ~ ~

Knowing the reader needs a bit of a head start, a brief description of each family member whose life is interwoven throughout this story follows. A detailed life chronology for Elsie appears at the end of this book.

ELSIE AT EBB TIDE

Elsie (1917-2000)

The heroine of her own life, Elsie writes letters to herself as a child and stuffs them into the barn wall until one year the mice eat them. Speaking only Finnish, she rides in a horse-drawn covered wagon to a two-room school in Finlayson, Minnesota, but ends up flying on Air Force Two—so named when the U.S. president is not on board.

She leaves Minnesota at the age of 19, ending her nanny job and her attendance at the Duluth Business School, when offered a free ride to New York City, to become a live-in "butler's girl" for a Wall Street executive whose family lives on Long Island. Using her meager earnings, she continues business school, garnering shorthand skills, and launches herself through seven clerical jobs in rapid succession.

Meanwhile, she dances the schottische at the Harlem Finnish Dance Hall and meets Herby—the man who turns every Finnish girl's eye.

When he disappears mysteriously from her life, she takes federal employment with the Census Bureau in Washington, D.C. Months later, after grieving and burying his mother, Herby shows up unexpectedly on her doorstep. Marriage soon follows and she continues in the workplace until their first child Sandra is born, and two years later, Barbara.

Rejoining the federal work force with the excuse she needs Christmas money, Elsie works for the Panama Canal offices in D.C., then at the State Department.

There, she inventories gifts given to U.S. citizens by foreign governments, eventually moving to the Office of Protocol. As a behind-the-scenes Protocol Officer, she manages foreign state visits to the United States and presidential delegations abroad, flying to every continent except Antarctica.

Accompanying the official delegations, she meets queens, kings, popes, heads of state, and even a would-be assassin. She oversees dinners, and maintains a "security system" allowing access to White House grounds—a custom-designed enamel lapel pin.

After twenty-five years, she retires with Herby to Florida. Eventually widowed and after a lifetime of travel, she faces a journey she never expected—one into mindlessness. Yet it becomes her most transcendent destination.

She holds onto life until Friday, October 13, 2000, then lets go of it in a lightning flash.

Herby (1913-1987)

Baptized Urjo Mertaniemi by his single, Finnish-born mother Ida in New York City, he has everything—intelligence, good looks, and a U.S. passport. Unable to support him, Ida returns to her parent's Finnish farm, only to become embroiled in Finland's Civil War.

Growing up during wartime, Urjo survives on birchbark bread. Upon returning to New York City (and being advised to take a more Americanized name), he becomes Herbert *Nurmi* (his new surname matching the world renown Olympic Finnish runner).

He leaves school at age 14 to crew sailing vessels carrying cargo between North and South America.

After burying his 47-year-old mother, he marries Elsie. When her career takes off, he tells her, "You have the best damned job in the world. I'll take care of the kids." Considered by many a genius without a degree, he reads voraciously, argues intelligently, raises two daughters, and provides an income as a self-employed carpenter. Many years later sensing his end, he settles Elsie safely with a new car and a home security system, and dies.

Sandra (1945-)

She bursts out of Elsie's womb like a sun-princess. Never once does it occur to her that she isn't radiant, fabulous, and perfect. When elementary school annoys her, she explains she has to go home at lunch every day to feed her sick grandmother (who lives 1,200 miles away). She hikes, explores caves, motorcycles her way through college, and graduates speaking Russian and Spanish.

Realizing she has good hips for childbearing, she marries "good genes" and over the year launches four boys into a world where they dig clams, skin animals, and tear apart anything mechanical.

Changing gears from genes to true love, she marries a second time, learns how to repair small aircraft, becomes an electrical engineer, works for the U.S. Navy, takes private Chinese lessons, clogs, and lives happily ever after in the house her husband builds by hand.

Barbara (1947-)

Unlike Sandra, when Barbara finds herself suddenly birthed, she immediately realizes earth life isn't nearly as comfy as womb life. Crabbing her little legs to her butt, she cosmically screams, *Beam me back up!* But it is too late.

She wears a perpetually puckered expression of worry throughout her childhood. But eventually as an adult she tells herself, *You went to all the trouble to get a human body. Get into it!* This mental conversation, much to her surprise, works. She finds friends, love, and laughter well worth the journey.

The sole dreamer among the logical intelligent practical Nurmis, she also explores caves and hikes her way through college garnering a library science degree. She marries young, designs some of the first automated systems for government and business libraries, and parents two sisters adopted from Korea.

ELSIE AT EBB TIDE

Although the marriage doesn't last, the friendship does, and she goes on to write two books, weave customized prayer shawls, and develop a jewelry business employing women in fragile circumstances. She discovers that she enjoys looking at the world differently so ... she never beams herself up.

January

The Journey Begins

January 1

Married Barbara ~ 1977 ~ You Can't Steal Memories

"Bill, the front door's ajar."

I look worriedly at my parent's house as we pull up. Mom and Dad now spend their winters in Florida. Bill and I check on their gray asbestos-sided house in Takoma Park, Maryland, just outside D.C., once a week.

We quickly walk under the rusty arbor, past the aging spruce trees, and up the brick steps. I look at the shattered wood around the brass latch, and push the white door open to the living room.

Everything seems okay. The desert cactus painting I hate still hangs over the French Provincial sofa; the drop leaf table where I did homework rests by the window; the baby grand piano sits tucked beneath the staircase. But we already know everything is *not* okay.

Bill and I slowly walk through the robbed house and see dresser drawers thrown on the floor, closet clothes in heaps, storage containers emptied out. Even the kitchen drawers have been ravaged.

"Boy," I turn to Bill, "how do we tell my parents?"

I walk back into the untouched living room, and plunk a few out-of-tune keys on the baby grand piano. It seems to anchor the living room in safety because of its sheer size. Atop it are the familiar signed black-and-white photographs.

I pick up the personally autographed Jack and Jacqueline Kennedy photo, the crown jewel of Mom's collection. I absentmindedly wipe dust off its frame. The piano is covered with twenty-five years of such photos: presidents, secretaries of state, foreign leaders.

"Well," I sigh, knowing the clean-up task ahead of us, "at least they can't steal Mom's memories. ..."

Retired Elsie ~ 1975 ~ A Christmas Letter

Dear Mim,

A belated Merry Christmas. Now at last I have time to drop you a note. Frankly, I feel like an unshelled crab. I have no place to go tomorrow. Nothing to do. After twenty-five years of having a glamorous life ... After all, I met the Kennedys, Nixon, Johnson, Bush, Reagan, Kissinger, Astronaut Borman—even Pope Paul VI.

I officially retire from the State Department on the 4th, but my desk is empty. I know it's the right decision. Herby gave me the career of my life when he promised he'd watch the kids and that I had "the best dammed job in the world."

Living in Takoma Park was perfect for my job, being on the north edge of D.C. The city's fortunes sure have risen since you moved. We were all blue collar then, weren't we? Now you can hardly afford the historic homes in downtown Takoma—they're being snatched up by federal employees who want a quick subway commute.

And imagine having a husband like Herby. There I'd be—calling Sandra and Barbara from the Philippines, or from the presidential aircraft just to see if they were doing their homework. Ah, *vanhoja hyviä aikoja*—the good old days.

But honestly, I felt a bit guilty especially after Herby retired. There he was, sitting home alone all day. He's sacrificed enough for my career. It's time for us to have a regular life together.

Herby took me outside early this morning before I even had my first cup of coffee. He blindfolded me and led me to the sidewalk before he took it off. WOWEEE—there was our camper all loaded and ready to go. He told me, "We're leaving tomorrow, Elsie."

He even went to the grocery store to buy food, and he put my clothes into the closets. "We're heading to Key West, and then ... who knows! That's the point of being retired. I can get used to this."

Married Barbara ~ 1968 ~ Winter Camping

"Wake up," Bill nudges my sleeping bag. I snuggle deeper into my down nest in our two-person tent resting on top of a foot of snow. This is our second winter camping experience.

Only my nose sticks out—it is that cold. I have *no* interest in greeting the New Year by unzipping my bag but I have to admit this experience beats last winter. That time, I crawled out of my bag to begin breakfast. I reached into my backpack to get the water bottle to start boiling water. My first "Oh no!" came when the water failed to slush. It was frozen solid. I dug out the oranges—now solid missiles I could shatter against a tree. I was hungry—and had *nothing* to eat.

That day my leather boots were frozen, my hands numb. We backpacked out, drove to the nearest restaurant, and I swore to Bill, "I will *never* go winter camping again."

But persistent Bill bought goose-down kits to make us subzero down jackets, down vests, down booties, down gloves, and he doggedly—without one kind word from me—sewed our winter gear. I didn't have the heart to turn down his request to try it "just one more time." Last night, we thoughtfully refined our wake-up routine. I put our water bottle and oranges into my down sleeping bag at night, using my body heat to keep them thawed. We placed the camp stove right outside the tent door so we could cook while still in our sleeping bags.

With breakfast finished, Bill encourages me, "Let's go." We leap out of our bags, quickly jump into our down booties and jackets pulling on our down gloves. We are blue-stuffed Eskimos flapping our bulky arms around, delighted with our warmth.

Amazingly, I love *this* winter camping experience: the blanket of snow smothering sound into silence, the brilliant blue sky above us, the crisp quiet weather with not even a hint of wind—the *stillness* of it all. The day seems open and endless.

Really, it *feels* as if a new year has been born.

Mother Elsie ~ 1961 ~ Rescuing a Babysitter

We went to the Smith's for their New Year's Eve party after dropping Barbara off to babysit the Svenson kids.

Ralph and Herby fired their rifles at midnight. Then I looked up the street and whom should I see? Barbara! Padding down in her bedroom slippers and plaid bathrobe.

She locked herself out.

She had gone outside to listen to the firecrackers and guns and shut the door so the kids wouldn't wake up. When she tried to get back in (it was *cold* outside) she realized she locked herself out.

Gus walked her back up and let her in. Well, it's hard to believe she's an apple off my tree. Maybe Herby's.

Caregiver Barbara ~ 2006 ~ Elsie at Ebb Tide

"I'm so glad you made it," Marilyn greets me. Taking my arm, she whispers, "Can you talk to Jim," pointing to a silver-haired man, his red-veined face speaking of scotch and martinis. "His wife has Alzheimer's. He got so exhausted caregiving, he collapsed. They hospitalized him. His daughter has taken her mother home with her to Florida. He's really upset."

I walk over, wondering if I'm intruding.

"My daughter stole my wife from me," he grouses as soon as I introduce myself.

I sigh with compassion. That is the way it is with Alzheimer's. Weighed with woe and loss, all he has left is the love he remembers.

~ ~ ~

One of the great problems with Alzheimer's comes to this—we think a solution exists and often believe we are the solution. Our care, love, and determination magically will rescue our beloved from this curse. We determine never to give up or abandon them to a nursing home.

This man got so mad at his daughter that he refused to speak to her. Now, his greatest anguish, his unabated guilt, is that he failed his marriage vow "in sickness and health till death do us part." Yet beneath the distress, there is one admission of relief: "*I am enjoying the break.*"

~ ~ ~

Before his daughter stepped in, he probably felt as though he and his wife were in a leaky rowboat alone in the middle of a very big lake. They had spent an entire life together in their sturdy rowboat, going here, going there, sometimes rowing together, sometimes rowing apart. That is marriage.

But then disease sprung a leak in the boat. Water seeped in, making it increasingly hard to maneuver. He bailed while she sat helpless, feet sloshed by slowly filling water, and the boat stayed afloat for awhile. But it went nowhere. No energy existed to row. That is how the marriage now goes, bound to the vow, "I'll never leave you."

Slowly it sinks beneath the surface.

~ ~ ~

If he sees this as an absolute tragedy, which it certainly is, then all of his reactions coalesce into save-and-rescue actions. It is like a tornado has struck his house, and he is gluing wood splinters back together to rebuild the frame.

But if he pauses and looks closely at his loved one, he may happen to notice something quite extraordinary. Her self-control, her socially acceptable guises, her false words begin to fall away. She can't *remember* how to camouflage her soul. He might begin to see that, like a flower at last emerging from its protective shell, she is stepping into a space between earth and heaven. If he simply sits by her side, perhaps holding her hand, he might be startled to see a transmutation from body to spirit.

Then he can love in a different way. An entirely different way. Because he *sees* in a different way, with deeper eyes—eyes that can witness the incredible beauty at the core of her spirit.

~ ~ ~

When my mother began to experience memory loss, one of the first things to go was her determined politeness.

Politeness serves as a societal lubricant. We fit into society, using politeness as the balm to squeeze through awkward and sometimes angry situations. That's what humans in society do. It seems essential and, as mothers and fathers, we determinedly pass on this social survival skill to our offspring. Then we die.

If we die too quickly with our armor of politeness intact, we lose the opportunity to experience telling our unvarnished truth, politeness be dammed. And everyone around us loses the opportunity to see a soul unveiled. *What made her tick? What is the core of her?*

But with Alzheimer's, one is allowed the grace of a stroll across a long, long bridge. The person who has the disease is drawn, as if in slow motion, into the Unknown.

~ ~ ~

My mother was a very organized woman but she *looked* carefree. She walked with no-nonsense briskness, but as though she were heading to a party. She wore tailored clothing to work but rarely in traditional business colors of black, gray, navy, or forest green. Her trim 5' 7" figure seemed to dance with life, her blue eyes twinkled, and not even her blonde hair obeyed strict coiffure. She loved action; she liked being in the middle of it; and she had a mind like a twenty-drawer filing cabinet—perfect for a State Department Protocol Officer.

She arranged delegations from foreign countries to the United States where kings, queens, and heads of state would meet the president. She coordinated the limousine processions down Pennsylvania Avenue. She managed hotel reservations, room assignments, meals, dietary restrictions, and touring agendas. Often she accompanied them on their U.S. tours becoming their diplomatic concierge. Eventually she began to accompany presidential delegations overseas—American leaders attending a king's death, a coronation, a dedication, a goodwill tour. These trips required the use of Air Force One, dubbed Air Force Two when the president was not on board.

When in retirement her memory began to slip, she wrote things down and taped them to walls, counters—anywhere that was near. Using her protocol skills, she arranged her hundred or so shoes in boxes, making an index card for each one.

When I visited her in Florida, she insisted I put everything back *exactly* where I found it. Nevertheless, an endless abundance of combs, staplers, or scissors blossomed in the house because she couldn't remember where she had put the last one. Money got put into manila folders, jewelry and coins into hidden cavities in the wall.

~ ~ ~

We can see tragedy, or we can enter into a strange kind of openness. Because in some forms of the Alzheimer's disease—not all—what happens is a *diminishment*, an ebbing away. As the loved one begins to shed the societal shell, slowly the granite-strong truth of their inner spirit and character emerges. They literally begin to glow, shining brighter and brighter.

One of our family's favorite photos shows my mother as a young woman. She has written her name *Elsie* in huge cursive letters on the beach. She dances in the water wearing a blue print dress. She looks back to shore, to her name boldly proclaimed on the beach. Nothing shows her spirit more clearly.

Yet the incoming tide will wash away *Elsie*. And at the ebb tide of her life, the woman once known as Elsie will also seem to disappear. But will her essence, her "Elsie-ness," be lost?

Eventually my mother no longer has the resources to pretend. She becomes her truest self, acting out of the basic material of her deepest, most strongly held beliefs. The conversations become simple and direct:

"Do you want to go to bed now?"

"No."

"Can I comb your hair?"

"Oh, that would be nice."

When I walk into her room sometimes, she opens her arms wide. Her eyes light up with joy. "Oh, come here." And her simian-grip fingers inch their way up my healthy 50-year old tanned skin until she can pull me down for a hug.

My *Finnish-American* mother—the woman who never hugged.

~ ~ ~

Back at the party, Jim lifts the lid of the ice chest telling me, "I'm ready for another glass of wine." And he adds, "I'm on depression medication. It isn't doing a thing. I think a martini is better. At least I feel better for a little while."

Retired Elsie ~ 1982 ~ Florida Diary

Watered honeybell, washed hair, defrosted refrig. Went to flea market and bought $4 typing table, $4 denim cotton shirt for Herby, & duct tape 75¢. Helen came along.

College Barbara ~ 1967 ~ Engaging Silence

Mom still isn't talking to me. It's like I don't exist, my engagement doesn't exist, Bill doesn't exist. She's *never* treated me this way. I keep replaying the scene. Bill gave me the most beautiful engagement ring on Christmas Eve, one we picked out together.

I'm so happy. Whenever I'm with Bill, I just relax. I first met him in Harper's Ferry, West Virginia. The Trail Club was digging out a virgin passage in a cave reported to once harbor John Brown's weapons. When Bill and I weren't digging, we sat scrunched in a small cavern and talked. I enjoyed listening to his low calm voice. I thought him handsome—tall and slender, light complexioned with brown hair and blue-gray eyes.

He's always upbeat and calm. I'm high strung. He settles me down and makes me laugh. I feel as though this is where I belong, even though I'm only 19.

It honestly didn't occur to me Mom and Dad might not be overjoyed—mostly because I did not give their reaction one single thought. I was in *love*.

When I went into the kitchen, Mom stood over the gas stove wearing her flower-patterned apron cooking hamburgers. Dad sat at the yellow Formica table smoking, with the newspaper spread in front of him. I soared in, thrust my hand between Mom's eyes and the hamburgers, shouting, "I'M ENGAGED!"

Absolute dead silence greeted me. Mom didn't turn to me. She didn't stop. As the silence grew longer, I quietly removed my hand. About to burst into tears, I saw my father get up. He walked over, hugged me and said, "Congratulations, Barbara."

I ran out of the kitchen to the only person who seemed to love me, and burst into tears. Standing in the living room waiting, Bill tucked me into his arms as calm as I was shattered. "It's okay, Barbara. Maybe you caught them by surprise. Give them some time. Do you want me to leave?"

I said, "Maybe that's best."

After he was gone, Dad came out of the kitchen. "Barbara, your mother wanted a college degree for you. That's what's upsetting her."

"I'll GET one," I blindly promised. How, I didn't know. In a few months, Bill would be drafted and likely sent to Vietnam. Who knows where I'd be living. I could see, through Mom's eyes, her shock. I'd be a GI wife with babies in diapers living in a barracks somewhere. Years later, I'd understand even more. She *knew* what it cost her to become a Protocol Officer. With only a high school diploma, the federal government required four *years* of employment to equate to one year of college. Mom sacrificed sixteen years waiting for a job she *knew* she could do all because she lacked a degree. Now I chose Bill over a baccalaureate. Or so it seemed.

She couldn't say anything nice so she said nothing. The silence lasted until I got married and left home.

Months later, I called her, ecstatic: "He's not going to Vietnam," I yelled. "I can graduate."

And I did. With honors.

Sister Sandra ~ 1984 ~ The Bunny Arrives

"Come *on,* Mom," Lisa insists tugging my hand. She is now 4 years old. Bill and I have learned to hold onto Lisa's hand because her feet seem to have minds of their own. She often goes flying and lands in a wailing heap. Her older sister Kendra has already dashed ahead.

We are waiting for my sister Sandra, her husband Ed, and the boys Mitch and Kier to arrive from Seattle. As we walk down the long ramp at the Baltimore-Washington airport, Kendra starts to shout, "THERE SHE IS!" Speechless, I watch as my sister skips up the corridor wearing a white fluffy coat ... a white fluffy hat ... white ski pants and white boots ... with white fluffy fur.

"She looks like a BUNNY, Mom!" Lisa screams.

Yes, the monochrome bunny girl. When she became an electrical engineer for the U.S. Navy, she decided life made more sense (to her) if her top, pants, and socks matched for the day. It could be a blue day or green day, often a red day, sometimes a black day. Years and then decades would pass without a single lapse. Today, it is *bunny* day, and it will be the first time my daughters truly get to know their aunt.

Actually they met her two years earlier, but that occurred during a layover the day we brought our newly adopted daughters (two- and four-year-old sisters) home from Korea.

"Barbara," Sandra began in her practical way, "you need to know how to wash your kids. I'm going to teach you."

Exhausted by the flight, emotionally drained from the roller-coaster high of seeing our children for the first time, I could care less about bathing. But soon I am sitting on Sandra's toilet as she kneels by the tub and turns the faucet on.

She grabs the naked Lisa, stands her in the tub, suds her from neck to toe, takes the detachable showerhead and sprays her clean (all the while Lisa is screaming). She flips her onto her back, cradles her head, soaps her face and wipes it with a washcloth.

For the finale, she squirts shampoo on her hair, rubs it vigorously, throws her head under the spigot—and in two minutes, Lisa is washed. She has entered and exited the Sandra Wash-O-Mat for Kids.

Now the vibrant bunny, trailed by her husband and sons, takes BWI Airport by ... white.

January 18

Caregiver Barbara ~ 1992 ~ First Signs

"Sandra," I call my sister long distance from Maryland when the kids are at school and Bill's at work. I'm on the kitchen phone pacing back and forth to ease my anxiety. "I'm worried about Mom."

"Why?" Sandra's sunny voice suddenly turns serious. In our family, Sandra and Mom vie for the position of first-class worrier. Growing up, I instinctively knew they were my first-alert warning system so I didn't have to bother. But now, I'm alarmed.

"Every time I talk to her," I try to put words to this vague anxiety, "she tells me how she is worried about her mind. That's not Mom. She never talks about her health. I just realized this has been going on for months. She talks about losing things. Making lists. Taping telephone numbers to the kitchen cabinet. I keep telling her that's normal. I do the same kinds of things. But this morning, I sat down and went through all those conversations. The point is she *never, ever* talks about that stuff. Health stuff."

"Yeah," Sandra agrees. "It's definitely not a Finn thing to complain." We'd eventually find out she'd cracked a rib, had a tooth pulled, gotten very sick for two weeks—but never when it was going on. Now that Dad has died, she has no one to talk to except us. And it seems we are about as sensitive as Finnish rye crackers without butter.

"I think she should be tested for Alzheimer's."

"Oh boy, she's really going to like that, Barbara." I hear Sandra's voice change in pitch—higher and tighter.

"Well, I've been researching," I say with forced hope. "It might be malnutrition. I think when you get older you just go with those instant meals and ice cream and stuff. She's sure not gaining any weight. I bet she skips meals all the time.

Or she might be having ministrokes, those TIAs, and that would affect her memory. But those things can be fixed. Maybe she'd listen." Even as I'm suggesting solutions, I fear the worst— Alzheimer's.

"Maybe," Sandra agrees. "Good luck."

~ ~ ~

So I wait. Until the next conversation. The next time she worries I ask, "Mom, why don't you get tested? Broward Hospital has this three-day process. They look for all sorts of things. It might be fixable—there are lots of causes."

I hear a long silence. Finally she says, "I'll go—but I *don't* want any diagnosis of *Alzheimer's*." In my mind, I see her on the kitchen phone, her mouth tightening, her eyes taking on a fierceness. I *know* she'd never go unless she was at stage-ten anxiety. We have Alzheimer's in our family. Her mother. Her uncle.

"I'll set the appointments for next month, Mom. It'll be okay. This is a good thing. Lots of things can be fixed. I'll fly down to Lake Worth and go with you." I hear the false cheeriness in my voice. Neither of us believes it's a good thing.

"Okay Barbara. ..." Soft anxiety floats in the air after I've hung up.

Child Elsie ~ 1927 ~ Black Bag Babies in Duluth

In the 1920s, few women, especially immigrant women, went to hospitals to have their babies. "Open the door when the doctor comes," my mother tells me, "and stay downstairs with Swante and Lucy." So I do. I let the doctor into the house. He carries a black bag with him.

I show him the room my mother is in, and then we three kids draw pictures at the kitchen table.

Mom told me that if we get hungry, there is food in the icebox. So we eat some rice pudding and drink some milk. Then we run outside and play in the snow for awhile. Mom told me, no matter what, not to bother her or the doctor.

I am brushing the snow off our coats when the doctor with the black bag leaves. Inside that bag—this is what I am told—was our new sister Alice. I take one look at her. She is small enough to fit into the bag. I wonder how she kept so quiet when the doctor brought her in. I'd be squalling like crazy—locked up in a dark black bag like that. We could have saved a lot of time if the doctor had just opened up his bag and given Mom the baby and left.

Career Elsie ~ 1946 ~
Gifts from Princes, Kings, and Queens
[A job description from Elsie's resume]

"Under the general supervision of the Assistant Chief of Protocol, I have charge of the extremely accurate and responsible work involved in the recording, administration, and maintenance of the records of persons entitled to the privileges and immunities in accordance with Public Law 291, 79th Congress and also the Headquarters Agreement as set forth in Public Law 357, 80th Congress, approved by the president August 4, 1947, effective November 21, 1947.

"Specifically, I have the immediate responsibility for the accurate functioning and expeditious processing of the work involved in maintaining the obligation which this Government incurred with the passing of the above mentioned legislation, which requires that no person shall be entitled to the benefits [of a gift given by a foreign government to a U.S. Citizen] unless he shall have been notified by the Secretary of State and accepted as such. In view of the delicate nature of these records ... which are used in arranging with Customs and Internal Revenue for free entry, customs courtesies, tax exemption purposes ... it is of the utmost importance that accurate, up-to-date records be maintained."

~ ~ ~

In plain English, this means that when Americans represent the president of the United States government overseas in an official capacity, and a gift is given to them by the hosting nation, they cannot take it home in their suitcase. It must be registered and left in a secured Gifts Department vault at the State Department.

And there it will stay until released by a Congressional Bill signed into law by a U.S. president.

Child Barbara ~ 1955 ~ King George

"I'm home," Mom hollers as she opens the door. "Herby, can you bring in the box from the car. It's large."

"What's in it?" Sandra and I begin to hover around the door. A present? Probably not. We are a blue-collar family on a tight budget. We watch Dad go to the car, open the tailgate, and carry in an enormous cardboard box.

That's how King George comes to live at Cockerille Avenue.

Elsie, in accord with her U.S. State Department job description, was ordered to "dump this animal skin in the incinerator." Presumably the gift recipient did not *want* an uncured, somewhat fossilized ocelot from Columbia whose eyes were so hard and chalky they were prone to losing tiny bits when shaken. Dutifully, Elsie wheeled the hide toward the incinerator in the basement. (Which, coincidentally, happened to be very close to her car.) ...

Nobody called him King George at the time. But Dad tacked him up diagonally on the wall in the tiny den where Mom had her after-work cocktail with Dad. Here Sandra and I heroically stood beneath the spotted ocelot whose creepy white eyes stared mercilessly down upon us. Here we made all of our childhood requests: to play another hour outside, watch TV, eat ice cream.

Two decades later our parents informed us: "We're moving to Florida."

~ ~ ~

ELSIE AT EBB TIDE

"I *love* that ocelot," Sandra insists over the phone, 3,000 miles away. "Can you guys store him for me until I get to Maryland next time?" Of course Bill and I agree. We untack him. "Wow!" I say, shocked by the smoke-free white wall beneath his skin. "We could have avoided a lot of secondary cigarette smoke if we'd been better friends with this guy and crawled under his hairy hide."

Bill artistically drapes him over a wooden sawhorse in our basement and another ten years pass until Sandra decides she does *not* want a crappy untanned ocelot skin. Bill suggests I dump him—only slightly delaying his original destination to the incinerator.

But now I have trouble letting go. I want to "place" him in a good home. What better spot than with my parish priest who, after all, has dead *fish* mounted on his wall?

"Dick," I enthusiastically suggest one day, "wouldn't you like to have an ocelot skin? He's a bit dry, but surely a taxidermist can soften his pelt." I envision a soft spotty animal with black glassy eyes, king of the jungle. King George! Father Dick, not yet having seen the pelt, agrees.

I prop him over the back seat of my station wagon so George can survey his kingdom as we drive to the skin specialist. We arrive. I unlock the tailgate and lift it. The taxidermist feels the pelt, stares at George's head, looks into his chalky eyes. … "Maybe if we cut off his head," he suggests without hope.

WHAT? Decapitate King George??? By now, twenty-five YEARS of love flow through my veins. THIS was the ocelot I grew up beneath. He might be ugly, but he was ours. I shut the station wagon door. King George is coming back with us.

Silence ensues.

After some time, I turn to my parish priest. "He is still a fine-looking ocelot," I say. I feel King George's fortunes diminishing in the prolonged pause as Dick searches for just the right pastoral words: "Maybe you should put him in the dumpster."

So that's what we do. We prop him alluringly over the green dumpster at church. I am SURE someone will want him—perhaps Sarah, the parish administrator. ... "He's a bit tough," I tell her, "and his eyes are a bit cloudy, but he's rare, he's exotic. He's King George!"

She enthusiastically calls her husband. I quickly leave. I really want to think that maybe, just maybe, King George has found his kingdom.

Retired Elsie ~ 1992 ~ Orange Theft!

I guess the thieves who stole our oranges didn't like the poor quality and threw them back over our fence. Indian givers.

Barbara called—she and my sister Alice plan to visit Finland. Do I want to go? I said yes and spent most of the day checking Delta Airlines.

Curious Barbara ~ 1995 ~
Trying Something New in Key West

I gaze out the car window with the ecstasy only a frozen snowbird can feel as I head out of Miami to transverse the Keys. I called Rosemary, my artist friend who lives three blocks from Ernest Hemingway's home before leaving. "I'll be there in about four hours."

Now I find myself amazed by the intensely turquoise waters as I concentrate on driving down this endless two-lane road. I even enjoy the rotten-fish smell that sometimes floats through my window.

As I drive, I think about Rosemary's unusual life. Once married to a disc jockey who became a medical-magazine salesman and eventually launched his own magazine, Rosemary went from frugal housewife and salaried nurse to a woman in fur and pearls. But now, decades later, her husband deceased, her children grown, she lives in an eclectic cottage with her own art studio filled with large colorful canvases.

What alternative healing thing is she into now? I wonder as I drive through the Keys. Once I asked her if she had any medical insurance. "No," she answered, "I use that money to keep myself healthy." Diet and bodywork constituted her insurance policy. Now she is in her late sixties and still healthy, vibrant, and alive.

I make a rash decision. *Whatever she is into, I'll try it.* I know it'll be different, interesting, perhaps even helpful. Just two days earlier, as I had been on my exercise mat doing leg lifts, I noticed an anomaly in my body. *Well, I'll mention it to Rosemary.* Soon, I pull into her grass-and-gravel driveway.

Rosemary, her face framed in wavy dark hair with silver streaks, opens the door, her smile lighting up her dark brown eyes. I walk into her magical house.

Right in front of me, on the wall, a huge vibrant-colored horse cut out of paper fills an area over six feet in length. Everywhere I turn, I see the color and light of an artist radiating out of this home. Each dining-room chair has its own painted design; the tiled table pops with energy. Soon I sit down to a splendid dinner of steamed shrimp and salad, replete with wine. I clean my plate, look apologetically at Rosemary and sheepishly admit, "I need carbohydrates or I'll die!"

Rosemary immediately leaps out of her chair. "Oh, Barbara, I read this amazing book, grabbing *Eat Right for Your Type* off her cookbook shelf. "I have the oldest human blood, Type O, and we're the hunter-gatherers so we thrive on meat and raw vegetables. What's your blood type?"

"I'm A positive. What am I supposed to eat?"

"Oh, you're the next one that evolved, when the hunters started to plant grain. You need … carbohydrates." She laughs, rummages through her cabinets, finds brown rice, and fixes me a pot.

Later as we sit in her living room under magnificent pieces of collage and abstract art, I ask, "So what type of healing are you doing these days?"

"Ohhhh, Barbara," she exclaims. "I've been working with an energy healer. She's *wonderful*."

"Yeah, but what is energy healing?"

She walks over to her birch wood bookcase and pulls off *Hands of Light* by Barbara Brennan, handing me a book with an image of light pouring out of cupped hands on the cover. As I flip through the pages, she tries to explain.

"She grew up on a Wisconsin farm and often went into the woods by herself. She would sit very still—even animals would approach her. Over time she learned she could sense things—like closing her eyes and knowing where a tree would be before she could touch it. The more she did it, the better she got.

"It was like she was feeling the *energy* of the trees and the animals." Rosemary took the book and opened it to a well-marked page. "She was sensing their energy auras, and she used the example of candle light to explain it. Here it is: 'Consider the candle and its flame. ... Where does the light begin and where does the flame end? There seems to be a line here but where exactly is it?'"

Listening to Brennan's words, I realize I want to understand. "I have to think about this," I admit.

Rosemary remains silent while I try to wrap my brain around Brennan's analogy. "Okay." I look up. "When I'm thinking a thought—like I've got to go to the grocery store—I'm the flame. It's a concrete thought and kind of like a flame. You can see the beginning and end of it. It has edges. But if, for example, I'm looking at a sunset and I sort of lose myself in the moment, then I don't know where 'I' begin and this sense of awe—this expanded state—begins."

"That makes sense," Rosemary agrees. "Really, she's asking us to think a different way. But it's not like she understood what was happening to her as a child."

Rosemary continues reading. "She got older, stopped going into the woods, and kind of forgot about it." She laughed. "She got a master's degree in *atmospheric physics* and worked for NASA. But eventually she became a counselor. She started seeing energies around her clients, but by now her scientific training made her skeptical so she just kept observing." Rosemary put the book down and picked up my empty wine glass. "I guess eventually she put two and two together and remembered her childhood experiences." She handed me a new glass of merlot and picked up the book again. "She says:

I saw that the energy field is intimately associated with a person's health and well-being. If a person is unhealthy, it will show in his energy field as an unbalanced flow of energy and/or stagnated energy."

Rosemary closed the book and handed it back to me. "Anyway, she found herself receiving channeled information. For example, she began to see cancer in people very clearly—and subsequent medical tests proved her right.

"She could also assist the healing process by rebalancing the client's field. She said that many times illness has a psychological or physical trauma associated with it, and in order to completely heal, the person must also address that issue."

"Well, do you work with her?" I ask.

"No, but Emily, one of her students who trained for four years under her, works in Key West. She comes to my house and I get healings about once a month."

Now I remember the experience I had back home. I tell Rosemary, "I was doing leg lifts the morning before I left. I noticed my right leg seemed energetically detached. It felt strange. My left leg went up and down just fine and physically my right leg did too, only it didn't *feel* right. Maybe Emily could work on that." *There! I think to myself. I picked something new.*

Two days later, tall slender soft-spoken Emily shows up with her massage table. Soon I am resting on my back, my legs slightly open, my arms apart from my body. She scarcely touches me. I feel gentle fingers on my feet, sometimes a light touch on my body. Afraid I'd want to wiggle or scratch my nose, I am surprised as I slip into this deep peacefulness no longer caring what she does. The hour passes quickly and afterward, she asks me to rest as long as I need.

When at last I slowly sit up, she tells me, "Your body is very divided, as though your waist was cut right through the middle, as though you haven't totally agreed to be on earth. I suspect you have trouble grounding yourself."

When someone says something to you that you've never heard in your life, either it resonates with your inner knowing or it doesn't. *You are so right,* I immediately know.

19

An image flashes through my mind and I share it. "This goes back to my birth. I am sure of it. It's as though I got born and all of the sudden realized I had made a *huge* mistake. I was like this little baby with my feet crabbed up against my butt screaming BEAM ME BACK UP! I MADE A MISTAKE! And then I realized I was stuck here. But I never put my feet down."

"Well, Barbara," Emily suggests, "you might want to try. After all it is amazing to have a human body. The Dalai Lama says there are so few humans, as compared to animals, insects, trees—all the living creations on earth. We have hands and feet and a mind; we can do so much on earth. But Barbara," she pauses to gently gaze at me with her soft blue eyes, "you have to get into your body."

When I share the experience with Rosemary, I feel a deepening curiosity about this kind of healing. I muse aloud, "Maybe this is why my right leg feels funny." *When I get back to Maryland,* I tell myself, *I am going to find another Brennan graduate and try this again.* It is a decision that will change my life, even my way of looking at it.

A few weeks later, Kenna will knock on my door.

Bored Sandra ~ 1972 ~
The Goat with a Brain Tumor

To prove my point about the adverse effect of a child living with an ocelot skin, my sister Sandra launches into an adult passion for skinning animals. "Why?" I ask one day.

"Well, remember when I was 16 and volunteered as a nurse's aide? The hospital let some of us see an autopsy. I didn't throw up so the pathologist asked me to weigh organs."

That was her explanation. I failed to see the connection between autopsies and taxidermy but she, bored with only one toddler to chase, decided to skin animals. Getting scalpels from her local pharmacist, she trained on a dead cow.

As the stench grew and flies swarmed, she soon realized scraping the hide off a one-ton cow in blistering sun was a particularly bad idea. Her husband buried the sorry mess.

Undeterred, she decides to take on smaller projects. After all, backpackers used *moleskin* for foot blisters. Why not make her own? She retrieves a cat-caught mole, skins it, and presents it to a seasoned hiker. He gazes at the mole stupefied by her stupidity. Rummaging in his backpack, he pulls out a cellophane package of thin pads with adhesive on one side. "Sandy, *this* is "moleskin."

Which brings us to ... the goat.

A hippy commune learns that Sandra likes to skin things. They arrive on her doorstep one day, tears in their eyes, a dead goat in their car trunk. "We *loved* this goat! He got a brain tumor and died. We want to remember him. Can you skin him for us?"

Happy to have another carcass, Sandra agrees, and they open the trunk. Sandra almost passes out from the stench. "WHAT IS THAT SMELL?" she hollers, staggering backwards, her fingers clamped onto her nose.

"Well," they admit, "he was in rut. You know, they roll in their own urine to attract females."

A tad more reluctant, Sandra tells them to drag the carcass onto the deck. The smell is so awful, she *loses* her sense of smell as she cuts, removes organs, and scrapes. The minute she finishes, she dumps the skin in to a vat of hot soapy water and scrubs it until she thinks the odor is gone. Then she has to leave for her dental appointment.

She showers, makes the 10-minute drive, and walks in unaware she is a proxy goat in rut. The dentist comes out, takes one whiff, looks at Sandra with horror, and incredulously states the obvious. "YOU STINK. Leave. Right NOW."

On the way out the door with stinky fumes trailing behind her and wild with joy at avoiding the dreaded dental appointment, she yodels over her shoulder, "I'm skinning a goat."

When the hippies arrive to receive their soft goat skin, Sandra—out of the extreme goodness of her heart—has gone the extra mile. She hands them a drawstring purse made out of tanned scrotum balls.

January 23

Retired Elsie ~ 1992 ~ Florida Diary

Maybe now that I have stopped worrying I can relax.

Career Elsie ~ 1950 ~ Flying Typewriter Platens

Elsie gets the desk next to the open door, the least desirable spot in the State Department typing pool. She's the new hire. Every morning, a stack of items to be typed shows up in her in-box. And sometimes, rarely, she takes dictation. She comes to work wearing white gloves, sensible heels, and a tailored blouse and skirt. She can't afford suits but buys attractive sweaters.

Her speed is excellent. Even under pressure, when required to take a timed test for her government service GS rating, she zips along, ranking in the 94th percentile for working from rough copy.

The secret to her speed, a skill she has honed perfectly, is the *SNAP* of the carriage return. With the metal manual typewriters, you need a certain *heft* to throw the roller, or platen, holding the typed paper back into position to begin a new line of typing.

Elsie has strong, short-nailed fingers. She grew up milking cows, once played the church organ, and always, the piano. Now she throws the typewriter carriage return with Olympian zeal.

So one day, launching into her in-box, she rolls a crisp piece of paper along with two carbons into the platen and goes into *the zone* where body and machine become one. She quietly zooms along, speeding along as her fingers limber up. Pretty soon she is cresting 100 words per minute when she whacks the carriage return.

She hears, before she sees, it crashing along the marble floor hitting the wall where the corridor turns. The entire carriage has flown off the bed, a lethal typing missile.

Elsie now has a platen-less typewriter. Nobody has ever seen one before.

The typing pool goes silent. Then slowly, one by one, giggles begin, drawing the supervisor out of her office. Elsie, convulsed with laughter, wordlessly points to her typewriter and the hallway.

The State Department maintenance office has no solution so Elsie gets another typewriter that same day.

"I'd suggest you go a bit slower, Elsie," the supervisor advises.

Anyway, all of this becomes irrelevant. Two months later, Elsie transfers to the Gifts Section of the Office of Protocol to work for the formidable Mr. Spruks.

Child Elsie ~ 1921 ~
Left Behind in Finlayson, Minnesota

"Get up!" Elsie hears her mother's voice and rubs her eyes. She sees her moving around the room, holding Lucy in her arms. She has her coat on. It's still dark outside.

"Elsie, we have to go now," Mom whispers. "Come downstairs. Your Dad wants to say good-bye. Here," she holds out a coat and boots for her 3-year-old daughter, "put these on."

Elsie pokes her arms into the holes and pulls it tight around her. She thrusts her bare feet into the boots and stumbles down the farmhouse stairs. The kitchen door is open. Snow swirls in. She watches her father put a suitcase in the black Model T. She shivers and runs outside.

He stops what he is doing and bends down to look at her. Years later, Elsie remembers the look on his face, seared into her young mind. It looks smiley-sad. She doesn't know what's going on. Why are they leaving her with her mother's parents?

"Elsie," he puts his hands on his daughter's shivering shoulders. "I want you to be good." He reaches into his pocket. She hears coins jingle. He opens the palm of her hand. "These are for you." She looks down. Two silver quarters lay in her upturned palm.

Her mother comes out the door, tucking Lucy into her bassinet in the back seat. Grandma and Grandpa Askelin stand at the kitchen door, watching. She walks over to Elsie, her eyes glassy with tears. But then she gives them a quick rub and looks at her firstborn daughter firmly. "Elsie, be good."

Elsie starts to cry. She feels tears streaming through the snow on her cheeks. She smears them away. "Why can't I come?"

"Elsie, Dad has to work far away. Grandma and Grandpa Askelin need you. It won't be that long." Her voice trails off. "We'll be back soon but I don't know when. You know your father is starting that new job." Her voice gets stern again. "Now stop crying, Elsie. You're a big girl now."

She tries. She rubs her eyes hard.

Her mother gives Elsie one last hug. By now, her grandparents have come down to the car. The sky is getting lighter. Elsie puts the cold quarters in her pocket.

Her mother gets into the car. Elsie hears the engine start. Her father looks at her from the open window. He waves.

The car disappears down the snow-covered road.

She watches until she can't see them any more.

"*Tule sisälle*, Elsie. *Minä kokki sinulle aamiaista*," Grandma tells her. Neither grandparent speaks any English. Elsie touches the quarters in her pocket and does as she's told. She goes inside and sits down to wait for breakfast.

Grandmother begins to fix it.

Mother Elsie ~ 1955 ~ Raising a Delinquent Daughter

"Mrs. Nurmi?"

"Yes." Elsie tucks the phone against her shoulder so she can keep filing.

"We hate to bother you at work. We know you must be busy. Things must be especially difficult with your mother being sick, but we simply can't have Sandra leaving school at lunch every day to take care of her."

Elsie puts down the files. "My mother is *perfectly* healthy," Elsie hears her voice coming out in chiseled syllables, "and she lives *1,200 miles* away." Elsie hangs up, amazed at Sandra's courage, creativity, spontaneity. Not.

Child Sandra ~ 1955 ~ I Am So Done with School

This is BORING. Ten-year-old Sandra *looks* studious in her class picture: thick blonde hair pulled into a tight ponytail, she wears a sedate plaid skirt and white blouse. But to her way of thinking, school is nonessential. *Nobody can expect a kid to do an hour of long division and then an hour of diagramming sentences.* She decides she can handle one—but not two. *I can't stand it. I am so done with school.*

So she leaves—but not like a runaway truant. No. She decides the school deserves *some* explanation.

"Mrs. Johnson," Sandra states the situation succinctly, "my grandmother is all alone at home. She's *very* sick. I have to go home and help her eat lunch." Now going home for lunch isn't against the rules—kids who live close often do this. But Sandra has no intention of coming back. To her amazement, it works.

"Oh, Sandra," Mrs. Johnson says, "I hope she gets better soon."

Sandra grabs her coat and lunch money. *I am out of here.*

Running down the school steps, she decides two homeless men she regularly sees across the street deserve to be the beneficiaries of her good fortune. She offers them her lunch money. The 35-cent transfer having taken place, Sandra realizes she can't go home. It wouldn't do for her to be watching TV when Dad walks in.

She walks to the country store and buys herself a Hershey bar. Then she goes to the creek and swings on the rope. Still more time. She scavenges through the dump and explores the abandoned Alleghany Street house. Finally it's 3 o'clock. "Hi Dad," she hollers coming in the door. "School was *great today.*"

Tomorrow was just as great. And the next day. And the next. She wonders how long her grandmother can be sick.

She learns, about two weeks.

January 31

Retired Elsie ~ 1990 ~ Testing One, Two, Three …

"Mom, we have to leave now to get to Broward Hospital on time." I anxiously glance at my watch, wanting spare time to find the hospital, the parking lot, the building, the clinic.

As she walks out of the bedroom wearing a blue knit top and a print skirt, she looks diminished … and scared.

At this juncture in my life, I see the world from a can-do perspective. I can *will* Mom to health—if only we can find out the problem. It *can't* be Alzheimer's. Not my mother. But in the back of my mind, in the deepest hidden recesses, I worry that it is. And so does Mom.

Forty-five minutes later, we pull into the parking lot. The doctors have scheduled three days of testing.

Mom will get a physical, blood work, a CAT scan of her brain, dietary analysis, logic testing, memory tests, an interview. She will be forced to decipher directions and geometric figures that baffle Sandra and me.

As we enter the building, Mom stops and freezes me with her eyes. "Barbara, I do *not* want to be told I have Alzheimer's." I hear the angry steel in her voice. "Okay, Mom. I'll tell them."

And I do. Right away. In very clear language. "You can test my mother, but you must give the results to me. She absolutely does not want to receive a diagnosis of Alzheimer's."

I don't think any more about it—I also don't stop to put myself in my mother's shoes. I handle emotional things by simply riding right over them, ignoring any hidden, volatile, or scary messages.

So the tests begin.

I sit in the waiting room filled with uncomfortable upholstered chairs. I stare at carpet stains. I flip through *Good Housekeeping* magazines. I drink coffee. We eat lunch in the hospital cafeteria. She resumes testing. I browse the gift shop, pace the corridors, stand outside. Finally the first day ends. The second rivals the first for boredom.

By the third, Mom looks as though the doctors have *extracted* her brain rather than examined it. Sandra and her husband Ed fly in that evening.

After Mom goes to bed, we uncork a big bottle of red wine. I glance at the telephone numbers taped to her kitchen cabinet, realizing how her life has changed. We put everything back exactly where we found it. Always organized, Mom's vigilance now even extends to trash.

Every scrap of rotting waste must be immediately put into the plastic wrapper her morning newspaper comes in. The bag must be knotted after each addition "to keep the insects out." It makes perfect sense—but I suspect every effort to control her world is an attempt to control her disintegrating mind.

We talk in hushed voices after she goes to bed. I know she must be terrified to subject herself to these tests—but her fear of *not* doing so seems even worse. *What if it is something that cannot be treated?*

~ ~ ~

It amazes me what the human being can ignore. I can efficiently make doctor's appointments. I can be pushy enough to get my mother to agree to tests. I can offer cheery platitudes. "Mom, it might be nutrition. You might be experiencing ministrokes. Then they can stop your memory loss. It won't get any worse." Hope. I offer hope.

None of us sleeps well. Today the doctors will give their assessment. Sandra, Ed, Mom, and I drive to the hospital. We park and walk to the waiting room. The nurse calls Mom in. We assume they are doing some final patient processing.

No.

Alone, without support, without our permission, the medical team announces to our Mother—against her *express* wishes—"Mrs. Nurmi, based on our tests, we have concluded you have Alzheimer's. We believe you should stop driving immediately. We strongly recommend you get some assistance in the home. We'll go over all our recommendations with your daughters." And she is ushered out, like an atomic bomb victim, left to sit alone in the waiting room while the doctors give us their "detailed conclusions."

Stunned with the reality of what we will be facing, I say, "Well, we'll tell Mom."

"Oh, we already told her," one doctor explained.

"You WHAT?" I ask incredulously. "The ONE thing we told you was to NOT tell her. She specifically told me she did not want to hear a diagnosis of Alzheimer's and that is exactly what I told you and you agreed."

Apparently somewhere during the three days of testing, they forgot. Their polite apology leaves us holding the emotional baggage of what we know would soon come—our mother's cold wrath.

To this day, I have not digested the emotional pain, shock, fury, anger of that day—all suppressed under a Finnish heritage. I can't empathize with my Mother because I cannot even get a handle on those emotions within my own self. Ed tries to hold the fort. "Let's just get Elsie home."

We drive in utter silence.

I can feel white rage pouring off my mother in the car. When we get home, I grab Sandra and Ed. "Let's take a walk around the lake, and let Mom be alone for awhile."

An hour later, we unlock the front door to an empty house. An unsigned handwritten note on lined paper lies on the dining room table. "I have gone to Helmi's. I won't return until Barbara leaves."

I feel my whole body turn to ice. This was my idea. Sandra and Ed were hesitant about it all along.

I take the doctor's advice literally. She lives alone in Florida. How is she to buy groceries, go to the bank, buy stamps at the post office, pick up prescriptions?

"We need to disable the Blazer," I say, thinking of the car my mother had custom painted school-bus yellow so no one would hit her. "We'll have to find a nursing aide to help." I am going into catastrophe mode, foreseeing an utterly incapacitated mother. I feel emotionally ravaged.

Ed and Sandra, together, finally put the brakes on my disintegrating world. They talk about the whole issue exactly the way two engineers would look at an engine that malfunctioned. *Can Elsie be repaired enough to get along on her own for a while longer?* They go through her entire life—driving, eating, finances, friendships.

"Barbara," Sandra offers, "you can't take everything away from her. Let me drive with her tomorrow and see how she does."

"But she could run over a kid. She could *kill* someone," I wail.

"Look," Ed tries to lighten things up, "she doesn't drive in rush hour. She takes back roads. For god sakes, she never even makes a left turn. She's got the weirdest routes to get anywhere just so she won't have to deal with traffic. Doris Holmes calls her every day. They go to dinner umpteen times a week."

Slowly I calm down. But to get Mom home, I have to leave. Feeling sucker-punched, emotionally drained, and numb, I book a flight back to Maryland.

After I'm gone, Sandra watches her drive and pronounces her safe. No one is hired to help her. We simply let Elsie continue to live alone in Florida—the only difference being that we now worry incessantly. Mom refuses to talk about her memory any more, and when I call, she answers and we talk—as though nothing has happened, as though Broward didn't exist.

Confused Elsie ~ 1992 ~ Florida Diary

I just found out I have a "muting" button on my remote control for the TV. The set was bought almost ten years ago.

February

Elsie Aboard Air Force Two

Journeys to Known (and Unknown) Destinations

February 3

Confused Elsie ~ 1993 ~ Match.Mom

"She needs a boyfriend," Sandra decides, "a companion, a friend—a *man*."

When I stop laughing, I suggest, "How about her Lutheran church? Surely there is a widower who is lonely. I'll call."

Now this isn't just any Lutheran church. It is a *Finnish* one, complete with Finnish sermons and Finnish *pulla* coffee cake after the service.

Reverend Matti listens to me and says, "I have just the person. Victor Salmela. He lost his wife last year. He's a very pleasant person."

"We'd be willing to pay him. We'd be hiring him to be Mom's companion—maybe take her out to lunch or dinner once a week, and call to check on her."

Sandra and I soon find ourselves enchanted with Victor who, in his eighties, does daily push-ups, raises roses, and cooks. He stands erect, has a full head of light brown hair, and a warm smile that makes his blue eyes twinkle. Now all we have to do is have them meet ... accidentally.

The next Sunday after the service we catch Victor's eye. Wearing a tan suit and paisley tie, he strolls over and introduces himself. Sandra asks, "Why don't you join us for lunch." Mom's eyes twinkle, the flirtatious spark not at all extinguished.

The next day Sandra and I fly home, and Victor steps in. No matter how often we try to pay him, he refuses. He and Elsie split restaurant checks. He often stops at her home just to share a cup of coffee or watch TV. He even offers to take her to Minnesota on his trip north.

On *that* adventure, they stop overnight at Victor's friends. Uncomfortable on the lumpy sofa, Elsie drags the cushions into the dining room. She arranges her new bed under the table so no one will accidentally step on her and promptly falls asleep, thrilled with her solution. Her mind correctly identifies problems, but her answers are becoming wildly unpredictable. From Sandra's and my perspective, she's safe—*and* she's having fun.

This arrangement buys us a year or so.

We get Meals on Wheels to deliver prepared food to Mom, which she throws in the trash because, "the chicken is too tough," "I'm not hungry," "I don't like meatballs." With Finnish practicality, Sandra admits defeat telling me, "We're going to have to wait till Mom crashes onto the floor." Exact words. I never forget them. And I agree.

That conversation opens the door to our first compromise with this disease. We have reluctantly considered court-ordered guardianship but it would strip Mom of any vestige of dignity and the disease is so stealthy and unpredictable, we realize we don't even *know* if she is incompetent ... yet.

Like an ocean at high and low tides, her mental acuity seems to go up and down, sometimes in a period of hours. In the end, we hope she'll stay safe until the inevitable crash comes.

Retired Elsie ~ 1982 ~ Florida Diary

Went to bank. Sandra called. Found body on beach. Chickens laying nine eggs a day.

Rescuer Sandra ~ 2011 ~ Beach Bodies

"Sandra, what's this about a body on the beach?" I ask. "It's in Mom's diary for 1982."

"Oh, yeah," Sandra remembers. "A man jumped off the bridge near our home on Bainbridge Island. I was outside with Kier digging mussels when the neighbor saw the body washing up on shore.

The policeman arrived pretty quickly. The tide comes in fast here, and the body was starting to float out but he insisted he couldn't move it without a coroner pronouncing him dead.

"I told the cop—he was young—'You've got to pull it up. He's going to wash away.' His face turned white. I thought he'd pass out so I said, 'Hold my kid. *I'll* do it.' Well, I guess that embarrassed him. He waded in and dragged the body farther up."

"Finally the coroner arrived. He went over and held a *mirror* under the guy's nose. Then he listened to his chest."

"But he's DEAD!" I told him.

"Yeah," the coroner agreed, "but we have to go through the protocol."

Career Elsie ~ 1965 ~ Dining in a Protocol World

[Official State Department Guidelines, as found in Elsie's papers]

"The main problem to be considered is seating the guests at table in order of rank and precedence.

"The simplest method is to make a list of the gentlemen and another of the ladies, strictly in order of rank, and place them thus:

> Gentleman No. 1 on the right of the hostess, Gentleman No. 2 on her left; likewise Lady No. 1 on the right of the host, Lady No. 2 on his left. Then Gentleman No. 3 on the right of Lady No. 1, and No. 4 on the left of No. 2 ...

"It could happen that when some gentlemen are accompanied by wives and others not, a lady is placed next to her husband.

In that case a slight alteration of the plan can be made, substituting the lady or gentleman next in line or immediately preceding.

"There is always a way to find a variant that will not upset the logic of protocol."

Children Sandra and Barbara ~ 1957 ~
Cuisine for Tomboys

Sandra and I are raised like tomboys. We wear striped T-shirts, not blouses, and constantly run around in dungarees or shorts, not skirts. This is not *my* idea of childhood. No. I want to play house with dolls, wear poodle skirts and cute neck scarves, and have *curly* hair.

Every Christmas Sandra reaches new heights of sport-equipment ecstasy while I dismally look at our new gifts—baseball gloves, badminton sets, bows and arrows, fishing rods. The most feminine thing I think I received was a baton for twirling. Oh, now that I remember, that didn't come from my parents.

When we aren't slugging balls or shooting arrows, I periodically bribe my sister to play house with me: "Sandra, let's play house." "NO." "Oh, come on. Just for a little while." "I don't want to." "What if I play baseball with you afterwards?" "You have to play for an hour *and* give me two of your cookies." It goes on until the contract, all in her favor, is sealed.

To make amends, Sandra sent me an Orphan Annie cloth doll for my 45th birthday.

She totally missed the point. Who wants something so infant-proof only a dog would want it? My dream doll would burp, talk, poop, and wear Barbie-doll gowns.

Imagine my dismay when Sandra decided her *sons* needed a gender-neutral doll experience.

For the first half hour, the boys were fascinated. They poured blue water in; they watched pee come out; they changed diapers. Then they got bored. "Well," Sandra picked up a hacksaw, "let's see how it works!"

At any rate, that pretty much covers my childhood—except when Mom decides we need better table manners. ...

~ ~ ~

We eat at a red Formica booth nailed to the kitchen wall. Dad got it free from a restaurant along with turquoise-painted benches. Occasionally we storm in, dirty from playing outside, to see the booth laden with Wedgwood china, real silverware, crystal, and cloth napkins. It's going to be one of *those* dinners.

Never does Dad's venison, squirrel, or wild rabbit get served at these meals. If it had, it would have been a double-hitter dinner—kind of a Daniel Boone moment at the White House.

We have two forks to the left of our plate, one knife, a soupspoon and teaspoon to the right of our plate, and a desert fork and teaspoon above our plate—all sterling, of course. We have a water glass (and lucky us) a wine glass once we are in high school. The Wedgwood serving dishes holding the food sit on the teak tea cart next to the table.

The first culinary chore we master is eating chicken with a fork and knife. After flipping these utensils back and forth a gazillion times, I complain, "What a stupid way to eat."

"Well," Dad turns the fork in his left hand upside down, "in Europe they hold it this way and use the knife in the right for cutting. They never change hands."

"You're kidding!" I respond with awe for the Europeans.

"I'm left-handed. I'm going to switch." Well it isn't easy but I master it. When Mom next drags out the Wedgwood, I flip my fork and balance the peas on the upside-down tines. I've gone euro.

At any rate, Sandra and I eventually can get a bone barer than a dinosaur relic in a matter of minutes. But then comes the cactus-looking vegetable ...

My sister, seeing the first disgusting looking artichoke sitting in splendorous isolation on a pristine white Wedgwood salad plate, turns to Mom and with a gourmand's irritation asks, "What? Artichokes *again*?"

Caviar on the other hand quickly becomes blasé; we have absolutely *no* problem drinking wine; and we never learn how disgusting raw oysters might be, because our father introduced them to us as baby food.

Under Mom's tutelage we learn *how* to eat but the experience stops with the silverware and china. Our everyday ware, which has faded fork-worn cactuses on it, holds meat, potatoes, frozen vegetables, and no desert at all.

By junior high, Sandra and I take over the kitchen and things go rapidly downhill.

I believe hamburger patties grilled five seconds above raw are cooked. Sandra eats pizza on prefab cardboard-like crusts. Needless to say, no Wedgwood plate can overcome such culinary disasters.

Confused Elsie ~ 1994 ~
You Have *Low* Blood Pressure

I hear the phone ringing and stop washing dishes to answer.

"This is Dr. Mizrahy's office. Is this Barbara Taylor, the daughter of Elsie Nurmi?"

Immediately I am on high alert. We know things are getting worse. Mom's sister Alice called me last week. "Your mother got so frustrated. She couldn't make the venetian blinds go down in the bedroom and I didn't know how to tell her over the phone."

Now, finally, *something* has happened.

~ ~ ~

"Your mother came to our office this morning. She felt woozy. We took her blood pressure. It was really low, so Dr. Mizrahy had her sit in the waiting room while we called 911. That's when she passed out. She's been admitted to Kennedy Hospital and she's stable. They're running some tests."

"I'll be there as soon as I can," I promise. That evening I fly into the West Palm Beach airport feeling catastrophe about to descend on our lives.

"Your mother was very dehydrated and malnourished. We are hydrating her right now," Dr. Mizrahy tells me in his deep soothing voice. "I'll tell her to drink more water and eat better. Then we'll discharge her."

"NO!" I stop him. "She's getting too confused. She doesn't know what dehydration *is*. She'll promise to drink more and then forget. She has Alzheimer's. Can you come up with something that sounds *very* serious—something she won't understand—and tell her she *has* to go into assisted living *now*?"

He studies her chart. "Well, I could tell her she has low blood pressure and it needs constant monitoring."

"That'll work. I don't think she'll understand blood pressure. She'll think it's a serious medical condition." From my perspective, it's our best hope.

"Let's tell her now," he offers.

We enter her hospital room. She looks so tiny and vulnerable in the hospital bed. I watch anxiously as Dr. Mizrahy bends over to put his hand on her arm.

In a very low slow *serious* voice he begins, "Mrs. Nurmi. You have very *low* blood pressure. It needs to be checked every 2 hours by a nurse. You *must* go to the Finnish-American Rest Home where they can do that. Is that alright with you?"

Out of the bed bleats a barely audible response. "Okay."

Like an unprotected lamb, she accepts having a fence placed around her, and I take my first non-hysterical breath in a long time. Finally Mom will be safe.

Curious Barbara ~ 1995 ~
A Different Way of Healing

Not forgetting my promise to continue energy healing after visiting Rosemary, I decide to interview three Barbara Brennan graduates. My last telephone call is to a woman named Kenna. "Hello," I begin, "I understand you are a Barbara Brennan graduate."

"Yes, I am," Kenna replies in a voice that sounds like a little wren.

"Do you have an office?"

"No."

"How do you work, then?"

"Oh, I come to your home."

"Do you have a massage table that you use?"

"Oh no, I'm too *little*. I couldn't carry it. You see, I'm not even five feet tall."

"So how do you work?"

"Oh, you lie on your dining-room table. That's best."

"Let me think about it. I'm interviewing two other Brennan graduates."

"Well, if you're meant to work with me, it'll just happen," Kenna cheerily answers, ending the conversation. No sales pitch. No "Let's set an appointment." No discounted six-treatment plan.

I find Kenna intriguing and the others much less so. They *do* have offices. They offer different modalities of healing, everything from massage to psychotherapy to Reiki. Brennan's approach simply is another tool in their healing kits. Kenna banks her life on it.

I choose Kenna.

~ ~ ~

Over time, I ask her questions about energy healing even though I don't always understand the answers. It requires highly intuitive telepathic skills. I am curious about how one trains oneself. "What made you decide to go to Barbara Brennan's school?" I ask one day.

"Well," she paused. "One morning when I was thinking about grocery shopping, a message flashed through: *Go to the library. There is a book for you.*

"You follow those messages?" I ask.

"Oh yes, that's how you come to trust your intuition. You see how well things fit together when you listen to that inner voice.

"Anyway, later that day, I walked in and said (silently of course), *Okay, I'm here.* I looked up and down the nearest shelf. The top of one book was tilted at a weird angle. I pulled it out and it was *Hands of Light,* by Barbara Brennan."

Keenly aware of serendipity, she began reading and quickly realized she had the natural healing gifts talked about in the book—but she lacked technique. When the time was right, she enrolled in Barbara Brennan's program. "Oh, the first time I performed a healing procedure on a fellow student," Kenna laughed, "I almost blew her over." It sounded like using a fireman's hose to drown a barbeque fire. "I learned to taper it down."

After 4 years of training, the final test required the student to do a very advanced healing. "Each of us has within our physical body a spot known in ancient oriental medicine as the *hara,*" Kenna explained. "It lies somewhat below the belly button, deep within the body. Our sense of vitality and life force comes from this. We feel grounded and balanced when this area is strong."

Now Kenna, in order to graduate, has to take her client into the deepest healing possible in the *hara* and *hold* that healing energy for an hour while the teacher observes. The aura must reflect the effectiveness of the healing being undertaken.

After graduating, Kenna decides to devote her life to this work. I become her client in 1992.[1] As we set the date and time, she reminds me, "I'm very small, Barbara."

The day for the healing arrives. I hear a knock on my door and throw it open. Gazing down at Kenna, I say, "My *god*, you are small!" She stands before me, blue eyes twinkling, a tiny gnome of a person dressed all in mauve, her soft brown hair curled into a pageboy that perfectly frames her heart-shaped face.

"Just lay quietly," Kenna explains as I hoist myself onto the solid walnut dining table covered with a folded quilt and blanket. "Keep your legs slightly apart and move your arms a little ways away from your body," she instructs.

I am once again in the classic Barbara Brennan healing position.

I feel tense, not yet sure I trust her. But then, I always have this hesitancy when experiencing new modalities of healing.

I well remember 1975 when I developed a slight fever and stopped absorbing food. Unable to find anything clinically wrong, the doctor referred me to an acupuncturist when hardly anyone had even heard of one.

The acupuncturist explained how I reached this digestive impasse and recommended a vegetarian, grain-based diet. When I protested I didn't *believe* what he was telling me, he replied, "You don't have to believe it; just eat it." Then he placed several needles in me.

Seeing no alternative, I bought brown rice, beans, miso soup, tofu, green vegetables, even seaweed, and cooked my first meal.

---

[1] Today, Kenna restricts her practice to existing clients and referrals. For that reason, I am not providing a last name. To learn more about how to contact her, go to www.ElsieAtEbbTide.com.

Forty-eight hours later, my fever broke. I could literally *feel* my body absorbing food. I never looked back and over time, gained confidence using alternative health care as a first option before pursuing doctors, prescriptions, and surgery.

Now, as Kenna begins her work, I close my eyes but peek out of them once in a while. She scarcely touches me. She stands at my feet gently placing her hands on their tops. I feel ripples running down my body toward her. Suddenly I *relax*. The scared tension I've been holding drains out of me like water from a tub.

After awhile, she moves to my right side. I see her waving her arms over me. If I were sitting on the sofa watching, I'd think she was a Druid priestess performing some bizarre rite. But this is *me* she is working on!

Again I feel a strange but pleasant rippling over my belly and chest. I fall asleep and remember nothing else. I have no idea how much time has passed, but suddenly and very gently I awake.

Kenna is now behind me. I feel tingling in my head though she is not touching me. Then it is over. I see Kenna sitting on a dining-room chair near me writing in her notebook. I lay in bliss. I feel as though I've experienced a deep *inside* massage, everything calm and quiet within me.

I eventually learn that some people experience more, some less. Those who are naturally psychic may even see the auras themselves. They *feel* the healing more directly. My experience never goes beyond this sense of ripples and tingling, of being drawn deeply into my body, and experiencing an overwhelming sense of Love pouring in as though I am being *filled* with Light.

Later Kenna tells me the same thing Emily had—"Barbara, you are *very* ungrounded. It took me almost 20 minutes to get you into your body."

I sense the difference. Rather than breathing in a shallow slightly anxious way, I now draw deep breaths. I feel safe, grounded, peaceful—unusual sensations for me.

For people naturally grounded, it must be almost impossible to understand how ungroundedness feels. But for those of us whose defense mechanism is flight rather than fight, energetically speaking we truly *know* the difference, and it feels *good* to be home in our bodies.

Career Elsie's Diary ~ 1969 ~ Astronaut Borman Goes Abroad

[On December 21, 1968, Frank Borman commanded Apollo 8 leaving the Earth's gravitation to become the first mission to orbit the far side of the Moon. A European goodwill tour for Borman and his family takes place the following year.]

~ ~ ~

I meet Colonel and Mrs. Borman, their sons Frederick and Edwin, and the seven other members of the party at 7 a.m. at Andrews Air Force Base. We take off in a Boeing 707, one of the president's fleet, which we will be using for the whole European goodwill tour.

Halfway across the Atlantic, we (the Protocol staff) start sorting out the gifts that seem to fill every unoccupied seat. I am writing out notations such as "queen," "de Gaulle," "pope" when I hear a very serious voice behind me. "Aren't you getting a bit informal there, Elsie?"

Anyway, the airport arrival in London is confusing since I've not yet experienced the repetitive functions I'll be performing throughout the trip: turning over passports, lining up the party in order of precedence, meeting the coordinating person at the embassy.

Our hotel is a block away from the Dorchester where Liz Taylor and Richard Burton stay. Today I get to the Wedgwood place and buy additional pieces for my set at a quarter of the cost. One of the embassy girls takes me to an English pub. It's really cozy—small rooms with heavy wood paneling and British characters wandering in and out. We have "bitters" (warm beer), a Scotch egg (egg baked inside of a biscuit), and shepherd's pie made of lamb.

We still have seven countries and nine additional cities to visit.

February 7

Career Elsie's Diary ~ 1969 ~
"Hey Seppällä, How's It Going?"

We were up and at it early two mornings ago—baggage to go, people to be called. We called one person three times. Each time he fell back asleep. Finally I sent a man to drag him out of his room. He told me, "I stood him up. He seemed awake. In fact he stood before the hotel window and said, 'Isn't Paris beautiful?' " (We were still in London.)

We took off at 8:00 a.m. Only one problem: the pilot had no idea where we were going. I had distributed the schedule in Washington to all concerned parties except the one *most* concerned. The White House pilot.

~ ~ ~

Ambassador and Mrs. Shriver held a reception at the Paris Embassy this evening. I decided to leave early. As I came down the steps I saw the former Finnish ambassador to Washington and out popped: *"Hei Seppälä! Kuinka se menee?"*

I guess yodeling "Hey, Seppälä, how's it going?" isn't quite what he expected. But diplomacy always trumps in these situations, so Seppälä and I had a pleasant chat in Finnish.

Yesterday there was a ceremony with Jules Verne's grandson, but I was too busy to go. Then last night we went to Ledoyne Restaurant. As we finished cocktails, the wall descended into the floor, and there was a beautiful table completely set with candles and flowers.

I had lamb European style (pretty rare) and spent most of the night sick as a dog.

This morning I wasn't sure I could go on with the delegation. Three times I went to the lobby. Three times I rushed back to my room. On the fourth try I made it (but carried a paper bag in my pocket).

I was mighty glad to see our plane. I ran on board, got a blanket, and lay down. WHEW!

On to Brussels.

Reflective Barbara ~ 2009 ~ Good Things to Lose

I arrive at the Missouri Department of Motor Vehicles to renew my tags. Last year I made two trips because I was missing a document, so I call ahead.

"You'll need your driver's license, proof you paid your county taxes, proof of inspection, and your insurance card," the clerk explains over the phone.

I collect them, arrive, and am told, "I'm sorry, we only accept personal checks."

"But this is 2009. *Everyone* takes credit."

"Not us. Sorry."

I collect my papers to drive home to get the bloody checkbook. Irritated, I start to tell myself, *Oh well, it's just 10 minutes*.

Then I change my mind. I decide, in an effort to feel my feelings, to stay with my anger. I pull up to the stoplight with this decision in mind. I hold onto it as I turn the corner. But by the time I am rolling up the hill to my home, 4 minutes later, I have completely forgotten. Delighting in the brilliantly blue sky, I have accidentally fallen back into a good mood.

I suffered a complete memory lapse in a mere 4 minutes. I can't even hold onto my rage.

I think of my mother's slow descent into Alzheimer's. She fought like a cougar but we both knew how it would end. I wonder if our "lower" emotions of anger, fear, greed, lust can keep their traction in us without the mind to remember them. Maybe emotion has no power at all without the memory to sustain it.

At any rate, as I crest the hill to my home to retrieve a blank check, the anger completely forgotten, I realize that memory loss allows us to lose a lot of things we probably don't want to keep anyway.

We all have been wounded, often far beyond the normal slings of life. We carry tender spots in our psyche, but they are carried *solely by memory*. Without memory, they do not exist. They cease to exist. They die.

Perhaps that is a good thing. I would like to cross over without the burden of anger, rage, hatred, bitterness, depression, and despair. I would like to cross over feeling buoyed by love, light, joy, laughter, and happiness. Somehow those feelings are not memory-based. They are *soul*-based.

Or so I believe.

February 10

Career Elsie's Diary ~ 1969 ~ Stealing Food in The Hague

We THINK we are going to leave. Ha! It's snowing. The plane can't take off from Brussels. Well there are trains. Off we chug to The Hague in a train with a walkway and glass-door compartments that make me feel like I'm on Poirot's *Oriental Express*.

What adds the final touch? A man from The Hague jumps off a train heading to Brussels and climbs onto ours just to reassure us that our itinerary has been adjusted. I nearly flip when we arrive and our American ambassador greets us dressed in century-old clothing—apparently the "current" fashion here.

The Hotel des Indes must have existed when Columbus sailed for America. The ceilings are double the height of ours with drapes coming all the way down. It takes the strength of a horse to close them. Everything is vintage—old and pretty worn out.

Here is where I meet my Waterloo on foreign money.

It is a rough morning. Without breakfast or coffee, I am like a cold worm. You can poke me but nothing happens. But there is no time to order breakfast.

I am beginning to feel the constant strain. We are about to leave but I still have to close the account and change guilders into German marks, all the while remembering U.S. dollars.

My stomach rumbling, I dash to the reception desk and run into the slowest human being on earth who lacks *any* comprehension of human language.

In frustration and hunger I get back on the elevator and burst into tears. At the fourth floor I turn off the faucet and get out with a protocol smile. I only have minutes to spare. While the Borman party is saying good-bye to their hosts in the private room set up for our breakfast, I see among the dishes ready to be cleared one plate practically untouched.

I am not proud, I say to myself. I reach over and practically vacuum in the plateful of food. Instant relief. Now I can tackle the world.

As we move toward the elevator, I see this man pick up the plate and look at it in utter disbelief. I have eaten the poor man's breakfast.

"I'm so sorry," I stammer. "I didn't know you hadn't finished." Just before the elevator doors close I shout, "Order another breakfast and put it on my account!" As we descend, I realize that won't do much good. I have just closed the account.

February 12

Marriable Elsie ~ 1940 ~ Where's Herby?

Elsie exits the restroom and stares down the empty marble hallway of the Warrenton, Virginia, courthouse. "Where's Herby?" she asks Ginny.

"Oh, he probably went to the men's room," Ginny Sadler offers. "Bob, go check." Turning back to Elsie, she beams with good wishes. "So you're tying the knot! How do you feel?"

"Well, I'd feel better if Herby were here."

"He's not in the bathroom. Let me go outside," Bob decides, pulling open the courthouse door. "Maybe he wanted one last smoke as a single man."

Still no Herby. Minutes pass. A half hour passes. Elsie waits. At last she sees him walk back into the courthouse dressed in the only suit he owns, a flattering double-breasted dark navy one. *He is a good looking man,* she feels her heart tingle with un-Finn-like giddiness. That feeling washes away the moments of anxiety she had experienced. He walks up to her and, with eyes full of seriousness, admits, "It's a big decision. I just wanted to make sure I was ready."

Elsie has taken Monday off from the U.S. Department of the Census to say her vows. Owning only two pretty dresses, one red and one black, the day before the wedding she turns to Herby to ask, "Which one do you want me to wear?"

Now, she stands next to him in front of Mr. G. D. Gaskins, a red-dressed girl waiting to say "I do" to a marriage that will last 47 years.

Their romance begins in Harlem, New York, in 1937. Back in the 1930s Harlem hosted not only the Negro dance hall (immortalized by the poet Langston Hughes) but also a Finnish dance hall.

It seems black Americans from a warm, sunny African descent and white Finns from a sunless, icy Scandinavian descent share a common, if segregated, love of dancing. The Finnish "band" consisted of one man who kicked the drums, pumped the accordion, blew the harmonica, and played faster than a metronome on meth.

Over 6 feet tall, slender with brown hair and blue eyes and smooth big-band moves on the dance floor, Herby is considered a catch. Whereas other Finnish men hop up and down to the schottische and the polka, he glides.

After going on a blind date with Herby, Elsie quickly steps into his dance arms. All goes well until one day he vanishes. Nobody knows where. When Elsie gets offered a clerk typist job with the U.S. Census Department, having no reason to stay, she moves to Washington, D.C.

On a fall day in 1938, as she wraps her wet hair in a towel, she hears a knock on her door. There stands Herby, the picture of Finnish reserve. Elsie, who could match him for understatement, welcomes him in as though she were dressed for a party instead of wearing house clothes with a towel wringing out her hair. She fixes coffee and slowly he explains his absence.

His 47-year-old mother had died. He made Ida's funeral arrangements, went through her personal effects, closed her business affairs, and grieved ... alone. He was 24 years old.

Decades later, Sandra and I learn snippets of Ida's life: She joined a massive exodus from Finland in 1903. She worked as a live-in cook, once for a DuPont family. In 1915, she returned to her parents' farm in Alajarvi, Finland, with her 2-year-old son. Her father, Daniel Mertaniemi, according to church records appeared prosperous. Ida returned to America 8 years later.

She took singing lessons, hoping to break into opera. I own her metronome; my daughter Lisa has her cookbook. The few pictures we have show a sturdy, plain, square-faced woman with brown hair and, likely, blue eyes. We also know from letters of the deep mother–son love that existed between them. On November 14, 1937, she was discovered dead in her furnished room from pneumonia.

ELSIE AT EBB TIDE

When Dad died in 1987, Mom pulled a trunk from beneath his built-in bunk, opened the lid, and handed us those letters—and Ida's ashes.

Retired Elsie ~ 1989 ~ Florida Diary

House cleaning: I proceed on the assumption that if you can't see dirt it's not there.

Career Elsie's Diary ~ 1969 ~
A Herby-less Anniversary in Bonn

Yesterday we arrived in Bonn, Germany, and drove in over the Rhine River, then on to the ambassador's residence where we are to stay, since he is assigned to Paris to see if he can talk the Vietnamese into a peace truce.

It is a beautiful place, watching the boats ply the river. I wonder why boats always ply the Rhine and float or do something else on other rivers.

Our trip is overlapping with President Nixon's advance party preparing for his European trip. Two of the president's aircraft are at the airport. We came in on the larger one. Now we are leaving on the smaller DC-6.

Tonight's dinner was very pleasant, especially the champagne ordered "in honor of Elsie Nurmi's anniversary." It's the first time Herby and I haven't been together in 29 years. Well, I toasted Herby *and* drank his champagne. HAPPY ANNIVERSARY!

Child Barbara ~ 1959 ~
Living with an Officer and a Gentleman

On workday mornings, certain rituals start the family's day. Dad bounces out of bed every morning at 5:30 a.m. Putting on his carpenter pants, black paint-specked shoes, and white work shirt, he goes into the kitchen, opens the frig, peels off four slices of bacon, tosses them into the frying pan, unpacks four pieces of Pepperidge Farm bread, pops them into the toaster, and falls asleep on a squat four-legged stool.

Awakened by the smell of burning bacon and now running late, he tosses the eggs in the pan, flips them over with the whites still runny, scrapes butter across the cold toast, and hollers up the stairwell, "Rise and shine, morning time," to Sandra and me. Then he waits for Mom to stagger into the kitchen and hands her a cup of gruesomely strong acrid black coffee from the two-tier drip pot. He cleans her windshield, tells her she looks beautiful, and walks her to the car every morning.

Looking back on those years, I realize Dad embodied the essence of manhood. "He was a gentleman," she insisted after he died. In our household, that meant manners—"He taught me real manners."

It seems inconceivable that our mother-of-Wedgwood wasn't born under some astrological sign of etiquette, but, if true, where did Dad learn his manners?

Perhaps from the Fred Astaire movies his mother took him to on her day off. Maybe Ida relayed stories of wealth and manners from the DuPont household. Whatever the source, he carried himself with an ingrained confidence without need to put himself forward. He stood in his own truth, as we say today.

He built up his one-man carpentry business, eventually taking several jobs on Capitol Hill.

As promised, he watches over Sandra and me, telling us repeatedly we can be and do anything. We learn how to skin an eel, eat squirrel, dive off his shoulders into the Chesapeake Bay, crew his somewhat leaky skipjack, and cook without recipes. We leave home confident we can establish ourselves in male workplaces.

When the movie, *An Officer and a Gentleman* comes to the theaters, I burst out laughing and call my sister. "Hey Sandra, have you seen *An Officer and a Gentleman*?"

Well, of course not. She never goes to movies. "It's a Tom Cruise movie," I tell her. He's the officer *and* the gentleman." Inspired by my own wit, I explain to my disinterested sister—"Mom was the *officer*. Dad was the *gentleman*."

February 15-20

Career Elsie's Diary ~ 1969 ~ Devil in the Moon

Yesterday, I faced a catastrophe! All of the Borman party, including me, received invitations to the Vatican, and there I was without a single dark outfit. I dashed across the street into *Luisa Spagnolli* and bought a $60 black suit [$350 today] for a good cause, then to the Vatican gift shop to pick up medals, and then downtown to get a black mantilla to cover my head.

This morning we drove through the archways onto the Vatican grounds. The pope's Protocol Officer met us and took us on a guided tour of the Sistine Chapel. I stood where the stove is placed to announce a new pope. After the tour, we were ushered to his office to meet Pope Paul VI. He was sitting at his desk. He read his welcome in English, which he seldom does, slowly but clearly. Pictures were taken. Then he shook our hands, giving each of us a medal. (Of course I had my purse chock-full of things I am going to bring back to my Catholic friends.)

Afterwards, all the cardinals and the Diplomatic Corps accredited to the Vatican watched as Colonel Borman showed slides. During the question-and-answer period, one of them asked, "Is there is a Devil on the Moon?" which had been misinterpreted because he actually asked if there was "Life on the Moon"—in Latin, *Diablo* instead of *Viable*. Colonel Borman answered both questions: "There is more on the Earth than on the Moon."

Career Elsie's Diary ~ 1969 ~ Sizzling Eels

Hard to believe, but here we are getting lost in the mountains of Spain. Colonel Borman and the men took off for a tracking station. We ladies were to follow. After miles on a slush-covered, snowy road, we decided we were lost. In the distance, we saw what looked like a tracking station and got there, but by then the men had left.

We got lost again. A man in a green suit driving a little white car came looking for us, so all was well.

In Spain you have to go to a typical Spanish restaurant, however I'm not so sure if what we ate was typical. For the first course we had live baby eels served in a sizzling pan (which they didn't like and kept on jumping up and down). We were told to stir them. (At that point I didn't know they were alive or I might have had second thoughts.) Absolutely delicious. I would recommend them to anyone.

Career Elsie's Diary ~ 1969 ~ Dining in a Stable

Today we headed for Lisbon, the final city on our goodwill tour. We stayed at the Hotel Ritz, where Zsa Zsa Gabor got thrown out and the hotel kept her luggage because she couldn't pay the bill.

After lunch I was given a tour up the mountains and to the coast, seeing castles, many in the Moorish style. At 7:10 p.m. I returned to the hotel only to be told the entire party had been invited to dinner ... at 7:00 p.m.!

I ran up the corridor, changed into dinner dress and ran back—in 10 minutes. Whew! A member of our party who saw me when I came in and out said, "That's the quickest I've ever seen *anyone* get ready for dinner."

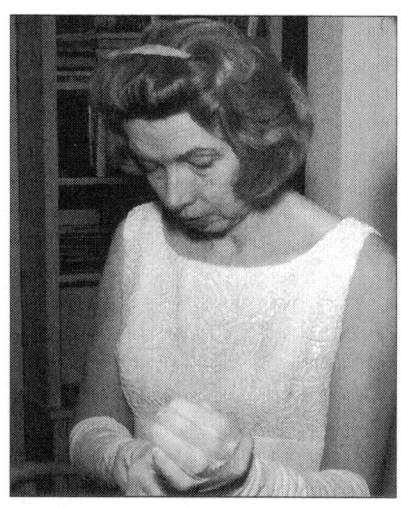

We drove and drove and drove—halfway back to the mountains. It was late. There, we were greeted by two horseback riders dressed in fancy clothes.

We walked into an immaculately clean stable where there were about ten horses. Then we went upstairs to be greeted by our host and hostess. We were served cocktails as we looked over the balcony into the "living room" which was actually a large arena.

Two riders had their horses perform in time to music. After that, a man pushed a wheel with a bull's head (complete with horns) to show how they train a horse in winter to fight bulls.

Career Elsie's Diary ~ 1969 ~ Air Force Two

Finally we're heading home. We were over the Atlantic before I knew it, eating a hearty American breakfast. Everyone looks sleepy and some climbed into the bunks that have been lowered.

My work is far from over. One official said, "I want you to make arrangements to connect with the Gulf Stream." I felt I had done enough on this trip.

This one stumped me until I realized it wasn't a *tail wind* he wanted but a Gulf Stream plane standing by at Andrews Air Force Base. The White House had asked the Bormans over for a debriefing. We ordered station wagons for the rest of the party.

I am to be the last one to leave. The people and baggage will soon be gone. ... And then me.

Injured Barbara ~ 1996 ~
How Far Can Energy Healing Travel?

"Let's go on another trip," I suggest to Sister Anita, a dear friend many years older than I. During her golden jubilee as a Carmelite sister, we had taken a "grand tour" of the United States and found we traveled well together.

Now, after much discussion, Anita suggests, "Let's drive to Chicago. We can stay with my family, then go on to Niagara Falls." Granted, not many people take vacations *north* in February, but it'd been a mild winter and fit our schedules. I planned to do most of the driving. ...

~ ~ ~

By the second day my right shoulder hurts so badly I can hardly turn the steering wheel. *I hope it's not a torn rotator cuff* I silently worry.

Unable to find a comfortable position for sleep, I am getting more and more tired. I need *sleep*. We still have 10 days of vacation to go. Lying in bed considering my options, I recall a recent conversation with Kenna.

She talked about experimenting with long-distance healing. *What have I got to lose,* I decide, *except a little money if it doesn't work?*

I call Kenna and we agree to work the next day at 5 a.m. Chicago time when hopefully I'll be asleep. I'm not. I struggle to relax, then suddenly—just as though she were actually there—I feel the familiar rippling, the deep relaxation. I fall asleep.

When I wake 2 hours later, I slowly sit up and rotate my arm. It's tender, but the sharp pain is completely gone. *Maybe just coincidence,* I admit, *but it's a huge difference.*

"Kenna," I call to thank her, "I think I'm okay." Once again, I want to know how she does this, especially long distance. "I just don't get it," I tell her.

"Oh," she laughs, "I don't know how to explain it. How is it that we are talking right now? We could talk about how the brain sends the signal to the mouth and tongue and how vibrations or waves go from your mouth into my ear."

I laugh. "I give up. Put that way, talking sounds just as strange."

I'd like to ask more questions, but I hear Sister Anita snapping her suitcase shut. It's time to go.

As we head out of Chicago, I turn the possibility of long-distance healing over in my mind. Most likely, we all have telepathic *possibilities*, but they remain unexplored.

We love our left brain—the part that analyzes, judges, and makes concrete decisions—and dismiss our right brain, that fertile area of intuition and insight. It slumbers on in our action-packed world. But Kenna not only retains a strong connection to her intuitive gifts, she hones and trains them.

Over time, Kenna and I will work exclusively this way. She saves travel time; I relax more deeply in my own bed. I still feel the rippling waves, the tingling, the experience of Light flowing in. I have the same grounded sensation and sense of deep interior massage. *I don't have to understand how this works,* I occasionally tell myself. Despite my scientific analytical nature that wants to intellectually understand, I realize my body responds to energy healing without any left-brain support from me.

February 26

Caregiver Barbara ~ 1994 ~
Visiting Mom in the Finnish-American Rest Home

I pull open the glass door to the Florida Finnish-American Rest Home glancing at the *Uuistet News* lying unopened beside a silk arrangement of yellow daffodils on the massive carved wood table.

A few nurses are chatting quietly. Piano music comes from the dining hall. It sounds like Charlie, the short, bald-headed man who once played with the Boston Pops. I hear his stubby, tanned fingers pummeling the keyboard playing ragtime music.

Having just arrived from the airport by taxi, I pull my suitcase down the long hall lined with built-in wooden benches that are empty.

By mealtime they will be filled.

Residents' doors will open: men and women will slowly emerge, some walking, some in wheelchairs, and others with walkers or canes. By the time they reach the lobby they will sit, perhaps to recover. The benches form the social heart of the Rest Home.

I leave my luggage outside Mom's locked door and walk to the dining hall. *She must be there. She loves Charlie's playing.* I remember seeing her at the family piano, anchoring the left pedal down with one foot, pumping the right, playing songs by heart--that slight off-rhythm beat I can never replicate. "Barbara," she'd say whenever I tried to copy her style, "what are you doing with your feet?"

I shove the door open. The music has stopped. Fragments of conversation in Finnish fill the air. I relax. This is the amniotic fluid I have swum in for years.

I find Mom sitting at a table in the back. She looks like a tiny-boned child with a neatly cut pageboy softly accenting her unusual blue eyes. Her eyes are changing. They still have a fire in them but it is like a fire burning in dense fog, a flame flicker that can only be seen up close.

I wave to her. She doesn't see me. Charlie starts playing again. Her fingers keep up the staccato pace on her blue-knit skirt. I walk to her table, stoop down and look into her eyes. "Have you got the key to your room?" I whisper. She shifts her gaze to me, answering brightly, "Oh, yes I do," then turns her vacant stare back to the piano and continues tapping her fingers on her leg.

For the first time, she has not recognized me.

Slowly I stand up, my knees crackling. *I'll ask the nurse to let me into her room,* I tell myself.

Quietly I trail after the RN down the hall, the happy music following us as she inserts the key, swings open the door, and leaves.

I go over to my mother's bed and sit down on the gold-and-white brocade spread. A new stillness has come into my life. And with it, the frightening sense that my mother is letting go, forever, of my daughter-child hand.

ELSIE AT EBB TIDE

Confused Elsie ~ 1995 ~ I Was There!

Rachel Hetico, the director of the Finnish-American Rest Home, pushes the door open. "Elsie, can we show your room? This couple would love to see your photographs."

On the walls, famous men and women smile out of their official, personally signed portraits. Elsie looks up from her green recliner, puts her hands on its wooden arms, and boosts herself up.

"Elsie worked for the Protocol Office in the U.S. State Department," Rachel explains. "She flew on the president's aircraft escorting delegations overseas."

Oh yes, I did do that, didn't I? "They signed that photo for me personally," Elsie tells the strangers, pointing to the smiling Kennedys. "I was there when he got shot."

The strangers turn toward this shrunken woman, her blue eyes still twinkling, intense but not quite focused, as though she is passionate but doesn't quite remember what she's passionate about.

"How amazing," they utter. "It must have been an exciting job."

"Oh it was," Elsie smiles. "I was in the car right behind him. I saw it all."

"You were *there*?" they ask, turning to the picture again.

Perhaps she was, they decide. After all, nobody ever shows pictures of who was in the car *behind* the president. How amazing.

They've met the very person who was feet away from the president when he was shot.

And I, her daughter, know that on that Friday, November 22, 1963, she was in Washington a thousand miles away from Dallas, alerting the diplomatic corps of his death and starting to help make arrangements for diplomats and heads of state to attend his funeral.

Caregiver Barbara ~ 1994 ~
Visiting Mom in the Finnish-American Rest Home
[Continued]

I hear the key slowly turn in the lock, the afternoon concert over. Mom carries her key on a string around her neck--*So I won't lose it, Barbara.*

I give her the cues: "Hi Mom, I just got in from the airport. You didn't recognize me with my new haircut."

"Oh, Barbara, you missed the BEST music today. That man."

"You mean Charlie? You love his music, Mom."

"Yes, Charlie. He was playing so good."

~ ~ ~

The next day, I let myself into her room. It is early afternoon. The curtains are drawn, the room sadly dark as though it has no life. My mother lies on her bed, one hand thrown over her eyes. I sit down quietly and watch her as she rests.

"Barbara?"

"Yes, Mom?"

"I don't know what's wrong with my head," she confides, rising up on one elbow to face me. "Can't you take me to some kind of doctor? I'm so confused." She pauses. "I didn't used to be this way."

"Mom," I answer, "it's a memory problem. Your mother had it. You have it. I don't think it will go away. It's your way of getting old."

She lies down on her bed and puts her hand back over her eyes.

I gaze at her tiny fragile body. Her funny sneakers with rainbow colors on them. Her white anklets. The blue skirt and aged V-neck cotton T-shirt. Her paper-thin skin with its lines and liver spots. I try to understand her silent world. "It feels like fog, Barbara."

I try to imagine. *A gummy world where thoughts get stuck. Mind stillfulness. Around her, people would keep moving and talking, loving and laughing. But she will be motionless in a vast strange land of inner silence.*

Neither of us speaks. The air conditioner clicks on. A wave of cool air begins its trek across the stuffy room. I sink into my own silent world––that slow moving river of quiet filled with strange flotsam of memories, emotions, dialogues. Her Westclox ticks its way like a river barge across a watery world.

Outside two women walk by chattering in Finnish. A peal of laughter bursts out.

Their voices catapult me into the past. I am a little girl where men and women dance, and vodka-loosened laughter rolls into the room. A woman bends down speaking Finnish to my sister and me. *Hyvaa yolua,* I reply. "Merry Christmas." My sister carefully intones the sounds *bah-nay might-toe yek-a-peen*: "Put the milk in the refrigerator." The woman laughs and walks away.

I feel safe in this cocooned world of sounds without meaning. Like a favored child in her mother's arms, I bob up and down on this sea of words, lost in my own silent world of fantasy.

"Barbara?" Mom sits up with a worried look on her face. "I can't find ... this thing. I use it to put things together." She forms her hands together in the shape of a ball. "It looks like this and you pull things off of it."

I open the drawer of her nightstand, pull out a little plastic storage box, and pry open the lid. "Do you mean this, Mom?" I ask, holding up scotch tape.

"Oh yes," she smiles with relief. "How did you KNOW where to find it, Barbara?"

She picks up a piece of paper with my telephone number written on it and tapes it to her wall. I reach over and turn her tape recorder on.

"Come on, Mom," I say, let's dance."

Student Barbara ~ 1960 ~ Clothes and Cloths

"Barbara," I hear Mom's voice sounding a tad too stern, "Come here."

This is *never* good news. I put down my Nancy Drew book reluctantly. Mom walks over and closes the bedroom door. Now I *know* I'm in trouble. But why? I've done the chores. My homework is finished. I'm home on time. What could possibly be wrong?

She's holding one of my school papers in her hand.

"Barbara, look at this." She shows me an essay I've written. "Your spelling is atrocious. If you don't spell better, you'll never get into college!"

But I'm in seventh grade, I think. *I'm not even sure I want to go.*

"Spell clothes, Barbara."

Jeez, what a simple word, I say to myself as I spell aloud, "C-l-o-t-h." I pause ... "s."

"Barbara," Mom looks outraged. "That's *cloths!* Kitchen rags. Clothes ends with es."

Decades later, I still stumble over this word.

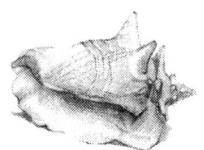

And Now, Another Journey Begins ...

Month by month, year by year, Mom loses ground until, nearing the last year of her life in 1999, time ceases to matter. One day I stop by to visit her. I bend over her bed to look into her eyes. Something is *very* wrong. She gazes at me like a trapped, wild, terrified animal.

"Mom, what's *wrong*?" I ask the one question she cannot answer.

I begin to panic. *Is she in pain? Is she trapped in some awful nightmare? What if she needs to go to the emergency room?*

I feel completely helpless. I will my mind to find a way into hers. I keep staring at her, increasingly anxious ... and in that moment the thought of *Kenna* flies into my mind.

"Mom," I say, "I'll be right back. I need to make a call." I rush from the room. As I hurry to the phone, I tell myself, *Kenna can connect with Mom.*

I make the call that will change everything about the way I think about Alzheimer's.

~ ~ ~

"Kenna," a whirlwind of words pours out my mouth, "Mom's in trouble. Something's wrong and I don't know what. She may be in physical pain, or she's in some awful nightmare. Can you connect with her right away and find out what's happening."

"I'll have to ask her permission, Barbara."

"I know," I answer. Kenna's standards for intervention are high. She treats each soul with the greatest respect. Mom, though damaged by Alzheimer's, still retains an intact functioning spirit. Kenna will be connecting with that higher self, asking permission to visit.

Now I have to wait. I pace. I wash dishes. I try to sit and calm myself. At last the phone rings.

"Your mother was very anxious, Barbara. When I asked her why, she said, 'I don't know where I am. I'm afraid I'm dying.' I explained everything to her. I think you'll find she's calmer now."

Overwhelmed with relief, I hang up. When I return, I find Mom's face once again calm, her eyes quiet and seemingly lost; she has returned to the only normalcy I know-- Alzheimer's.

After this frightening episode, Sandra and I agree. We hire Kenna to connect regularly with Mom.

We reserve judgment. It may be "real"; it may be sheer fantasy. But if it gives Mom comfort, we are willing to explore this avenue of communication. "I'll write down whatever Kenna tells me," I promise my sister.

And so, a door opens.

Child Barbara ~ 2002 ~ Purple-Colored Memories

Purple. It is a color my father hated. ...

"You remember that old icebox in your kitchen?" Mom's oldest Finn-American friend Mim asks me.

Of course I do. Our beloved little icebox. It squatted in the kitchen corner on four clubbed metal feet and its door gave a satisfyingly solid thunk when we pulled the stainless steel handle up. It clearly predated our need to have trays of frozen ice cubes. To its credit, it was electrified. A motor sat on the top purring away.

Eventually the icebox was moved to the furnace area like a shunned date, to make way for a more cavernous refrigerator. I visited it on occasion in the dark scary unfinished portion of our basement because it held excess food when my parents gave a party.

Then one day, after I was grown and gone, I made a nostalgic trip downstairs and noticed the icebox was missing. This beautiful four-footed goddess had probably gone to the dump. I felt the sadness one gets when parents disassemble our childhood memories.

I look at Mim, this petite rounded matriarch filled with stories. "Yes, it was our first refrigerator. What about it?"

"Well," Mim answers, laughter pouring out of her button blue eyes, "your mother painted it because she was so mad at your father."

"Huh? It's white."

"Did you ever look at it closely?" she asks.

"Ohhh," I say as a memory flashes by. "it was *painted* white instead of factory white. I never thought about that."

"*Repainted* to be white once again!" Mim exclaims.

I put my chin on my hands, "Okay, what happened to the icebox?"

"Well, it had a habit of walking," Mim explains. "The motor vibrated so much, and the kitchen floor wasn't level. By the time your mother got home from work, it walked halfway across the room--as far as its cord could reach."

"When Herby got home, Elsie would tell him every single day to fix it. Nothing ever happened though Herby always promised he'd get around to it."

I grin, remembering the kitchen drawers filled to overflowing with nails, hinges, oilcans--potential material for fix-it projects. Instinctively I knew the walking icebox would have safe sanctuary in our kitchen until its legs fell off from stress metal fractures.

I begin to wonder how I would have handled the situation. Whining? Rage? Refusal to cook?

"Well, Elsie painted it *purple*. You father *hated* purple."

I can see the whole scene. The claw-footed purple icebox vibrating its way into the middle of the kitchen like a Parisian model on meth coming down the linoleum runway.

"Then merry as a Cheshire cat knowing a mouse is coming, she waited for Herby to come home. ..."

Now this would be standard Finnish practice in our house. Silence. Maybe it's a tundra thing. Maybe if your gene pool spent most of its evolutionary life in a sunless world, it evokes the only possible response--silence. Finns are not known for heated arguments. White-hot anger comes out of Finns in perfect monosyllabic ice-cube form.

For a Finn to even *think* of painting an *expensive* kitchen appliance purple ... well, it probably hadn't ever been thought of by a single Finnish person in the whole United States. It would be like a Finn smiling—for no reason.

"Your Dad didn't say a word," Mim continues. "But," she finishes the story, her tinkle-like laughter rippling out, "that refrigerator never walked again."

"Okay, that kind of explains *the dress*," I tell Mim.

I never saw Mom wear purple until I was a teenager. But one day on her lunch break, she decided to shop at Garfinkels where stylish Washington women bought their clothing. There on the sales rack hung the most beautiful Jacqueline Kennedy style wool sheath dress with a full-length matching coat. It was lovely, affordable, and purple.

Mom just couldn't leave it, marriage vows or not.

Lugging her oversized box back to the Protocol Office, Elsie fretted. "What will I tell Herby?"

Her coworker Mary Edith, being imbued with a true Protocol Officer's heart, quickly solved the problem. "Just tell him it's *blue*. He'll never notice the difference."

Mom sailed home with her box—buoyed by this slight ripple of hope. I, personally, would not have been buoyed.

"What's in the box, Elsie?"

"Oh, just something I got on sale."

"Well, let's see it."

No amount of dodging could get her out of this moment, so she takes a deep breath, opens the box, holds up the dress, and says, "Isn't this a beautiful blue dress, Herby?"

He takes one astonished look and says, "That's PURPLE."

Elsie the skilled Protocol Officer quickly negotiates, "I'll only wear it to work, Herby. I promise."

So Mom would put on her Jacqueline outfit, becoming the most beautiful purple-clad mother in the world. I remember those days with fondness. They were the *good* fashion years.

Then one day, a Scandinavian furniture store aptly named SCAN opened its doors in our neighborhood. This visionary forerunner of IKEA introduced America to the beauty of an unembellished line. Suddenly I found myself sitting at a utilitarian teak Scandinavian table on minimalist Scandinavian chairs picking up food with Scandinavian stainless steel cutlery, all placed upon a Scandinavian rya rug. Then one day Elsie saw a dress rack in SCAN.

That was the beginning of the end.

ELSIE AT EBB TIDE

Picture an A-line dress made of fortified cotton so thick it could stand up wondering why it would need a hanger. Then add *huge* geometric printed objects on it, like Calder mobiles flattened into garish reds, oranges, greens, or blues. Next, pop a skinny 5' 7" blonde into it with sensible pumps and a handbag, and you have Elsie-in-the-70s.

What possessed a furniture store to think it could furnish women? The dresses made Mom look like a lampshade. I grieved the loss of the purple Elsie.

March

Life in the Finnish Lane

March 5

Child Elsie ~ 1928 ~
Before Riding on Air Force II, There Was ...

Finlayson, Minnesota winters are dark dreadful things. Elsie tries to hide under a pile of blankets in the futile hope her grandparents will somehow overlook her. She scrunches down mouselike, still as a winter tree on a windless night. She hears noises downstairs, feet shuffling, coffee pot clanking onto the wood stove, her grandmother's voice hollering up the stairs, "Elsie, *herää!*"--"Wake up!" She ignores the first holler up the stairs. "Elsie, *herää* " goes sailing out the thin-paned window over the barren farm fields. That call is for some other Elsie somewhere ... maybe a thousand miles away.

"ELSIE," she hears the thunderous voice in her ear; she feels her toasty warm skin unceremoniously exposed to frigid Minnesota air. It is morning. There is nothing she can do about it. She pulls on every piece of clothing she can lay her hands on, each piece colder than the last. She shivers uncontrollably as she dashes downstairs, heading for the hot stove and huddles in misery by its side.

"*Istu alas ja syödä.*" "Sit down and eat, girl," Grandma Liisa reminds her, and Elsie leaves the last bit of real warmth to be a proper girl—to eat eggs and bacon at the kitchen table, which is too far away from the stove's warmth. She knows worse is to come. Dazed by sleep, half frozen, she muddles through breakfast and heads out the door with her books to wait for the wagon to pick her up. Out of the pitch black, she hears the horses whinnying, the hooves clomping, and soon the covered wagon glides into sight.

Decades later, she will see humor in this. A *covered wagon*--who goes to school in a prairie wagon? During the summer, wooden wheels roll down dirt roads to the two-room schoolhouse. At some magical moment in November or December, one day she won't hear the creak of the wheels; she'll hear the cutting glide of the skis. Then she'll know they're in the dread dead of winter and, for the next several months, she'll be miserable.

Today, Mr. Erikson handles the two-horse team pulling the school bus.

The farmers take turns driving the wagon stored in the barn behind the Finnish Lutheran church. The wagon floor is covered with straw. Elsie scrambles in, finds her seat on the wood plank bench running from the rear to the front, and quickly puts her hot stone on the floor so her feet won't freeze.

Through the still-falling snow, the wagon jostles over hard bumpy ice that is now months old but still unmelted. The horses pick up speed. It'll be 15 minutes before they get to the next farm. She dozes, slumping over her books.

It's been snowing hard. The twelve students jerk back and forth. The wagon suddenly hits an icy bump and they start to tip. They try to lean to the other side--they've been told to do that--but too little, too late. The hitch breaks and the wagon tumbles over, leaving Mr. Erikson and the horses atop the hill.

Suddenly, her body crashes against the canvas wall. She is rolling, books and hot stones flying.

She careens into Bobby, sending his glasses flying in the air. One girl keeps hollering for her mama. Then silence. They land on their side covered in snow. Josephine, the redheaded first grader, ends up next to Elsie, screaming and screaming.

Torn out of her sleep, unceremoniously dumped into a bank of snow, cold and unhappy about winter in general, she turns to the tear-streaked hysterical Josephine.

"Oh, SHUT UP."

Career Elsie ~ 1958 ~ Testing Telephone Etiquette

"Mr. Spruks," Elsie pokes her head into her boss's office. "Can I speak to you for a moment?" Spruks, a tall ex-military man with a square-cut face looks up from the papers on his massive wood desk. "Come in, Mrs. Nurmi."

When she accepted the promotion from State Department typing pool to personal secretary, coworkers warned her, "He's really difficult to work for."

Duly warned but undaunted, she entered the Office of Protocol for the first time and found a party in progress. Elsie began to network right away, chatting up the man nearest her saying with newfound authority, "I'm Elsie Nurmi. I am Mr. Spruks's secretary."

He glared down at her. "Well, it's nice to meet you, Mrs. Nurmi. I am Mr. Spruks."

A few weeks into the job, Elsie's confidence soared. One day when the phone rang for Mr. Spruks, she put the caller on hold and yodeled into his open doorway, "Mr. Spruks, you have a call on line 2." She returned to typing. After a minute or so, Mr. Spruks called her on the extension. "Would you come into my office, Mrs. Nurmi?"

She picked up her steno pad and walked over to his desk. He still had the phone receiver in his right hand.

"NEVER EVER yell through that door again, Mrs. Nurmi," Mr. Spruks chiseled out each word, slamming the receiver into the telephone cradle so hard the phone began to fly across his massive walnut desk. Elsie stood ramrod straight, not moving a muscle, not flinching, not blinking. They both watched the heavy rotary phone flying straight for her belly. Inches before collision, it stopped.

"Yes, Mr. Spruks. Is there anything else?"

And that, if you can believe it, was the start of a great relationship. So when Elsie walked into his office this day, he calmly waited for her to speak.

"Mr. Spruks," Elsie begins, "the room where we keep the gifts is getting crowded. How do we ever clean it out?" She was, of course, referring to gifts given to American citizens by officials of foreign governments.

"It takes an act of Congress to release them," he explains. The president has to sign it into law.

"So how does one do that?" Elsie persists.

"You have to make a list of every item--what it is, who it is intended for, which government gave it, and so on." He smiles. "The only thing that *hasn't* gotten into that room is the stallion Jacqueline Kennedy got from the president of Pakistan."

"Would you mind if I try to do that?"

Spruks raises his eyebrows in surprise. "You can try but you have to deliver it on the first day of Congress for there to be any chance it'll make it to the president's desk. And," he looks pointedly at her, "you can't let any of your other work slip."

"Let me see what I can do, sir." Shortly thereafter, Elsie requests a State Department car and driver to take her to Capitol Hill. She walks in with a massive sheath of typed paper. It becomes Senate Bill S.3198, the first step toward becoming a law.

Career Elsie ~ 1956 ~ Traveling in a Travelall

"Mom, Dad," I run into the kitchen, "someone wants to see our car." *Who drives all the way to Takoma Park to see a new car,* I wonder as I trail my parents out the door.

The middle-aged couple peer through the windows of our new International Harvester Travelall.

Polite enough not to comment on the colors (pink on top, gray on bottom), they marvel at how sturdy it looks. "The dealer told us you bought the first one in D.C. They don't have any on the lot so we thought we'd drive over. Hope that's okay."

My father swings open the driver's door proclaiming, "It's built like a truck. I wanted Elsie to be safe, especially when we get snow or ice." (He cared considerably less for his own safety. He threw his carpentry tools into cantankerous, partially rusted wrecks with semi-bald tires.)

"You'll have trouble insuring it," Mom admits.

"Why?"

Mom breaks into her mischievous smile. "It's got *three* doors--two in the front and one on the back right passenger side. The insurance agent will tell you that's impossible."

Fifty-one years later, a September 2007 *New York Times* article will report that Travelall was America's first SUV. The International Harvester company "initiated a marketing campaign directed at *suburban* families [but] ... unfortunately the timing wasn't ideal."

Mom eventually replaced that "SUV" with a newer slimmed-down, red-and-white model that she and Dad once drove to the White House for a reception.

Career Elsie ~ 1962 ~
U.S. Constitutionally Quarantined Gifts

Four years after stepping into Mr. Spruks's office, Mom appears in an *American Weekly* article "Gifts to the White House," an insert magazine in the *New York Journal American*.

The article begins, "To keep or not to keep, that is the question. Whether 'tis nobler to turn all gifts over to the government, or to save a few for oneself."

The problem, of course, arises in the Constitution. "No person holding any office of profit or trust ... shall, without the consent of the Congress, accept ... any present ... of any kind whatever, from any king, prince, or foreign state."

That's why Elsie had to type up a law. But the article puts flesh on the problem--not only on Jacqueline's stallion called Sardar from Ayub Khan of Pakistan. There's a spinning wheel from the shrine of Mahatma Gandhi, a priceless five-strand pearl necklace, *Don Quixote* printed entirely on cork, a jewel-encrusted dagger, a harem dress, and even a deep freezer. Then there's the question of first ladies who are not employees of the U.S. government. They hold no "office of profit" though perhaps one of trust.

At any rate in the article, a black-suited, smiling, bouffant-coiffed Elsie twists the dial on the combination lock of the door securing the gifts. The caption reads, "The State Department puts most gifts from foreign countries to public officials into this special storage chamber. Every four years Congress passes a statute allowing those people no longer in government service to claim their property." (If, that is, anyone takes the time to type up the law and deliver it to Congress in the first place.)

Confused Elsie ~ 1996 ~
You Go Your Way, I'll Go Mine

"Barbara," Rachel Hetico calls me from the Finnish-American Rest Home. "You're going to have to move your mother elsewhere."

"Why?" I hold the receiver numbly, my body suddenly frozen. "What's wrong? I thought Mom could stay there forever."

"Barbara, your mother's bothering Victor Salmela. She goes to his room, visits, leaves, forgets, and goes to his room again. He finds it upsetting because he likes Elsie but now that he lives here, he needs his privacy respected.

"Also," Rachel's voice turns matter of fact, "I'm retiring."

"You're WHAT?" I ask, sitting down to calm myself.

"Barbara, the board of directors begged me to straighten things out two years ago. I gave in, but really I wanted to retire then."

I hear the determined readiness in her voice but the pauses seem tinged with sadness. She goes on, "it's better if you place her while I'm still here. She no longer fits our assisted-living guidelines, but I just made it work because I'm so fond of you and Sandra and Elsie."

"Oh Rachel," I sigh. "That means a lot." And we hang up.

Whenever I feel the earth shift beneath me, when my emotions go into free fall, I sit in my Amish rocker, sometimes still as a fragile piece of glass. Now I sit in shock, not moving, hardly thinking. Slowly I accept this new reality. I'll have to tell Mom and the only way will be in person. I call Sandra and book a flight.

One week later, I stand outside the West Palm Beach airport, giving the taxi driver Rachel's address. Soon we are sipping wine by her pool.

"Well, I'm not looking forward to tomorrow," I admit anxiously. "I know what this is going to cost her--loss of friends, loss of Victor, dependence on me, staying in a strange new facility. She'll somehow know this is a very BAD thing. I'm afraid she's going to fight me all the way." Later I fall into a troubled sleep.

~ ~ ~

"Mom," I say gently the next day as we walk out of the dining hall and begin the stroll towards her room.

"Yes," she absentmindedly answers. "What?"

"Rachel Hetico is leaving. She can't watch over you anymore. I want to move you to Maryland so I can take care of you and visit more."

"I don't want to leave. In fact, I have no intention of leaving."

I can see that Finnish *sisu* rising up in her.

"Mom, I wish there was another way. But I can't take care of you far away like this."

"Barbara," she icily glares at me, "I've never told you this, but I don't like you. I never used the word love with you or Sandra. I reserved that word for Herby. I think we should just part ways. You go your way. I'll go mine." She walks into her room and clicks the door shut.

I feel I may fall to the floor. Her words slam into me like an emotional earthquake. Tears welling up, I run out of the Rest Home afraid others will see me. Hardly able to see where I'm going, I drive to Rachel's house. Sobbing, I pick up the phone and call Sandra. I sound like a bottled frog.

Our well-thought-out strategy hasn't worked.

In fact, *none* of our strategies work. *Our* plan was that Mom would stay in the Rest Home forever, and Rachel would watch over her. We assumed Mom would move to their nursing wing but no beds are available. Even so, I can't do close monitoring from 1,100 miles away. Victor no longer can help. Each plan we've devised eventually crumbles because the disease itself relentlessly makes them obsolete.

I finally get the words out. "She's *really* mad, Sandra. She said she never used the word love with you or me, and I should just go my way and she'll go hers."

After Broward Hospital's testing, Sandra and I made decisions about how Mom's care would be handled. With Sandra in Seattle, me in Maryland, and Mom in Florida, we realized we had *no* plan in place and no one to keep an eye on her.

This was the beginning of Sandra and I melding our different temperaments together. I saw crises around every corner. I projected *way* into the future. Sandra, on the other hand, remained cheerfully optimistic. She saw Mom at her highest possible functioning, I, at her lowest.

Because I was closest geographically to Mom, and Sandra was still raising her sons and dealing with a full-time engineering job, I became the de facto care manager. As things unfolded, Sandra's job was to support *me* emotionally.

Now as I sat weeping in Rachel's chair, Sandra went all out. "I'll fly there *right now. The bitch.*"

Now there is nothing quite as heartening as having your sister call your mother a bitch--it seriously lightens up the mood. I burst into teary laughter. Then Sandra, relieved I was feeling better, laughed too. We hung up.

When Rachel came home, puffy-eyed I quietly told her what Mom had said--that she never used the word love with Sandra or me. Rachel leapt out of her chair, swept me into her ample bosom, and said, "*I love you.*" I truly felt better.

When I flew home, I felt emotionally paralyzed for 3 days. I sat in my walnut rocker. I did nothing to analyze my feelings or fix them. I felt the stunned shock. I felt the helplessness. I felt the anger. I let everything flow through me, holding on to nothing. Often I sat staring into nothing. But miraculously after 3 days, I got up feeling whole and peaceful once again. *She fought like a cornered wild animal,* I knew, and despite her declaration to the contrary, she loved me. *It's a different love than for Herby,* I decided, *but it's real.* Nevertheless, I had to admit that compared to emotional battering from earlier trips, this had been the harshest.

A few days later I pulled out the greeting cards I had kept from Mom and opened them. She had never signed a single one of them "Love, Mom."

I hadn't noticed.

Kenna and Elsie ~ 2000 ~ *Is It Today or Tomorrow?*

It is the last year of Mom's life. With mother-daughter conversation no longer possible, Sandra and I ask Kenna to continue connecting with Mom. I turn over questions in my mind. *Will we know if it's really Elsie? What do I want to ask her? Does this help her?* I see it as an experiment. I have few if any expectations other than a *hope* that Kenna can indeed meet with Mom on a spirit level.

When Kenna asks me, "Do you have anything you want to know from your mother?" At first I say no but then I pause, "Kenna, we have no idea what she wants for a funeral. Does she want to be cremated or buried? Does she have any special songs she wants at her memorial service? We never asked her and now it seems too late."

"Well," Kenna offers, "Let's see what she says."

~ ~ ~

Elsie: *I want to kick up my heels and ride out of here. I just want to move. I feel like fish soup. Once the fish is in the soup, it's not likely to go anywhere else.*

Kenna: You can go places in your mind.

Elsie: *Yes, that's the only book I read now. Reading the mind with its jumbled pages. Short stories instead of a long novel.*

Kenna: I'm experiencing these little scenes with you, Elsie.

Elsie: *I feel lost and found. You can always find me here in this body but my mind is often lost.*

Elsie: *Why doesn't Sandra come to visit?*

Kenna: She is far away.

Elsie: *I'm getting old and I am not really enjoying this. I am all right but this is no fun. Sometimes I feel like I will be here forever whether I want to be or not.*

Kenna: Yes, but you are staying.

Elsie: *I feel safe here.*

Kenna: I can help you feel safe on the other side.

Elsie: *I am not ready yet.*

Elsie: *My thoughts used to be quite orderly. I liked plans, knowing what to expect when. Now time runs together for me, like rivers into oceans. Is it today or yesterday? Time is something I have so much of, but I do not know what to do with it or where to put it. I do not need to save it because it is always available. The monotony is unbelievable and I am a part of it. I used to be very busy, but now is now.*

Kenna: Do you want to tell Barbara anything?

ELSIE AT EBB TIDE

Elsie: *I'm actually okay. I'm feeling better. I want to tell her that it is not just that I do not make any sense but not much of anything makes sense, so how can I?*

Kenna: Do you want me to help you here, or there?

Elsie: *I don't know. I like the in-between.*

Kenna: Barbara worries about what you will want for your funeral.

Elsie: *You know it really does not matter that much to me now. I suppose a church is nicer and Barbara would like it, don't you think? But I am really only interested in music. I still want to dance, you know. I like piano better than organ.*

Elsie: *You can bury ashes, can't you? I certainly could stand being a little warmer. Then, I don't know. Whatever is easier for Barbara. I used to worry about such details.*

Kenna: You have lots of family [deceased] around you. You can tell the angels what you need and they will help you.

Elsie: *My husband liked the beach. My days are like this. Reminiscing.*

Kenna: Is there anything I can do for you?

Elsie: *Can you sing?*

Kenna: I really cannot sing. But I will sing a little lullaby.

Kenna: There are four angels. Can you see them?

Elsie: *No, but I feel them.*

~ ~ ~

As I listen to Kenna read her notes about her conversation with Elsie, I am struck by how a new relationship begins.

Mom speaks in her trademark somewhat-humorous voice. She's an action person. *I want to kick up my heels.*

Kenna prefers the subtle spiritual approach ... *You can go places in your mind.* Clearly, Elsie doesn't know much about that world. She begins by talking about fish soup, something Americans would rarely if ever eat but something with which Finns would be well acquainted.

She explains to Kenna that Herby loved the beach. True. She tells Kenna she loves to dance. True. That she prefers the piano to the organ. True. She always owned a piano and played it, while she only used the organ during her teen years for the Finlayson church.

When asked about funeral arrangements, she admits she longer cares much about it. The woman who designed her own monument down to its last chiseled letter now admits *I used to worry about such details.*

To my surprise, she asks about burying ashes.

Sandra and I have presumed, having no guidance from her, that she preferred burial because she wanted to wear the black suit she wore when meeting Pope Paul VI. But now she jokes, *I certainly could stand being a little warmer.*

"So what do we do?" I later ask my sister.

"I think she wants to be with Dad in every way," Sandra answers. "He was cremated. It makes her feel closer to him."

Knowing our mother, that makes absolute sense. She will be buried in accordance with her long-standing wishes in Finlayson Lutheran Cemetery. But not in body—in ashes.

Most important from a caregiving perspective, I learn her level of awareness. She wonders why Sandra is not visiting.

I feel for the first time that we have a link to Elsie--a way, however tenuous, to communicate. A process begins that we will use until Mom dies. In fact, Kenna will be connected to my mother within an hour of her death, and then within hours, on the other side.

Retired Elsie ~ 1991 ~ An Intruder!

Thundering trains, ambulances, cars--nothing disturbs my mother when she sleeps in her Lake Worth home. But on this particular morning at 3 a.m., she hears something scratching in the bathroom. Gingerly she opens the door--and *there* is a water rat so big its head touches the toilet and its tail swishes the opposite wall.

She slams the door shut. What to do? After all, it is ungodly early. Who can help her? Only one person: Doris Holmes, her practical no-nonsense friend.

"Doris," she hisses over the phone, apparently afraid the rat will hear. "I've got a gigantic RAT in my bathroom. I don't know what to do!"

"Call the police. It's an intruder."

"It's not an intruder; it's a RAT."

But Doris insists. After all, who would invite a rat into their home?

So Mom feeling somewhat sheepish calls 911, doubtful her plea will bring a real policeman. To her amazement, two burly men arrive, holstered and ready for the kill. Five hundred pounds of police against one hefty rat. Mom wonders if they can all fit into her small bathroom. But in they go. The war-of-the-rat is on.

Seconds go by, then minutes. Finally one policeman comes out and asks, "Do you have rat poisoning or anything?" Mom hands him a spray can of mosquito repellent. The man sighs and reenters rat land.

More minutes pass. The policeman comes out and reports, "He is getting tired. He's not jumping as high in the bathtub. Have you got something we can put him in?" Mom hands him a grocery bag.

Fifteen minutes later the police emerge triumphant with one very tired rat that will probably never get a mosquito bite.

When I think of all the years that Mom determinedly put every scrap of garbage into plastic bags to thwart cockroaches, it doesn't seem fair to have a rat crawl out of your toilet bowl.

The next morning as Mom fixes breakfast, she turns her head to glance out the living-room window and sees a green tail hanging over her shoulder. "Oh *no!*" She yells, "No No NO!" marching irately out of the house with a gecko perched on her blouse.

The wild-animal saga not yet over, later that morning her neighbor alerts her, "There's a large black snake sitting on your front step."

Tackling the snake with a broom, she flings it into the grass, slams the door shut, and for good measure locks it.

Career Elsie ~ 1974 ~ A Mother and Daughter Talk

"Why did you leave me at your parents, Mom?" Elsie sits at the kitchen table in the Duluth boarding house her mother Jennie manages. Elsie works as a Protocol Officer and wears smart clothes but she still remembers. *They took Lucy. Why not me?*

Jennie sips her black coffee. "Your grandmother kept after me to leave you. She wanted you to stay because you had a way with your grandfather. He'd do anything for you. She wore me down," her voice falters, "but I shouldn't have given in."

"You *wanted* to take me?" Elsie replies, surprised.

"Elsie, we had no money. None of the men could get jobs. A friend got your dad the granary job in Duluth. He had to take it. All we could afford was a two-room flat. Lucy was still nursing. I *hated* leaving you, but ..." her soft-noted voice fluttered to a halt.

Elsie suddenly remembers all the times her grandmother would call her, "Elsie, *kerro ukki* ... tell Grandpa, and out would pop her request. Visit Mary. Go to town. Attend a church event.

Of course, Elsie could care less about most of those outings but she'd run to grandpa. He'd stop milking or plowing or hammering, look at Elsie's tow-headed straight-cut hair and mischievous blue eyes, and melt. "We'll go later this afternoon if you want."

Then Elsie'd run back to her grandmother: *"Hän sanoo voimme mennä iltapäi vällä "*--"he says we'll go this afternoon." And her grandmother would smile.

Turning to her mother, Elsie admits, "I felt like you didn't want me." Elsie twists her empty coffee cup around. Then she laughs. "She was really strict! It wasn't much fun."

Grandparents Henry and Liisa Askelin

"Don't you *ever* play cards, Elsie. It's *pahaa*." Evil. "We don't do that sort of thing. We're Lutherans." *Luterilaiset*.

Oh, but everybody else plays cards, Elsie thinks to herself. *It must be because they're store-bought! That's what makes them bad. I'll make a set. Then they'll be okay.*

Elsie cuts out card-sized rectangles and meticulously colors each one. Aces, deuces, kings, queens. Slowly the deck emerges, card by card, until she holds her handmade deck. She is shuffling her artwork, inordinately proud. Her grandmother walks in.

"What's that in your hand, Elsie?"

"I *made* them, Grandma. I didn't buy them.

"Elsie," Grandma's voice storms. "I said they're BAD." Taking the cards out of Elsie's hand, muttering *Esitän heilli juuri ny*, "I'm going to throw them away," she walks over to the woodburning stove and opens the door. Inside, Elsie can see the bed of glowing hot coals. In one second, all the cards land in a heap atop them. They smoke. The edges curl. And in a minute, they're gone.

~ ~ ~

Jennie collects the cups and puts them in the sink. She has her life and Elsie has hers. They are nothing alike. Jennie keeps a boarding house for single men and has a man to keep her company. She has her German cuckoo clock in the sitting room, her hand-crocheted doilies on the stuffed furniture, orchids blooming in the bay window. Elsie plans trips for important people. She travels around the world.

She's left the farmhouse far behind.

Nervous Barbara ~ 2003 ~ First Encounter of a Psychic Kind

"Would you like me to do a reading for you, Barbara?" my new friend Angelita asks.

NO, I am thinking. *Absolutely not*. I don't want to hurt Angelita's feelings but I don't want someone messing around with my psyche, peering into secret portals, seeing stuff I don't want *anyone* to see. *How did I get in this fix?* I wonder.

The first step, of course, was moving to Poulsbo, Washington. Forever believing I truly wasn't a Maryland girl, on vacations I'd wonder, *Is this my place? Or this?* I remember standing in the middle of Durango, Colorado, one morning, the sun burning down on me. I stretched my arms wide, threw my head back, and exclaimed, "I'm a DURANGO girl."

I never got there.

~ ~ ~

My move to Poulsbo comes in a roundabout way as things of importance often do. While visiting my sister, I pop down to the little craft-and-coffee town of Poulsbo. I wander through stores, once again smitten by the quaint beauty of this village perched aside Liberty Bay with the Olympic Mountains in the background.

I chance into a nook-sized New Age store and pause to look at jewelry, pick up crystals, browse books, smell incense, and read the signs advertising psychic readings.

Eventually I begin to talk with a woman named Angelita. She makes drums according to the Native American tradition, showing me a beautiful twelve-sided cedar drum covered with elk skin. "The wood is taken in a sacred way," she explains, "hand timbered. This is the last drum coming from that tree."

I find myself drawn to the drum *and* to Angelita, a petite woman my age with long silver-gray hair and dark, shining eyes. As we begin to chat, I mention my wanderlust. "I *love* Poulsbo," I admit.

"Well, why don't you move here?" she suggests. *What a ridiculous idea,* I think.

The storeowner chips in. "Envision exactly what you want and let it materialize. Draw it on paper."

I hate New Age talk. It sounds so woo-woo to me. I say my good-byes and move on to other shops. But the next morning, with my sister and brother-in-law at work, I'm alone with nothing to do. I find myself picking up a cocktail napkin left on the kitchen table and sketching a dream apartment. I lay out where the two bedrooms, kitchen, living room, and bath would be. I even include closets. I position the apartment so I can see the mountains.

With a sense of whimsy and napkin in hand, I look at apartments. When I walk into the Hilltop complex perched above town, I nearly drop from shock. The *exact* apartment I drew exists, with the view I want. Though I hadn't included price in my reveries, it is right. I can take a 6-month lease.

Back home, I examine possibilities. I am single once again. My beautiful nineteen-year-old feeling of love slowly collapsed under the weight of reality. Never had two people tried so hard to make a marriage work. After years of listening, my therapist gently suggested, "You are two great people in a wrong relationship." I ended our twenty-five-year marriage, and we coparented our daughters through their teens with a daily arrangement. As difficult and painful as the divorce was, we worked hard to parent our children and keep what *was* healthy. A friendship.

Now with our daughters grown, I feel free to leave Maryland. *If I rent my house, I can use that money to pay for the apartment rental. It will be a cost-free experiment.*

I buy a fifteen-year-old van from my ex-husband, sell my RV to a man called Mr. Godlove, load up my loom, mattress, pots and pans, clothing, dog, cockatiel, and canary, and with my friend Ann supporting me, head west.

That's how I end up in Poulsbo. After settling in, I renew my acquaintance with Angelita. I soon learn that not only does she make drums, she offers psychic readings. I never ask for one because it seems a bit scary to me.

Now she is offering a free reading as a thank-you for my helping her haul some furniture in my van. Not a fast thinker, I cannot come up with a polite way to say no, and find myself entering her private reading area.

~ ~ ~

I sit nervously on a wooden chair with a soft cushion across from Angelita, shielded from store customers by a bookcase and blue curtain. She lights a white candle. "This tells the spirits what we are about to do." She places it on a table covered with a blue-purple velvet cloth. A solitary blue-gray stone, which looks like a squat wand rests on the table. "What's that?" I ask.

"Kyanite," she says, picking it up and handing it to me. "It helps cleanse and balance your aura."

I put it down. "It sounds like Superman's kryptonite." Frankly, I am doubtful. I don't believe that kyanite balances anything; I am not convinced a lit candle opens the door to spirits. I am perhaps the psychic's worst customer--a frightened skeptic. Yet Angelita seems entirely unconcerned.

I find myself perplexed. When she talks about Native American sun dances, the sacred tree, the moon lodge, blessing what you take, sweat lodges, eagle feathers, though it is not my way, I feel profound respect for her. That tradition seems so *grounded*. The alcove I now sit in seems so *ungrounded*. I have no idea how Angelita makes sense of these two worlds. The only common denominator I can see is her devotion to the hidden sacred nature of life. To her kyanite is as alive, in its own way, as a soaring bird.

I realize how extraordinarily different my world is from hers. I grew up under the tutelage of a father who leaned toward atheism and repeatedly tried to understand Einstein's theory of relativity. I absorbed my mother's organized and efficient get-it-done attitude. In my work, marriage, and circle of friends, I never encountered anyone like Angelita. But there had been tiny moments when my life view was shaken. My husband's near-death experience; my own spiritual awakening; the divorce—none of these fit my childhood worldview. Now a simple social encounter with someone who admits to psychic abilities further erodes my way of viewing reality. I am about to have a psychic reading.

She begins by asking that whatever comes through her bring only an increase in love and goodness for ourselves and the world, and that this time and space be protected. Then she begins to channel.

~ ~ ~

That first time, now many years past, surprised me. No soothsayer, she made no predictions about my future--no early deaths, no new boyfriend in the next few months. Rather, she gave insights into my character that I hid well beneath my ego. It felt as though she talked *directly* to my soul, bypassing my mind with all its worries and restrictions. The specific advice seemed relevant, pure and unencumbered, naturally *right*.

I remember feeling safe. Completely different from my belief that my psyche would be stripped naked with my worst characteristics revealed, I found myself clothed in a new reality--an affirmation of giftedness and value.

Years later, I laugh at that first encounter-of-a-psychic kind. Of course, I cannot remember what she said, but the gentle nonintrusive respectful wisdom allayed my fears.

I think how often we want to fit in, be successful, attract wealth, find love—yet these may not be the things that nurture our spirit *or* bring forth our gifts. How often have we heard people lament later in life how they sacrificed their dreams for economic security? That day, I felt as though she peeled back my ego layer so I could better view my soul and follow its urgings. Angelita opened a door I chose not to shut.

March 16 ~ St. Urho's Day

Finding-Roots Barbara ~ 2010 ~ A Bit of Finnish History ...

In 1981, Connecticut Governor O'Neill declared March 16 to be St. Urho's Day because Urjo drove a plague of grasshoppers out of Finland (presumably before St. Patrick chased snakes out of Ireland) chanting, *"Heinasirkka, heinasirkka, mene taalta hiiteen"*--"Grasshopper, grasshopper, go away." (Finn-Americans like to say he told them to go to hell.)

I *never* heard about St. Urho until I saw Mom sporting his T-shirt. In seriousness achievable only by a Finn, Mom solemnly related the "legend" (actually birthed in 1956 by a Finnish clerk in Ketola's department store in Minnesota). In fact, the true patron saint of Finland is Bishop Henry who ended up with a peasant's axe in his back.

~ ~ ~

Growing up as a Finn-American child meant taking saunas, eating *pulla* and pickled herring, and dancing the schottische. Once a month, the Forsbackas, Pellinens, Luhtanens, Nurmis, Saarinens and others gathered in a rented hall, abandoning English at the coat rack. That didn't mean they understood each other.

Their Finnish depended on their parent's immigration date. Mom's Finnish dated to the late 1800s; Dad's, the 1920s. Cut off from the mother tongue, these Finns found themselves stuck, like passengers dropped off at an abandoned railway spur, speaking increasingly archaic Finnish.

I know of no parent teaching Finnish, with its convoluted words like *koulupussimme, palveluspaikassa,* and *vakuutusyhtiöissä,* to their children.

My sister detests the language; I love it. Who wouldn't like to say *koulupussimme*? But there are only six million Finns in the world, roughly the population of Missouri. The chances of me finding a Missourian-Finn to converse with seem slim.

With this effective barrier between parent and child, Mom and Dad freely talked about us, switching to Finnish mid-sentence. It was an unbreachable defense. We had no such protection from the sauna.

Whenever we visited the Pellinens, inevitably someone would say, "Let's go sauna." Uttered exactly that way.

No prepubescent or teenage child wants to do this. Off we'd trek to the aunt's farm where we were hailed by wildly flapping chickens. Women first, we'd go to the sauna behind the barn, strip in the dressing room, step into blistering heat coming from wood-fire-sizzling stones, sit on benches, and toss ladles of cold water onto the crackling rocks, causing billowing steam to explode in the air.

Sweat trickled down our sternums; our foreheads bubbled with perspiration. Sandra and I vied for highest bench to see who could win the title for the first recorded death-by-sauna.

Luckily we always missed sauna night when visiting Minnesota relatives. Instead, we learned about outhouses. I spend countless minutes enjoying the rough-hewn solitude of a two-holer I'd never have to scrub.

Uncle Swante even owned a cow I coveted as much as a puppy--a front-yard bovine I could milk every day--though I didn't care much for Bessie's *pitkä piima.* Mom once convinced me to try this thick stringy fermented yogurt-like drink. I started to sip and suddenly realized it was like swallowing cloth. You couldn't stop without gagging. Mom stood there grinning as she told me, "There's a Finnish saying: It's so thick you need scissors to cut it." Despite the *pitkä piima,* I still loved that cow. Imagine my horror when two years later we returned and I sprinted across the yard to the barn only to find Bessie's stall *empty.*

"Where is she?" I asked my cousin. Pat threw open the door to their deep freezer and triumphantly said, *"Mojakka!"* I saw numerous white-papered packages. Bessie. Such is Finnish humor. That evening we chowed down on my defrosted friend, *Mojakka* Bessie.

There is one last thing no Finn-American quite escapes--the *Kalevala*--that heroic poem that launched Finnish nationalism. In 1845 Elias Lönnrot collected sung poems of ancient Finnish lineage. Consider just one scene from this epic: old man Väinämöinen watches a man rise out of the sea no bigger than a woman's hand, dressed in copper hat, gloves, and boots, carrying a copper axe, the handle only a thumb-length long. "He's an odd one," Väinämöinen admits.[1]

It's a bit hard to see this as the song you sing going into revolution. Nevertheless, this epic inspired Finns to seize their nationhood in 1917.

Confused Elsie ~ 1994 ~ Limping Along

"Barbara, look at me!" I glance up from my magazine. Mom leaps from her chair and begins to drag her leg behind her saying, "O-LIMP-ALONG!"

"What?" I ask, totally confused.

"Well, everyone in the Rest Home kept talking about the Olympics and I couldn't remember the name."

I start to laugh as she keeps dragging her leg. "Mom, that's *brilliant*!" I announce. Watching this diminutive woman score yet another victory in life, I am bursting with pride for her. The unsinkable Elsie Nurmi, the unquenchable Protocol Officer. I wonder if I have half the *sisu,* that stubborn Finnish determination.

Later when she lays down to rest, I pop into the director's office to share the story. As I drag my leg across Rachael's carpet, she roars into laughter. We both *get* it--the *force* of Mom wanting to stay in the game of life.

The head nurse Sheryl walks in.

"Tell her," Rachel exclaims, wiping tears from her eyes.

I repeat the story, complete with dragged leg.

---

[1] *The Kalevala: Epic of the Finnish People*, trans. by Eino Friberg, Otava Publishing Company Ltd., 1988, Runo 2, p. 49.

"Ohhhh," Sheryl's face drops into mournful compassion. "That's so *sad*."

How, I wonder, can we have such opposite reactions? I am awestruck by Mom's intelligence, her feisty spirit, her fight to stay mentally engaged. Sheryl only sees disease, decay, loss.

March 17

Name-Changing Nurmis ~ 1913 ~ Mixing Up the Melting Pot of Names

Growing up, I never notice the missing grandfather from my father's Manhattan 1913 birth certificate, but eventually I wonder if I am more like *him* than a Nurmi or a Norlund. From a Finnish perspective, I am inappropriately emotional. As a child, I cried; I laughed out loud; I hurtled myself onto the floor in rage; I worried about the poor in Appalachia and believed in civil rights.

Even Sandra and Mom have doubts about my heritage. "Where does she get it from?" Sandra wondered one day to my mother. "Not from my side of the family," Mom adamantly answered. Silence stretched out as they thought of every relative. Suddenly (I am told), they looked up and in the same breath said, "She gets it from *him*. The Manhattan Grandfather!"

My father's birth could not have made things easy for his mother Ida, a first generation immigrant living in New York City. One day I get the urge to find out where Dad's ancestors had been born and mention it to Mom. "Give me time," she promises. "I'll try to find out."

One year later, the phone rings. "I got it!" Mom exclaims. "What?" I ask, perplexed.

"Your father came from Alajärvi."

Now why would it take a *year* to find out such a simple fact? Well, Dad refused to talk about Finland. When his mother took him back, Finland was a peaceful Grand Duchy of Russia. But by the time he was 5 years old, it was convulsed in civil war; people starved; he lived on birchbark bread.

Years after he died, Mom and I visited Alajärvi, stopping in the Lutheran church seeking Mertaniemi records.

The secretary brought out a dusty oversized volume. I requested a photocopy but unable to decipher it, filed it away, forgotten. Now having access to online translation, I doggedly type in the entry for Ida and hit "Translate:"

"America was first visited in 1905, and again in 1923 with son Urjo."

Imagine my surprise when I discovered that my father, Herbert Nurmi, had once been *Urjo Mertaniemi*. First his mother, born of a Kallen, somehow became a Mertaniemi. Then she jettisoned the *Merta* upon returning to Manhattan.

I discover I have a *Niemi* grandmother and a *Nurmi* father named after Paavo Nurmi (the "Flying Finn" of the Olympics) because he decided Americans could pronounce it. Urjo was scuttled for Herbert. Why? Nobody knows.

Mom, raised as a Norlund, was actually a Kangaanpää descended from a Finnish meat-hunter for railroad workers, though she took excessive pride in all her names: Elsie Julia Elizabeth Norlund, or EJEN.

ELSIE AT EBB TIDE

Genetically wired to dislike one name for life, I happily abandoned Nurmi (which rhymed with wormy) for Mrs. Taylor. Sadly when my marriage didn't last, the fatal Finnish name-changing disorder set in.

Eventually I went to the Finnish dictionary, looked up single (*erakko*), added Bella, and became Bella Barbara Erakko.

Thus my cremated remains should read:

HERE RESTS

BARBARA (a.k.a. BARBY) ELIZABETH NURMI

+

BARBARA ELIZABETH TAYLOR

+

BARBARA ELISABETH ERAKKO-TAYLOR

+

Recently Changed to BELLA BARBARA ERAKKO

+

DAUGHTER OF ELSIE JULIA ELIZABETH NORLUND NURMI

a.k.a. EJEN

of KANGAANPÄÄ DESCENDANTS

And

HERBERT NURMI

Once Known as URJO MERTANIEMI

Dust to Dust

Ashes to Ashes

Names to Names

March 27

Caregiver Barbara ~ 1995 ~
She Needs Someone to Hug Her

As I begin to research places where I can place my mother, one Maryland facility in particular sounds exciting. I've never heard of a place architecturally *designed* to make life for the mentally impaired more secure. Three different carpeted corridors help residents find their room by color coding. The long hallways *seem* shorter and visually more intimate by the little turns structured into them, which creates the effect of small clusters of rooms. Locked doors to the outside secure the residents except for one leading to an enclosed patio.

Most importantly, the facility maintains an on-site psychiatric/nursing unit so residents can easily be monitored. Just the thought of 24-hour medical care gives me enormous relief. In addition to her dementia, Mom has advanced osteoporosis.

While impressed with much of what I see, I feel uncomfortable when I walk through the empty lobby so unlike the Finnish-American Rest Home. Here, wingback chairs look too new, the sofa too isolated, the décor too chic. But then I visit a typical resident's room. Its cream-walled smallness appeals to me--less confusion. I love the double-wide casement windows that fill the room with light. Limiting the residents to one dresser and a small closet minimizes decisions. The sliding bathroom door lessens the possibility of a resident getting trapped. I also think that the split entry door is innovative. The lower half can be closed to give the resident a sense of privacy and protection; the upper can be left open so they do not feel isolated. Or the entire door can be left open or shut.

After meeting the on-duty nurse with her office full of patient files and trays containing residents' pills, and the activities coordinator who bubbles over with affection for the residents, I believe this facility is doing its very best to help mentally impaired residents.

It certainly differs from my beloved Finnish-American Rest Home where the furniture is old and comfortable, the hallways long and tiled in institutional linoleum, the pictures on the wall uniformly unattractive, the staffing much more minimal.

Of course, the Rest Home supported more independent living. Some residents owned cars and most socialized with one another every day. Mom is now past that stage.

After the visit, Sandra, Ed, and I talk over the phone. "The doctors can monitor her," I tell them. "There's 24-hour nursing. It's been architecturally designed just for people with Alzheimer's. Can you fly out and see it?"

One week later, Sandra and Ed go on the same tour.

Looking at the plush furniture, polished tables, lush carpeting, art, Ed reacts. "She doesn't *need* all that stuff, Barbara. She just needs a big woman to hug her."

At that moment, Ed and I could be on different planets. He had said the same thing before in Florida. I still can't *imagine* that anything as simple as love could possibly be the best care solution for Mom.

"I should be taking care of her," Sandra anxiously insists. "I'm the firstborn."

"But Sandra, I *want* to and anyway, I'm not the caregiver; I'm just managing her care. You know I don't have a job right now. It gives me something to do."

"Well," Sandra admits, "she's got the money. We can use her pension and the rent from her Florida house to cover this. But you've got to pay yourself something."

The next day I sign a contract, admitting Mom as a resident.

~ ~ ~

Rachel accompanies Elsie from the Rest Home to Maryland. She has mothered me as much as Mom. It's hard to realize that the deep link between us will become more distant.

She goes over Mom's care with the nurse while the admissions staff suggests I *not* see my mother for the first two weeks. I resist, but Rachel explains that many facilities want the transition handled by professional staff. "Barbara, it's hard on the family because the one being admitted might lash out at them."

I understand the logic, but I've already been through her bouts of rage and anxiety. *She'll feel safer and more reassured if I stick it out with her,* I tell myself and decide to visit Mom every other day. But after unpacking her suitcase, sitting with her on her bed, *nothing* makes it any easier for me to leave her alone in a strange room on the mauve corridor.

~ ~ ~

Six months pass. I worry that I'm not proactive enough. I fret over her loss of weight. Mom, with an unusually small mouth, eats food in very tiny bites. The plates I've seen placed before residents have large hunks of uncut meat. When I complain, the nutritionist explains that by law, they have to provide a specific number of calories in certain nutritional proportions.

The aides tell me Mom comes to the dining room, stares at the food without touching it, and walks away. The cooking staff then can legally offer her Ensure and they find she likes Rice Krispies.

After hearing this, I make an appointment with the nutritionist. I explain, "You have to puree her food. She can't eat it this way. It needs to be put into an applesauce base." The nutritionist agrees, promising, "I'll tell the kitchen staff." Nothing happens. I call again. "Yes, I'm sorry," she admits, "I was out of town at a wedding. I'll write an order." Nothing happens.

One day I walk into the kitchen. "Why aren't you pureeing my mother's food?" "We haven't been told to do that." I make the request again, and then leave on a trip. When I return, Mom is still drinking Ensure and eating cereal. I feel increasing anxiety. Are these mishaps or an emerging pattern?

Her mental score has plummeted by 50 percent. I tell myself, *it's the disease*. But sometimes I feel I am failing as her care manager.

I should pay closer attention. I should be more vigilant. I should come every day. I'm trusting them too much to take care of everything. I'm not monitoring things as closely as I should. On and on the litany goes as I struggle to cope with this disease.

"Mom," I rub her blue-veined hand, "so how do you like your new telephone?"

"Oh, I *like* it, Barbara. I like to call you."

I think to myself, *at least I got that right.* When Mom's calls become incessant, I install a second telephone line into my house, a second phone, and an answering machine. When Mom calls, the machine cheerily answers, "HELLO, Mom! I'm not here right now. But talk as LONG as you want!"

At Sandra's suggestion, I buy Mom a phone with oversized automatic call buttons. I program one to dial my house and label it BARBARA. This works amazingly well. I monitor every call as I work from home. If anything alarming happens, I pick up and talk to her right away.

Looking at Mom wearing a white jersey and tan pants, I have to admit, *she isn't* always *miserable.* She still loves the piano. I can play for her. We go on outings at least once a week, usually to the local diner. ...

~ ~ ~

"Mom, let's go to lunch."

"Oh, that would be nice, Barbara."

I sign Mom out of the facility. Soon we are sitting in a booth waiting for hamburgers and fries, watching the place fill up with the lunch crowd. Mom begins to complain. "Barbara, I don't feel good." I look at her. She does seem pale. She starts to slump over the table.

"Drink your coke, Mom. You'll feel better."

She takes a few sips. "I still don't feel good."

"What's wrong?"

"I feel weak. I need to lie down." She begins to slide off the booth seat.

I stop her. I wonder, *is she having a heart attack? Is she going to faint?* I really believe it's hypoglycemia--Sandra, Mom, and I all have it--but I won't know for 20 minutes until the sugar from the coke gets into her system. If not ... I feel anxiety slowly constricting my chest.

"I need to lie down," she moans. I see her eyeing the floor.

That's it! I leap out of my seat, race to the waiter and frantically tell him to call 911. If it's low blood sugar, she'll start feeling better in a few minutes. If not ...

"Mom, you need to sit up." I hold the straw to her lips, "Drink some more coke."

Ten minutes later, the paramedics look like a SWAT team bursting through the doors of the restaurant. Everyone stops eating. But Elsie sits in her seat perkily enjoying all the attention, sipping her coke.

"How are you feeling, Mrs. Nurmi?" the paramedic asks.

"Oh, I feel just FINE," she replies.

I glance around the restaurant. Most talking has ceased as the diners watch; but a few seem determined to respect our privacy, averting their eyes, continuing their conversations.

The hunky handsome paramedic smiles at Mom and takes her vitals that are completely normal. Now knowing it's a hypoglycemic episode, I elect *not* to have her transported to the hospital. Rattled by the experience, I also decide not to stay for lunch, and ask the waiter to put our lunches into carry-out containers.

I maneuver Mom into the car, shut the doors, turn on the engine, and burst into tears. Mom looks at me and asks, "What's wrong?"

"MOM!" I blubber through my tears. "You almost passed out. I had to call the PARAMEDICS! You tried to lay down on the restaurant FLOOR." I am screaming.

"Oh," she says, "I don't remember that."

I continue to cry. She pauses for a moment and then adds, "I'm feeling pretty good, but you don't look like you're doing too well."

I start to laugh. I blow my nose. I pat her knee. "Let's go home, Mom."

~ ~ ~

About two weeks later, a resident named Betty walks into my mother's room and thinking Mom is an intruder in *her* room, attacks her. The color-coded corridors don't work. She has the right room, wrong corridor. I separate them, call the nurse, and then completely fall apart. *My mother could have fallen.* In disaster mode, I see her lying on the floor helpless with a broken hip. *If I hadn't been here ...*

I lash out at the institution blaming them for poor care. I now see the hallways with their hidden angles as death traps. I go ballistic over the Rice Krispies. I am so angry I would fault the wingback chairs in the lobby if I could think of a reason to hate them. Instead of sleeping, I pound the computer keys writing Perry Mason–tinged diatribes. I am in a living hell of rage, fear, and anxiety.

I haven't come to grips with the basic fact that no one can protect my mother from this dying process. I live in a brochure world of happy residents and perfect care.

This moment becomes the absolute lowest point in my struggle to deal with this disease. I hit rock bottom. I cannot fix it. I cannot control it. I cannot stop it. I want every one of my care-management decisions to be impeccable, flawless, perfect. I am not yet ready to look at the underlying *emotional* issues.

Mom made an angry descent into Alzheimer's. But much of her anger came, I eventually realize, from feeling anxious, fearful, unloved, and helpless. These aren't disease issues--they are emotional issues as a result of the disease. Emotions *can* be treated with love.

Finally I shift gears from my mind to my heart. At last I land where Ed and Sandra had tried to pilot me all along. I realize that all I can do is accompany her with love.

In order for me to step across the threshold from my mind to my heart, the disease itself had to break me. It broke my mother down; it broke me down; it broke my sister down. Each of us, in our own way, had to face this death. I *could not* keep my mother safe. She would have to undergo this journey. I would have to accompany her. Sandra would have to accompany us.

I wasn't sure I had the capacity for the kind of love Ed talked about. Raised by Finns to *not* have emotions, after years of learning to quell vulnerable expressions of love--how would I awaken them? Recognize them? Surprisingly, Mom helped me. One day she grabbed me by the arms, stared fiercely into my eyes and said, "I don't know what I did to deserve a daughter as good as you."

Both of us were on a journey, and ...

Both of us had a long way to go.

Confused Elsie ~ 1996 ~ Perilous Journey Ends

Today, my mother lives a two-bedroom assisted-living facility in Columbia, Maryland. The ratio of caregiver to resident is 1:3. She has the same aide 24 hours a day from Monday to Friday, and another from Friday evening to Monday morning. These women handle her as gently as a baby.

They wash her clothes while she is sleeping. They fix ground meats for her and cut her food. They serve her little portions, and sit with her to encourage eating. They let her do what she wants when she wants. She continues to take frequent naps. But the biggest change is in her disposition. She is relaxed. Her face has lost that anxious fearful angry look. Her eyes twinkle. I saw her late last night. She was in bed dozing, her bedspread up around her nose. I leaned over to kiss her forehead and she opened her eyes--and they twinkled. Like a mischievous child.

April

The Measure of a Life

April 5

Married Barbara ~ 1982 ~ Becoming a Mother

"Are you still okay with adopting sisters?" our social worker Sally at Catholic Charities asks me over the phone. In actuality, Bill and I initially wanted one toddler because we had little experience with children, but with hesitation we agreed to *consider* siblings. Now Sally tells me over the phone, "We have Korean sisters, aged 2 and 5, ready for adoption."

I feel my heart leap with excitement. "Sally, let me call Bill. I'll get right back to you." I hang up. As I dial Bill's work number, I realize that repeating the application, interview, home visit, and long wait for the second child we already know we want makes no sense. "They'll be bonded to each other," I tell Bill. "There'll always be a blood link between them. We wouldn't have to go through another adoption." I seal the deal: "It's cheaper."

Four hours later, we are driving to the social worker's home to pick up files on Sun-Hee and Sook-Hee. Later the social worker admits she was perplexed by our silence as we look at our daughter's faces for the first time. But Bill and I believe this moment belongs to us, alone. In the car driving home through the dark night, our excitement starts cautiously to bubble over. "What do you think?" I ask Bill, about to burst with newfound love for these two tiny children.

"I think they're our daughters," he immediately answers. We grin like village idiots. After months of interviews, house visits, classes, applications, fees, we will be parents! I open the top folder of the older girl Sun-Hee. Gazing without a smile directly into the camera, she looks so strong—and vulnerable. Almost immediately, I seize on a name.

"Let's call her Kendra: *ken* for your father Kanardy, and *dra* for my sister Sandra." Somehow the name sticks. There will be no second guessing.

I gaze much longer at the younger child. She looks forlorn, sitting atop a table, her hair sticking straight up, bound in a rubber band. I can't *see* her personality. Perhaps she's too young. I keep thinking of family names. Elsie. Alice. Elizabeth. Liisa. "What about Elisa?"

The next day, we announce our adoptions. *Everyone* in Bill's family stumbles over Elisa because our niece is named *Alicia*. Even I have problems. So Elisa becomes Lisa.

And the wait begins.

Career Elsie ~ 1954 ~ "Why not Elsie?"

"We have to do something about Betty." Three Protocol Officers discuss the visit of a dignitary to New York City as they stand by Elsie's desk.

"She can't handle the stress. She got so excited she wet her pants in the ticker tape parade. We need someone more mature."

Elsie's ears perk up.

She wouldn't pee. *She* has an excellent bladder. Rather than being blunt about it all, saying something like "How about ME?" (that would be *much* too feminist for the times),

She begins to smile. She beams. She shines like a megawatt blonde-haired light bulb. She types fast and furiously on the metal keys with great noise and clatter. She straightens her back. She practically leaps out of her secretarial seat.

At last, one of the gentlemen notices her. "Well," he wonders out loud, "Why not Elsie?"

Indeed! Why not!

And that's how Elsie moves out of Diplomatic Operations into the far more interesting Visits Division. Elsie admits in a speech given decades later at her high school reunion, "I thought I would be willing to work there for nothing."

She soon proves her mettle.

The Shah of Iran is feted with a ticker tape parade in New York City. Elsie remembers, "It looked like a white blizzard. I saw hundreds of people throwing confetti out their Fifth Avenue office windows. It all seemed to fall onto the Shah as he stood waving from his open limousine. I guess I acted a bit too awestruck. One of the party with me in the last limousine said, 'Turn around and look behind you.' We were being followed by the sanitation-department vacuum truck."

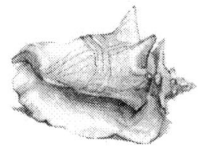

Kenna and Elsie ~ 2000 ~ *The Cluttered Room*

Kenna continues to give me clues about how she receives information. One day she tells me, "Oh, it's like Dr. Spock."

Thinking of the show *Star Trek,* I ask, "You mean when he touches another person's head and the two minds temporarily meld?"

"Yes. It's as though I see what your mother sees."

~ ~ ~

<u>Elsie</u>: Know what I've been thinking about? About all the time I have now. And when I could make use of it, I didn't have it. Now I can't do much with it. I do get bored but what can I do? The pleasures and pains of old age—I have to accept it. There's nothing else to do.

<u>Kenna</u>: What's in your heart tonight?

<u>Elsie</u>: Oh, I like the piano. I wish I could play it and dance like I used to. Dancing is not just exercise for the body; it's a way to clear the mind too.

<u>Kenna</u>: You seem tired.

<u>Elsie</u>: I got a chill a few days ago.

[Kenna did brain balancing. She could see that her brain looked like dead-end streets—no information could go through.]

Elsie: [referring to her brain, said]: *You could make a playroom out of it.*

Kenna: What do you mean?

Elsie: You know how a child plays with a toy and then leaves it and goes to the next and leaves it and the room can get cluttered with toys—but there's no one to clean up my play room. The toys are left there to clutter my mind. I can't walk through easily.

I can't find what I'm looking for. I generally have to wait until I bump into it. It becomes like a new discovery. I know there's so much in my mind, but I can't find it when I want to.

Kenna: We can clean out the clutter.

Elsie: Thank you. Thank Barbara too. When is she coming back? I've forgotten.

Kenna: In a few days.

~ ~ ~

As I write down Kenna's conversation with Mom, I keep one anxious eye on the clock.

I'm running late for a meeting but I want to hear everything. As soon as we hang up, I grab my purse and keys and dash out the door. Once I ease into beltway traffic, I mull over Mom's comments: *"I like the piano. I wish I could play it and dance like I used to."*

Tears sting my eyes. Mom loved music. Her simple way of speaking, so familiar to me, matches the way she responded to life.

But I also notice how Kenna, as Elsie's translator, sometimes uses her own vocabulary for describing things.

Mom never said she "had a chill" (she always had a "cold"). As I think back to Kenna's Dr. Spock image, I realize that somehow Elsie telepathically conveys her thoughts to Kenna. Kenna may see Mom dancing and pointing to her body and then her mind and then Kenna hears phrases like *exercise* and *clear mind*. It's up to Kenna to match what she's receiving with a specific translation I might understand. Mom lives in a different world now, one dependent on oblique communication.

I pass a slow-moving truck continuing to think about dancing. *Maybe that was the only way she could let go and just enjoy herself without worry, without being responsible all the time*, I tell myself.

I am struck by Mom's image of a cluttered toy room. It seems some aspect of Elsie (her soul? her spirit?) remains undiseased. She can describe how she uses her wits in an increasingly witless situation: *"I can't find what I'm looking for. I generally have to wait until I bump into it."*

Later, I will read about a neuroscientist who suffers a devastating stroke, recovers, and gives a very similar explanation. But now, in many respects, Kenna is Mom's only portal to the outside world.

Child Barbara ~ 1955 ~
And Jesus Called the Fisher Children ...

"Can't we at least stop at the church?" I whine, absolutely inconsolable.

Finally after years of trying, I have gone to Sunday school every single Sunday for a full 3 months and I'll get an attendance pin. I really want that pin. Mom and Dad seem equally resolute—we are going herring fishing. But at the last minute, they have a turn of heart and we head up the highway to the red brick Lutheran church.

Our pink-and-gray Travelall pulls up beside the building. I dash inside in my striped T-shirt and dungarees. "I'm here to get my pin!" I tell my teacher with sheer happiness written all over my face. "I can't stay. We're going fishing. But my family stopped so I could get it."

"But you can't get the pin unless you stay for Sunday school today," the teacher-of-no-mercy emphatically explains to me. I begin to cry. She pats me awkwardly on the shoulder. I sense *she* would have showered me with pins but implacable church policy forbids it.

So I am sent away.

I probably became a halfhearted Lutheran at that point. In *my* church, I'd have overflowing boxes of attendance pins.

At any rate, within an hour or two, Dad, Sandra, and I stand on the muddy banks of a branch of the Potomac River, casting our bare hooks into the water to snag herring. Upriver, an old man in a worn brown jacket fishes all alone with a bamboo cane in his hand.

My enthusiasm barely lasts an hour before I wander into the woods down one muddy path after another, not enjoying nature or the cool spring dampness. I secretly believe that Mom, like me, prefers restaurant dining to pickled herring. Meanwhile we eat bologna-and-cheese sandwiches on Pepperidge Farm bread with cold muddy fingers.

Eventually all days, even herring fishing days, come to an end. Sandra and Dad together catch eleven fish. As we pack up, the old man strolls down. "Would you take my herring?" he asks. "My wife will kill me if I bring any more home," he admits with a wry almost apologetic smile.

"SURE!" my father agrees, and follows him upstream.

"I think I caught about a hundred," the man says, dumping the fish into our bucket. Astonished by this unexpected bounty, Dad vigorously shakes the man's hand and thanks him.

The trouble with a hundred herring is the fact they must be scaled, gutted, washed, chopped, and pickled. Childhood bedtimes aside, we have a mountain of smelly fish to clean. Mom lifts the hinged kitchen counter to reveal the double laundry tubs beneath, puts two plugs in, dumps in the pickling spices, and fills the open tubs with vinegar and water. (This becomes our new routine until her sister Alice one day throws her clothes in the washing machine, not knowing she's drowning our latest batch of pickled fish in soapy rinse water)

Sandra and I scale, Dad guts and chops; Mom rallies us on. The evening passes into the wee hours. Slowly a vinegary smell overtakes the kitchen until the last fish is dumped into its brimming brew. Like hunters and gatherers, we now face a winter of pickled herring and boiled potatoes with butter.

~ ~ ~

Decades later, I recalled this wonderful herring bonanza to Mom when she commented, "Well, you know we always went herring fishing on Easter Sunday."

No, of course, I don't know. "Why?" I ask.

"Your Dad and I couldn't afford to buy you Easter outfits so we went fishing instead."

I think back to my religious education. My father's attraction to atheism kind of put a damper on religion, so Sunday school was a hit-or-miss affair. Mom, who made certain Dad got baptized before he went to war, had equal concern that her children be confirmed. So while childhood Sunday school tended to be sporadic, the two-year confirmation process was not.

During those years, I never made a single friend. We had absolutely no social connections to anyone in the church community. I held a particular fear of Bible quizzes. We stood up. Each of us was asked a question: "Who was Matthew?" "What was the name of the Promised Land?" "How many days did it take God to create the world?" It really didn't matter what question I got. I mumbled, "I don't know," and sat down, alone until some other hapless Bible student goofed. Though I personally had religious curiosity, churches then were ill equipped to handle stray spiritual children.

Up to confirmation, one of my parents dutifully delivered me to church. I remember waking up the Sunday after confirmation, putting on a white blouse and blue skirt, slipping on nylons and two-inch heels, ready to go. I came downstairs to an empty living room. I walked into the darkened kitchen.

Dad's soft snores rumbled out of the bedroom. So I fixed coffee, got the paper from the front steps, and took out the comics.

I think, overall, I was happy with this turn of events. But occasionally I walked 3 miles to church, never entirely certain whether religion or the freshly baked honey-dipped donut I bought on the way home was my motivation. In all honestly, I think it was the donut.

At any rate, I decided one year I should go to an Easter service. To my complete amazement, there were more people in attendance than on Christmas.

In my still-childish world, Christmas was *the* Christian holiday. I sat in the pew, surrounded by Easter-hatted ladies. The pastor heatedly berated CE Christians. I eventually learned a Christmas–Easter Christian only comes two times a year. I wanted to yell, "Hey, nobody took me. I *walked three miles* just to see what it was all about!" As I left, the minister glanced at me and said, "Thanks for coming, Sandra."

Sandra? That was my last walk ... for a very long time.

Career Elsie ~ 1939 ~ An Armored Brink's Moment

Elsie lets no grass gather under her career feet between 1937 and 1939.

She leapfrogs her way through three Manhattan jobs beginning with Lexington Manufacturing at $5/week for 4 months, the North American Accident Insurance Company at $12/week for 19 months, and the Kieckhefer Container Company at $16.25/week for 10 months.

She collects letters certifying she is efficient, diligent, honest, capable, and valuable. Kieckhefer puts it best: "Her capabilities unquestionably justify more remuneration than we are willing to provide at this time."

Indeed. Elsie moves to Washington, D.C., doubles her salary, and her trustworthiness is soon put to the test. She works as a clerk typist for the Treasury Department Census Bureau. Employees receive their pay in envelopes filled with cash. Once every two weeks, Elsie picks up the envelopes and makes her rounds, office to office, personally handing out thousands of dollars. She becomes the walking equivalent of a Brink's armored truck—only her truck consists of a holstered guard.

One day, Elsie being as we now know efficient, capable, and honest, roars off the elevator and down the corridor in her staccato tapping heels. After about twenty strides, Elsie pauses. She realizes she isn't hearing the slap, slap, slap, of her guard's leather soled shoes. She looks down the empty marble-floored hallway. *Where is my guard?* Oh well. Elsie-the-Brink's continues unloading money, with a devilish smile on her face as her armed protector shortly comes careening out of the stairwell. "MRS. NURMI," he pants. "Do NOT ever do that again."

Anyway, eventually the U.S. Government gets a better idea: Checks.

Confused Barbara ~ 2008 ~ Lost in Traffic

I decide to fit in a quick errand. I relax as I drive along Hannibal's main business drag. My mind wanders. I cruise past fast-food restaurants and gas stations. I suddenly realize ... I have absolutely *no* idea where I'm going.

I slow the car. I near a traffic light. *Do I need to turn here?* Mental silence. Not a peep from the brain.

I turn left for no better reason than most stores come off this artery. It is probable I had wanted to go to one of them. I still have absolutely no idea why I am driving this way. I hope some circuitry will get connected soon or I'll be hapless outside Aldi's or Sutherlands or Farm & Home.

My brain feels so pure, so completely empty. I haven't taken in panic or anxiety, frustration or anger. I just am in this vast mindless landscape of ... nothing.

So this is how Alzheimer's might be, I think to myself.

Strangely, it has an appeal—like a portal into a Narnia-like world—like spring rain falling on pure white sand, the openness and abundance of the landscape capturing my attention completely.

Then I remember I wanted to go to Kroger.

~ ~ ~

I continually surprise myself with my instinctive reactions to such a seemingly dreadful disease. Here I am saying, *WOW, this looks like a neat place to visit* when any rational person would be haunted by the mental lapse.

Now at age 61, I could be experiencing the first moments of a synapse running into a roadblock of plaque obstruction. Why am I so unalarmed?

Perhaps meditation has provided a bridge—not that I often meditate or meditate "enough." When I do, sometimes I quiet my mind into utter silence and emptiness—but it is a deliberate practice. I *choose* to become still. I am in control. I return in time to sip a nice cup of morning coffee from my favorite chair overlooking the Mississippi River.

All of us experience moments when time seems to fall away: gazing at a sunset, holding a newborn. Such moments have a glow that fills us beyond the dimensions of our physical world. It never lasts long—a tiny flirtation with *more*—and then we slip into the mental cogs of who and what, when and where.

I begin to wonder about my mother's journey. We fretted about her diet, her skin, her happiness, her quality of life. We wanted to *make* it healthy and filled with life. But she dwelled in a timeless heart-glow we could not see or join. Then, like a feather, she floated to the other side—with one last exhalation of breath.

Retired Elsie ~ 1977 ~ Alcohol and Taxes

"Herby," Elsie hollers from the bedroom to the kitchen where he reads the newspaper. "I'm going to stop drinking. I drank too much last night at the Kippers. I can't even add these numbers up."

She pauses from the income taxes spread on her vanity to look through the open door at her husband. He glances up from reading. "Okay," he agrees.

Elsie goes back to the taxes, he, to the paper. Hours fly by and now completely sober and confident that her numbers add up, Elsie wants a celebratory drink. *But,* she reluctantly thinks, *Herby's been drinking a lot lately.* So she stays silent ... but hopeful. Four o'clock, when Herby usually leaves for the liquor store to pick up a six-pack and pint of vodka, comes and goes.

As grown, married, and moved-out children, Sandra and I no longer have any idea about their drinking habits. We both remember their after-work cocktails but that was years ago. Certainly, the Finn crowd drinks. It's a badge of honor to hold your vodka. Our parent's tolerance always seemed fine.

The next day arrives. Now Elsie *really* wants a drink. Not a word is said. Herby remains in his naugahyde recliner, reading a book as 4 o'clock comes and goes. The next day and the day after that, and frankly all the days for the next 8 years pass the same way.

They both go stone-cold sober on the same day because they are both too stubborn to be the first one to give in.

April 14

Worried Barbara ~ 1987 ~ She's *Catholic!*

The phone rings, and I stop stirring the dinner stew to answer it.

"Barbara," my mother's voice sounds tense, unnatural. "Your father had a stroke. He's in the hospital." I hear the anxiety in her matter-of-fact words: "I think you should come down." My heart stops.

~ ~ ~

Eighteen hours later, I punch the elevator button to the intensive-care unit. *It'll be okay,* I try to convince myself as I walk into my father's cubicle. I feel my whole body tremble when I see him weak and fighting for his life.

Shocked by the tubes and wires, I push my emotions down and go over to him. "Hey Dad, I'm here," I announce peering down into his blue eyes and sallow, grizzled face. Mom warned me of his delirium. *Will he recognize me*, I wonder.

When I'd visited my parents during the past year, I noticed odd things: Dad going over the whole security system for the house, checking the bars on the patio doors, teaching Mom how to use them. Dad insisting on her buying a new car. Dad tearing down a partition Mom never liked. I thought to myself, *he's preparing to leave. Somehow he knows his time is running out and he wants her safe and comfortable. It's his last gift to her.*

I felt like I was reading an open book no one else saw. If Sandra and Mom were seeing the same thing, they too kept a vigil of silence, hoping the silence itself would protect us from loss.

Three weeks before he died, Dad cornered me in the kitchen with a question asked almost in fury. "How can you believe in God?"

I looked at him dressed as always in his dark work pants, short-sleeved shirt, black Penney's shoes, his face as yet unshaved, his eyes piercing blue. The eyes stopped me. They had a searching vulnerable quality I'd not seen.

I felt tiny in front of this towering intellect, this man who brooked no stupidity, who stood firm in his disbelief. Dad challenged me on so many things, edging me into debates I could not win. But now I sensed an urgency, almost a plea for me to come up with one convincing argument.

I paused asking myself, *What does he need to hear?* Then, in an intimacy I had never used with my father, I looked straight into his eyes. "It's not about churches, Dad. It's about love. I know you love me even if you don't say it. If you were to die tomorrow, I'd know it. Mom knows you love her. That's all God is ... Love."

A silent pause grew between us. I watched as his eyes snapped out of their questioning gaze. He picked up his coffee mug. "What the *hell* are you talking about?" he said, and walked out of the kitchen. I watched him leave, thinking, *He's going to die believing there is nothing beyond. What courage.*

That was the last time I saw him as my strong intelligent kind father.

Now standing beside him in the hospital room, I only hope for some sign that in his delirium he knows I am there. Suddenly he rises up, looks at the nurse with the eyes I know so well, and announces, "She's *CATHOLIC*."

I laugh. He *knows* I am here. I well remember the day I told Dad I'd decided to become Catholic. Apparently after I hung up the phone, he turned to Mom and asked plaintively, "Elsie, where did we go wrong?" with that droll Finnish understatement.

Clearly, in his delirium, he knows his youngest daughter has arrived at his bedside.

~ ~ ~

Six hours later, Sandra arrives, her face ashen. She hesitates in the doorway, as though about to burst into tears. Then I watch as she resolutely smiles and walks over to Dad. Just before we leave for the evening, Sandra drags a chair over to his hospital bed, stands on it, and closes the overhead vent blowing cold air on him.

Usually cringing at even the thought of a hospital and phobic about checkups as ordinary as blood pressure or cholesterol, she seems to have lost all fear. Her face set with strange determination, she marches to the nurse's desk and asks for extra blankets, swaddling him tightly before we leave. She leans over to kiss him on his forehead. She acts very un-Sandra-like.

The doctor comes in one last time. "Mrs. Nurmi," he updates, "He's doing better. We'll have to talk about where he can go for rehab." With those hope-filled words, we file out of the hospital. Once Mom has gone to bed, Sandra turns to Ed and me. "Let's go get a drink."

Minutes later we are sitting in a restaurant with wine. We go over the day, detail by detail. "Well, it sounds like he'll pull through," I say.

"No," Sandra looks at me. "He's going to die tonight."

I feel all the air go out of me. Confused, I turn to her. "How do you know?"

"His breathing," she answers seriously. "I watched. He stopped breathing for long periods of time. I remember seeing that when I was a nurse's aide. It was always just before they died."

Suddenly I was very worried. We finished our drinks and went home to a restless night.

April 15

Bereaved Elsie ~ 1987 ~ A Husband and Father Dies

At 4:30 a.m., the phone rings. Mom answers.

"Your husband suffered another stroke," the nurse tells her, "I think you might want to come to the hospital as soon as possible." Ten minutes later, we get into the car and silently drive through the night.

The neurologist gently explains, "The stroke was very severe, Mrs. Nurmi. We need to know how much brain damage has occurred, so I've ordered some tests. Let's wait until those results come back and then we'll talk."

For the next 2 hours, we take turns holding Dad's nonresponding hand, sit in the waiting room, pace the halls, drink coffee. Mid-morning the doctor returns.

"I am so sorry, Mrs. Nurmi. There is no easy way to say this. I see no brain activity. It was truly a massive stroke."

Unable to speak, Mom looks utterly lost in her chair. Sandra finally asks, "What about the life-support equipment? Can he live without it?"

A long pause fills the room. Finally the doctor answers, "No. He might live for a day or two, but it won't be long. Most likely his body will shut down right away."

He walked over and took Mom's hand. "I know this is a lot to take in. I've scheduled another neurologist to stop by, and I think you should talk to your family physician as well."

As the day goes on—in our now soundless, timeless world—every hope ebbs away. Herby, Elsie's husband and our father, will never come back. We can keep him alive with machines. "He'd hate that," Mom says with a sudden fierceness.

I watch as she holds the pen in her hand. Then with swiftness, she signs the release papers. Life support will be stopped.

~ ~ ~

I gaze down on him sleeping in a mindless sleep. The air seeping out of his mouth forms the bubble of a soft snore. *Where are you?* I wonder. Outside the cubicle in intensive care, I hear the atonal sounds of ICU equipment beeping strange alarm languages and the hushed voices of nurses. The attending doctor's words echo in my mind, their two syllables keeping pace with the spikes on the heart monitor ... brain dead ... brain dead.

You were supposed to come home.

~ ~ ~

"I want to be with him," I tell the nurse.

"I don't think that will be possible," she gently explains.

"He shouldn't die alone," I look at her with quiet determination. "I'll be okay."

Now we stand together in the cubicle. I take Dad's right hand in mine. *You're still warm.* I enter a silence where meaning loses meaning. Standing at the very bow of the human ship of silence, I can go no further. Only he can.

I gently rub the back of his hand. I haven't held hands with my Dad in decades—not since he boosted me onto his strong, dark-tanned shoulders at the beach so I could soar off them like a flying porpoise into the Chesapeake Bay.

It's time, Dad.

Perhaps he is tethered to this earth—an out-of-body being, waiting. I look up into the eyes of the ceiling with love. *We're letting you go.*

All the years he guided me, opening the doors of life for me. "Just stand straight and fall backwards," he coaxed when I stood on the diving board, as my 10-year-old toes clenching the sandpapery surface in terror. "If anything goes wrong, I'll get you," he promises. I believe and let go.

Now I am standing beside him in a curtained cubicle. *Go, Dad,* I silently whisper knowing all he needs now is the springboard.

The nurse removes the oxygen tube. "This helped him breathe," she says, laying the translucent green tubing aside. His 73-year-old tanned face still shows that rugged Finn strength, the jaw now stubbled with beard. The fine dark hair. The high cheekbones defining his slender face. Still a handsome face after all these years. Even in this last repose he seems poised—ready to draw you into his world of intelligent scrutiny and dry mirth.

"This provided the intravenous glucose." She stops the fluids flowing into his body.

I think of the Finnish pancakes he made only 3 days ago. Yesterday, I warmed and ate them. I had stared at my plate stupefied, unable to comprehend that I nourished myself on food he, now dying, cooked.

The silence in the room begins to expand.

"This supported his heart," the nurse touches the final machine with her hand. With a gentle stroke, she shuts it down.

"Click."

Together we begin to watch. "It will take about 15 minutes," she whispers.

The spikes coursing across the fluorescent screen begin to stretch out, like a long-distance swimmer stroking slower and slower across a vast lake.

The room is utterly silent.

Life begins to seep out into some mysterious beyond, trembling in its chrysalis, as though life is transforming itself invisibly in our midst.

I feel *Light* so bright it is more intense than anything I can see. The room is *filled* with it. It is as though a trapdoor between eternity and life has opened and a beam of *Light* has come straight for my father's soul and gathered him up. He is leaving. I can actually *see* him leaving. He gazes back on me with such joy, happiness, love. My heart, no longer flesh and blood, is crying out to eternity in mindless amazement.

Somehow we are saying our final good-byes.

Then *poof* ... the door between us closes and I drop back into my body.

Only the shimmering shadow, the echo-mark of his soul, remains.

~ ~ ~

Alone with my dead father, his hand imperceptibly growing cold in mine, I cannot feel anything but joy. The *Light* blocks my grief.

Years later, I will explain it: When two hearts are joined in love and one crosses over, the other goes with it. The love itself transcends time and space ... but only so far. Then the heart of the living falls back to earth because it is not yet its time.

Or, it is like we are in a sealed sphere and when one soul is leaving, a portal in the sphere opens up and a blinding *Light* connects to the soul. As the soul is ascending, the living soul that loves also begins to ascend. But then, very quickly, it falls back to earth and it watches as the dying soul goes through the portal, and the opening is slammed shut.

Or, it is like my father and I have tickets to a theater. We queue in line. At last it is our time to go in. He goes before me, and suddenly—against my will—the door slams shut. I glimpse the inside. It is exactly where I want to be. I am angry. I realize decades must pass before I'll go through that door. Some soul-part of me *knows* eternity.

But I soon come back to earth, forget, and dread that door.

Bereaved Elsie ~ 1987 ~ Diary of a Death

On Thursday: Went to Dorsey's & made arrangements—Many visitors & calls including Irma from Finland who heard by ham radio.

On Friday: Telephones busy. Lunch @ Hawaiian restaurant on A1A.

On Saturday: Bill arrived.

On Easter Sunday: House on this street robbed today.

On Tuesday: Services @ Dorsey Chapel. Barbara delivered eulogy. Friends visited house 7-9 p.m. Reverend Eisold of Our Savior Lutheran Church spoke. Very nice.

On Wednesday: Herby's ashes were buried at Gulf Stream out of Boynton Beach. We used Chris Holme's boat—Barbara, Ed, & Sandra, Doris, Chris Holme & myself.

... Then the diary falls silent for 8 months.

~ ~ ~

Nine years later, I set about going through Mom's personal papers—the ones we'd stored in boxes after moving her out of the Lake Worth house. I took out several black 5" x 8" bound diaries with gold-embossed years on their covers. I retrieved earlier spiral-bound notebook diaries. I flipped open manila folders, binders, notepads, quickly throwing them into the trash. I hardly paused over a tiny blue spiral-bound notebook. I almost tossed it without looking, but then sticking to my rule of checking everything, I flipped it open—and found Mom's secret diary.

~ ~ ~

I have no intention of dying until I get everything straightened out—then I will think about it.

~

If he were healthy, he would not have died.

~

He lived a full life until the final week.

~

ELSIE AT EBB TIDE

Physical activity without mental awareness would have been devastating for survivors.
Mental awareness without physical function would have been devastating for *him*.

~

609
This is my home
This is where Herby is.

~

After the funeral everyone comes out of their shell
and all feel close.
Afterwards, each goes back to his daily circle and routine,
but I don't have my shell anymore.

~

He lived a full life and didn't just let time drift by.
He demanded a great deal from life and seized it.

~

As difficult as it was,
I am grateful for the grieving and adjustment period provided
by the stay in the hospital.

~

The evening before he died,
he talked with the wife of his roommate.
She told me later that he said, "I had a very happy marriage"—
then he cried a little.

When Herby was in the hospital under medication,
and with restraints to prevent injury, he said,
"I want to escape."
Yes, he did.

~

It wasn't me when Herby was alive—
I was what he wanted me to be.

Now I am my own rotten, pushy, independent self that I always was—suspicious, cautious, stubborn, negative & possessive, hoarding material things—

I need help?

~ ~ ~

Her last entries were Herby's humorous or inspiring insights ...

How much beach does she need?

Have you forgotten how to dance?

Do you know what you are talking about?

and ...

What's to lose?

April 16

Uncertain Sandra ~ 1987 ~ To Marry ... or Not?

"Let's take a walk," Sandra suggests, and we head two blocks north to Lake Osborne. We've been overwhelmed by funeral arrangements and Mom's grief. Soon we're walking the paved path around the lake, circumventing Muscovy ducks. Joggers and bicyclists zip by. Wind rippled waves cross the lake creating white caps.

"I can't get over Mom believing Dad made her who she is," I say, thinking back to last night's strange conversation. Mom adamantly told us, "I'd be nothing without Herby. I was nothing but a stupid Finnish farm girl. He taught me everything."

I turn to Sandra, "What do you think?" We both know Mom as the unflappable commander-in-chief of the household, the woman who made her life from scratch. After all, *she* was the Protocol Officer, not Dad. *She* got the job, held it, flourished in it, and flew around the world because of it.

"It doesn't make sense," Sandra agrees on the enigmatic mother, and we walk on in silence for a while.

"Barbara," Sandra looks at me with an anxious frown creasing her forehead. We are cresting the top of a footbridge. I stop. "What's wrong?" I ask.

"Ed's asked me to marry him."

"WOW," I turn to her wondering why she looks so unhappy. "That's cool. So are you going to accept?"

"I'm not sure. He's asked me about five times, but I don't believe him."

I stare at her. She starts to walk again.

WHAT? I think to myself. *Guys don't offer to marry someone with four teen and preteen boys if they're not serious.* I hurry to catch up. She sets a fast stride.

"Do you love him?" I ask. "Are you worried things will go wrong again, like with Buzz?"

I think back to her first marriage. Buzz—the hero of the University of Maryland Trail Club, the guy every girl wanted to catch—the caver, hiker, motorcyclist, mountain climber—the handsome rugged brilliant engineer who fathered four sons—the man who worked too late, parented too little, had a mean temper—the one she divorced.

"I'm scared. I'm not sure I'm ready to get married again."

"I can understand that. I'm not sure I'd trust anyone after Buzz." I look her square in the eye, "How do you *feel* about him?"

"I think he loves me more than I love him. I've told him that."

If it were me, I thought, *I'd have a hard time too sorting out love from fear. It's hard to trust if you've been badly hurt.* Now I study my sister silently. She looks like a lithe animal. She walks like a panther, lean and muscled, intent and forward moving, strangely beautiful and attractive to men.

"Does that bother him?"

"No, he said he doesn't care. He loves me and wants to be with me, and that is that."

"And four boys," I laugh.

"Yeah, me and Chad, Donovan, Mitchem, and Kieran."

"Well, why don't you ask if he really means it?" I couldn't think of anything brilliant to say because I find love to be a minor miracle in all its forms.

That night, unable to sleep, I decide to read in the living room and find Ed up as well. We talk about Mom and the funeral. There is a lull in the conversation.

"You know, Barbara," Ed begins, "I've been asking Sandra to marry me but she never gives me an answer. I don't know what to do."

I feel awkward at the suddenly intimate turn of conversation. I glance over at him, a rugged well-built man's man with brown hair and blue eyes and wonder if he will be my new brother-in-law. I love the way he makes Sandra feel, the way they tease each other until we are all convulsed in laughter. I almost giggle thinking of this afternoon. Mom's fetish for knotting every scrap of kitchen waste into her daily plastic newspaper wrapper as part of her personal war on Florida bugs drives us all nuts.

In her absence, Ed scrupulously follows her instructions. He drops a half an eggshell into the bag, knot, the other eggshell, knot, toast crust, knot, greasy paper towel, knot—soon we all have visions of trash mobiles swinging from the kitchen ceiling. My loyalty to my mother makes me feel guilty for laughing so hard my sides ache but I also wish he'd help me laugh more often.

A self-made man, once a Navy SEAL, and now a computer-systems troubleshooter, Ed finds himself at a loss with regard to my sister.

He really loves her, I absolutely know this. *He's a good man.* I know that too. "Why don't you ask her one more time?"

~ ~ ~

Mom and I just finish our eggs and bacon when Sandra and Ed emerge from the bedroom. They stop in front of the dining-room table holding hands. "We're engaged," Sandra admits with a grin. When I get her alone later that day, I pry. "So what happened?"

"You know, I realized life doesn't last." Her eyes looked reflective, then she smiled. "I asked *him*. I said, 'If you *do* want to get married, let's do it.'"

A decade later, Sandra will tell me, "I wish every woman knew what it is like to be really loved." That love is captured in one photo. He gazes at her with adoration; she flirtatiously teases with her eyes, and between them in the background are the stenciled letters—PICK-UP—on a store glass window.

Career Elsie ~ 1960 ~ Takoma Park or Helsinki?

After an evening Protocol event is over, somehow Mom wangles a chauffeur to drive her home. "So, where do you live?" he asks.

Tired but happy, Elsie offers to tell him the quickest route from the State Department to Takoma Park. Now no DC-Takoma highway exists but some streets at least have four lanes. The driver *never* sees those.

Elsie chirps out "left here, right there," taking him through the absolute poorest sections of D.C. It is her favorite way to work precisely because there is *no* rush hour traffic—ever.

As he contorts his limo with increasing frustration through broken-down streets, he says through chiseled teeth, *"Where* do you live? In *Helsinki?"* To which there is no need to reply, because he has just turned off Elm onto Cockerille Avenue, and Elsie is home.

Nostalgic Barbara ~ 1983 ~ Dancing, Finn Style

"Let's go to Kenttä Hall," I suggest, nostalgically remembering the Finnish dances at the Takoma Park Recreation Center.

Mom immediately agrees. "Raino's still playing, isn't he?" she asks Dad.

"Who's Raino?" I ask, getting no answer.

Kenttä Hall houses one of *two* Finnish dance halls in Lake Worth, Florida. These dance halls have a long history in America. If you're a Finn, regardless of how many generations removed, you've probably been dragged to one.

When Sandra and I were growing up in the 1950s, the Takoma Park Finns rented a community center once a month. I'd stand on my dad's feet and he would glide me, mop-like, across the floor as the accordionist and fiddler pumped out Scandinavian music. Mom-the-practical gripped my shoulders with her inescapable clamping fingers repeating to her bouncy errant child, "Step, step, glide, glide, glide."

Sandra and I were trained in the peculiar *Nurmi* style of Finnish dancing. "But Mom," I'd complain, "Everyone *else* is bouncing. Why can't I?" They looked like happy, hopping drunk people. I looked like a squashed jack-in-the-box because we g-l-i-d-e-d.

My parents danced the schottische and even the polka with big-band Finnishness. A Suomi Sinatra would have been proud. But why were they so different from other Takoma Park Finns, I wondered. The answer, I eventually decided, had to be found in the Harlem Finnish Dance Hall where they met ... and I was right.

Sixty years later at a Finnish picnic, one curly haired wrinkle-skinned Finn exclaimed, "You're *Herby's* daughter! Oh, we *all* wanted Herby! He was the *best* dancer." She sighed, "But Elsie got him."

When Mom and Dad retired to Lake Worth, Florida (the international outpost for frozen Finns), imagine their delight at finding a Finnish dance hall—albeit a one-story no-frills building on a dead-end street. After a few years of attending, they walked in one evening to the strangely familiar sounds of an accordion pumping, a drum booming, and a harmonica wailing. It could only be ...

Yes, now blind and half-deaf, Raino, the man who once played in Harlem, moved to Lake Worth. His rapid metronome beat had slowed a bit, but not much. So Sandra and I meet the original Harlem one-man now-blind band that serenaded my parents.

~ ~ ~

Now let me explain how the dance in Kenttä Hall works.

First, all the blue-haired, gray-haired, and dye-haired ladies come creaking in with their husbands or paramours, usually carrying canes or at least shuffling (though an occasional bony-legged beauty will carefully walk in on high-heeled sandals).

The dance hall is a large, wooden-floored room about the size of a basketball court, ringed with built-in benches and a shelf above those benches.

All the Finns soberly sit down, talking in respectable tones.

The music starts.

The Finns slowly stand up. They put their canes and purses on the shelf. They inch their way onto the dance floor.

I watch as dozens of slow-motion Finns start to move like rusty wind-up toys, not quite in step with the now not-so-lively schottische. I'm thinking *broken hip, stroke, heart attack.*

Then it happens.

They start to move. It's like watching hinges getting lubricated. The legs are bending. The toes are wiggling. They're going faster and faster. Suddenly the Finns are *whirling* around—limbs flying, bouncing up and down, and *smiling*!

The music stops. Like a broken movie film, they stop.

And now get this ... they *shuffle* back to their benches.

Needless to say, I absolutely love this. It's all so ... Finnish.

It's not long before Sandy and I are cherry-picked by some old tubby Finnish men feeling *sorry* for us because we're ... not moving. So they take us to be aerobicized around the floor in breathtakingly fast polkas.

I have had my feet knocked out from under me as I've been polka'd to exhaustion. My mother has gone crashing to the floor with post-Dad partners. You can <u>not</u> take the hop out of a Finn until they're absolutely laid out, dead.

Nor can I hope to hop happily. A disappointed and frustrated Mom once again suggests we dance, pushing her bony viselike grip into my shoulders.

"*Barbara!*—Step, step, glide, glide, glide."

April 18

Bereaved Elsie ~ 1987 ~ Widowed

The boat bounces across the rough waves. BAM. BAM. BAM. The bow hits each crest, slamming us up and down.

I sit in the foredeck of the 20-foot cruiser, my arm steadying the marble urn holding my father's ashes. Mom and Sandra, weighed in grief, huddle against the cabin. Mom seems shrunken, as though part of her has died. In her arms, she holds dozens of red carnations.

"We should be in the Gulf of Mexico soon," Chris yells above the engine.

"He wanted his ashes to be buried in the Gulf Stream," Mom revealed the night he died. Every day since his death, she has sat in his brown naugahyde recliner beside the white marble urn on the brass table next to his reading chair. It is as close as she can get to him.

"Mom, you can wait. We don't have to do this yet," I urge her.

"No," is all she will say.

Now we are coursing through rough afternoon waters beneath a blue sky. Sandra and Mom have both asked me to say a final prayer and put the urn into the ocean. *How can I let go of you?* I beseech him. *I cannot do this,* I scream silently. *I can't let go of all we have left of you.* I hug the urn tightly to my side. Suddenly the motor cuts off.

We're here," Chris says as the boat bobs up and down.

The urn is heavy, a sealed solid white marble cube.

I steady myself, pick up the urn, and join Mom and Sandra at the railing.

"Lord, this is the man we loved," I begin to explain, casting my words onto the sea, where the waves and wind will slowly unstring them into fragments floating into the vast ocean, never to be connected again.

Silence falls over us, our hearts and eyes looking for one last time on the precious gift I am now surrendering.

How, Dad?

Then once again I see myself standing on the diving board, my toes clenched in terror. "Just lean back and fall in. I'll get you. I'm here. ..."

Now I am holding him. *Go, Dad,* I silently whisper, knowing all he needs is the springboard.

I raise my arms and with all my strength throw the urn into the air.

It arcs for a moment, then falls into the shadowy depths and is gone.

Bereaved Elsie ~ 1987 ~ Secret Diary of a Loss
[Continued]

There is a sad little corner in my mind—
I wish I could cover it up and put a flower on it.

~

I hitched my wagon to a star
and the star burned out.

~

I used to be a wife—
now I am a <u>house</u>wife.

~

Part of me died when he died.

<u>Yet</u> ...
In the midst of despair there is happiness—
In less than a week
I lost a husband and gained a son-in-law—
A loving balance.

Child Sandra ~ 1951 ~ A Truculent Reader

Sandra didn't really like her second-grade teacher, Mrs. Johnson, so she refused to read. "I was a stubborn child," Sandra admits to me, decades later.

"I had been reading since around kindergarten. I memorized whole words by seeing the *look* of the word.

"One day I saw the sign NO SM-KING. I told Dad, "That sign is WRONG. That's not the way to make that word. Dad stared at me, his eyebrows going up. I don't think he knew I could read until that moment."

At any rate, for the first parent–teacher conference with Mrs. Johnson, Mom shows up in her work outfit. Sandra remembers, "I adored her because she always looked so beautiful. She was slim; she had great posture; and she was so much prettier than any of the other mothers. She wore a suit; she had heels; she wore hose. I was so proud of her."

~ ~ ~

"Sandra, sit outside and wait," Mrs. Johnson points to a wooden chair outside the classroom door. Sandra sits.

"Mrs. Nurmi," the second grade teacher explains to Mom, "We're going to have to put Sandra in the yellowbird reading group. She's not reading at all."

In the 1950s, if you attended J. Enos Ray Elementary, you were either an advanced "bluebird" reader, an average reading "redbird," or a very stupid "yellowbird."

Meanwhile back in the hallway, Sandra kicks her feet against the chair, bored. Suddenly the door opens. *We can go home now*, she thinks. She stands up with her lunch box and starts to walk out the door.

"STOP right there, Sandra." Mom's words freeze her midstride.

She turns around. One look at her mother, arms akimbo, tells her things aren't going too well for her.

"Come HERE."

Sandra comes into the classroom and stands in front of the teacher's desk. Mom hands her a book. "READ."

The next day Sandra is put in the bluebird group.

Curious Barbara ~ 2003 ~ A Detour Out of Time

Eventually psychic readings with Angelita become a part of my life, albeit sporadic and infrequent. Occasionally I'll have a life issue gnawing on me. It might be something simple—how to commit more deeply to my weaving business—or thorny, perhaps a rough spot in a relationship I value.

One day as Angelita is allowing information to flow through her, she begins to laugh. "Barbara, your mother's here. She wants to say hi."

"You're kidding!" I exclaim. "Mom's been dead for 3 years. She's actually coming through to you now?"

"Yeah, she's pretty strong too. I don't usually see spirits on the other side come in like this. She wants to thank you for all you did for her."

"Whoa...." I am too stupefied to ask Mom any questions. "Well," I lamely tell Angelita, "tell her hi and that I love her."

"She's showing me that she's there for you all the time, Barbara," Angelita explains after the reading concludes, "supporting you and sending you love."

I find myself feeling two completely opposite reactions. "I find that a bit creepy," I admit to Angelita. The idea of a spirit hanging around me—it sounds too much like ghosts and poltergeists and exorcisms. But surely Mom is a *good* spirit. Right?

The other reaction I don't say out loud. I feel skeptical about the belief that "we are all connected."

On some level, I understand; but then I live in a world of human separateness. No one can see my thoughts; no one can live my life. I realize I'll be part of the next generation to die.

But now, it seems I have *not* lost Mom—just my ability to see her.

If she can burst into my reading from the *other* side uninvited, I have to rethink things. Clearly I'm not alone. If so, I'm *never* really alone. Love—in ways I don't understand—envelops me.

Up to now, I divided love into two parts—this life and the afterlife. Now it seems that line is blurred.

It's a bit much for me to digest.

I file it away. I always felt certain her soul was at peace and in a better place, so it never occurred to me to ask Angelita to connect with her.

Perhaps she, now living outside time and space, could foresee a time in the future when I would be making a very unusual request of her. ...

April 20

Confused Elsie ~ 1998 ~ Measuring a Life

"Barbara," I hear the owner Hilaria Cooper's worried voice over the phone at the Cooper Group Home. "Your mother fell. I think you should come."

My worst nightmare is finally happening.

She has advanced osteoporosis. Has she broken her hip? "I'm leaving right now," I put the receiver down, grab my car keys, and run out the door. Fifteen minutes later I slam the car into park and run inside.

"Mom," I look at her ashen pain-filled face. She gazes at me like a terrified stunned rabbit. Hilaria lifts up the blanket and I see the obvious—one leg distinctly longer than the other. She has broken her hip.

"We need to call 911," I say sharply, politeness be damned. *Why hadn't Hilaria done that right away?*

The wait begins. "Exactly what happened?" I want to know.

Hilaria looks as upset as I am.

"She was sitting on the toilet seat. Janice was with her and turned away for just a moment. Your mother tried to stand up and fell back onto the seat. But she seemed okay. Janice helped her back up and she actually *walked* to her easy chair. She resisted when Janice wanted to walk her to the bedroom, which was unusual. But she gave in and allowed them to put her to bed. And that's where I found her.

She hadn't crashed to the kitchen floor. I never dreamed you could break a hip by a five-inch fall. But it had happened, and an ambulance arrived moments later to transport Mom to the hospital, thus ending forever her stay at Hilaria Cooper's Group Home.

~ ~ ~

We've scheduled surgery for tomorrow morning," the doctor explains. "We're keeping her sedated right now." I sit by Mom's side holding her hand. She drifts in and out of consciousness. I go home late and arrive early in the morning to kiss her forehead before she is wheeled into surgery. The wait begins.

~ ~ ~

"Most patients in this condition die within a year," the doctor speaks over the din of a metal food cart rattling down the gray-tiled hospital corridor. "The statistics show," he adds, "that 80 percent do not survive."

Dr. Henderson had just replaced my mother's hip. Surgery served no other purpose than to put her out of pain. Realistically, though he would prescribe therapy, she would probably never walk again. After all, she had Alzheimer's. Not in its beginning stages, but in the final stage. She'd failed the basic cognitive tests long ago, looking at a pencil with absolute perplexity.

Yet I stand there in disbelief. Why is death so inconceivable? I have walked the Alzheimer's walk with her. I have heard enough stories about "the fall" and its inexorable consequences. With osteoporosis so severe X-rays startle doctors with her sheer *lack* of bone mass, and a mind that has no idea what is happening, why should she survive? What would be the purpose?

So, I think to myself, *this is the way we measure lives*. Machinery breaking down. Ignition barely turning the motor over. The body mechanism—the air, food, liquid that moves it along—has less than a year of engine-life.

Initially I accept the doctor's verdict. I absolutely believe my mother will die. I am ready to let her go. We've reconciled as mother and daughter. We've broken through painful memories together and entered into a simple relationship as adults. It is tiring to worry about her.

1 walk back to my mother's room and stare at her shrunken childlike figure asleep on the bed, encased in foam restraints to keep her hip in perfect alignment.

The rehabilitation site picked, she will be transferred in a couple of hours. The obvious facts face me: Alzheimer's. Osteoporosis. Broken hip. Aged. Good life. Time to go.

The medics hoist her onto the hospital gurney. I watch as they roll her down the hall, out of the hospital and into the nursing home.

April 22

Caregiver Barbara ~ 1998 ~ Switching Gears

Two days later, I arrive early at the rehab unit. Worried about skin breakdown, especially with the cloth diapers the staff provides, I buy adult disposable ones.

I walk through a wave of cloying antiseptic odor and step into my mother's darkened room. Asleep in the raised hospital bed, her head dangles awkwardly to one side, contorting her neck muscles. Her diaper reeks of urine. Her food lays untouched, the spoon still in cold congealing oatmeal.

That's when I wake up. *No.* Life is *not* a machine breaking down. Life is a *spirit* that decides when it is time to leave earth. And my mother's spirit is not ready to go. Yes, her body is giving me all the messages but her *self*—the complete and utter total of her decisions to make and form her life—is demanding overtime in the game. One last shot.

How in the world do you know that, Barbara, I ask myself as I angrily adjust my mother's head, lower her bed, tuck her in, and run down the linoleum corridor looking for an aide to change her diaper.

We are no longer talking on a verbal level. That passed long ago. But I *feel* her *energy*. Her life force, her desire to live, has not abated at all. Here I am faced with seemingly irreconcilable opposites: A body I am told will die within one year, and a will that wants to go on forever.

I realize nothing separates her from death except me. Without my affirmation and belief in the value of her life, she *will* die. That is obvious. I see death rushing towards her. At this rehab center, each patient gets 5 minutes of assisted feeding. It takes Mom that long to open her mouth. It takes twice as long for her to chew and swallow. She'll die of starvation, not a broken hip.

Or her paper-thin skin will slowly break down beneath the stench of urine creating bedsores more painful than her broken hip.

Or she'll die of sheer neglect. Of *knowing* she is no longer wanted or valued in life—having no more worth than an untouched orphaned infant helplessly dying because of an absolute lack of human love.

~ ~ ~

I walk to the nightstand with a certainty building inside me. *It's not her time yet. Somehow I'll know when. But it's not now.* I pick up the phone. In minutes I hire a nursing aide to make sure she eats and is clean while I continue to think. At what point, what juncture, do we say farewell? I can't simply ask her, "Mom, are you ready to let go?" So here we have the heart of the issue. Where, really, is "Elsie?"

That afternoon, Mary, a private-agency nursing aide pulls up a chair beside my mother. She will feed her, clean her, turn her, and massage cream into her skin while I turn my home into a health-care facility.

Mom is coming home.

May

Mothers and Daughters

May 1

Caregiver Barbara ~ 1998 ~
From Home to *Nursing* Home

Okay, I tell myself, *you can turn 1,200 square feet of Cape Cod architecture into a nursing home.* I walk around carrying my hot tea, willing silent walls to answer me. As I glance toward the bedroom and office, I realize I can partition off those rooms along with the bath and laundry for Mom and a live-in. Of course that means I'll have to move upstairs.

"Joe," I call the wiry carpenter who left the priesthood for marriage and six children, "my mother broke her hip. She'll die without home care. I need help!"

"I'll be there tomorrow," he promises. That night, I start a list. Mom's room needs cable, the aide's room, a telephone. I need Internet upstairs. Virtually every piece of furniture needs to be shifted or moved. I pick up the phone and make more calls.

Two days later, as Joe hammers, the electrician wires, and a moon-faced man with an earring tunes Mom's piano, two white-haired men arrive, one wheezing from emphysema—the movers. Too incredulous to tell them to leave, I hope they survive. My bed goes upstairs, the guest bed, downstairs. We shove the spinet piano against the new partitioned wall. There's no space for my rocker. The emphysema-stricken man doubles over in coughing spasms every time he moves a piece of furniture. He restores himself by smoking Camels on my front steps.

They anchor a wood plank to the wall in the upstairs 4' x 6' closet. I now have no view, no ventilation, and my files are reduced to storage cubes on the floor. Somehow I see merit in this. I plop myself down at my new desk, swing my arms through this sensory-deprived space, and declare it a writer's paradise. No distractions. I can reach out and touch … everything.

With draconian efficiency, I dismantle my house and move upstairs in 10 days. I begin sleeping under an eave. I bath in a shower the size of a telephone booth. I peer out tiny dormer windows. Everything in my house and life has changed. Every inch of counter space, every appliance and utensil—even the refrigerator—have been turned into duty stations for attending my mother. Medical supplies line closet shelves. A hospital bed, toilet chair, and La-Z-Boy with a built-in chair lift are on standby. Physical therapists are scheduled. With Sandra's approval, I use Mom's savings for round-the-clock care. Her skin is so thin, her eating needs so unusual, her dementia so advanced, we believe she has little time left and want the best care for her.

Joe stops me one afternoon asking, "How do you plan to get your mother into the house? Those front stairs are steep."

"I hadn't thought about it," I admit. We go outside and stare at the stone steps, six in all. "Let me call some equipment-rental companies." I quickly find we can't afford, or even get, a metal ramp in time.

"Sandra," I call my problem-solving sister, "I'm building a dammed nursing home and I can't figure out how to get Mom inside it."

"Hoist her through the window," Sandra proposes. "You know, run a rope out, stick her in a bucket—she's tiny enough—and just haul her in."

I start laughing. I've become a micromanaging general of stupid details. Somehow a bucket sounds *perfect*. Immediately we both imagine the diminutive Protocol Queen swinging precariously in her bucket, her flapping hands regally waving as we tote her to her kingdom.

Then Joe and I stand outside some more.

"You know," he says, "All you really need are two long boards." He unclips the tape measure from his waistband, stretches it to 16 feet. I hold one end and we study the angle. "It's moderate enough." he concludes. "The ambulance driver can stand between the boards and walk up the steps while she rolls up."

"Okay, done. Go build them."

"I'll add guards on the sides so she won't roll off."

I think to myself, *Last problem. Solved.*

Three days later, I pick up the phone to call rehab.

"I'm ready," I tell them.

May 5

Princess Sandra ~ 1989 ~ A Queen-in-Waiting

I get into the back seat of the car. Ed nudges Sandra. "Tell her," he prompts.

Tell me what? I wonder.

Sandra turns around and stares at me. I see fear in her eyes ... and anger. I tense up, worried. *Have I done something to hurt my sister? Did I say something?*

She pauses, opens her mouth, and I hear hot angry words coming from her lips. "I HATE the bitch."

Having delivered her one-sentence speech about Mom, she anxiously looks at me. Silence fills the car while I take in this momentous news. Then I begin to giggle. She watches transfixed as I laugh so hard, tears stream down my face. I howl till I'm clutching my belly.

After all ... Mom isn't the easiest person to live with.

~ ~ ~

As firstborn, Sandra is both the apple of Mom's eye and the primary source of her ire. The reason is easy to see. In my favorite picture of Sandra, she seems to be about 2 years old. She's sitting on our front brick steps.

But sitting doesn't quite express it. Her arms are thrown wide, and her face is wreathed in a smile conveying to all the world that *she* is queen of the universe.

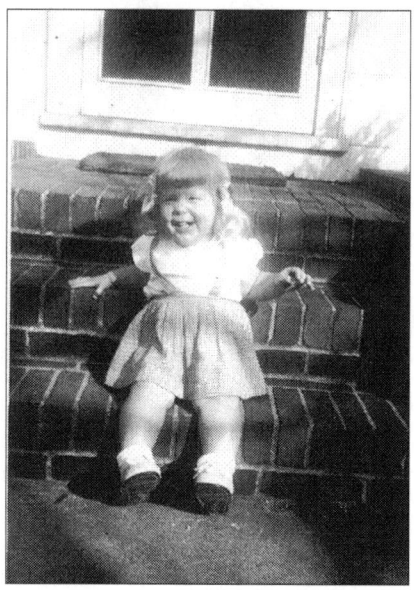

Unfortunately, my mother logically assumes that *she* is queen ... hence the slight problem.

Now I have no such issues. I absolutely know my place—daughter/sister-in-waiting. In the case of my mother, it means being quiet and staying out of the way. With my sister, it means enduring truly awful games of Monopoly, losing at cribbage, attempting to play softball, and even accompanying her on high school dates with guys she doesn't favor.

Admittedly Sandra—because, after all, she is a *benevolent* queen—makes all things fun. But Mom has a household to run. Inevitably the two queens clash. ...

~ ~ ~

First of all, Sandra-the-child-queen considers all household treasure—including lunch money—to be hers. One day, Sandra suggests we go on a treasure hunt. I enthusiastically agree. We head to the ball field and rock outcropping in Spring Park. Soon Sandra is finding quarters and dimes. After several minutes of trailing the increasingly rich queen, I burst into tears complaining, "I'm not finding *anything*." THEN ... all of the sudden I find a quarter! My spirits brighten considerably.

We continue on in this fashion, with my treasure amounting to little and Sandra's amounting to much. At last it is time to go home. I race ahead, ecstatic with my good fortune. I burst through the kitchen door and yell, "MOM, you should see all the *money* we found in the park!"

The wealthy queen follows behind me, her pockets bulging with coins.

Without a pause, without even leaving the bedroom, Mom addresses the purloining queen: "Put the money back in the lunch jar, Sandra."

See, two queens just know each other.

~ ~ ~

Sandra's fiefdom extends to school. One day, her fourth-grade teacher picks Sandra and another student to fetch school supplies from the closet. Once there, Sandra notices a rat trap loaded with cheese. Being hungry, she drags the boy over. "See that? Why don't you get the cheese and we'll eat it."

"It's a *trap*," the boy replies.

"But if you're real quick, you can get it. You'd be faster than me. I'm a girl."

The boy, proud of his prowess, decides to go for it. He reaches for the cheese. SLAM.

Soon he is on the way to the hospital with two broken fingers. Meanwhile, the queen has to face the teacher. "So, Sandra," Mrs. Franklin looks through her rimless eyeglasses. "How long do you think you should stay in detention *this* time?" (Sandra had thrown rocks out an open classroom window the week before.)

Sandra ponders this. One hour seems too long, but she wants to give a respectable number of minutes for her crime. Finally she decides, "37 minutes."

Sandra *thinks* she sees a hint of a smile. The silence stretches on. Sandra reevaluates. *Maybe 38 or 39 minutes would have been better. He* did *break two fingers. ...*

Just then Mrs. Franklin looks at her watch. "I'll let you know when your time is up."

Sandra sits down, satisfied with justice.

Child Elsie ~ 1935 ~ She Was Smart, *Real* Smart

Oldenburg Jasberg, the only Finnish-speaking land-sales company in Minnesota in the late 1800s insists it has "the best interests in mind for the Finnish people." It admits its land is no good for wheat, but "potatoes and rutabagas will do well," along with cows and chickens. For $200 paid over 5 years, buyers get 40 acres and a donated cemetery plot so that they can live in perpetuity in Finlayson.

Farming and burying take off. A century later, Mom strolls through the cemetery. "I dated him." "Oh my, him too." "Well look at that, there's Carl. I dated him." In later years when she is too ill to come, I run into an elder Finlayson man who admits he also wanted to date Elsie.

Named after sawmill owner David Finlayson in 1895, the town does attract Finns. They come, settle, and set up a pickle factory, two potato warehouses, a train station, and a post office. Elsie's maternal grandparents, Liisa and Henry Askelin must have been among the first wave. They have three children and their daughter Jennie marries the fiddle-playing, band-leading Hjalmar Norlund, setting the stage for Elsie's birth.

~ ~ ~

Tow-headed Finn-speaking Elsie sits in her first assigned school seat in Duluth and promptly realizes something is terribly amiss. The teacher doesn't speak Finnish. Elsie patiently explains, *En puhu Englanti*—I don't speak English. She gets dunced and demoted, slowing but not derailing her path to valedictorian.

By 1926 Elsie has a sister, Lucy, and a brother, Swante. Her father works in the Duluth granary, and her mother is pregnant with a fourth child. Then one day in December a man knocks on their door. "Your husband's had an accident. His arm got caught," he explains, twisting his cap in his hands. "We took him to the hospital."

ELSIE AT EBB TIDE

Jennie leaves the children in Elsie's care and disappears out the front door. The kids see little of her over the next 3 days. A snowstorm blankets the city. Hjalmar fights for his life. Gangrene sets in. Nothing stops it. Then one day Jennie, carrying the weight of an 8th-month child inside her, walks home with the crushing sorrow of death on her. Hjalmar is dead.

Elsie is 9 years old.

Jennie falls into deep depression and Elsie's childhood is over. Her fun-loving father—the sunshine of her young life—is gone. At the funeral, her grandmother tells her not to cry. "Crying isn't nice." Elsie remembers standing at the window as Christmas approaches, saying to herself, *I'll never cry again.*"

Alice is born the next month with a clubbed right foot that is soon encased in plaster. Elsie, now emotionally responsible for a whole family, carries her little sister up and down steps and around the home. "I felt closer to her," Elsie remembers decades later. "I guess that's why."

The family soon ends up back in Finlayson. Probably they live on the Askelin farm for a while. Elsie, the only child who still speaks immigrant Finnish, acts as the go-between for her siblings. As Alice gets older, she tries to teach her grandparents English. Picking up a serving spoon, she goes to Grandma Liisa and says in her limited Finnish, *Tämä on* SPOON." Grandma replies in Finnish, "Go teach your grandfather." *Tämä on* SPOON," she tells him. He pats her on the head, "Go tell your grandmother." They never speak English, or even Finn-lish. Not one word. Ever.

~ ~ ~

In this strict Lutheran household, church constitutes the only entertainment, so Elsie (who loves music as much as her deceased father), ends up as a teenage organist at the church built by Finns (including the Norlunds) in 1895 on property donated by the St. Paul–Duluth Railway. Unfortunately, Elsie often falls asleep over the keyboard because of her late-night dates.

147

As graduation approaches in 1935, Elsie racks up A's in every subject from algebra to deportment, American history to physics. During her senior year (spent in one classroom) under the hands Mrs. F. Mannelin, Elsie and Charlie Smith vie for top dog. Elsie edges him out to become class valedictorian.

She draws little inspiration from her autograph book: "Tulips in the garden, tulips in the dark, but what could be more sweeter than tulips in the dark?" or, "Think of me far, far away in the woods when the woodchucks die of whooping cough."

But an adult inscriber, in elegant script, writes, "You have charm, poise, even temperament, and willingness to work. Cultivate them and they will bring you many things." Everyone agrees even decades later that Elsie was smart, so in her yearbook she bequeaths her A's to "anyone who feels the need to get them."

When graduation day arrives, Elsie—resplendent in a full-length white satin dress—promises the class, "We stand at the threshold of infinite opportunity. It is not enough that we go meandering through a long curriculum in a halfhearted way."

She ends with a poem concluding, "We have a firm foundation; we have not worked in vain. We feel a sad elation to forge ahead again."

Forever after, whenever Elsie writes a poem, it rhymes—as though life itself should have a rhythmic movement progressing forward, never looking back. But a future in this tiny town usually means classmates marry one another, take jobs in Minnesota, shoot deer, eat walleye, own all-terrain vehicles, and birth Garrison Keillor–type children.

Elsie heads to Duluth Business School, earning money as a nanny. But the "honest, thoroughly reliable, of fine character, and very efficient" Elsie soon takes employment at the Great Northern Candy Co., the only time in her life she *looks* as plump as the chocolate-covered marshmallow products she sells.

Surely there has to be more to life. Soon she'll be one of the first Finlayson High students to leave Minnesota, shedding the pounds as she goes.

Caregiver Barbara ~ 1998 ~ Mom Comes Home

This morning, the hospital bed and other equipment arrived. I've arranged for Mom to be picked up from the rehab center at 2 o'clock. I stopped by Mom's room early this morning to tell her she's coming to my house. Cognitively she shows absolutely *no* sign she understands; but I feel better treating her as though she does.

Now I'm sitting on the stone steps waiting. I hear a vehicle turn the corner on my isolated street. As it rounds the curve at the top of the hill, I see the handicapped transport vehicle. I stand up and wave it to a stop.

"Here's how we plan to get her up the stairs," I explain to the driver who looks incredulously at the 16-foot long 10-inch wide planks with corner molding on each side. "We're going to tie a rope to the wheel chair. You push it onto the planks while I pull."

"I don't know if this is safe or not." He scratches his head. I'm afraid he's going to take Mom back to rehab.

"It'll work. She only weighs 113 pounds. But you might want to get a running start."

He unloads Elsie, and eyeballs the two planks. I'm holding onto the nylon rope tied to her chair. "Okay," I holler, "let's *do* it," and the driver picks up speed on the flat walkway, bounces her over the plank edge and shoves her hard up the tracks while I'm reeling in the rope as fast as I can.

Mom *flies* off the top of the ramp onto the stone porch. The rest is easy. We leverage her over the doorstep and roll her into the living room, past her piano, through the new door into *her* home, the master bedroom.

Mary, the nursing aide I've hired, transfers her from wheelchair to bed and tucks her in. I sign the papers the driver hands me. "Well," he admits, "I've *never* delivered a client this way."

We are now family: Mom, Mary, and me.

Mother Elsie ~ 1957 ~
Hiring the Pint-Sized Cleaning Crew

"Kids," Dad hollers out the front door. "Come in the kitchen for a minute." We abandon our Monopoly game on the front steps. That suits me fine. It takes a torturously long time to always arrive at the same result—bankruptcy.

We dutifully and a bit nervously stand in front of our parents.

"We've decided you're old enough to watch each other so we're not hiring another housekeeper," Mom tells us. "But in order to do this, you'll have to clean the house and we'll pay each of you $5 a week."

"FIVE DOLLARS!" Sandra and I shout in astonishment and stare at each other. Our quarter allowance has just shot up four, eight, twelve, sixteen ... TWENTY times. We are child millionaires.

"We think you're old enough to supervise yourselves. We'll never find someone like Mary again." Here we all pause. Mary. ...

~ ~ ~

When Mom returned to work, the 4' 8" Irish Mary became our surrogate mother. Irish mothering included lumpy breakfast oatmeal. Initially, Sandra and I greeted this with horror and grumbling until Mom overheard us. Thereafter we learned the childhood art of gagging down food.

Every afternoon, Mary disappeared into our pink-and-gray tiled bathroom and let her gray-white braided hair fall loose to her waist. As I stared, she brushed, braided, and rewound it. When she wasn't doing this, she slapped us with wet washcloths—Sandra more than me because I was the *good* child. Sandra was well on her way to being the wicked *Sandrella*.

One day Sandra and I ran out to play, heading up to Spring Park. The boulders bordering the baseball field became our imaginary transportation vehicles, furniture, or household appliances. All went well until a rock sailed over our heads.

Once again the "Ralphie boys"—two bully brothers in the neighborhood—launched an attack sending us scrambling. We began to tear across the field with the boys in hot pursuit, when Sandra stopped dead in her tracks, bent down, picked up a stone, aimed well, and nailed the rotten Ralph. He went screaming home. We went home very satisfied.

Shortly thereafter, Mr. Ralphie-the-father roared down the street filled with rage. He stormed up our sidewalk and hammered on our screen door. Mary was ready. Eyes flashing, washcloth flapping, in full Irish brogue, she dressed him right down to his shorts.

And *that* was the end of the Ralphie-boy episodes.

Mary's days with us ended when her elder sister became ill and she needed to tend her. She brought us a container of ice cream and, with tear-filled eyes, left. She was our last "mother" and we rapidly went through housekeepers. Florence ignored us unless we were sick. Judy let us climb out our dormer window onto the roof for a picnic. (In sublime stupidity, I told my mother.) With Edith, we simply lost half our household—one linen tablecloth, sheet, towel, and washcloth at a time.

Unlike every other kid in our neighborhood, we preferred being latchkey children. Neither of us could imagine an at-home Elsie. First of all, Mom never baked. Second, she didn't sew. Lastly, her boredom would have bored holes through our lives in unanticipated (but dreadful) ways.

~ ~ ~

"So," the pragmatic Sandra asks, "what do we have to do?"

"You need to do the laundry, iron, vacuum, dust, scrub down the bathrooms, and wash the kitchen and bathroom floors every Saturday morning," Mom explains. "You'll do the dishes every night, and sometimes help with the cooking. And we expect you to watch each other. We are placing a lot of trust in you."

Somehow it all sounds wonderful. After all, how long can it take to do that stuff? Two or three hours? We immediately agree and Mom reaches under the sink for the Bon Ami, wash rags, and a bucket. We are in training.

We especially like the part about watching each other. Sure. We can do that.

We often watch each other successfully from about 30 feet up in our fir tree, hoping our parents (who once unexpectedly arrived home) won't notice their striped T-shirted kids way over the roofline.

We launch all-day adventures, bicycling to the D.C. zoo, or taking public transit to unknown end-of-line destinations.

The cleaning part, however, quickly loses its luster: picking up your parent's stinky socks and underwear, scrubbing toilet bowls, becoming ironing drones. I convince Sandra that washing clothes is much more laborious than hanging them up (in the dead of winter). Sandra agreeably goes along until I get sick ... after that we share.

We never learn how to properly clean a house—it becomes a 10- and 12-year old's version of "how much cleanliness is $5 worth." Not much. The house retains a clean patina scarcely covering forgotten floorboards, corners, cobwebs, and concealed dust balls.

We settle into our domestic drudgery including nightly dish washing. To while away that chore, we usually belt out a Swahili song Sandra has memorized: *my-a-nakapiki-mun-da*—clueless of what it means.

Though we grumble, we never turn in our resignations. Frankly the fringe benefit of freedom far outweighs Saturday chores. We become the envy of the neighborhood. We are rich. We are liberated. We sing Swahili.

Many years later, I realize that once again, Mom trumped us. She knew we hated the practical clothes she bought us—plaid jumpers, solid colored shirts, dungarees, T-shirts. Now we could buy *fashionable* outfits such as my beloved Dr. Kildare shirt. Mom no longer bought us clothes; we used our allowance. So basically, as I see it, we were a line-item transfer.

I'd have to say Mom was a *child-whisperer* because, like people who silently talk to horses or dogs, she herded us successfully into places we had no interest in going. For example, living without television. ...

~ ~ ~

I loved TV. I clung onto it with all the enthusiasm of an addict. Even though it was a little black-and-white screen stuck in a tasteless mahogany box, I'd sit in front of it, mesmerized by *I Love Lucy, Leave It to Beaver, Father Knows Best,* and *The Lone Ranger*. One day I came home, twisted the ON dial. Nothing happened. No sound, no picture. I ran to my parents. "The television is BROKEN!" I wailed.

My parents looked very sad, Mom especially. They seemed to feel my pain. "Oh Barbara," they lamented, "we can't afford to fix it right now."

For TWO years, the television set remained broken. I was slowly and relentlessly forced off my viewing addition. It took me 6 months before I gave up looking forlornly at its black screen. To fill in all that empty time, I began to talk to my parents. I read books. I played outside. When the TV finally flickered into life again, I rejoiced that my parent's finances were better.

Decades later, Mom tells me, "Oh, we pulled a vacuum tube out of it. You were watching too much TV."

Career Elsie ~ 1967 ~ Her Dress Is Missing!

Elsie pokes her head into her boss's office. "Would it be possible for me to attend the airport arrival ceremony for President Kekkonen?" This is not a whimsical request—Kekkonen after all is the Finnish president and Elsie wants to see him in person.

"I'm afraid not, Elsie," her new boss replies, not looking up from the pile of papers. "We're too busy right now."

The next day Elsie, with some irritation, works at her desk while the arrival ceremony commences without her. She knows Urjo and Sylvia Kekkonen will be escorted to the Blair House where her friend and coworker Mary Edith presides as hostess for presidential visitors. *Maybe I can talk to her and just get a chance to greet them while they are there,* Elsie thinks.

Close to lunchtime, the phone rings. She picks it up and hears Mary Edith's voice. "Elsie, you've got to get over here right away. Mrs. Kekkonen is hysterical and nobody understands what she's saying."

Elsie leaps out of her chair and dashes into her boss's office.

"They need me at Blair House! Mrs. Kekkonen is very upset and nobody understands why." (All the translators are at the White House with President Kekkonen's party.) "Mary Edith asked me to come right away!"

"They'll have to get someone else. I need you here," he replies.

A shocked Elsie returns to her desk, picks up the receiver and gives the bad news to Mary Edith. Elsie, now more frustrated than ever and entirely dissatisfied with her new boss, returns to work.

Fifteen minutes later, her boss walks over to her desk. "The Chief of Protocol orders you to go over to the Blair House immediately," he says, turning his heel to go back to his office.

Wow, Elsie thinks, *Mary Edith pulled rank.* She grabs her purse, calls for a State Department car and within minutes jumps out at Blair House directly across from the White House.

"She's upstairs," Mary Edith gestures, and follows Elsie as she breaks into a run up the steps.

"*Mikä on vialla?*" Elsie asks.

"WHAT's WRONG?!" Mrs. Kekkonen screeches. "*Minun illallinen mekko puuttuu!* My dress for tonight's White House dinner is MISSING!"

Now *that* is something Elsie can handle. She calls Andrews Air Force Base, describes the box the dress is in, and soon a team scours the cargo bay searching for Mrs. Kekkonen's dress. Still containing numerous boxes carrying gifts for the state visit and staff luggage, every likely box has to be checked.

Minutes tick by.

Any woman can understand the first lady's distress. After all, she is not meeting just *any* president and his wife. She is meeting Jack Kennedy and the stunningly beautiful Jacqueline. It simply will not do to arrive in an off-the-rack gown—even from an upscale Washington, D.C. department store—after she has spent months fretting over her outfit.

Elsie chats with Mrs. Kekkonen in Finnish to keep her distracted. Within the hour, the phone rings. "We found the dress. It's on its way," an Air Force staff sergeant assures her. Mrs. Kekkonen begins to relax.

Elsie stays, even doing touch-up ironing at her request until the first lady, coiffed and dressed, takes the arm of her husband and leaves for the White House.

In the meantime, Mary Edith calls Angier Biddle Duke, Chief of Protocol, to insist that Elsie stay at the Blair House until the Kekkonens leave.

Raised in a world of manners where his father was heir to the American Tobacco Company and his grandfather helped found Duke University, Duke instinctively understands that seamless comfort constitutes good diplomacy.

Because of his sense of the obvious, Elsie gets her first taste of life as a Protocol Officer, though it will be years before she carries the title.

May 11

Child Barbara ~ 1960 ~ A *Very* Good Deed

I never remember Mom sewing. However, a photo exists of me wearing a gray mouse costume. I suspect the only way I got it was through some heroic Elsie effort at a sewing machine.

But I never remember seeing such a machine. Despite my mental lapses, I vividly recall the time my mother made a slipcover for our Queen Anne chair. The fabric, with garish saucer-sized pink flowers trapped in swirling green vines, completely dwarfed the modest club-footed chair, but Mom absolutely loved what she had accomplished, right down to the forest-green piping and zipper holding it perfectly tight.

Looking at the chair the week before Mother's Day, I decide to do a *very good deed* for my mother. Her coveted slipcover could use a bit of washing—this despite the fact that no dirt could possibly be seen, given its garishness.

I unzip the cover, toss it in the washing machine, dump in soap, set it on the hot wash cycle, and run out to play. When I come in a couple of hours later and lift the slipcover out, it looks considerably smaller than when I put it in. I stand very still, taking in the enormity of this situation. My heart lands somewhere around my knee caps.

Heroically, I begin to tug at it, attempting to stretch it back into shape. I decide that if I let it dry, things will only get worse, so I run over to the Queen Anne chair and begin to force it over the back and seat.

With all my effort, it barely fits. I tug and tug the zipper and can only force it halfway down. All afternoon, I look at that chair and feel very sorry for myself. It stands sentinel by the front door—the first thing my mother will see when she walks into the house after an exhausting day of work.

At the appointed hour, Mom steps through the front door, beneath its good-luck horseshoe.

I stand stoically by my disaster. I tell her it was meant to be her Mother's Day present and I am so sorry I have ruined it. She listens to me in absolute silence and then very *quietly* walks into her bedroom and shuts the door. It is the first and only time I ever hear her cry. When she comes out, an hour later, she never says a thing about that chair. That night the slipcover disappears forever.

May 14

Caregiver Barbara ~ 1998 ~
Learning the Ropes of Home Care

I find myself increasingly uncomfortable with Mary. She insists on washing my mother in private. "You shouldn't see your mother like this." "You don't have to worry about anything." "Please stay out of the kitchen while I'm preparing your mother's food." "Let me know when you want to visit with your mother so I can get her ready for you." "You should knock before entering."

When the home-health nurse came today for a scheduled checkup, I insisted that she examine all of my mother's skin with me present to make sure no bedsores were starting. Sure enough, when we turn Mom onto her side, we both see ominous red spots around her tailbone and hip.

I once saw these horrifying open wounds clear to the bone on a woman whose elderly husband did not know how to care for her. As soon as the nurse leaves, I call the agency, explaining Mary's behavior and what the nurse and I have witnessed.

"You are *always* allowed to be present at any time," he tells me, clearly upset.

"I had no idea what to expect," I wearily reply. "I've never hired a nurse's aide."

"Look, I am going to remove her immediately," he informs me. "Don't say anything to Mary. I don't want to take any chance she might hurt your mother. This is how we're going to do it."

Now I am alarmed, but agree. He calls Mary. She walks into the living room abruptly informing me, "I have been offered a better job," and disappears into her bedroom to pack.

Two hours later, we hear a knock on the door. I open it. In steps Hawa with a big grin on her mahogany-skinned face, and tan, lace-up leather boots on her feet.

"So," she turns to me, "if it's okay with you, Mary can explain how she's been taking care of your mother." I agree, and they lapse into their native Sierra Leone tongue while I retreat to the kitchen to start dinner. After Mary leaves, Hawa talks to me, saying she understands the situation and not to worry.

That evening, she hops into the hospital bed, cuddles my frail mother, and spoon-feeds her one slow mouthful at a time.

Retired Elsie ~ 1989 ~ Elsie-isms

Be what you iz
And not what you aint
If you iz what you aint
You aint what you iz.

~

I have seen what I want to see
I have done what I want to do
I am just riding out the rest of my life.

~

My body doesn't know
I'm getting old and I'm
Not telling it.

~

I'm going to be
all I can be
as long as I be.

Caregiver Barbara ~ 1998 ~ The Way We Anticipate Death

I force myself today to make funeral arrangements. It's not that I am squeamish. After all, Dad once suggested we plasticize our loved ones: "You could store them in the closet and bring 'em out for Thanksgiving and Christmas."

But right now, I face its reality. That's the sticking point—admitting my *mother* is going to be part of it: dressing the body, embalming the body, beautifying it with makeup and curled hair. The *death*.

How many times will my mother be transported in a hearse?

How many obituaries do I want printed, in which newspapers?

And of course, which coffin will be the one to contain my mother. I am stepping through a portal from which I cannot return. I *agree* to this death.

Which of course I do. I do not. I do. Not.

~ ~ ~

I want the service in my home, I tell the funeral official, wondering what he is called. There must be a title and I imagine it is something soft and reassuring. Not death-specialist or end-of-the-road placement counselor.

"How large are your doorways?" he asks. Of course, I don't know. We measure coffins. Oak coffins. Temporary cardboard ones destined for cremation.

The 10-pound cardboard is infinitely lighter to carry up the steps into my house than a rental 150-pound oak casket. I rather like the blue-gray floral-imprinted cloth-covered cardboard coffin. It seems more like Elsie. I find myself saying, "It will match her eyes."

But there are so many problems to untangle. Sandra does *not* want to see a dead body, but our mother (we think) absolutely *wants* to be viewed. After all, she insisted we dress her in the black suit she wore to the private audience with Pope Paul VI.

On her last visit, Sandra unearthed that suit. "Barbara, there's a moth hole in the jacket. Mom would *never* want to be seen like that."

I think to myself, *magic marker,* but what I say is, "I'll weave in some threads." We are each translating our anticipated grief into making her last moment "right."

~ ~ ~

I come home with the price list and immediately get a tape measure. Will the coffin go through the door to her bedroom?

No.

I visualize a cantilevered Elsie and then give up. I walk around the living and dining rooms, trying to figure out how I can have the visitation I think Mom wants *and* protect my sister. I silently lament, *Mom, you were the Protocol Officer. You dealt with this stuff all the time. What do I do? And by the way, are we even burying you or do you prefer cremation now?*

It is, in a way, ridiculous to have the funeral in my acutely small home but easier for her older friends. They can pay their respects, attend the memorial service, visit with each other, and have refreshments. We can also play songs she loved on the piano.

I measure spaces where we can place chairs and come up with forty (with ten in obscured-vision locations). Then I consider who might come. Well, one never knows. But if all those who might come did—well, we would run out of chairs, room, food—everything.

I stop and sit down. *This is crazy,* I tell myself. *Mom is alive. I don't want to be doing this.* But then I remind myself, *When the time comes, I don't want to be signing contracts, filling out forms, making decisions. I want to sit, just sit.*

So here I am, measuring walls, figuratively moving furniture, envisioning coffins coming in, coffins going out, people flowing through this tiny house.

That is, I suppose, the way we anticipate death.

May 19

Bride Barbara ~ 1967 ~ Are You Sure?

I stand in the narthex with my father, listening to the beginning notes of the *Wedding March*. Dressed in a knee-length, lace-covered satin dress, I tug at the veil netting to make sure it hangs straight over my face. My fiancé Bill and his brother Alan stand at the altar waiting.

"Barbara, are you sure?" Dad turns to me. "If you have *any* doubts, we can stop right now."

I look at him confused. *Why would I want to stop? I want to run down the aisle into the arms of this man. I am IN LOVE.*

"No, Dad," I answer. "I'm sure." He tucks my arm into his, and we begin the walk. I am 19 years old.

Granted, my announcement 5 months earlier was received like Titanic hitting the iceberg. Decades later, I easily understand Mom's sorrow.

She *knew* what lay ahead for a girl with only a high school degree. The one thing, the only thing really, Mom and Dad wanted for Sandra and me was a college degree. Month by month, Mom set part of her paycheck aside, preparing for the expenses. When we seemed utterly disinterested, Mom anxiously talked to coworker Mary Edith Wilroy at Blair House, whose children all attended institutions of higher learning.

"Elsie," she explained, "just say, '*when* you go to college,' and they'll go like lambs."

Soon our household conversations revolved constantly about when we'd go to college, where we'd go, what it would be like, what a wonderful opportunity it would be. Both Sandra and I, too stupid to know differently, simply filed our high school diplomas into our vanity drawers and registered for college. Now halfway through, I choose to marry a U.S. Army draftee with the Vietnam War raging, knowing with absolute certainty my husband will be shipped overseas.

From Mom's perspective, her teenage daughter opted for half a degree, a husband who might be killed, and diapers on a clothesline in some godforsaken military base. The highest support Mom could give me was to say absolutely nothing. Being in love, I easily chose to ignore the icy soundlessness of our household. Through sheer good fortune, Bill got assigned to Ft. McNair in Washington, D.C. and I graduated from college with high honors.

May 25

Kenna and Elsie ~ 2000 ~ *I Want to Dance*

Kenna and Mom are slowly establishing a relationship. In a way, the conversations become more concrete—about everyday things, about wishes and needs.

~ ~ ~

<u>Elsie</u>: *I don't feel like I will be living much longer. I am feeling weak.*

<u>Kenna</u>: Why?

<u>Elsie</u>: *I don't know. I am just weaker than before. I feel strange.*

<u>Kenna</u>: You could live much longer.

Elsie: I'm just growing more tired of being here like this.

Kenna: What would you like?

Elsie: I want to leave something for my grandchildren. I want them to remember me.

Kenna: I'll tell Barbara.

Elsie: Well, Barbara can do anything. Don't tell her she can't—that is just when she will! Can you tell Barbara to hold my hands more? It is only when I am touched that I know that I am here.

[Kenna starts to cry. She continues to connect with Elsie, filling her with Light.]

Elsie: Oh, that feels so good.

Kenna: So what's in your heart, Elsie?

Elsie: I want to dance. I wish I could. I liked to fly. But my husband preferred the water and boats. Sandra and Barbara have been good daughters. I am like an old leaf on a tree.

Kenna: Can you see angels, Elsie?

Elsie: Yes. I am seeing them now. I am getting tired. I will be ready when Barbara is ready.

Kenna: Would you like me to come back to visit?

Elsie: The door is always open. Right now I want to get some sleep.

~ ~ ~

After Kenna finishes her session with Mom, we talk and I write down the messages.

I go into Mom's room and watch her as she sleeps with her face at peace, her mouth ever so slightly open, a tiny smile seeming to tug at the corners. *Perhaps you are talking with the angels,* I think. *Or maybe you're flying on Air Force Two.* Kenna received one message clearly: Dad loved water; Mom loved air. How true.

I wonder about her words, *I will be ready when Barbara is ready.* Does she know how I've fretted about the funeral? Strangely, even during these declining stages, I still find moments when she seems briefly lucid.

About 2 weeks ago, I walked in and saw her cheeks wet with tears. I bent over her and asked, "What's wrong, Mom?" To my surprise she answered, "I'm sad because I'm going to die."

How do we explain these things? Even though she is in the last stages of Alzheimer's, she emerges from her confusion. She *knows* her life is slipping away. Today she feels tired, weak. Is the end nearing? I don't know. But with Kenna's help, she is learning to navigate across that mysterious bridge between life and death.

May 28

Caregiver Barbara ~ 1998 ~ Tending A Fading Cornflower

I am weary. I transformed my house into a perfect sanctuary for Mom but it has taken an emotional toll on me. Not yet accustomed to living upstairs, I feel I am scooping up handfuls of myself, like feathers that have escaped from a down pillow, urging them to float up the steps.

It takes time, I find, to create new household routines. My writing gets pushed aside with nursing needs: "We need more diapers." "Can you fix this?" "How does your mother like …?" "Where is the blender, masher, beater, frying pan, spatula?"

My solitude is sliced, diced, and flipped every day. But actually I'm my own biggest distraction. I like to play the piano for Mom. I sit with her. I watch TV with her and Hawa. By the end of the day, I go upstairs in some ways happy—and in some ways frustrated.

On the other hand, I am beginning to realize I have the undeserved honor of knowing my mother in the deepest possible way—the inner mainspring hidden beneath her manners, history, habits, prejudice. She becomes more *her* as the disease eats away the useless stuff she had to bear because of culture or guilt.

Alzheimer's is an expensive, lengthy, and debilitating disease. Unlike cancer or even heart disease, no measurable medical chronology exists for Alzheimer's. It consumes the intellect slow or fast. It subverts personality or leaves it intact. Mom moves gradually through its corridors. She is fading like a cornflower in a vase. The water is changed daily; nutrients are added to preserve the flower. But slowly the vibrant blue begins to dim; the petals curl downward.

Mom's eyes are blue, but they seem strange now. People talk of the vacant stare—lights out—but this is no lights out. It is lights elsewhere. She is seeing something we simply cannot see. It is not a vacant look but a gazing look.

Child Barbara ~ 1959 ~ Piano Practice

"Have you done your piano practice yet," Mom calls from the den where she is having her after-work vodka and tonic with Dad.

"Not yet," I admit, and resignedly put my Nancy Drew mystery down and head for the piano bench. Now in my third year, I loathe the 30 minutes of daily drudgery. I flip the Thompson piano book open to another boring classical piece with three sharps. I wind up the mechanical metronome hoping to sort out eighth notes from quarter notes and grind my way through the piece.

What makes piano practice particularly irritating is that Mom taught me how to play by ear last Christmas. After spending 3 years reading music, I now find there's a much easier way.

"Here, Barbara," she said, sitting beside me on the bench. "It's easy. Try "Silent Night." The notes either go up or down. So the right hand is easy to figure out. Then you just add a chord to the bottom with your left hand. If you play in the key of C, then you can use a C-chord (she plays it) and a G-chord (she plays that). Try it," she says, and goes back to the kitchen.

For the rest of the afternoon, I compose my own version of "Silent Night" and move on to five other Christmas carols. *What the heck am I learning sheet music for?* I wonder. *This is so much easier.*

After that, my days as a trained musician are pretty much over. I become less enthusiastic day by boring-practice day.

Now Mom, still clad in her tailored blue-gray suit, comes out of the den and sits next to me on the piano bench. "Barbara," she begins, "We can't afford to get you braces *and* pay for piano lessons." *Huh?* I think. *I don't even want braces. They are so completely dorky. Stupid. Ugly.*

"So you'll have to choose," she continues. "Do you want to keep taking piano lessons or get braces?"

I am so stupid I don't even realize this is a SET ... UP. "Oh, I'd MUCH rather have braces, Mom!" Only decades later do I realize that I had been hoodwinked once again by the *child whisperer.*

Confused Elsie ~ 1999 ~ Poor Joan

Hawa and I decide to watch a TV special on Joan of Arc. "It'll be like a pajama party," I promise. Of course, Hawa (having been raised in Sierra Leone without American-style slumber parties) looks at me and laughs at the idea. "Okay," she agrees and transfers Mom to her La-Z-Boy.

We want her to sit up more. Wrapped in a blanket, she looks elfin-like with her strangely platinum-silver hair and otherworldly eyes. Her irritated face says *I want nothing of this! I want to go to bed.* But we ignore her body language determined that she join us watching this movie.

Soon the TV is clicked on and Hawa curls up in Mom's hospital bed. I sit in her wheelchair. With bowls of popcorn on our laps, Hawa feeds kernel after kernel into my mother's mouth.

We watch the diminutive Joan as she grows up, hears heavenly counsel, leads military battles, and rescues France. But now Joan is about to be tried.

Peter O'Toole, thundering through the screen as the bishop, begins his harangue. He violently gestures toward Joan as he warns the judges:

"Do NOT be deceived."

"She will say that GOD has spoken to her."

"She believes it."

"She will tell you the SPIRIT tells her things."

"She believes it."

"Do not judge her on those things."

"Judge her on one thing only."

"HER PRIDE!"

~ ~ ~

"We WILL!" Mom chirps.

(So much for Joan...)

May 31

Caregiver Barbara ~ 1999 ~ Love Melts a Finnish Heart

When tall well-figured, mahogany-skinned Hawa laughs, it's a *big* warm-hearted laugh that brightens the whole house. She is so un-Finn-like.

Every day, Hawa leaps into Mom's bed—her golden brown long legs stretched out, her eyes laughing, her face as happy as a pea tucked inside a pod.

She wraps Mom in physical closeness and warmth. She sits by her, touches her, curls up in bed with her. She laughs, teases, and snoozes with her in a hospital bed wide enough for two when one is a frail woman who rarely eats.

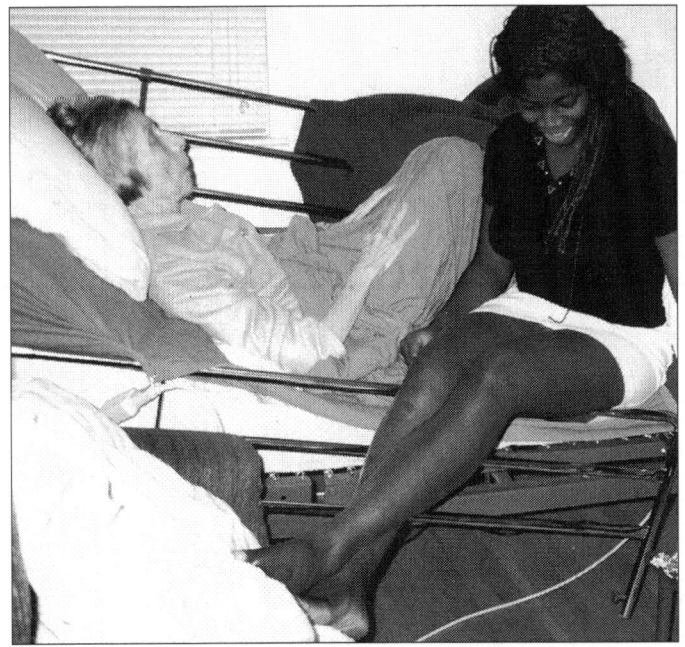

Hawa is a complete enigma to a Finn. After all, such effervescent love could melt an ice cap (a scary thing indeed to a reserved Scandinavian). And Hawa never leaves the house, often staying indoors 5 or 6 weeks before taking a break.

Initially both Hawa and I fully expect Mom to walk because she had made reasonable progress in rehab. When the therapist came to the house, Mom initially stood and took a few steps, until one day she lost her balance. She threw her butt out to compensate; the therapist surrendered her grip; and Mom landed in the wheelchair, exactly where she wanted to be.

For a clinically demented woman, Mom became an instant learner. I could almost see the mental cogs grinding, grumbling, *"Where the hell do I think I'm going anyway?"* The therapist continued to come; Elsie perfected her rump revolt; the therapist wrote, "no change" on her Medicare reports; and the federal government soon dumped her from therapy.

So, we lost that one. But I kept the wooden planks on the edge of the steps ready to wheel Mom out for a nice ride through the neighborhood. It never happened. Hawa and I feared we'd lose our grip on the wheelchair and Elsie would go careening down the street dodging cars.

One evening we wheeled Mom onto the glass porch facing the backyard. She stared vacantly into a fragrant garden filled with blooming flowers, but for her, it no longer existed in reality or in memory. Mom liked her room best and as *she* disconnected from the larger world, so did we. Hawa and I simply *forgot* to take her outside. We built a totally happy world within her four walls.

~ ~ ~

Slowly I learned more of Hawa's life in Sierra Leone. It almost never began.

With virtually no medical care, premature babies are generally left to die beneath a tree—especially girl children. But Hawa's mother wrapped her against her chest, protecting Hawa's life with her own heart. So Hawa survived.

As she described her everyday life, I wonder if I could have flourished in an African village. For example, in the morning *everyone* opens all their doors. To keep them closed would be considerably rude. All day and into the night, anyone and everyone walks in. I wonder how introverts survive. A lot of the congregating also occurs outdoors where the women cook.

Slowly my kitchen in Catonsville, Maryland, goes African. A new deep-fat fryer sits on the counter, spitting out home-cut French fries. One day Hawa decides to show me how to make a spicy green African sauce. Even though I'm a bit leery, I turn the kitchen over to her. Hours later, she hands me a spoon with less than a thimble-sized portion of her labor. I put it in my mouth, expecting Mexican-style spicy. My head explodes. I spew it all over the kitchen. My mouth burns with volcanic remnants of the sauce. Not even water douses it.

Even Hawa is surprised. "It's not *that* hot, Barbara."

"Oh YES IT IS," I gasp. Never again do I eat the seductive green sauce that appears on and in everything Leone.

When Hawa and her fiancé Mike insist that one day I accompany them to their motherland, I have only one thought. *I will DIE. My body will burst into glowing hot, green particles.*

I decide that perhaps hot food accounts for Hawa's warm heart. I have not crawled into bed with my Mom. I do not clamber across the bed rail and throw myself full length next to her and make jokes with her. I stand at her side, put my hand on her head of still-thick platinum-aged hair, stroke her cheek softened with lotion, and smooth her furled brow.

Everyone in poverty-stricken Sierra Leone townships believes American streets are paved with gold. Seeing America from Hollywood DVDs, Hawa begs her mother to let her go. When she turns 17, she boards a plane to visit her sister.

"I want to see your office," Hawa demands. "Let me see where you work." She envisions her sister working in a professional building with her own secretary—and certainly American wealth pouring into her purse.

"Okay," Fatima agrees with a hint of a smile. "I'll take you." They set off in her car. They pull up to a home. They enter. She takes Hawa to the bedroom where an elderly bedridden man lays, spittle drooling down his chin. She pulls on rubber gloves, strips down his pajama bottoms, undoes the diaper, and begins to wipe him. "THIS is my OFFICE," she says to the shocked Hawa.

What America is THIS? she wonders. The ones who come home to visit Freetown always dress so expensively. And they talk big. They say they have fancy jobs—but it's not true.

They're first generation immigrants struggling—just as she, now, will begin to struggle. She too will receive endless letters and calls from relatives begging for money. She will send every single penny she can to her mother. It will never be enough. But unlike the others, she will never lie.

Blunt reality hits with the force of a two-by-four. "You have to get a job," her sister explains. "The only thing you can learn quickly is how to be a nurse's aide. It means you'll wipe old people's bottoms just the way I do."

Teenaged Hawa eventually finds herself sitting in class learning how to lift, transfer, wash, and feed the elderly.

Meanwhile back home, a violent civil war erupts and Hawa's mother forbids her from returning. The State Department grants temporary "protective status" to all Sierra Leone citizens because of the genocide.

Stories of men, women, and children being slaughtered, their limbs macheted off, make it to the back pages of Washington newspapers. Left for dead, limbless children become wards of overrun orphanages. Yet the war rages on—over blood diamonds. Diamonds harvested with forced labor and violence are accepted knowingly by European diamond merchants. The "girl's best friend" is, in fact, a murderer.

Hawa's mother though illiterate owns gas stations, orchards, and houses. Perhaps because she sells gas unwittingly to a rebel, she is arrested and thrown into prison. Released after one year, she flees to Guinea leaving everything behind. Suffering from diabetes and high blood pressure, she seeks asylum in the United States. Approved, she will soon be reunited with her daughters in America.

"When I take care of your mother," Hawa explains to me one evening, "I always pray that someone is taking care of mine." She becomes quiet. "My mother once told me, 'All I can give you is an education. Everything else can be lost.' She enrolled me in the best school she could find—a Catholic missionary school in Freetown."

"Did you do well in school?" I ask.

Hawa laughs. "Oh yeah, I stayed at the *top* of my class. I got my high school diploma."

Months later, her mother would be dead. She'd never reach America. But she gave Hawa what she promised—an educated mind.

Confused Elsie ~ 1999 ~
Knowing Before *We* Know ...

"Your mother said something unusual," Hawa tells me as we eat dinner together. "When she woke up from her nap this afternoon, she said, 'I can't stop him. He won't listen to me.'"

Hawa continued, "Your mother was so clear I decided to ask her who, and she answered, 'My brother.' Then she sank back into her crazy chatter again."

Hawa pauses, her fork halfway to her mouth, "I never knew she *had* a brother."

"Oh, yes," I answer, "Swante. He was the third-born—the only son. He stayed on in Minnesota.

We finish dinner and decide which Monday night shows we want to watch and give Mom's strangely coherent conversation no more thought.

~ ~ ~

I'm upstairs trying to work in my office-closet when the phone rings. I pick it up on the second ring. "Barbara?" I hear an unfamiliar voice on the line.

"Yes?" I answer, mentally scrolling through my brain's voice-recognition data bank.

"This is Pat," the voice goes on. *Oh! Now I'm connected—it's that flat Minnesota accent.*

"Well, hi there," I answer, surprised by the unexpected call. Being distant cousins, we only exchange annual Christmas cards. I've never received a phone call.

"Swante died."

I hold the receiver motionless, my whole body falling into a strange silence.

"When?" I ask.

"Yesterday afternoon."

~ ~ ~

I hang up the phone, stunned. *Swante was passing over,* I realize, when Mom told Hawa, *"I can't stop him. He won't listen to me."* She *knows* she has lost her only brother.

I feel like I've stumbled into an Alice-in-Wonderland world—one that cannot be replicated by scientific experiment or by wiring Mom's brain to neurotransmitter monitors. She not only became lucid, she relayed information I wouldn't receive for another 24 hours. How is this possible?

This event, more than any other, convinces me that Kenna's work is real, that psychic communication is possible, and that the world is much larger than what our limited senses sometimes perceive.

Now I walk into Mom's room. "Hawa," I say, still in shock. "Mom's brother died on *Monday* afternoon."

"That's when your mother told me," Hawa gazes over at her, sleeping peacefully. "Well," Hawa adds with a laugh, "She's better than AT&T."

Mother Barbara ~ 1982 ~ Meeting Your Children for the First Time

Bill and I debark in Seoul clutching 3 x 5 cards. On one side indecipherable script indicates our Korean necessity, the other, an English translation.

I pick through the cards till I get to "hotel address," and hand it to the taxi driver. Soon we're navigating through streets that become smaller and smaller until he stops at a three-story plain looking aged building. "Well," Bill reminds me, "we needed a cheap hotel."

We step into a very clean, very small room with a sagging mattress, one battered wooden dresser, a fan, an openable window, and a bath down the hall.

ELSIE AT EBB TIDE

After a 13-hour flight, we could care less and fall asleep.

That night we produce another card, eat eggs and rice, and try kimchi, a Korean mainstay of spicy fermented cabbage. Tomorrow we will meet our children, and I'm trembling with nervousness and excitement.

~ ~ ~

"Would you like tea?" the director of Sung Roe Won orphanage, Mr. Kim, asks us. "Yes," we politely reply, wanting our daughters a great deal more than tea.

"We thought it best if you meet Sun-Hee first," he begins. "She's in the 5-year-old group, and they'll be in the large room soon for singing and dancing." I sip my tea, realizing the moment is about to arrive.

We've received other photos of her. In recent weeks, I've sat holding these pictures, so afraid something would go wrong that I hadn't even prepared a children's room beyond the bare essentials. A prior adoption failed because of an administrative error.

We walk up the stairs through an open door into a large room. A young woman plays the piano. Children stand in a circle singing. I immediately spot Kendra, her thick black hair tightly bound in French braids.

She breaks from the circle, running to us, and leaps into Bill's arms, later settling into my lap. Mothers of adoptive children try in many ways to express their awe of this moment. But really there are no words.

I feel stunned, inadequate to the task, thunderstruck that she will be my *daughter*, and completely in love.

She grasps both our hands and ushers us into lunch in her room.

We sit on the floor, eat at a low table, smile and laugh. She brings us the photo album we had sent her, pointing out each picture of us, our pets, our family, and her future home, chattering away in Korean.

After lunch, she takes us to her sister's room. The *bomo*, or caregiver, is holding Lisa in her arms giving her a cookie.

We quickly learn this child has a temper, and the *bomo* calms her with candy and cookies. Now the *bomo* tucks this hot heavy child into my arms and hands me a cookie. She wears a pink knit dress and cotton tights with embroidered children dancing up the sides. I worry she'll burst into tears, but she grabs a cookie and contentedly munches. I now have two children.

We stay for a week. One day Mr. Kim suggests we take Kendra to the zoo. We agree and off we go. We look strange— two tall light-haired adults with a Korean child—but we are intoxicated with our first family outing.

Then suddenly Kendra pulls her hand from Bill's and races down the hill, laughing. We tear after her. She thinks it's a game. She keeps running. We can't cry for help; we don't know Korean. People start to stare. Suddenly Bill stops. "She has to come to us," he breathlessly tells me.

We stand like terrified frozen statues. Kendra stops. She stares at us, then runs up the hill, and takes Bill's hand again. We never attempt another outing, and 2 days later we leave Korea.

Caregiver Barbara ~ 1999 ~
To Treat Pneumonia ... or Not

A year has passed since Mom entered my home. She may be dying—or not. I mean actively dying, in the last stages where after all this time of the gradualness that never seems to end, her life *will* end. The hospice nurse suspects Mom may have a touch of pneumonia, or perhaps the signs of heart failure, or both, or neither. Without hospital tests, the signs are not clear.

Being with Mom now has suddenly taken a jolting turn, one I never really thought I'd come to in my 12-year journey with her and this disease. Perhaps in the weeks ahead, she will finally die and be utterly gone from my life. I find that incredibly sad and mentally incomprehensible.

We have been joined together by this disease for *so long*, it has *become* us. It is she, and me, and *it*. We have all made friends, though sometimes painfully, with each other.

There is almost a love for the dementia itself, as though it has its own personality, its own quirks, its own love and laughter, humor and sadness.

We are a family.

Each member has a place at the sacred table of love. And Alzheimer's is not denied affection, and a fork and knife, in this dwelling. But I have pulled up no chair at the table for death. It is not invited or welcome, for it breaks the bonds that have become stronger even as the ravages of the disease tear deeper into her body.

~ ~ ~

I was not expecting to make any decisions about actively letting go of my mother's life: of placing her in a deliberate sluice that will lead, absolutely, to physical death. Yet pneumonia brings the question. *Do you want to treat her?*

It is not asked in a euthanasia way, but in a letting-go way—trusting the *body's* wisdom to know when to say goodbye to this life.

I find myself wondering, *Where is she in her journey from body to spirit?* And what lies ahead if we *don't* accept this invitation to let go?

I don't think there is ever such a thing as no quality of life. The longer I sit with Mom, the less convinced am I that a measuring stick can be used to determine when a life is not meaningful.

I see less and less—but I also see more and more.

Each physical loss comes as a blow to me, something I grieve deeply—like birthdays going backwards. To feed her even 3 teaspoons of soup takes Hawa nearly 2 hours. Mom starts babbling in such a verbal torrent it makes it impossible to put food in her mouth. Or Mom simply rejects it, pushing her tongue out with determination.

The hospice nurse gently defines nutrition differently for us. She explains we are no longer trying to *make* Elsie live. There is no cure for this disease. We are trying to make her content, happy, peaceful. We are asked to envision "life" from a different plateau.

In this different realm, it feels as though Hawa and I have become ghostly holographic images to Mom, while her spirit world has taken on lifelike reality.

One evening recently, Hawa and I both stood close to Mom talking in our loud human voices.

Obviously auditory noise was going into Mom's ear. But *she* was talking to something roughly cutting into one-half of Hawa's body—as though a spirit was in that precise space. It was the focused direction of her eyes; the cognitive attentiveness she gave to that space that made it more real than Hawa or me.

She could not hear us; but she could hear this spirit. We no longer existed. We were the ghosts; the spirits were real. What seems less and less is more and more.

I do not see any point on the continuum where her "quality of life" is too low to continue because I see spirit-life *growing* right before my eyes. It would seem wrong to injure that natural process by amputating the physical body before it is naturally done and complete.

On a *human* level, she sleeps more; she no longer wants to chew; she only occasionally claps her hands to music when I play the piano.

It is the piano that has always been my last and final barometer. Mom played it all her life—at her childhood church, home, and nursing homes, at Republican meetings, theatrical productions, and retirement events. No matter where she was, she sat at the keyboard, her fingers rippling through the small repertoire of songs she committed to memory as deep as the first cells of her body.

If she is irritable, afraid, thrashing, unsettled, I play the piano. I play her songs, her music, and her face relaxes. She clap, clap, claps in perfect staccato beat to the music.

Yesterday I played for her and she clapped softly for a while. I finished and walked over to look at her. Her face is beautiful now. It has a quality I can't describe. It is as though she is in the center—the absolute center point—of human life and spirit life. She holds *all* of it in her body frame, and her face is the mirror into the absolute miracle of it all.

It must be the most precious, the most amazing point a human being can feel: to be human, and to be knowingly in the eternity of love.

I feel it, a tiny portion of it, pass into me when I am near her like this.

It is not always there; it has a rare quality about it; but it is becoming more real than her body, than her earthly life, than any loss she is suffering.

I am in absolute awe of what is happening.

~ ~ ~

What lies ahead? What distress, what suffering?

I act as the gatekeeper, the vigilant guard who wards pain away: *You cannot enter here. I will not allow it.* This is where the holy rage of compassion comes from within me.

I will allow death to sit at our table. I will pull out the chair. I will make friends with it. I will let her body wisdom and her death have the last dance. But I want for her a good death, a gentle death, a peaceful death. I will bar suffering with the body block of every resource at my hand. So I act vigilantly, and that is why the question, "Do you want to treat the pneumonia?" takes on a dimension of love.

I look at all of this and wonder. Is pneumonia the guest that is to be invited to table with us? Or kidney failure? Heart failure? Will her skin begin to rot with bedsores because the inner body cannot create skin anymore?

What lies ahead?

Our faith tells us we cannot be God. We cannot control the forces of life and death. All we can do is accompany.

But the medical establishment often whispers, *We can heal. We can push death back one more time. With antibiotics. With stronger antibiotics. With hospital admission and intravenous drips. With stomach tubes. We can push death back one more time.*

And the hospice nurse gives me the space to ponder, *Is it time to let go? What is the quality of her life? Pneumonia is an old person's friend. A gentle death. A kind death.*

I have no answers. None whatsoever. No decision fits. I cannot *see*. My world is limited to three dimensions confined by time and space. I must make living human decisions out of that earthbound perspective. And I *know* I am using the wrong measuring stick.

That is why I listen quietly. Is she spiritually ready? What is the quality of her life? What lies ahead? Somehow, in the between of those three questions, lies her true path.

~ ~ ~

I begin a 10-day course of antibiotics. We inject pink liquid with a needleless syringe into her mouth. She is getting better. I see an ease about her face, less pallor. But as soon as the 4 hours pass, her cough begins. A weak woman trying to expel something that cannot be expelled.

We give her another dose, and the cough begins its 4-hour sleep. Again.

~ ~ ~

I think we will know when death approaches. It will have a way of being emphatic, an insistence that cannot be overlooked. Within us all, I believe, we *know* death. Like a gene within our own coding that is slumbering, it waits till it is time to speak to us. Not to scare or frighten us, but to be *real* with us about the *More* that has always been in us and with us and part of us.

When someone we love dies, that *More* within us, that tiny "gene carrying death" blinks at us. Not like a Halloween ghoul, but like the dearest closest friend. It blinks because if it didn't, we'd be terrified when it awoke.

As I quietly watch Mom, something has blinked within me.

June

Traveling Distances
Short and Long

June 2

Caregiver Barbara ~ 1999 ~ A Late Spring Evening

Hawa rolls Elsie onto the glass porch tonight in her wheelchair. I perch on a stool eating sautéed asparagus and mushrooms while my mother downs gingerbread soaked in Häagen Dazs ice cream.

The backyard roses overwhelm us with color. Mown grass scents the air; pink impatiens carpet the ground. It's an intoxicating evening and Mom sees and experiences ... nothing. These sensuous sensations no longer reach her mental awareness.

While Mom and Hawa remain on the porch, I go inside to play Mom's Messinginger piano. Not exactly a name-brand (in fact, no one seems to have ever heard of one), the rainy May hasn't helped the keyboard. The G above middle C sticks; the A below middle C is temperamental. I have learned which songs use those keys in excess and pop them up while still playing. I sometimes feel like Albert Schweitzer who, I once read, played the most dilapidated pianos in the African hinterland.

So I begin. Out roll Sousa marches, patriotic songs, "Camptown Races," "When I Wore a Tulip." I go full bore—no subtlety, nuanced pedaling, or soft tones.

The creaky un-oiled ceiling fan cuts through my songs at roughly the same cadence. Oreo, my canary, joins in trilling through his repertoire. Hawa rolls Mom to the piano. She beats the lower octaves with flat hands, pummeling the keys in perfect time.

As I sit there, rolling through "You Are My Sunshine," I think to myself, *it doesn't get much better than this*.

And it doesn't. The music, Mom slapping the keys, the bird singing, Hawa laughing, me being free to play truly bad music—all on a June evening with the windows open and the fan blades clacking.

Confused Elsie ~ 1998 ~ The Art of Hugging

Like many Depression-era families, Elsie had a rough childhood bearing the common scars of an immigrant family in America. Separated from her parents, losing her father, being forced to harvest fallen coal from passing railroad cars—love didn't come packaged in Hallmark cards that she could open.

In some ways perhaps, she had the classic abandoned personality. To not quite believe you should exist. To try to be seen, rather than relax knowing you don't need to be. To achieve in order to convince yourself you have value. As daughters we never saw these uncertain thoughts until Mom said, after Dad's death, that she was nothing but a stupid farm girl. But whatever thoughts she carried in the privacy of her mind, Alzheimer's reduced them to rubble.

~ ~ ~

Being Elsie's offspring meant we'd get no demonstrative declarations of love. If we hugged her, she responded like a limp fish. Since it seemed so unpleasant to her, Sandra and I spared her. We grinned our greeting: "Hi, Mom!" Truth be told, after we learned to walk, we were never hugged or held on laps or cuddled. Apparently, I didn't notice, but Sandra felt devastated by this tactile denial. I decided I *must* have been deprived even if I hadn't noticed, and one day I shared our childhood trauma with Mom's sister Alice.

"Well, Barbara," Alice put down her coffee cup. "Finns don't hug. I never hugged my kids either."

I started to giggle. I started to laugh. I thought of all the pain-in-solidarity I had gone through, all for naught because I was born to a Finn. Go figure.

Anyway, for whatever perverse reason, Sandra and I agreed that our mother, now in her sixties, needed to be hugged regardless of whether she liked it or not. So bucking up our courage, we began to hug our mother-the-jelly-fish. Elsie would stand there, almost shuddering. We would wrap her in our sturdy arms, but not for too long. We didn't want her to melt or fall to the floor or anything. Eventually when she realized we would not desist, she began to lift her cold bony hands and *slightly* embrace us.

Progress.

Daughters have to—it's a mandatory requirement of offspring—analyze *what makes Mom that way?* Okay, putting the Finn thing aside, Mom's parents *did* leave her with Lutheran fundamentalist grandparents. Here, Elsie learned to *never* crawl into a lap seeking comfort. In front of a whole room of Lutheran women, Grandmother Liisa shoved Elsie off her lap, saying in Finnish, "Stop acting like a baby looking for a titty."

But he died suddenly and violently when she was 9 years old. She not only gave up hugs; she gave up crying. It didn't bring back people from the dead. It didn't make anything better.

So Sandra and I grew up learning not to need emotions, at least not to succumb to them. Now Sandra was breaking *all* the rules—breeching the emotional fortress—by hugging our mother.

One day when Mom was still only slightly demented (and I say that with the fondness of love), she grasped my forearms in her bony grip. She looked me in the eye with intense blue-eyed fierceness that felt like light shining out of a foggy night and said, "I don't know what I did to deserve a daughter as good as you."

Whoa. And that was only the beginning.

After that, she reached up to Sandra's or my face, caressed our cheek, told us how beautiful we were, held our hands with a simian-like grip, and *loved* being held, kissed, hugged.

She reminded me of a 2-year-old sitting in a little plastic pool flapping her hands up and down in the water—water being all the love that had always been there for *her*.

Sandra was the one who turned the hose on.

Retired Elsie ~ 1982 ~ Florida Diary

Herby is putting up a new antenna for the ham radio on a 26-foot bamboo tree. Beautiful day. The grapefruit are falling so loud they wake me up at night. Tried to take a nap. Same thing happened. Grrr.

Sandra called—Kieran has said his first word. "Goddammit."

June 5

Retired Elsie ~ 1992 ~ Loving Your Roots in Finland

"Barbara, your mother almost missed the plane." My aunt Alice turns to me after hanging up the phone. "Doris went to pick her up and she wasn't even packed."

"That doesn't sound like Mom." I turn my coffee cup around in my hands. "She's anal about packing." I remember her glee when she packed a grocery bag or suitcase until not one square inch remained. Perhaps it was a leftover Protocol thing—packing fast and traveling light.

"It's worse." Alice continues. "She had all her flight information wrong. They had to run like crazy to get the plane."

Neither of us can make sense of it.

~ ~ ~

Forty-three hours later, we debark in Helsinki, tired and excited. For the next 2 days, we'll be staying at the Hotel Satakuntatalo. Presumably we can walk to it from the railroad station where the Finnair bus shuttle dropped us off.

We pull our suitcases down the sidewalk, orienting ourselves (we think) with our trusty Helsinki map and promptly get lost. "Elsie," Alice decides, "ask someone how to get to the hotel." True, Mom's dated immigrant Finnish doesn't match today's Nokia world, but how different can it be to say, "How do you get to ...?"

Elsie readily agrees and walks up to a Japanese man and woman, politely asking, *"Miten pääse tähän hotelliin Satakuntatalo?"*

"ELSIE," Alice hisses. "They're JAPANESE! They don't speak Finnish."

I feel my heart thud, silently watching my mind, like a computer, whir through what has happened in the last 2 days. "Alice," I pull her aside. "This is really wrong."

ELSIE AT EBB TIDE

Tired and disoriented, we shove Mom toward a blond blue-eyed man, and say, "Ask HIM." Graciously he escorts us personally to the nearby hotel and we register, hoping that Elsie's lapses are caused by nothing more than travel exhaustion.

We are wrong.

~ ~ ~

"How do I open the door?" Elsie stands helpless in front of the bathroom. It has a European lever-like handle. "Mom, you push it down," I gently say, opening it for her. She goes in. I continue unpacking.

"I can't get out," she hollers.

I walk to the door and open it. "Mom, let me show you from the inside. You just push this lever down. Now you try it."

After dinner, she needs to go to the bathroom again. "How do you open this door?" she asks.

~ ~ ~

Eventually Elsie begins to softly snore. Alice and I sit on our beds looking at each other, alarm written all over our faces. "What's happening?" Alice asks. "What's wrong with your mother?"

"Alice," I answer with a logic I don't want to admit to, "she's been complaining about her memory. But I had no idea it was this bad. This is awful. It's scary. I don't know if we can even continue."

Neither does Alice. But what can we do? We are what—6,000 miles away from home—with no return ticket for the next 14 days. "Maybe it'll be better tomorrow," Alice sighs. "Let's get some sleep."

~ ~ ~

The next day unfolds with only little mishaps. We begin to hope it is all just a bad nightmare, a temporary insanity brought on by travel fatigue. We go to a nice restaurant for dinner and order soup as a first course.

"Oh, this is DELICIOUS," Elsie exclaims slopping the broth out of the bowl held up to her mouth, the soup spoon lying untouched by her plate. I don't even look at Alice. Already my rules are changing. Is there any harm, after all, in her drinking soup from the bowl in a fine restaurant? No safety issue. Odd. Decidedly. Embarrassing. Definitely. But worth making her eat her soup with a spoon?

"Elsie," Alice says with a mother's firmness, "use your spoon."

"Oh, I don't need that. I do it this way." She grins and takes another slug out of the bowl. Thankfully, she eats the meat, potatoes, and vegetables with her fork and knife.

"Let's get some dessert," I suggest. We order vanilla ice cream. It comes in a family-style bowl with various toppings around it. I ladle mine into my dessert dish as does Alice. Mom picks up the empty ashtray from the middle of the table, puts ice cream and crunchy topping into it, and licks it.

We can no longer pretend that what we see is not happening. We realize we are facing a full-blown version of what doctors will later tell me is "organic brain disorder," commonly called Alzheimer's or dementia.

~ ~ ~

The horrors never stop. In the end it is Alice and I, not my mother, who adapt. What shocks us eventually becomes acceptable. What amazes us becomes funny. We learn that you can "park" Elsie—and she'll stay put. We also learn that Elsie is always hungry.

"Elsie, you just ATE!" Alice looks at her sister incredulously. Elsie looks a little diminished ... but still hungry.

"I'll take her to that café over there," I tell Alice. "You go ahead to Tourist Information. I'll head to the bank and exchange money." We are ready to take the risk—leaving Mom unattended for a small period of time. We've already tried it several times, always keeping her in eyesight. Now we entrust her to an unsuspecting waitress. We are figuring out how much we can salvage of our vacation without losing Elsie somewhere on the streets of Helsinki or Alajarvi or Kuopio.

ELSIE AT EBB TIDE

Not reading Finnish, I leave Mom to order and head for the bank. Twenty anxious minutes later, I return. Elsie sits utterly contented in front of a plate of bread crumbs and an empty coffee cup. The price is outrageous and I could care less. We have a system!

Next stop? Picking up our rental car.

"It's outside by the curb," the agent tells us. Alice and I sign the papers. I'll be the first driver. I pop into the driver's seat, put the key in the ignition, and *then* notice the three pedals. I roll down the window. "I don't *do* manual," I explain. "Well, I did about 20 years or so ago. If I don't crash the car in the first few blocks, I guess I'll be okay."

He quietly takes this morsel of information in with total Finn-like composure and says, "Wait a second," and disappears back into the rental storefront. Two minutes later, he's back at my car window. "We're driving another car over for you to use." We unload our bags from the Ford Fiesta and wait. Soon a black, sleek four-door Volvo glides to the curb. The driver hands me the keys. I begin to stutter, "We can't afford this."

The agent explains, "There's no additional charge. It's automatic."

Our first bit of luck ... our compensation for dealing with the trauma of Elsie ... at least we'll be doing it in comfort. Once we discreetly pull away from the curb, we all burst out laughing. We've hit the *Suomi* lottery—the Finn highlight of our trip. Even Elsie, not quite understanding, at least knows we're happy. Off we go, out of Helsinki, onto a two-lane road heading to Rauma. We plan to spend the night at a farmhouse. As twilight approaches and we have backtracked two times in pursuit of garbled written directions, once again we need to rely on Elsie, our only translator.

"Mom," I tell her, pulling the car to a stop next to a man out walking. "Ask how to get to Poroholma." She asks. We get rambling instructions neither Alice nor I understand. I burst into tears. Mom, clueless about what is wrong, offers comfort: "It'll be okay, Barbara." Alice reapplies herself to the map. Thirty minutes later, we stumble across the farmhouse entrance as the last vestiges of dusk disappear.

Alice and I fall into our bunk beds. My last vision before my eyelids float shut is of Mom unpacking every item from her suitcase and telling us, "I have to organize things."

The next morning, we encounter our first smörgåsbord-style breakfast: salami, boiled eggs, oatmeal, yogurt, cucumbers, tomatoes, buttermilk, juice, black-tar coffee, hardtack rye crisps, and bread. I don't want to say it, but I'm thinking it: *Yuck.*

~ ~ ~

It's an international music festival," Elsie exclaims, translating a Finnish sign as we approach the town of Kankanpää. We circle through the streets of the small town looking for this international event. Eventually we find a tiny town hall that appears to be having a music program. We go inside and sit in the auditorium. The empty seats far outnumber the audience. Suddenly Elsie slips out of her seat. We watch curiously as she goes right up to the woman on the stage, who is dressed in a traditional Finnish costume. They engage in a long conversation. Elsie comes back and sits down. Before we can ask anything, the lights go down and the woman moves to the center of the stage. As she begins to speak in Finnish, I find myself relaxing as I always do when surrounded by the sounds I have heard all my life. Suddenly I hear ... "Elsie Nurmi!"

And my mother is out of her seat, walking to the front, climbing up the steps, and then standing next to the woman. Elsie begins to speak ... in Finnish. Alice and I laugh. "I wonder what she's saying?" I whisper to Alice. The only word we understand is "Protocol." I guess Elsie doesn't know the Finnish equivalent for that. When my mother finishes, there is a big burst of applause. Elsie beams like a glowing Christmas tree and eventually returns to her seat. "What did you say?" I ask. But the "international" concert—consisting of four accordion players—begins.

~ ~ ~

Eventually we arrive at the small town of Alajarvi to answer Mom's question: Had Herby been baptized in Finland? We knew so little. All we had left of his mother's short life was a battered cookbook and a metronome.

We go to the Lutheran church and ask for the family baptismal records. The secretary returns with an accountant-type book filled with names, dates, relationships. There he is—Urjo Herbert Mertaniemi. I turn to Mom. "He *was* baptized."

"Ida's father?" she asks.

"No, Mom, it's the baptismal record for your husband, Herbert."

Mom never realizes she's found the answer to a decades-old question. The question itself has receded into a foggy murk I can't access. I request photocopies and we leave.

~ ~ ~

Somewhere in the latitude and longitude of Finland, my landscape forever changes.

Elsie—my mother—steps across some invisible boundary. I truly do not expect her to ever step back. I have to immediately adjust everything in my world. Perhaps it's best to do it in a foreign country where I am as confused, in a different way, as she. I speak no Finnish; customs are different. After all, who eats pickled herring and beets for breakfast?

For utterly different reasons, we are all in the same boat. Mom, who was to be our anchor, our translator, *drops* her moorings before she even touches down at the Helsinki airport. Our tour guide has gone AWOL.

But something miraculous happens. We give up. Alice and I simply give up. We can't *make* Elsie be normal—and nothing bad seems to come of it. We just live in a world different from the one we thought we lived in. Frankly, it's a bit more fun.

When she doesn't know the front end of a car from the back, we say it's not important. When impish Elsie sticks her head between two carved bears grinning from ear to ear, we laugh.

When she has *no* idea where Finland is, we say, "Well, who cares anyway." And when she explains, "I am confused," we double over in laughter admitting, "So are we."

Off we go to the Arctic Circle, chasing after reindeer. We leave her in the cabin packing and repacking and repacking again while Alice and I argue over *when*, precisely, to photograph the midnight sun. "You have to wait until midnight," I insist. Exasperated, Alice replies, "But Barbara, the sun will be *beneath* the horizon at midnight." We each click photos according to our own stubbornly Finnish definition of the midnight sun.

The trip becomes magical, unpredictable, filled with laughter. We find Elsie endlessly entertaining. She might not know where Finland is, she might be waving $50 bills around trying to buy a sandwich, she might be going onstage to give speeches, but we realize being together is more important. Years later, I will retrieve and need this hard-won perspective. But right now we are in Russia after an overnight cruise from Helsinki. We are about to visit a world-famous art museum.

~ ~ ~

"Mom," I patiently explain after we wake up in our cabin berth, docked in St. Petersburg, "the trip to the Hermitage will be too tiring for you."

"I can do it, Barbara. I'm not tired at all." Mom springs up from her bunk. "See. I've got more energy than you."

I try again, several times, to no avail. She *will not* be deterred. She *will* go on the charter bus and guided tour. Worried, I give in.

This is my second attempt to get into the Hermitage.

The first occurred 20 years earlier during the height of the Cold War, when my husband and I camped throughout the Soviet Union. On a communist-controlled itinerary, we had only one day to visit the Hermitage, and that was the day Bill vomited.

The camp administrator called an "ambulance" which arrived with a Soviet doctor who administered we-know-not-what, and he spent the day convulsed with diarrhea. So, my passion for art went unrequited. Now I am finally here, inside the Hermitage, and we are about to begin our tour.

"We go up these stairs," the guide points to a long flight of white marble steps.

"Oh Barbara," Mom wilts right before my eyes. "I can't do *that*. I'm too tired."

"But MOM!" I begin, "you said you had lots of energy."

"I don't remember that. This is too hard. You just go on ahead."

The tour guide, now at the top of the staircase, tells us, "Hurry. This is a long tour and we must get started."

Elsie doesn't move. Alice has held back. I size up the situation. Alice, older than I, probably will never have a chance to come back. I *might*. "Alice, you go. I'll stay with Mom." She hurries up the steps after the guide and they disappear from view.

I take Mom by the arm. "Let's look for a place for you to sit." I find an upholstered chair in an almost-empty gallery. We sit down. I try not to think of my disappointment.

It's my second disappointment this morning. On our bus tour, I had seen a set of nested matryoshka dolls for which Russia is famous—each one an exquisitely painted religious icon nestled into the next, seven in all. The street vendor wanted $40. I couldn't decide. The bus driver hurried us. I got on the bus.

Now, sitting with Mom, I wonder if I could find my way back to that vendor. He sold his wares right outside an Orthodox Church with shutters, whose name I thought I remembered. In 15 minutes, surely, I could just run over and buy those dolls. Then this whole day wouldn't be such a dismal failure.

"Mom, sit here. Do NOT move. I have to run an errand. I'll be right back."

I dash out the Hermitage doors and race across the plaza. As I run, I yell out the name of the church to each passer-by. Nobody understands me. I keep running, mentally remembering the streets. If I get lost and don't get back, the bus will leave the Hermitage without me, and the ship will leave St. Petersburg without me. I keep running.

Finally two children understand bedraggled English. They point. I follow their fingers. A man carrying a briefcase listens. "I speak English. Go this way." He quickly walks me down a block. "Over that creek. The church is there," he says. I see the bulbous gilded top. I cross the muddy stream on a wobbly wood plank, foot by foot, then run again.

"I want those dolls!" I yell, thrusting money at the vendor. I grab my prized souvenir and begin running—back across the plank, my mind whirring with street names, turns, and corners. It is way longer than 15 minutes—maybe 30 or 40. I am careening back into the Hermitage. There, patiently, sits my mother. My whole body collapses with relief. What I have done is risky—for her and for myself. But we're both safe.

"Let's go find the bus, Mom." I silently say good-bye to this amazing unseen place. We come to a vast plaza. I see a brown bear held by a gypsy. Other gypsies gather to beg. I dodge them and get my mother on the bus. I watch the children's hands reaching toward my window. What can I say in my defense? I get off the bus to part with some money. This raises, rightfully I think, the ire of my fellow tourists. But after seeing the paint-peeled buildings, the chain-pull toilets without seats, the streets empty of cars, I just feel they can do more with that little bit of money than I. There's tourist promotion and beggar promotion. I support both.

~ ~ ~

ELSIE AT EBB TIDE

At last, the trip ends. We have driven 1,800 miles. We've almost run over a reindeer as Alice slams on the superior Volvo ABS brakes. We have traveled the entire circumference of Finland. Now we queue up for our flight home.

As we board, Elsie steps onto the plane first. Neither Alice nor I want to sit with her. She chatters like a magpie all the time. We are like two brawling children. "*You* sit next to her," I hopefully suggest to Alice. "Barbara, I'm too tired. I can't deal with your mother all the way over the Atlantic Ocean."

Finally we agree. We *both* suffer the same fate—we'll put Elsie between us and share the joy. Meanwhile Elsie has plopped herself down in the window seat.

"Elsie, get back out. I'm sitting by the window," Alice orders.

With that trademark mischievous grin, Elsie says, "I don't have to get out." She promptly steps onto the middle seat. If that weren't enough, she takes her knitted fishnet bag, puts it over her head, and starts making funny faces as the passengers—now at a dead halt—wait for us to get seated.

"Oh, Elsie," Alice tiredly hisses, "Sit *down!*"

And Elsie sits.

~ ~ ~

To my utter shock, once back in her Lake Worth home, Mom quickly gains command of her routines, habits, patterns, and life—as though the memory lapse never happened. Needless to say, my sister thinks I am utterly demented.

"Barbara," she repeatedly tells me, "she sounds just fine." When Sandra visits her later that year, she truly thinks I have gone over the edge. "There's absolutely nothing wrong with her."

Of course, she's wrong—but the oncoming disease has acted like a chameleon hiding in our very midst. Years later, I will turn the pages of Mom's diary looking for clues, and find them:

> March 14: Alice called. She and Barbara are going to Finland. Did I want to go? I said yes. I spent most of the day checking with Delta Airlines.

April 20: I got ambitious & got together my *whole wardrobe* for the trip to Finland!

April 29: This evening I started getting things together for the trip to Finland & putting them separately into one closet.

May 17: I put in a real tough day but accomplished a lot. Selected all items I'm considering taking to Finland. Packed them into the carrier on wheels to see if they fit & then hung them back in the closet.

May 26: I organized the "Finland papers & notes" that I had collected all over the house.

May 30: Finally—getting *started* packing what I need for the trip.

I doubt I would have noticed anything strange had I read her diary in 1992 because the trip-related entries were spaced apart. Taken together, a pattern emerges: the redundant packing, notes left all over the house, calling the suitcase a "carrier." We didn't know that, in her case, memory loss triggered a need to organize, reorganize, and organize again. In the end, Doris threw her clothes into a suitcase as they raced to the airport.

Apparently she took her diary with her but the entries shrank to notations: "Stayed as Stakuntatalo, a dormitory, and had meals there," "Explored Helsinki," "Off to Lapland," and then, "From here on I forget—except we covered northern Finland, St. Petersburg, Russia & Sweden (the last two by boat)."

Looking at the diary once she returned:

June 22: Back home. What a trip!

June 23: All worn out. Just resting.

June 24: Trying to catch up.

June 25: Still worn out.

June 26: Had appointment with Dr. Mizrahy—general checkup to see if I'm normal. Results next Thursday.

June 30: My memory is coming back. I think I stressed it a bit & have been confused.

She deals with this all by herself—perhaps a typical Finnish thing to do—but as I call and talk to her on the phone, she seems once again to be normal. I know with certainty what lies ahead; my sister happily does not.

June 11

Career Elsie ~ 1960 ~ Mistaken Identity

Two presidential delegations are in New York City at the same time. Elsie's group, at the Waldorf Towers, is scheduled to go to Hawaii. She looks at the sea of suitcases, now crammed with souvenirs from Manhattan and glances at her watch. *Two hours before departure,* she notes as she rummages through her folders and manila envelopes looking for the luggage tags. *Where the heck are they?* She mutters to herself getting more anxious by the minute. She flips through the last folder. No tags. *Maybe I left them in my room,* she hopes, and scurries to the front desk to reclaim her key.

Over the years, Elsie has developed a staccato-heeled walk of such speed and determination that she looks like Moses parting the sea—only she parts people rather than water. I experienced this personally when Mom took my daughters to a Christmas-crowded mall in Florida. Diminutive Elsie looked at Kendra and Lisa and said, "I can make all those people move."

None of us believed her. The wall-to-wall crowd of Christmas shoppers looked like rush hour in a New York City subway station. "No you can't," Kendra pipes up.

"Watch me," she says. Head erect, eyes blazing like search beams, Elsie picks up speed—her size 7 feet stampeding into the crowd. This bite-sized bullet of flying humanity heads into the mob like a human hurricane. Startled, people leap out of the way. It is just about the funniest thing I've ever seen. *MOVE,* the flying Elsie Julia Elizabeth Norlund Nurmi appears to be telling the crowd, *or I will mow you over*. Kendra observes, calculates, and takes off, Lisa right behind her, then me as we sweep through the shoppers, laughing at the wide berth she has cleared.

At this moment, however, Elsie has a real crisis. No baggage tags. She picks up the phone and quickly calls The Plaza across town where Jane is leading another delegation. "Have you got extra luggage tags," she abruptly asks.

Sensing an emergency underway, Jane quickly answers, "Yes, I've got plenty. Come to the Crystal Ballroom. I'll go to my room right now and get some. How many do you need?"

"Forty-seven. I'll be there in 15 minutes." She slams the phone down, and dashes out the door. The doorman flags down a taxi. A man standing next to her asks to share the ride. "I'm a reporter," he explains on the way down.

They jump out, and Elsie thinks she's left him behind as she runs for the elevator. The reporter heads for the stairs.

Slowly—too slowly—the elevator operator closes the door, pushes the button, and it begins its upward glide. Eyes ahead, she *wills* the doors to open, and speeds out.

Seeing a dark-haired man in a blue suit standing several feet apart from a group of men, she stops him thinking he is a hotel employee.

"Where is the Crystal Ballroom?" she asks him, her eyes frantically gazing down the long hallway.

"Oh, I was just there," he answers with polite kindness and raises his arm to point, "Go to the left at the end of the hall and then make your first right."

She thanks him without even bothering to look at him, and keeps running.

"Oh, Elsie," Mary Edith hands her the tags, "You just missed Vice President Nixon."

Elsie feels a tap on her shoulder.

It is the reporter who, unbeknownst to Elsie, followed her to the ballroom. He stares at her, his brown eyes bursting with merriment, his mouth beginning to erupt in laughter.

"That *was* Vice President Nixon," he said, deep-bellied laughter spilling out. "That's who you asked directions from."

Elsie stood stock still for a moment, aghast. Then she started to giggle. Soon she was laughing so hard tears burst out her eyes. The trouble was, she didn't have time to laugh. She turned her heel and headed for the door. She had to get those bags tagged.

Caretaker Barbara ~ 2000 ~
Hawa Returns to Sierra Leone

"Barbara," Hawa catches me in the kitchen while I wash dishes. I glance up. Her voice sounds solemn—not the usual sunny sound that always seems to accompany her voice.

"I'm going home to Sierra Leone. My mother's suffered a stroke."

"Oh Hawa." I feel my heart ache for this 20-year-old woman who's been separated from her mother for so long.

"Is it safe?" I ask.

"Safe enough. Most of the fighting has stopped. Freetown is okay."

"When are you going?" I ask.

"My last day will be Friday. I'm going to catch a flight on Saturday."

"How long will you be gone?"

"About a month. But Barbara, when I get back, I want to go to the community college and get a nursing degree. I've been saving all my money."

I feel my heart thud. "So you won't be coming back?"

Sadness crosses the space between us. "No," she answers.

"I guess I'd better contact the agency about a replacement." I end the silence with practical considerations. "I hope I don't get another Amy."

Despite her anxiety about her mother, Hawa bursts out laughing—that deep-bellied golden laughter I love so much. "Oh, yeahhh," she says in her Leonian accent.

I laugh too.

A few months ago when Hawa took a long weekend off, the agency sent me a big-boned large woman, Amy. In 3 days, hefty Amy crashed into the only furniture inherited from my grandmother—a folding rocker—which suffered immediate death-by-splintering. She threw the lid to Hawa's beloved deep fat fryer into Mom's soiled diaper pail and refused to retrieve it. Her last contribution was to lodge a bar of soap in the neck of the toilet. I plunged, snaked, and finally poured scalding water down, re-plunging, re-snaking, until at last the soap went to sewer heaven.

"Well, Barbara, my Aunt Comfort and Cousin Tata could work for you much cheaper than the agency...."

~ ~ ~

I soon find myself dealing with all sorts of employer issues: getting an employer ID, figuring out withholdings, creating time sheets, opening up a special bank account, writing checks, dealing with the IRS, printing W-2s. I agonize over this, none of which comes naturally to me. But I *want* to give these two women an opportunity.

Hawa's last day comes too soon.

"Well, that's everything," Hawa says, taking her overnight bag out of the bedroom. For the first time, I will be alone with my mother since neither Comfort nor Tata plan to stay overnight. I worry about emergencies but feel I am ready.

We look at each other. It's been over a year since her arrival. Naively I believe the next caregivers will be as good as Hawa. She has trained them. I will find out later she even gave them hints on how to live with me. "Barbara needs her space. Don't interrupt her too much." *How did she know that?* I wonder.

I would come to realize the home ran smoothly because Hawa flexed as easily as a willow branch. She fit herself into my routine out of kindness and understanding.

But right now, the house seems empty and I wonder if the new caregiving arrangement will work. I don't yet know that only one Hawa will ever exist.

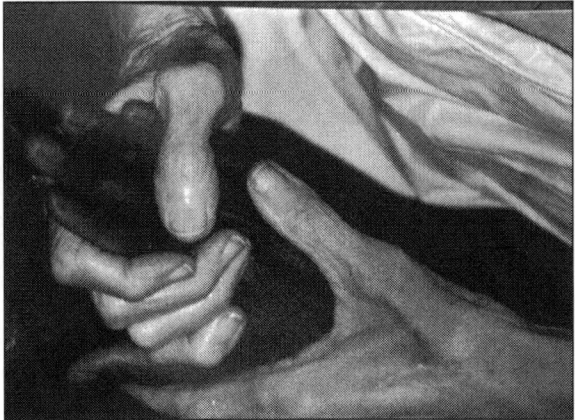

Elsie, Secure in Hawa's Hands

Graduate Elsie ~ 1936 ~ Leaving Home

"Why don't you come with us to New York City?" Helmi suggests to 19-year-old Elsie.

Why not indeed, Elsie thinks to herself. Working as a nanny in Duluth and that stint in the candy store certainly aren't the grand horizons she envisioned when giving her valedictorian speech. *New York City can't be too far away. Probably just a day's drive,* she assumes.

Every year, Helmi, a homesick Minnesotan, and her husband, drive north from New York City to rent a cabin at Island Lake Resort managed by Elsie's mother outside Duluth. Helmi befriends Elsie, beguiling her with the excitement of big-city life.

"Why not drive back with us, Elsie, and look for a job. You can sleep on the sofa till you find one."

Elsie never thinks twice. She gave notice to the Great Northern Candy Company, and tells her mother she's leaving.

The bond between them isn't close. After Hjalmar died, Jennie goes to work while Elsie as firstborn watches the children. Jennie eventually remarries only to find her new husband an alcoholic. She eventually settles into a third long-term relationship and runs a boarding house in Duluth.

When I meet her, adult to adult, I see a typical grandmother with a perm and graying hair who has stuffy old furniture with doilies on the arms, orchids in the windows, and a cuckoo clock on the wall. I find her laughter as soft and enchanting as a wind chime. I realize I know absolutely nothing about my mother's relationship with her except for one chance remark from Mom: "I wasn't close to her." I never thought to ask why.

The leave-taking is practical: "Let me buy your black patent shoes," Jennie suggests to Elsie, handing her $5. The shoes don't fit Elsie and may not fit Jennie, but it's a way of giving her daughter financial support for the trip. There is a sadness, perhaps, at seeing her firstborn daughter travel so far away—but anyone knowing Elsie also knows she'll never be content in Minnesota and likely will never come back.

As they barrel down two-lane roads towards Manhattan, Elsie finds the trip far longer than she envisioned. But thoughts of distance melt as a flask filled with vodka passes from front seat to back. Amazed at the ever-growing distance, Elsie feels a bit uneasy—but there's no turning back. The memories of growing up on a farm, of that quiet sweet pastoral childhood, of small town life, and valedictorian speeches are over.

~ ~ ~

"You need gloves and a perm," Helmi explains, opening her dresser drawer and handing Elsie white gloves. "Then you go to this employment agency," she explains, giving her a piece of paper with an address written on it. Blonde, blue-eyed Elsie sets out to get her perm, assuming Minnesota prices match Manhattan ones. The haircut, metal rollers, ammonia solution, electricity, and styling take 3 hours. The only thing left is payment.

"That'll be $7 dollars, please."

"SEVEN DOLLARS?" Elsie gasps. "But I only *have*"—and here she empties out her coin purse and counts—"$6.32." They stare at each other, the male owner and Elsie, whose cheeks burn. It seems hopeless and neither one has a solution. Finally, precisely because no solution exists, he takes $6 and Elsie scurries shame-faced out the door.

The next morning, she appears—a rouged, permed, and gloved Finnish girl—at the employment agency. The interview commences with more questions about her physical health than the A's she received at Finlayson High or the typing course she took from the Duluth Business School. Apparently employers want *healthy* domestics, not necessarily valedictorian ones.

"Please step into the salon," the agency owner opens the door to a sumptuous wallpapered room with large mirrors. On a chaise lounge a woman rests with furs draped over her shoulder sipping coffee. Awkwardly, Elsie stands in the middle of the room.

"Would you walk around," the owner suggests. *I feel like a dammed horse,* Elsie thinks mutinously to herself. The lady stands up, walks over to Elsie and asks to see her teeth. Elsie obediently widens her tiny mouth, not giving way to the urge to whinny. They pass muster, and she receives a one-way ticket to Long Island. She is about to become a "butler's girl."

Single Herby ~ 1925 ~ First Job Short-Lived

As an only child of a single mother, Herby quits school in 1925 and works the Manhattan docks. One Sunday he takes his best friend Aarti Antilla to show off a bit. As luck has it, he notices one of the forklift trucks his company owns is still on the dock. He turns to Aarti. "Hey, let's take it for a ride," adding enthusiastically, "What's to lose?"

He hops into the seat and soon has the engine running. Slowly it rumbles down the long dock.

"I guess I'd better turn it off now," Herby yells. He tries to twist the key to the OFF position, but it refuses to budge. A bit panicked, he keeps trying.

The edge of the pier looms larger and larger. He frantically looks at the pedals, gears, switches—clueless. About three feet from the edge, he jumps off. The forklift keeps going. In horrorstruck awe, they watch as it pitches forward into the Harlem River with a stupendous splash and sinks to the bottom.

Herby turns to Aarti. "Guess I'll be leaving town now."

Retired Elsie ~ 1982 ~ Florida Diary

Today Herby's antenna fell. Too much rain. Rope contracted and broke bamboo.

June 19

Child Barbara ~ 1959 ~ Breezy Point Beach

Breezy Point Beach fills our summer days—but not always agreeably. Today, it's going to be hot. As we crest the hill and I see the Chesapeake Bay, I smell its brine-tinged odor as it pours into the open car windows. We drive down the white, dusty gravel road to the piers. With only a small outbuilding housing the fuel, no one could call this a marina. Rather, it serves the working class whose boats looked aged and worn. Ours is no exception—though of classier lineage.

The *Bonnie Fay*, one of the few remaining wooden Chesapeake oystering boats, became part of our family years ago. Our Sundays soon revolved around this rarely sailed, always worked on, skipjack. Dad worked; Mom relaxed; Sandra and I played.

"Why is Ralph waving at us?" I ask from the back seat, watching Dad's best friend. I helpfully add, "Gee, the mast looks kinda low, Dad." Indeed. The *Bonnie Fay* has sunk.

It's best at times like this to become quickly invisible. Leaving Dad, Ralph, and Mom to bemoan the sunken hull, Sandra and I yell, "We'll get the picnic table, Mom," and grab our swimming suits out of the canvas bag.

We race through the clubhouse past the ratcheting sound of one-armed bandits into the paint-peeling bathhouse. We shrug off our T-shirts and shorts, wiggle into swimsuits, drop our stuff on the favorite family picnic table, and hit the water at the same time, racing for the anchored raft near the edge of the netted area.

Any child swimming in the Bay quickly learns how to choreograph swim strokes with jellyfish. Eyes ever vigilant, we circumnavigate the floating globs. The hemp net strung around the swimming area after Memorial Day keeps out the biggest ones but storm-torn tentacles still float through the net. No swim ends without scraping wet sand over stung skin.

Soon we are diving off the wooden planks, playing water games. An hour later, we emerge, waterlogged goblins-of-the-brine to stretch out on our towels.

This is family-time heaven. Later, after lunch, we'll take the dinghy, the *Bonnie Fay-ette*, into tiny overgrown channels, counting water moccasins slithering happily through the warm green water.

Meanwhile, Mom has abandoned Herby and Ralph and gotten into her red plaid swimsuit buttressed with frontal foam padding. She cannot get her ruptured eardrum wet, so she bobs like an unsinkable cork while we take turns diving under her, losing points only when we have bodily contact.

Thus goes our weekly Sunday ritual, which actually began years earlier when Dad decided to teach us to swim. He encased us in multi-tubed plastic life preservers, taught us to paddle, then slowly punctured our vests, section by section—until even we realized we were actually swimming—and tossed the deflated things in the trash.

Toward lunchtime, our somewhat discouraged father shows up by our beach blanket. "So what are you going to do?" I ask.

After all, this is *our* paradise. We hunt for sharks' teeth. We fish. We take the dinghy into the smelly backwaters. We find prehistoric dinosaur bones. We hunt crabs. We are little sun bunnies.

"Well, I'm getting it hoisted out of the water. Then Ralph and I will sail it to a place that can repair it."

I wonder how, exactly, one sails a just-sunken boat—maybe by bailing. He turns to Mom. "Would you mind following us in the car ... just in case we sink?"

"Of course," she agrees and then turns to us. "Barbara, go get the ice chest. Sandra, get the table ready." I scurry over to the pink and gray International Harvester, hoist the Styrofoam cooler from the back, lug it over, and dump it on the wooden table.

"Someone open the cooler and bring me the hotdogs," she orders as Dad gets the Coleman stove turned on. Starving, we both pop the lid off the cooler. "Hey, Mom," Sandra hollers out, "where are the hotdogs?"

"They're in the cooler."

"No they're not."

Mom walks over to peer in. No meat. The master organizer, the Ph.D. packer-of-things, the woman who never forgets, has left the doggies 70 miles away from our empty, raging tummies. We, as children, are shocked. WHAT? Buns, ketchup, mustard, relish, chips, potato salad, cheap generic soft drinks, quarters for ice cream ... but NO HOTDOGS?

This day isn't going very well but since we have to stay out of the water for an hour after lunch, Sandra and I decide to go shark's tooth hunting. Our skills are exceptional. Either of us can spot, easily, a tooth 1/16th inch. I firmly believe we have rescued teeth 1/32nd inch, so small they look like wet dots on the tip of our finger.

The only super-sized shark's tooth we ever found happened 2 years earlier when we sailed down to Calvert Cliffs.

As Mom walked along, she saw a dry, gray stone tip jutting out of the stand. Prodding it with her toe, it soon took on a tooth-shape of gigantic (to us) proportions. Holding the 3" treasure, she did absolutely nothing. She did not shriek. She didn't dance the schottische in the sand. She didn't even smile. She walked back like a proper Finn, toting the treasure in her hand. Being a fourth-generation Finn, I screamed and danced and did the whole WOW routine.

After tooth hunting, we decide to go crabbing.

We untie the dinghy from the pier, and head out the channel to the Bay. Water moccasin beady eyes follow us as we row. Dad has taught us not to fall out, or jump out, or swim in the marina—so we don't. Once we took Gloria, a very athletic sixth grader, in the dinghy and gave her the basic snake rule. When she screamed, "TAKE ME BACK," I thought (for the first time) that perhaps she had survival skills I lacked.

At any rate, the pilings surrounding the swim area are full of crabs eating whatever crabs eat on mollusk-laden piers. We scoop them up in our net, throw them in a cardboard box, and keep hauling them in until we have about fifteen. We row ashore, carry the box to our beach blanket, return the dinghy, and go back to swimming until we look puckered and waterlogged.

"Let's go," Dad yells from the picnic table. I look up to see him hoisting the ice chest onto his shoulder. "Grab the box," Sandra bosses me while she flaps her towel, throwing a ton of sand in my face. "*You* get it," I snarl back taking my towel and throwing sand at her. She walks over, picks it up, the bottom collapses, and fifteen crabs fall out scurrying toward dozens of sunbathers.

"DAD!" we both start screaming. "DAD, the crabs are getting away."

Sunbathers seeing crabs spidering their way in all directions, jump up, scream, grab towels, run. If they weren't our hard-earned dinner, I'd have run too.

Dad drops the ice chest and races down to the beach. "Catch them like this," he says, stomping on the back of a crab with his bare foot. Sandra immediately slams her bare foot on the nearest crab. I just as instantly have less enthusiasm for this and grab the soggy box, flip it over so the dry side is closed and down. Within minutes, all the crabs are re-quarantined. Dad fetches a beer box from the beach restaurant; we transfer the poor exhausted crabs, and head home.

Two weeks later, Dad successfully sails the *Bonnie Fay* south to have it repaired. It is the boat's longest voyage under my father's captainship. It comes back, and 6 months later disappears again into the marina murk. Dad never says a thing—not a word of remorse or anger or disgust. But the *Bonnie Fay* is never seen again.

"Where did you take it, Dad?" I ask. "Into the swamp," he says, offering no navigational clues.

Sandra and I often take the dinghy into the swampy wetlands looking for the sunken *Bonnie Fay*, but we never find her. She has gone "to the oysters," which I guess is only fair. Once she caught them. Now they claim her for their own submerged haven.

Retired Elsie ~ 1982 ~ Florida Diary

Rain again. Herby's antenna broke again. Tough luck. Tomatoes are rotting on the vine.

June 22

Career Elsie ~ 1941 ~ Panama Canal

Now 34 years old, Elsie has risen to senior clerk-stenographer with a salary of $1,260 per year. Her job, however, sounds nothing like the title.

In her own words, she "lays out, directs, and reviews the work of clerks in purchasing general and technical supplies," and "supervises assembling, preparation and review of formal contracts and bonds." She looks for contract "omissions, errors, or inconsistencies, and confers with scientific and professional staff when incomplete and conflicting data is received." She ensures that contracts meet General Accounting Office procedures, and even drafts contracts for equipment rentals. "Considerable independent action and decision are required," she notes, yet she leaves 5 years later. Why?

She succinctly states the reason: "UNEMPLOYED. To raise family."

Psychic Julie ~ 2009 ~
Disease versus Essential Elsieness

I'm sitting in Julie Madill's kitchen lamenting my inability to write this book. Julie, a yoga teacher, who has recently been told she has psychic gifts, suddenly feels Mom blasting in and sheepishly admits, "I think your mother is trying to connect with me." I almost laugh. It seems that Elsie is a psychic's dream come true.

"Just tell me what she's saying—then I can tell you if it's probably her."

"Okay," Julie begins. "She wants readers to know that she was funny. She wants her ... *Elsieness* ... to come through. She doesn't want you to write about her as a diseased, dying person."

~ ~ ~

For the first time, I realize that I can never minimize the devastation this disease causes. I observed the disease; Mom suffered it. I saw the transcendence; she saw the loss. I witnessed beauty; she experienced horror. Somehow, all of it is true.

In the end, I realize the only way I can honestly write this book is to listen. To her. To me. To our unspoken conversations. To my heart.

Retired Elsie ~ 1982 ~ Florida Diary

Toimi Vaananen and Herby worked on antenna again. I typed a visa letter for Toimi—hope it works. Picked up watermelon for Herby to give teacher (he graduates from his ham-radio class tonite). He dropped it. It cracked ... but stayed together.

Daughters Sandra and Barbara ~ 1945–1987 ~ Father's Day

A word about Father's Day a bit belatedly since he is deceased. True, my father got the usual array of shirts and cards. But now, years after his death, the day evokes memories.

I can walk right back into my childhood home with tremendous mental ease.

~ ~ ~

I see him, lean and dark-haired, moving quietly around the kitchen fixing our breakfast, carving a roast, smoking a cigarette, reading. Over the years, he builds the turquoise-painted wooden cabinets and Formica counters, installs the progression of refrigerators and stoves, adds a restaurant booth, tiles the kitchen floor, and creates a formidable array of storage places for brooms, spices, dishpans, and cookie sheets.

Mom inhabits one side of the kitchen, keeping her pots, pans, spices, and pantry. Dad overtakes the other side, stuffing drawers to overflowing with hinges, bolts, nails, screwdrivers, and brackets that will rust as surely as we will age.

As an independent carpenter, Dad's livelihood depends on the economy. When a recession hits, Dad and the kitchen become inseparable. "Bye, Dad," we holler as we head for high school or college, checking our book bags to make sure he hasn't stolen any of our texts. We see him sitting at a new yellow Formica table in the middle of the kitchen, coffee cup in one hand, cigarette dangling from the other, ashtray empty, elbows on table, bony legs crossed, book opened. "Have a good day," he enthusiastically encourages us, even though he's already engrossed in his reading. Usually he sticks to history or science.

Seven hours later, we walk in the kitchen. "Hi, Dad, we're home." If I were to snap photos in the morning and afternoon, the only difference would be an ashtray overflowing with Camel butts and a book advanced by many, many pages. As we fix snacks, he disappears into the den to await Elsie and their shared vodka-and-tonic cocktails.

The den owes its existence to the day Mom finds Sandra dressing in a closet because of her sudden need for privacy. Soon after, Dad lifts our roof, and adds two upstairs bedrooms and a bath because, after all, he is a carpenter.

With Sandra's privacy resolved, Mom and Dad gain a den which becomes his second-most frequented place for learning. Technically speaking, his brown naugahyde recliner earned enough hours to get a Ph.D. if it hadn't ended up unceremoniously in the dump.

Of course, when the economy is good, Dad heads out in his short-sleeve white shirt, heavy-cotton blue work pants, white socks, paint-splattered black Penney's shoes, carpenter's overalls, and pumpernickel sandwich slathered with butter and slabs of blue cheese, wrapped in wax paper.

He hops into his bald-tired, lamentably old truck, guns it up the short, steep dirt driveway, turns left onto Cockerille Avenue, and heads into his carpentry day.

The most memorable truck, by far, is the white Quonset-hut beer truck bought on the cheap, with a dead pig thrown in. Dad immediately invites neighbors to eat the pig, which no one does because it reeks of fish. (Apparently the pig's owner fed it rotting fish offal.)

Dad rarely enters the living room with its upholstered chairs, mahogany end tables with marble-based lamps, and French provincial sofa. I can do homework and read Nancy Drew mysteries, unseen and forgotten by the entire family.

The only time that room gets attention is on Christmas Day, at parties, and when I play my 45 rpms drawing my father irresistibly into singing counter-lyrics to my love songs.

We are all self-contained, each in our own happy world ... until dinner. Once at the dinner table, we are expected to talk politics, history, science—anything—but *not* high school dances, boyfriends, pulp fiction, gossip.

"So," Dad begins, "what kind of science project are you thinking of?"

Dumb me, interested in swiftness rather than prizes answers, "Well, I thought lima beans might be interesting."

Dad can hardly muster an answer. He tries a different track. "What do you know about the Coriolis effect?"

Huh?

"Why does water going down a bath drain circle *clockwise* in the northern hemisphere and *counterclockwise* in the south?" He pauses as I stare at him blank-faced. "It's the Coriolis effect! Wouldn't it be interesting measuring that?"

And lamb-to-slaughter that I am, I agree.

Soon I am watching people enter department stores, movie theaters, museums—my little Brownie camera in hand—to see if they unconsciously abide by the Coriolis effect by entering clockwise. Apparently they don't care, and I win no prize.

Meanwhile Sandra gets hooked into building a barometer filled with liquid mercury. It towers several feet in the air and all goes well with her winning second place, until she carries the exhibit out and drops it in the parking lot, turning it into a toxic waste site.

What Dad gives Mom, Sandra, and me, however, doesn't reside in rooms or breakfasts or science projects, but in identity. He *insists* that each of us has *infinite* value—and he never lets us lose sight of it. "Be all you can be" becomes the mantra we live under. In an extraordinary way, he exudes a quiet confidence, an absolute certainty, an adamant satisfaction in each of us.

Part of *being all we can be* also means knowing how to play softball, bicycle, roller skate, shoot a bow, sail a skipjack, catch a fish. On the learn-to-bike day, Sandra and I head to our elementary-school playground with our brand-new Schwinns. Dad ties a rope to Sandra's while I sit alone by my shiny blue one, ignored and dejected. After a couple of hours Sandra flies, ropeless, around the parking lot, screeching to a halt. The sun is setting, but at last it's my turn. I eagerly wheel my bike over to him.

"It's getting late, Barbara." He looks a bit tuckered out. "Maybe we should try another day."

WHAT?! I am so overcome with disappointment, I begin to cry. Little tears drip down my face. I sniffle. I look utterly forlorn.

Girding his rope-run loins, he looks down at me. "Okay, we'll give you one try." He ties the rope to my bike, slackly dragging my bicycle behind him. I kind of get it, in a wobbly sort of way. Clearly Sandra and he want to go home.

"I think we should start you out on *training wheels*," he suggests. I am outraged. Incensed. The idea of *me* on baby wheels while my sister soars around on her Schwinn is too much to tolerate.

"Let me try it just *once* on my own, without the rope," I beg. He agrees. I push my bike to the top of the playground. I pray. *Please, God, don't let me fall off.* I mount. I push off.

Wobbling but still upright, I start to gather speed. I'm screaming with glee. "I'm DOING it, Dad, I'm DOING it." The parking lot is whizzing by. Suddenly I notice the school. The *brick* school. "How do I STOP?" I scream. Dad and Sandra are yelling at me, running as fast as they can.

KaBOOM. I hit the school full speed. Nobody has mentioned brakes.

Granted, learning to bike is an adolescent version of *being all I can be*. But all the Nurmi women persevere and thrive under Dad's mantra. Mom becomes a Protocol Officer. Sandra speaks Russian, Chinese, and Spanish—with a dash of Swahili—and goes on to another degree in electrical engineering. I develop an information system for the White House Executive Office and then design more for various federal agencies and corporate organizations. All because we believe in this man's belief in us.

Caregiver Barbara ~ 2000 ~ Home Care Ends

Comfort, I am finding, needs too much comfort from *me*. She's in her sixties. She's trying so hard to please me. I feel I spend all my time reassuring her. She needs constant companionship, it seems. I end up watching TV I don't want to watch just to keep her company.

It's exhausting to keep explaining how this house works. She interrupts me endlessly throughout the day—little questions about where I keep something, how I do something, what I would like. I feel my routine, minimal as it seems, is being torn to shreds. Comfort takes good care of Mom, but I worry about a sixty-something woman transferring her from the bed to the recliner and have ordered a hoist.

On the other hand, Tata called me last week to tell me she had no transportation or child care for her infant. I left Mom utterly alone that day in a locked house at 6 a.m. in order to drive 40 minutes to pick up Tata, and bring her and her child back. Mom apparently slept through the whole thing, but Tata no longer has guaranteed transportation.

It's the kind of disaster that spirals into desperation. I am hitting an emotional rock bottom. I can't multitask caregiving and writing. I've put off my own needs—virtually all of them—for over a year. Now I see that one year can become two or three or more. Will I have the patience and determination to continue?

And right now, what do I do? Tata can't continue. Comfort needs too much *comfort*. I call the agency that provided Hawa. The owner tells me most aides want weekends off; Hawa was the exception. That means endless substitutes every weekend, with none of them knowing how the kitchen works or how to handle Mom emotionally.

~ ~ ~

I had a dream last night. In it, I am asleep with Mom's bed right next to mine, her head touching me. Suddenly I feel my bed violently dragged halfway across the room. Still in the dream, I see myself waking up the next morning and looking at the wall where the bed had stood. In its place, she has left a blueprint of her entire DNA etched upon my bedroom wall.

I've never completely interpreted that dream—even after a decade. Once again I wonder, *what did that dream mean?* It suddenly occurs to me to ask my mother. Since beginning this book, when I get stuck, I often sit quietly and simply ask for help from Mom.

I don't consider myself psychic, but I do believe she wants to help me. I envision an open channel between us, hoping something will come through to help. Sometimes it's hard for me to remain open-minded about this. After all I live in a very concrete world. But then again, perhaps we have more psychic abilities than we realize, especially with loved ones—but we never *ask*, or open up a dialogue.

So I sit, quiet myself, and ask Mom.

~ ~ ~

<u>Barbara</u>: That DNA dream—what was that about?

<u>Mom</u>: *It was about how <u>you</u> felt. You felt you were being consumed, that I was overtaking your life <u>so</u> much you were even becoming my DNA.*

<u>Barbara</u>: Why was the bed being yanked from the wall? It felt like you were doing that.

<u>Mom</u>: Barbara, yes, I did. You weren't paying attention to your own needs. You <u>wanted</u> to be able to give your entire self to caring for me, but you <u>couldn't</u>. I had to shake some sense into you. So I did. (laughter).

<u>Barbara</u>: How did you feel about leaving my house?

<u>Mom</u>: I didn't really care by then. As you know, I lived in two worlds. But in your world, kind and gentle touch was all I needed. I was beyond relationship in the human sense.

~ ~ ~

Mom had passed her first anniversary of hip surgery in my home. Contrary to the surgeon's predictions, Mom thrived. Not physically, of course. She *did* reject physical therapy, and the same with chewing. I could almost hear her say, *I'm not going to live through this anyway. Why go to all that work?*

When I began managing Mom's care, I spent a great deal of time considering my role. Some daughters or sons are all-in, all the time. I admire that, but it's not me. I wondered what advice Mom would give me. Immediately, I realized she would have said *two* things to me:

"Barbara, live your life. I lived mine."

"Barbara, I'll do whatever I can to keep you glued to my hip socket."

The second message needs a little interpreting. Mom liked to get her way. Getting her way now would mean I would always be there for her, always make sure she was as happy as she could possibly be, as well taken care of, as *alive* as possible.

So I thought about it, but not for long. I chose the "good mother" message: "Live your life. I lived mine."

I sat in Mom's room that night. Comfort had left. "Mom," I began, stroking her hand. "I need to have my house back. I love you but I don't know how to take care of you anymore. Hawa's gone." I started to cry.

Mom looked at me and as always, I wondered if her hovering soul understood. "All these people coming in, Mom. I can't keep training them. It just isn't working."

ELSIE AT EBB TIDE

We sat together as the sky darkened into night.

I had come to love this frail, demented woman in a way that I had never learned how to love my controlling mother. But all I could feel right now was exhaustion, frustration, and hopelessness.

The next day, I picked up the phone and began dialing.

I interviewed various places, at last choosing an assisted-care home where a friend's mother resided. "I need a home for my mother. Do you have space?"

Retired Elsie ~ 1988 ~ Ode to Obsolescence

[Letter to the Editor]

For 40 years I have been in good health, due in part to the fact that I have been taking Gevral, a multivitamin every day.

Much to my disappointment it has been squeezed off the shelves by hundreds of new products. Not only that, but I can no longer find round toothpicks. They are either square or a rough-hewn imitation of round.

I have an Instant Kodak Camera, which I love and have used for many years. Now the company is prohibited from making and selling film for this camera under a court order.

Last week I looked for Fruitful Bran cereal and found it had been pushed off the shelves by other unknown products. What next?

Swedish Pancake Mix! My husband makes pancakes every Sunday morning but will not use any other brand. There goes my Sunday breakfast.

Once I had quite a supply of Annase that cures every twinge and muscular spasm, making me as good as new in a few moments. I contacted every pharmacy in the area and not one was able to provide it.

I have come to the conclusion that I am of the wrong generation. In my circle of friends they don't even make babies anymore.

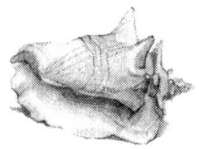

Kenna and Elsie ~ 2000 ~ I Haven't Given Up

As time goes on, Kenna's visits take on a routine. She always does the energy healing. Sometimes Elsie has more to say; sometimes less, slowly sharing more of her inner feelings.

Kenna uses her energy healing to make a path for Elsie's thoughts—like clearing a way into the wilderness, or taking a flashlight into a dark room.

~ ~ ~

<u>Elsie</u>; *I feel like the trees, standing in the same place day after day. I am like an autumn leaf. But my heart is not heavy.*

I really do feel reconciled. I want Barbara to know I am at peace most of the time in terms of the past. Yet there are many questions as to why things happened as they did—like how I got into this condition.

Acceptance is a major learning task in old age. Perhaps when we are young we know we have strength to fight in adversity, but in old age, we're confused and weak and have to give in to our situation. Here is where my stubbornness is losing. I've given in, but I haven't given up. See the difference? This realization is a great blessing.

<u>Kenna</u>: Do you see the angels around you? They're with you every day all the time. Whatever you need, ask for it.

<u>Elsie</u>: *Like a cup of tea?*

<u>Kenna</u>: Well, try it!

~ ~ ~

Clearly, transformation is taking place even as Mom succumbs to Alzheimer's. She tells Kenna she's accepted her circumstances and the effects of this disease—but she hasn't given up on life itself.

I find myself curious. *What more can life hold for her without a working mind?*

Though I have glimmers of it, I don't yet understand that she now lives in two worlds, not one. She has a safe harbor in her physical body that she is not willing to abandon. But her spirit-soul is beginning to be drawn to the other side, to explore a life without a body.

June 28

Caregiver Barbara ~ 2000 ~ Grieving Mom's Move

Two days ago, I moved Mom into Barbara Reddick's group home to live with two other elderly women both suffering from Alzheimer's. Margaret screams out a two-toned YOO-HOO. Emily smiles brightly and agrees with whatever you say. Mom waves her fluttering hands toward the ceiling and carries on her intently self-engrossing conversations. And I am in my house, alone.

It all happened so fast. Barbara arrived with her nephew John in a transport van at 1 o'clock. They wheeled Mom out of my house for the first time since she had arrived over a year ago. They carefully bumped her wheelchair down the stone steps, rolled her along the sidewalk, and gently lifted her into the front passenger seat. They closed the door and drove her away. Hours later, the hospital bed followed.

~ ~ ~

The house seems strangely empty, her room so bare. The oyster-colored walls are scarred from the countless times the hospital bed scraped against them. The chairlift, with its rubber guards, has left black stripes. Once inaccessible dust balls now tumble across the scuffed wood floor. But hardest of all, *life* has gone out of the room.

My mother and Hawa, once the nuclear heart of my tiny brick home, are both gone. I am truly home alone in an empty house.

Today, I painted the walls. Not oyster, but powder blue. I set about the project with determination, remaking the room in one day. I hung paintings and polished the desk, turning the room into something utterly different and new.

I still haven't *sat* with all of this. I know how much I loved having Mom in my house, and I know she will not come back. I feel like I am sitting in the silent vortex of a terrible emotional storm. I remember as a child when the eye of a hurricane passed over our Takoma Park home. It was so eerily still.

That is how I feel right now.

Perhaps I am in shock. My truth, what I need right now, and my desire—how much I would like to be a wonder woman who could single-handedly take care of my mother *and* write *and* take care of myself—don't match.

I feel the raw edges of powerful emotions: sadness and relief, anger and hope, guilt and understanding. I don't want to be swamped by them right now. I know I will have to wrestle with all of this. Just not now. Not today.

Mom will continue to decline. I have seen the small losses month after month. But Hawa needs to get on with her life. I do too.

My mind goes over the story again and again, like a revolving Rolodex, trying to find a better ending. When I get to the last card, it always reads the same: *It was time.* Then I flip the cards and begin again. That is how caregiving goes. Reality and desire don't always dance to the same tune.

~ ~ ~

When I look back on Hawa's and my time with Mom, I think I understand why Mom recovered and flourished. She came to us like a shrunken balloon—the kind that wilts when left alone and gets puckered rubbery skin. But Hawa and I kept blowing our life energy, more importantly our love, into her. On some level I guess I knew that without this continual flow of love, she would gradually shrink away from us.

The one thing I cannot fix is dying. Even today, a decade later, I feel such sadness. It was the hardest thing for me to learn. Mom *had* to travel down this road, and I could not stop her. It felt so awful, so dreadful.

The *disease* wasn't dreadful. I'd have kept my mother, demented as she was, forever because I found so much *light* in her.

She had such an incandescent radiance. It filled the room. She was no longer "physical" in any meaningful sense. But she was *Elsie*. She never left, and was never really diminished.

The soul-spirit seems to have an inerasable imprint—something that cannot be lost regardless of the ravages of disease. It doesn't rest in habits or memory. Rather it seems to be raw, radiant energy—a love generator—uniquely tuned. Elsie could not lose her *Elsieness*.

Alzheimer's slows dying down so much the soul has time to flicker brighter and brighter into spirit in our midst. I know this is not everyone's experience. When psychics connect to her years after her death, Mom talks about anger and explains why it occurs. The soul, encased for so long in a mind that insists on controlling and choosing, feels completely thrown when the brain slowly grinds to a stop. In this increasing vacuum, the soul doesn't know where it is, or what to do. There can be a lot of thrashing around, a lot of fear and anger.

But consider the hatching of an egg.

To be born, the bird must batter the shell with its beak. If the bird were our soul, and the shell our functioning mind (within which we felt safe and wanted no change), the soul would slumber forever unawakened.

But aging and illness awaken this strange eternal soul-spirit.

It is dying itself that arouses it from its happy slumber. Angry at its fate, the weak, wet little creature begins to strike the shell, wanting to battle death itself. Yet as it does, it becomes stronger.

At last it realizes that, because of illness and age, it is in a terrible cage. Suddenly it wants freedom.

Perhaps this is the way of the soul in an aging body. In the initial stages of Alzheimer's, Mom threw her anger and intellect against it. She fought the disease thinking she could destroy death itself. But as time went on, her spirit got stronger. She seemed to see the other side. She forgot this world. She entered a period of extended time, with a foot in both worlds.

Alzheimer's gave Mom all the time in the world, it seemed, to make this soul-to-spirit journey. There is a kindness in this. It is as though the *Higher Force of Love* whispers, "No hurry, Elsie. We know you love your human life. So we are not rushing you out the door, here. You've received this disease as a gift of life really. You'll have plenty of time to say your good-byes. You can return to your childlike play. You can be loved like a baby one last time.

And when you choose, one last peck and the shell will simply crumble and you will fly away."

July

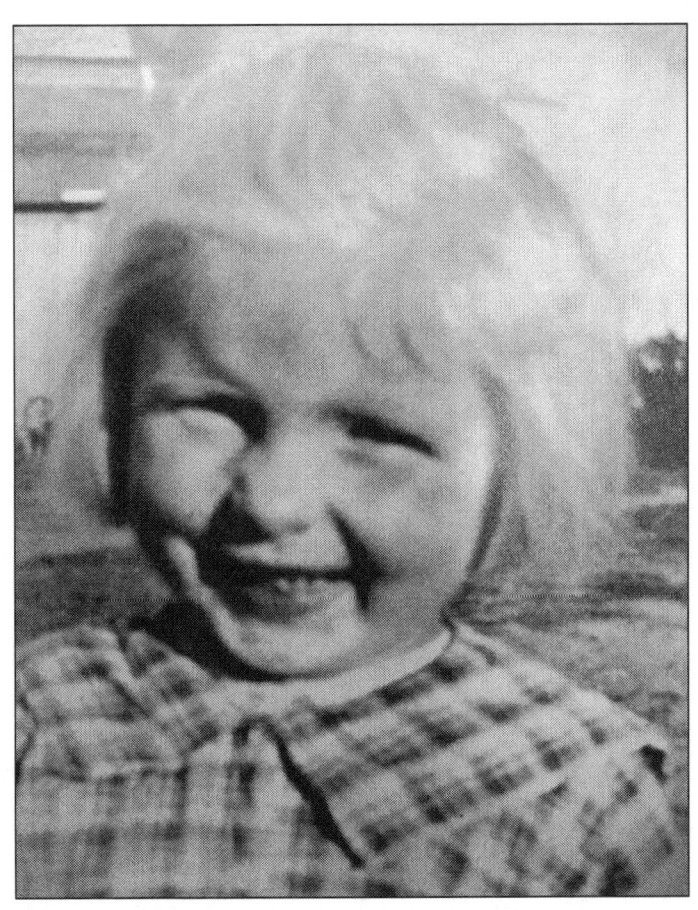

Living Life

July 1

Career Elsie ~ 1963 ~
Hotel Protocol Meets State Department Protocol

Top-tier hotels such as The Plaza in New York City employ their own Protocol Officers. When the King of Morocco arrives, *Pageant Magazine* decides to cover both Mrs. Ivanka Nina Lytle, the Plaza Protocol Officer who speaks six languages and considers a mink stole, black sheath dress and white gloves everyday garb—and State Department Protocol Officer Elsie Nurmi wearing off-the-shelf, on-sale suits and a ready-to-go wig. Yet ...

Just like Elsie, Mrs. Lytle is on call 24 hours a day.

Just like Elsie, she vouchsafes gorgeous flower arrangements, exquisite cuisine, and instant translators with seemingly effortless grace.

The photo-studded article shows this tall slender woman coiffed in an elegant golden-blonde French twist working with Elsie to prepare for King Hassan II, who as a Muslim "may not eat pork nor drink alcohol" so lamb and orange juice are served.

Visit complete, the reader sees Mrs. Nurmi and Mrs. Lytle leaning against each other, exhausted, shoulders touching, "in giddy giggles," at last released from the stress of a state visit.

And how do they unwind?

Mrs. Lytle in stocking feet deftly pours her businessman-husband a dinner drink from a crystal decanter. But no such photo exists for Elsie.

She dashes out the Plaza door, jumps in a taxi, naps on the night train to D.C., drives to her blue-collar neighborhood, and faces rush hour and the new delegation the next day.

Retired Elsie ~ 1982 ~ Florida Diary

Storm knocked down antenna again last night. Tough luck. Today, went to flea market and bought typing table $4, and duct tape 75¢. Tried typewriter on the table. Works good.

Caregiver Barbara ~ 2000 ~ Detours or Dead Ends?

I sit by Mom's side, watching her sleep as I hold her hand. In the next bed, Eleanor who yodels YOO HOO when awake, slumbers with slight snores. I find it comforting to be with Mom as our energies quietly merge.

More often than not when I visit she is dozing. Whereas I could take advantage of her sporadic moments of wakefulness in my home, my visits here always seem to miss them. She is entering the thirteenth year of the disease since those first conversations of memory loss.

Sometimes she goes into a *deep* sleep—way beyond normal sleeping. When it first happened, Hawa got scared. She could scarcely wake Mom for meals, and Mom would sometimes fall asleep with food in her mouth.

I thought that perhaps she was going somewhere deeper than sleep—to the spirit world. My council was always the same. "Let her explore."

But it took me time to get that perspective....

~ ~ ~

I expected death when I brought her home because of the doctor's diagnosis. At someone's recommendation, I read about Kubler-Ross's stages of dying, I matter-of-factly decided to prepare Mom. After all, could I rely on my *sense* she wanted to live when I saw her in rehab?

"Mom," I'd begin, "it's okay to let go. Everyone is fine. Everything is fine. You can go." Of course, we weren't having a *conversation*, but I believed I connected with some intact essence-of-Elsie. I droned on, day after day, reassuring her.

What absolutely did *not* occur to me was the simple fact I might have been right in the first place—she wanted to live.

So here I was, posting a dead-end sign at the foot of her bed. I should have remembered the time *she* pointed to the DEAD END traffic sign at the entrance of the Finnish-American Rest Home, and with Finn understatement remarked, "Aptly named."

But she wasn't dead or even close. I just hadn't learned the subtle signs of life. So I invited my ex-husband Bill who had a near-death experience to talk to her about the other side and how much she was loved there.

If Mom had an ounce of coherency I think she would have used it to glare at me and say, "SHUT UP!"

Still on my death-march, I called Sandra and Ed. "You better come and see her ... for one *last* visit." So they flew in from Seattle for the death vigil. I took them into Mom's room. While I blathered on about death, Ed drew up close to Mom. She began to babble, loudly. Ed leaned over, listened, and looked up. "She's saying: "I have *no use* for that word!"

My poor mother!—a Rapunzel trapped in her Babel, begging for someone to rescue her. And Ed, like a prince, grabs one strand after another, weaving a tiny braid of coherent thought.

I never doubted that Ed *got* her garbling because it was classic Elsie—*exactly* how she'd say something. And Ed didn't know her that long or that well.

After that, I shut up.

July 7

Newborn Elsie ~ 1917 ~
EJEN a.k.a. Elsie Julia Elizabeth Norlund Arrives

This is to certify that a *Female* child named *Elsie Julia Elizabeth Norlund* was born to *Hjalmar Norlund* and *Jennie Sophie Askelin Norlund* on the *7th* day of *July* 19*17*, at *11* a.m., at *2613 W. 1st St.,* Duluth, Minnesota, and registered as No. *1430B*.

Birthplace of Father, Wyoming, Age 26, Carpenter

Birthplace of Mother, Minnesota, Age 19, Housewife

~ ~ ~

Elsie *loves* her birth date. After she's forgotten Herby's, Sandra's, and mine, she still remembers the classy rhythm of 7.7.17.

After her birth, however, her baptismal identity gets muddied. *Hjalmar* becomes *Jalmar*. *Norlund* becomes *Norlundin*. Baby Elsie becomes *Elsie Julia Elisabeth*. Nevertheless, the elaborate gold-and-green document with Moses, several Jesuses, a dove, and even a butterfly ensure Elsie's eternal identity and salvation. She is on her way.

Elsie soon begins to document her own life. In early Finlayson years, she writes a birthday letter to herself, pokes around her grandparents' barn, finds a secret niche, and hides her missive. On every birthday thereafter, she writes a new letter, pulls the old ones, reads them, and adds the new one.

Elsie on front left

All goes well for a few years, but then disaster (in the form of a mouse) strikes. She pulls out paper nesting. One might hope the mouse educated itself—kind of a Renaissance mouse exploring other cultures. Irate Elsie never entrusts her life to a mouse again.

Midwest mice, however, face far-greater threats than little girls poking around in barns. No one in Finlayson forgets the September 1894 Hinckley fire that lapped at the township line. The newspaper reported, "A Cyclone of Wind and Fire Bathed Northern Minnesota ... Hundreds of Human Lives Are Sacrificed." The fire reached Sandstone, 8 miles from Finlayson. In one afternoon, both Hinckley and Sandstone burned to the ground. "Though there were hundreds of people burned to death, thank God there were survivors. ... Many saved themselves in a gravel pit which contained several feet of water." Others survived by crawling into an open well, or drenching blankets with water and lying down in open potato fields, covering themselves with dirt. But in one spot, rescuers found 96 bodies burned beyond recognition.

When a fire starts in Finlayson in 1922, it reaches Askelin pastureland. Elsie's mother grabs 5-year-old Elsie and 3-year-old Lucy and drags them out the door. "Elsie," she orders quickly, "Take Lucy and go to the Pekkanen's." Terrified to leave her parents, but seeing the flames in the field, she obeys. She leaves her parents, grandparents, aunts, and uncles to fight the fire. Alone, tugging Lucy's little hand, she runs down the long farmhouse dirt road toward town.

The house and barn are saved.

Retired Elsie ~ 1982 ~ Florida Diary

Took typewriter to be checked—neck switch or capacitor. Went to the Post Office—little frog on hood rode w/me. My brother Swante came over 4 days ago. He told Herby that he "was bringing a 5th on the 3rd for the 4th. We drank it on the 7th.

Birthday Elsie and Barbara ~ 1987 ~ A Celebration of Years

"Barbara," Mom asks me, "how many people did you say were coming?"

"Oh, I don't know," I casually answer from the kitchen. "I think there are about a hundred names on my address list. I invited them all."

"BARBARA," Mom's voice cuts through the air, "You have NO PLACE to PUT a HUNDRED PEOPLE."

My thought is ... *Huh?* I lamely offer, "But it'll be a nice day. It's not raining. Everybody can go outside. We have the deck." Eyes widening in horror, Mom marches out of my kitchen and starts shoving furniture willy-nilly against the walls.

My sister-in-law Kay also greets my news that I want 110 candles on the sheet cake with dismay. "Because Mom is turning 70 and I am turning 40," I explain. Our birthdays are 1 day and 30 years apart.

At times like this, Mom probably wonders *why* she considered having a second child. Sandra, after all, is so funny, smart, cute—and organized. Perhaps she thinks, like many mothers, she'll luck out twice.

And I'm sure that when I was born on July 6, 1947, one day before her own birthday—she radiated hope. There was only one tiny little thing. Even as a newborn infant, I looked worried. Beneath a head full of black hair, I lacked the self-assured glow of sunbeam Sandra. If I'd had a vocabulary other than wailing, I might have said, *Oh my God, I've made a horrible mistake. Beam me back up. Let's undo this thing right now.*"

Of course, I don't notice this anxious aspect of myself until decades later when I actually spent time poring over my baby album and early childhood pictures.

No matter the occasion, no matter the age, I look seriously worried. Certainly unlike every other member of my family, I chronically worried about the poor, the dispossessed, the disenfranchised, the sad and lonely—from Appalachia to the inner city to worldwide starvation. It just came natural to me. Good-hearted family members quickly give up on me once they hear this litany.

Since I did not get beamed back up, I end up in a bassinet next to my sister's crib. She looks through the wooden slats and drags me over to her side so she can stare at me. She absolutely does not think this is a baby. I am a very strange thing with black stuff pouring out of my top.

Although I worry about world events, I pay scant heed to everyday matters such as 110-year birthday parties. Without saying a word, Kay devises the least incendiary solution, positioning candles in color-coded groups of ten. At *the* moment of lighting, *eleven* people each set their bank of candles aglow. Mom and I blow out 110 years worth of life over the rising flames that are actually squelched by a horde of candle-snuffing kids.

That was a *great* party," I exclaim again and again, even years later. My husband thinks otherwise.

"Too many people. You couldn't really talk to anyone." I agree—it was sort of a mass of happy humanity pouring through every portal to, from, and within the house. But for one *glorious* moment, Mom and I blew into a blazing inferno of togetherness—all ONE-HUNDRED-AND-TEN YEARS of it. We never get another double-decade birthday, no 80/50. By then, Mom no longer knows the word. Birthday.

Mother Barbara ~ 1982 ~ Parenting Begins

Kendra sobs for hours, screaming *nik-o-ya*. We can't put her to bed. Desperate, we call one of our new Korean friends. It is past midnight.

"Let me listen to her," Teresa says.

Bill puts the mouthpiece to Kendra's mouth as she continues to wail. He then puts it back to his ear. "I don't know what she's talking about," Teresa admits, "but she's screaming, 'It's MINE.'"

Bill hangs up. We have absolutely no idea what *mine* is, so Bill starts walking around the house carrying Kendra in his arms. Suddenly she points to the blue rayon blouse with a blue ribbon attached to the collar—the one she wore from Korea. He picks it up; she thrusts the ribbon in her mouth; the tears stop; she falls asleep.

July 16

Career Elsie ~ 1969 ~ Liftoff

Even Herby's excited for me. The State Department sent invitations to the embassies to attend the Apollo 11 liftoff for the moon. State Department chartered a plane—every seat now reserved by a diplomat—and I'm on the Protocol team.

The bus I ordered met us when we debarked. NASA provided bleachers for invited guests and press. Each of us has a pass to get into the cordoned area. We're sitting at Complex 39-A staring at this mammoth Saturn V rocket waiting for liftoff from the Kennedy Space Center. I never ever in my life dreamed I'd be present at a moment like this. Ever.

The loud speaker has been announcing the countdown in minutes. We are very close to liftoff. Finally we are hearing TEN ... NINE ... EIGHT. I know Herby's watching. All of America is holding its breath. I can hardly stand the tension.

Now the ground is beginning to rumble. I am seeing enormous flames shoot out. Nothing seems to be happening. A thought races through my head, *Is it too heavy to lift off?* It seems seconds are passing, but the rumble is building and building. Suddenly I feel way too close. *What if it explodes? We are only a couple miles away. Thousands of tons of explosives...*

The rumbling now shakes the spectator stand so violently I fear the whole structure will collapse.

It's becoming unbearable—and frightening.

I can't move. I can't get out of my protocol head. *What if the stand collapses and diplomats are killed?* Just then, I see it. The rocket is slowly lifting off the pad. It is rising, rising, rising. My heart begins to soar with astonished joy. It is happening. America is sending a man to the moon.

The ground slowly silences.

You can hear a pin drop. Not one of us moves. We scarcely even breathe. We watch and watch as the rocket rises into the incredibly blue sky until at last, it is out of sight. Even then, we remain silent, awestruck by what we've seen.

Retired Elsie ~ 1982 ~ Florida Diary

What a day. No telephone. No Datsun (no gas, no brake lights). No Scout (battery died). They can't even fix my typewriter.

Saw Mabel—back on the juice again.

RVing Barbara ~ 1997 ~ I am SO Over It

It's been a long time since I've taken my RV on the road. During the year Hawa lives with me, I take a couple short trips. But for the past year, it's been moldering under oak trees behind Bill's garage. I usually don't think about getting away. And I remind myself, I can hardly say I have *fond* memories of every trip ...

~ ~ ~

My RVing days began in July 1997 when I fell in love with an RV in Poulsbo, Washington—smitten enough to buy it. Sandra graciously stored it until I could figure out how to get it cross country. Months passed, but eventually October looked like a good month. *Fall colors,* I thought to myself. *Nice cool weather.* I'd fly west, drive my RV along Route 2 from Seattle to Duluth and then cut down to Maryland.

~ ~ ~

On October 20, I pull out of Poulsbo in my Winnebago Warrior and head for the Kingston ferry. On board, I buy coffee and 40 minutes later debark into my autumn adventure.

Washington State goes from ocean shore to soggy, fern-thriving woodlands to Sahara-like hills to thriving orchards, badlands, and then rippling grain fields—all in 300 miles. But eventually that visual entertainment gives way to Montana's ranges and its dirt-road towns. It isn't until I near Glacier National Park that I have second thoughts.

I have no generator. Campgrounds are shutting down day by day for the winter. I have Charlie-Girl, my corgi/beagle puppy, with me.

Just short of Glacier, I think about scrapping my northern route and heading south. But the next morning, I scotch that decision. I don't *want* to do interstates. *I might have to ask for help,* I admit to myself—a gas station, church, even a stranger's home for a hook-up. *People are pretty good,* I decide. *I think I'll be okay.*

Montana is a lonely, hauntingly beautiful state. The road takes me around Glacier National Park, with golden-needled larches lacing the hillside and wheat fields in the plains. Campgrounds now are about 350 miles apart. Every evening, I study the Good Sam directory. Hook-ups are electric only. Owners have drained the water pipes for the winter.

Then comes news of a snow flurry. Now I am in North Dakota. The Dakota plains, I know, will go all the way to Minnesota. I am increasingly nervous. Snow raises a tremor within me. *I don't* do *snow—not in an RV.* The next morning I head south not knowing I am aiming right into the edge of a vicious early winter storm.

The flurries begin. Wind whips dry snow across the two-lane road like tendrils of a spider web. I begin a 70-mile stretch of absolute desolation. No towns. No weather channel. No *USA Today*. No cell-phone coverage. I keep telling myself, *It's only dry snow. I can handle this.*

I keep my eye on the odometer. Sixty miles to go. Forty. About every 15 minutes, a car or truck passes me on the other side. No one is going my way. At last I pull onto I-94. Night is falling. I relax. I am finally on the interstate.

ELSIE AT EBB TIDE

~ ~ ~

It happens so fast. A pick-up truck shimmies on the exit ramp. I can't figure out why. The road is bone dry with faint snow blowing across it. Then I see another truck in a ditch. *What's going on?* Then the semi in front of me hits the hazard lights and slows. I try to brake—and can't. I am on ice.

A mist of rain has glazed the entire interstate with the thinnest veneer of black ice. Cars are all over the road. Five are in ditches. I creep along. The only open campground is 12 miles away. I drop into second gear and keep going, mile after mile. It is now pitch black. No moon, no stars, just red taillights, and cars spun weirdly into ditches.

Three miles later I leave the interstate terrified. Conditions are deteriorating by the minute. I begin the ascent up the mountainous hills. For 5 miles, I climb. I see the crest of the mountain coming and realize with a sickening thud I have to go down.

Coming up I have traction, but going down? How can I stop a top-heavy RV? I can see the whole thing—the curve, the inability to stop, the panic, the RV flipping and rolling, myself and my dog inside.

My nerves utterly give out. I pull over frozen with exhaustion and fear. Just in front of me a road leads toward what seems to be a factory. I see a car and gesture wildly. The woman rolls down her window. I sob, "I can't go on. I don't know how to drive on ice. I'm only 3 miles from the campground but I can't get there."

I no longer look like a cocky RVer. She points at the building behind her, "Maybe the security guard can drive you down."

I pound on the locked door of the showroom where a woman is tallying up cash-register receipts. I gaze at her frantically, tears pouring down my cheeks. Alarmed, she hurries to the door and unlocks it.

"I don't *do* ice," I sob. Incoherent, I babble hysterically for several seconds until she extracts the campground information from me. She ripples through the yellow pages, and dials.

"I have a woman here alone who's about 3 miles away from your campground but she's afraid to drive down the hill. Can you come up and drive her RV down for her?"

"Sure," Jim Czywczynski from Happy Holiday Campground says. "I'll get my son and we'll be over in a few minutes.

Out of the swirling snow about 15 minutes later I see a pick-up truck. A kid about 17 years old piles out with his father. The boy, also a Jim, plops himself in the driver's seat, takes my keys, turns over the engine and out we roll onto the treacherous downhill road.

With no sign of concern, he wields the rig down the hill as though it were a dry sunny day, even putting on more speed than I would have dreamed—an incredible 35 mph.

Starting to relax, I say, "Gee, you're good at this. Do you ever skid off, or is it just knowing what to do?"

"Oh," he says, "we all end up in the ditch once in awhile around here. You can't help it with these kind of storms."

By then, luckily, we have turned off into Happy Holidays. Jim drives me to my site and I swear I will not move till summer. That night the winds howl, and I finally get to listen to the forecast: minus nine degrees, 30-mile-per-hour gusts, a freak storm.

Three days later, the pavement is completely dry and I head east.

With my sewage frozen beneath me, I am *so* over being an RVing woman. When I pull off the interstate that night, completely exhausted, I go into the campground gas station. "I'm sure glad you're still open. I need a site." The man looks at me incredulously. "Lady, there's a foot of snow. My camp's closed."

I resort to begging. "All I need is a 3-prong outlet." That's how I end up tethered to the bottom of a towering interstate CITGO sign. I nuzzle right up to the semis—truckers catching a quick nap—like an orphaned pup. A tiny orange cord snakes out of my little brown RV into a socket somewhere in the vast dark universe. Light. Heat. I fall asleep.

My sewage doesn't melt until I get home but I don't care. *I survived.* I wonder if I'll do a major road trip again. Ever.

Caregiver Sandra ~ 2000 ~ It's My Turn

"Sandra," I call my sister. "Mom's doing pretty good at Reddick's, but I want to take an RV trip. It's been so long since I've been away. (Obviously time heals all RV trauma. ...)

"Hey, that's great. Come out here!"

"That's the point. It'd take 2 months to get out there, see a few national parks, and get back. I don't feel comfortable leaving Mom for that long."

I don't mention something else. I feel like I'm being hit with an intuitive brick: *Get Elsie to Sandra. Mom needs to say good-bye to her.*

"Look, Barbara, it's my turn. You've done all the caregiving, but I'm the firstborn. I feel guilty you got stuck with all of this. You should be able to travel if you want. What if we move Mom out here to a group home? When do you want to go?"

"Well, *not* October," I laugh. "Never again. It'd be great to go in August and September, I think. But Sandra, taking care of Mom isn't the easiest thing—even to see her. She's pretty much bedridden. It can be depressing. She's wasting away."

Sandra, like Mom, gravitates towards life, not the *end* of life. I remember her horror when she entered the hospital room thinking Dad had died, only to have the nurse put his hand in hers and say, "He's not gone yet." She shrinks from death, but has an amazing amount of energy for raising children. I, on the other hand, can sit with Mom, somehow facing death with her but am easily overwhelmed by parenting.

Now I find conflicting emotions inside me about Sandra stepping in as caregiver. *What if Mom dies and I am not there?* After all these years, I feel like I have lived with a baby monitor that keeps beeping at me—*my mother's needs, my mother's life*. I can't separate myself from it. When I started her care management, I never realized that caregiving permeates your whole life. *Do I believe anyone can take as good care of Mom as I have?—and* had *I taken that good of care?* I give myself no gold medals. I haven't forgotten all the missed calls: the disastrous testing, the institutionalized neglect in the shiny gleaming Alzheimer's facility, the delay in getting emergency care after the broken hip. *Do any of us ever take good enough care of our loved ones?*

"Barbara," Sandra insists. "It's my turn. Let me research this and see if there's a place near me. I'll get back to you."

"Hey, Sandra, before you do that, let's get Kenna involved. It'd be an interesting experiment. Maybe Mom can help us make the decision. I mean, she can stay right here at Reddick's if she's okay with me not being here for 2 or 3 months. Let's ask *her* and see what happens."

"Okay," Sandra, equally curious, agrees.

Truant Herby ~ 1925 ~ Getting On With Life

After deep-sixing the forklife, Herby leaves town to crew sailing vessels up and down the Atlantic, going as far as Brazil. He sends money to his mother until she dies, and then marries Elsie. One story (told by one of their best friends) goes this way: Elsie handed Herby a hammer, taught him how to drive a nail hard and fast as only a farm girl could. She suggests he take up carpentry. Whatever the truth, after a World War II stint in the Merchant Marines, he did—his strong suit being speed and practicality, not elegance. Bookcases and closets were eyeballed, not measured, crammed not slid, into Capitol Hill houses and various embassies.

July 20

Retired Elsie ~ 1982 ~ Florida Diary

Lousy day. Got battery for typewriter. $25. It still doesn't work & store is closed. Had turkey meatloaf, gravy, baked potatoes, salad, & asparagus—all lousy. Dessert wouldn't even jell.

Grand Tour Barbara ~ 1969 ~ Europe on $5 a Day

"So, let's go to Europe," Bill suggests one afternoon as we hike one of the trails in Shenandoah National Park.

"You're kidding," I shout over my shoulder. I always take the lead climbing up the mountain because, hikers tell me, I pace myself well. *Yeah,* I think, *like a turtle.*

"Well, it'll be our only opportunity. Once you graduate, I get out of the Army, and we get jobs, we'll only have 2 weeks of vacation a year."

"Do we have enough money?" I ask. After 2 years of marriage, I know Bill is famously frugal. Our idea of a date is a large cheese pizza and water. But that's partly because Bill paid for the remainder of my college education.

"We have about $4,000. If we camp, we can live on $5 a day, buy a VW Squareback for $1800, and ship it back. I've checked. It's cheaper than getting the same car here."

~ ~ ~

Six weeks later, we land in London, with two fully loaded duffel bags. One contains a canvas tent complete with center pole and wire frame, backpacking stove, cook gear, and sleeping bags. The other holds our clothes, and two aluminum folding stools, and a shelf-sized piece of plywood cut in half and hinged (that will be attached with a bungee cord to a third stool). Two homemade dollies complete our inventory—built to tote everything.

Our VW is in Germany. We heave our custom-checked duffels onto our dollies, roll out of the London airport, check them onto the train, and settle in for our trip to Wolfsburg.

We get off at Dover. Bill looks to make sure our duffels get transferred while I babble on about the beauty of the English countryside.

We get on the Dover ferry. No bags. We debark in France. No bags. We board our train for Germany. No bags. We get off in Germany. No bags. Two 70-pound Army green duffels are hard to miss.

Now we sit in the station waiting our final departure to Wolfsburg when Bill leaps up—"I left the dollies on the last train!" Off he races, leaving me alone in the darkening night. My body screams for sleep—I look at the train clock. *We've only got 5 minutes.* I want my husband—not some stupid dolly. Meanwhile, he scans cars, makes his best guess, gropes under seats. Bingo! Grabs them and runs.

Four minutes. Three minutes. I watch the second hand sweep by. I hear the incoming train whistle. *Who abandons his wife in a foreign train station to get some stupid dollies?* I don't have to answer. Bill pants to a halt beside me.

We board the train. "I haven't seen our bags once," Bill worries.

"They've gone to Tajikistan," I suggest, still considering the dolly-versus-husband question. When the train stops, the ever-efficient German-crafted luggage door springs open and our two duffel bags tumble out.

Car retrieved, gear stowed, we arrange our Fodor Europe maps: Germany, Denmark, Sweden, Finland, Soviet Union, Poland, Czechoslovakia, East Germany, West Germany, Austria, Switzerland, Italy, France. Home.

~ ~ ~

It's funny what things one remembers from long-ago trips. It seems I retain one fact for every country. The mermaid in Denmark. The shiny modernity of Sweden. The lack of modernity in Finland (plus the gypsies taking saunas with me). Then there's the Soviet Union where every day is scripted by our Intourist visa....

In 1969 the Cold War seems to be coldest. I *believed* in the Cold War. I had gone through the Cuban-missile crisis.

I'd ducked under my school desk. I earnestly assumed our survival depended on winning the race to space. The Soviet Union was an armed-to-the-teeth monster.

Imagine my shock. Rain pours through the roof of Moscow's most prestigious science museum. The art galleries use seatless toilets with pull chains in grimy cubicles. We are told we must "tank up" before leaving Leningrad because there are *no* gas stations between that city and Moscow. The only road between them is a two-lane washboard-jarring route.

I think to myself, *What Cold War? Just bomb the gas stations.*

When we take a wrong fork in the absolute middle of nowhere, we spy a *real* village and for 5 minutes (the time it takes a Soviet officer to apprehend us), we enjoy rural Russia—before being forced back onto our chassis-rattling route.

Nothing prepares us for the architectural decay in Moscow: buildings crumbling, paint peeling, boarded-up mausoleums, eight-lane boulevards absolutely devoid of cars ... and insanely inefficient grocery shopping.

We were warned to buy all our food before crossing the border. We soon learn why.

Venders set up their stalls in one great warehouse. Say you want to buy bacon, milk, bread, potatoes, and some fruit. You stand in the meat line. When your turn comes, you point to what you want. The man writes a number on a slip of paper and hands it to you. You continue to the next vender and the next until you have a handful of slips. You go to the cashier and pay. She stamps each slip. You return to each vender, again standing in line, to retrieve what you purchased. This can easily take 2 hours. We do it once, and then surrender to our stash of kippered herring in tomato sauce.

We meet two American students in a battered VW bus whose windshield blew out when a rock hit it in Moscow. They grin and bear it, even as torrential rain pours into their cab. We next see them in Kiev. "Our VW died. We don't know what to do. We *have* to exit in 2 days, and we can't leave without our VW—Intourist won't let us."

I wondered if Intourist would put you in the gulag for this. The subtleties of a police state hadn't escaped my notice: being stopped on the street; having to prove we had the right to be in Kiev; keeping passports always ready.

"There's *no* VW dealers, no way to get this fixed," the student couple exclaims, stating the obvious. Bringing a VW into the Soviet Union is like inviting Brad Pitt to stand on the street. Crowds instantly gather. Guys peer with unabated envy in the windows. "We're thinking of burying it and making a run for it," they desperately admit.

Sadly I didn't think to get their addresses—gulag or U.S.A.?—so I have no ending but logically assume the Russians didn't want to add two kids to their state welfare system.

While we are in the Soviet Union, we nervously accept restrictions without comment. We play campground hopscotch with three VW vans filled with Harvard students. They *love* Communism until they see women their mother's age hand-painting passing lines on potholed roads. Shocked, they become radically patriotic.

Camping gives us much more freedom than staying at Intourist hotels. We receive less Soviet attention, presumably being unworthy of recruitment. (When we return home, however, an FBI agent materializes at our apartment knowing our *entire* itinerary, and asks if we were "approached." We are suspect. Bill has completed his army tour; I have graduated from college. We meet an FBI profile for spy recruitment.)

When we cross the border into Poland, I feel my muscles unknot.

~ ~ ~

With the Soviet Union behind us, we now experience "satellite Communism," which is considerably more relaxed. We no longer need an itinerary; the Poles know how to party, and soon we are picked up. "Oh, you MUST come to the club," our new Polish friends insist (especially since none of them owns a car). We drive to the countryside. Soon the guys teach Bill and me how to throw back shots of vodka. I never get the hang of it, and am left to put four staggeringly drunk men to bed—on the premises.

Which brings us, a bit drunkenly, to the 20th of July.

ELSIE AT EBB TIDE

~ ~ ~

"You *must* come with me," one of the young men who hangs around the campground insists. "The Moon," he keeps saying. "The Moon."

Traveling for over 6 weeks now, we are completely clueless as to the imminent landing on the Moon. Of course we *know* about Apollo—but not exact dates. Now he insists we follow him.

The campground abuts a crowded neighborhood of aging apartment buildings. "COME! COME!" he insists. "HURRY!" Soon we are running toward a dingy, yellow-painted apartment building and rushed indoors.

"I got them," he announces proudly to his parents who are glued to a small black-and-white TV with rabbit ears. "In about 20 minutes, your astronaut will step onto the Moon," our Polish friend proudly tells us.

Bill and I gaze around the apartment. We see no kitchen. "Oh," he gestures toward a wall, "this apartment was divided into two living spaces. "We got the bathtub; they got the kitchen sink. So we have to get all our water, and wash our dishes, in the tub. We use a hot plate for cooking."

I turn to Bill in utter amazement, immediately wondering who got the toilet, if anyone. I was just about to ask when our hosts shushed us.

Six thousand miles from the United States and 250,000 from the Moon, in a cramped Polish apartment, we watch Neil Armstrong step onto the Moon.

I hear Houston Control—achingly close in the background—drowned out by a Polish translation.

I watch the grainy screen, having no idea that Mom, 4 days earlier, watched Apollo 11 blast off.

Kenna and Elsie ~ 2000 ~ How About Seattle?

"Kenna, I'm worn out," I admit. "I just want to get away for 2 to 3 months.

"I've talked to Sandra about this. I was trying to come up with some options. Sandra decided she'd like to step in if we could get Mom to the West Coast. She'd put her in a group home near her."

"Well, *that* would be a big step for your mother," Kenna noncommittally answers.

"You know," I add, "I would never tell Sandra this, but I keep having this feeling that Mom *needs* to be with her—to make sure Sandra's okay before she leaves." "Anyway," I continue, "we've come up with three choices. We want you to ask Mom which she prefers.

"She can stay at Reddick's, but she won't see me for 2 or 3 months. Or she can move to Seattle to be near Sandra. Or (this the surprise choice) she can move back to her Florida home and Hawa will take care of her."

"I thought Hawa was still in school," Kenna interrupts.

"No, she's taking a break to earn more money."

"Ohh!" Kenna exclaims. "That's the choice *I* would make. Florida and all that sunshine."

I don't tell Kenna I'm absolutely certain Mom will *not* pick that option. She'll want to be near one of her daughters. But let's see what Mom thinks....

~ ~ ~

<u>Elsie</u>: *Hi, Kenna. I know who you are. I feel you.*

<u>Kenna</u>: Well, Elsie, Barbara is going to be away for 2 to 3 months and she is making plans for you. She has some ideas and wants you to decide.

ELSIE AT EBB TIDE

So here are your options: You can stay where you are, but you won't be seeing Barbara for a long time. You can go to a group home in Seattle to be near Sandra. Or you can go back to your own home in Florida and Hawa will take care of you.

Elsie: *I don't like that. My daughters wouldn't be there. I don't want to move.*

Kenna: But if you stay here, you will be alone for 2 months.

Elsie: *I don't like that.*

Kenna: You don't want to be alone?

Elsie: *No. I like having people around. It's more exciting than living alone.*

Kenna: Well, here are two other options. Seattle near Sandra ...

Elsie: *Or ... ?*

Kenna: You can go to Florida and stay with Hawa and Sandra and Barbara will visit when they can. You would be alone with Hawa. She would take good care of you.

Elsie: *I like Hawa.*

Kenna: She likes you. It was her idea to take care of you in Florida.

Elsie: *I like Florida.*

Kenna: When Barbara gets back, you could live near her again, but it might be in a new place [not the Reddick's Group Home].

Elsie: *Why can't Barbara see me now?*

Kenna: She's traveling.

Elsie: *Oh.*

Kenna: Barbara needs to travel and do some new things.

Elsie: *Barbara's always doing new things, isn't she?*

Kenna: Yes, I guess she is. She works hard to take care of you.

Elsie: *I know. I'm thankful.*

Kenna: Well, Elsie, what's it going to be?

Elsie: *I don't want to be away from my daughters.*

Kenna: I understand. Do you think you want to go to Seattle?

Elsie: Seattle sounds like it's near the sea. Have I been there before? I like to be practical. I also want to be thrifty. How practical is this? Barbara is the planner. What does she think?

Kenna: I don't know. Barbara wants you to decide.

Elsie: And Sandra would visit and play music? I like to dance. I miss dancing. I dance in my dreams around and around. I could dance all night but I get tired.

Kenna: I don't know, but Sandra would visit.

Elsie: Well, let's go. [Kenna "sees" her kicking up her legs in excitement.]

Kenna: Are you sure? You could be with Hawa.

Elsie: She's not my daughter.

Kenna: I know. Sandra's children could visit you too sometimes.

Elsie: I'd like that. When would we go?

Kenna: If you move, it will be by August.

Elsie: Absolutely meaningless to me.

Kenna: Well, soon. I'll tell Barbara what you said and I guess you'll go to Seattle unless you change your mind.

Elsie: I'd like my family to be near me. I'm old, aren't I? How old am I?

Kenna: Well, you're in your eighties.

Elsie: Do you have to go?

Kenna: Yes, but I'll be back.

~ ~ ~

Does Mom truly participate in the decision to move to Seattle? Frankly, I don't know. She doesn't remember Seattle, and Sandra doesn't play the piano or sing. But she adamantly refuses the Florida option. She knows Hawa is not her daughter. She tags me correctly as *always doing new things* and being *the planner*.

As I believed, she clearly states *I do not want to be away from my daughters,* later adding, *I'd like my family near me.*

And then there's the trademark Elsie: *I like to dance ... I dance in my dreams.* And ever ready for adventure, she kicks up her legs and uses the phrase I've heard her say so often, *Let's go!*

But in no way does Mom express an end-of-life *need* to be with Sandra. My strong intuitive sense might be pure imagination. But of course, we didn't ask her *that* question and wouldn't know the answer until a psychic asks her, years later, when she is on the other side. ...

Mother Sandra ~ 1981 ~ Summertime Snow

"Hey, come with me!" she says to her four sons with all the enthusiasm of a woman who wears mono-colored clothes to work and tans rancid goats. "We're going to have a snowstorm," she announces.

"But it's JULY, Mom!" Donovan protests.

"Yeah, well, look what Christie gave us," Sandra holds up an oversized carton of powdered milk. I've got *four* of these—one for each of you.

"How did she get it?" Donovan-the-analyst persists.

Sandra decides the kids didn't need to know that Christie, newly divorced with two children, needs food stamps and takes advantage of the U.S. Government surplus-food-distribution program—in this case, powdered milk. Considering it a staple, she nabbed four cartons.

"It doesn't dissolve," she tells Sandra in despair. "It's CRAP."

If *anyone* can make milk out of this stuff, Sandra can. After all, she's an engineer. What can be so hard about dissolving powdered milk? But when cold, lukewarm, warm, and finally boiling water fail to transform the powder into milk, she gives up.

"All I get is lumpy blobs. Do you want it back, Christie?"

"Hell, no," Christie snaps over the phone. "Throw it out!"

So now Sandra's saddled with several pounds of undissolvable powdered milk and four bored sons—hence the inspiration for a snow party.

Sensing white blizzards of fun, the kids finally charge out the door enthusiastically hoping presents will be buried beneath.

By now, Sandra has sawed through all the tops with her box cutter and handed one each to Chad, Donovan, and Mitch. Infant Kier is mercifully saved ... for the moment. They start dumping it on the deck, still glistening with morning dew.

Soon the kids are constructing roads, building highways, pushing their dump trucks, matchbox cars, trains through the snow. Intersections are constructed with dew-congealed milk, hills mounded up, traffic tickets given. The kids are having an absolutely great time.

"Wow," Chad exclaims. "This is COOL. It's like Christmas in July." And on they go until Mitch begins to cry. "MY EYES WON'T OPEN," he is screaming.

Sandra rushes over and sure enough, his lashes are covered (laden) with milk powder. The tears have turned the milk into lactose glue. Now all the kids are screaming that their eyes are sealed shut.

A little bit worried (after all not even boiling water dissolved it), Sandra is wondering if she'll be carting four kids to the emergency room trying to explain why she was emptying boxes of powdered milk on her deck.

She picks up Mitch, throws him clothes and all in the tub, turns on the spigot and begins rubbing and rubbing and rubbing his eyes ignoring his howling protests. She's picking at it with her fingernails, slowly scraping it off. Meanwhile, Chad, Donovan, and Kier continue to howl, tears running down their milk-caked faces.

Finally the last kid has been de-dairyed and she's toweling them off.

"Mom," Chad glares at her red-eyed, "I don't ever want Christmas in July *again*."

ELSIE AT EBB TIDE

Injured Barbara ~ 2002 ~ Psychic Surprises

"Don't move," the paramedic tells me. The vacation rental car lays crushed against a tree. Shattered windshield glass and fresh dirt cover me.

Everything had gone fine till we left Chicago. We visited Anita's family, strolled city streets admiring architecture, headed north, and ended up in an accident, more bruised than hurt. For safety reasons, I was taken out on a backboard; Sister Anita, though seriously shaken, walked away.

At the hospital, I learn I've received a concussion, bruised ribs, and a broken toe. Sister Anita suffered severe bruising. I lay on the emergency-room bed shivering from shock as I remember the weird foreboding I'd felt for months. *Something would disrupt my life and I wouldn't be able to stop it.* I couldn't dispel the feeling, but now it's completely gone. If I weren't so disoriented, I'd be mad because I don't believe in premonition, yet it seems to have happened despite my disbelief.

Discharged from the hospital and now in the hotel room, I refuse to think my life is on some fixed trajectory. I decide to have a tête-à-tête with ... *what? Who?*

I open up the desk drawer, find paper and a pen, and sit in the hotel chair unrepentantly angry yet strangely open. *Well, why did this accident happen?* I ask.

To my complete shock, a "conversation" begins....

I honestly cannot remember (nor did I write down) what transpired, but I was shown *myself* in a *different* way. It was as though I was shown *two* ways of communicating. In the first, my mind pondered things. It asked questions. It sought rational answers. It had to see to believe. But now that mind became silent—as though it hardly existed.

I discover another *me* exists, one that is far more open, curious, and receptive. *This* me poses questions. *Why did this happen?* Immediately I feel answers *flowing* into my consciousness. While I can't logically make sense of it or even justify it, the answers calm me in some deep, soul-satisfying way.

It was time, I am told, for this portal, this way of communication, to open. *It could have happened much easier than an accident—but I would have resisted.*

That explains some of the accident's strangeness. As the car rolled, I felt as though Pillsbury doughboys padded my body. Then there was the toy electronic violin....

I'd brought it along as a gift to be given to someone on the trip. It played Mozart when you touched the tiny bow to the strings, one note for each tap. It also had a recessed button that performed an entire selection. When the crash began, the violin began to play—ending its selection precisely when we slammed into a tree.

I could never remember the accident (the worst of my life) with fear, because of that violin. Always, I hear that crazy toy playing Mozart as I crashed through the air.

Since that day in the hotel, I often sit with a notebook, asking questions, receiving answers. This soul communication—perhaps connecting with either my own higher soul and/or guides who agree to help me—began that day and continues to this.

July 26

Retired Elsie ~ 1982 ~ Florida Diary

Well, typewriter is "Kaput." Belt can't be replaced locally. Herby had a rubber band but didn't know if it would work. But voila! He has fixed it. A modern miracle!

Wartime Elsie ~ 1944 ~
Brother Swante Missing in Action

"Swante's been shot down somewhere over Yugoslavia," Elsie hears her sister-in-law Mayme's tremulous voice over the phone.

"When?" Elsie holds the phone motionless.

"I don't know the details yet. I'll let you know."

~ ~ ~

Is he alive? Elsie puts the phone down, feeling sick with worry.

Her only brother, the third-born child, the last one born while her father was still alive, has crashed behind enemy lines. *What will Mayme, alone with their infant Patty, do?*

Then she thinks of Herby on a ship in the north Atlantic, protecting war-supply transport. *Will he survive?*

Swante and Mayme

~ ~ ~

We took off from our base at Foggia Airfield in southern Italy to bomb the German fighter airfields. We thought it would be a milk run but it was our last mission. A burst of flak knocked out our two right engines.

I was in the waist gunner's position. Antiaircraft shells were exploding all around us. Shrapnel hit my left arm. I noticed holes in my flight jacket. The shrapnel broke my arm.

I opened the door to the bomb bay. A strong smell of gas hit me. I returned to waist window. The three gunners were huddled on top of the escape hatch with no earphones on. It could be dangerous to send a message; a spark of electricity could cause an explosion. I put my headset on. The copilot was yelling "Everybody bail out!" I yelled to the guys but they didn't move. I threw down the earphones and jumped out the waist window, thinking the other gunners would follow, which they did.

The wind was roaring as I tumbled, seeing sky, ground, sky. I thought we were pretty close to the ground so I counted to 5 slowly and 6, 7, 8, 9, 10 real fast. I pulled the rip cord, and when the chute opened all was still. I saw our bomber hit and burn. The ground came up fast and when I landed it knocked me out.

Caregiver Barbara ~ 2000 ~ Letting Go

When Mom first came into my home, if anything bad happened to her, I would have taken her to the hospital in a New York minute. I would have called 911 and had her whisked away—and cured.

Then I slowly realized her body had passed a portal. I posted a DO NOT RESUSCITATE order on the front door. Every bone in her rib cage would break with the slightest pressure. My new mantra became *over my dead body will she experience pain*. I began to let her lead; I learned to follow....

I let go of the retirement home in Florida.

I let go of the Alzheimer's facility in Maryland.

I let go of the group home.

I let go of resuscitation.

As she lets go, I let go.

I've let go of her laughter, her naughty playful eyes.

I've let go of her wakefulness.

I've let go of her coherence, and her saying I am beautiful.

Wherever she goes, I follow, fascinated.

ELSIE AT EBB TIDE

If she goes into deep sleep, a slumber beyond slumber. I stand at her bedside and stare at her, wondering *where are you now?*

She leads, as she always has as a mother.

And I, as always a daughter, follow.

BARBARA ERAKKO

August

Left: Elsie at Work, Gift Unit, Office of Chief of Protocol
Right: Personally Signed Photo of Kennedys

Life is a Lived Event

August 5

Retired Elsie ~ 1990 ~ First Time for Everything

"Barbara," Mom calls me on the phone. "I went to another funeral yesterday."

"Anybody I know?" I ask.

"No. He's Canadian. I sat with a close friend of the widow and she started telling me how unhappy the widow was with the presiding minister. She didn't like this and she didn't like that. Finally I asked, "Well, where did her husband *used* to go to church?"

"Oh," she said, "this is the first time."

Wartime Elsie ~ 1944 ~ Swante Missing in Action

"Herby," Elsie writes in her weekly letter to her husband, somewhere in the north Atlantic protecting supply ships, "Swante got shot down in Yugoslavia. That's all we know. He's been declared missing in action." Writing makes it more real—*Is he alive?*

~ ~ ~

When I came to, I found myself surrounded by white nylon. The chute collapsed on top of me. I got the parachute clips off but couldn't get the harness off because of my broken arm, so I hid the chute under some bushes and started walking toward a farmhouse I had seen from the air.

When I got there, an old couple and teenage girl started gesturing toward a certain direction yelling *Tedeschi, Tedeschi!* I soon learn that means *Germans!* in Italian. They wanted me to leave, but I insisted they help me get off my harness. They wrapped a cloth around my bleeding arm, and I took off across the field towards the woods.

I saw an old man with a black patch over one eye tending sheep. He came running at me and pulled a pistol. I found out his intention was not to shoot but guard me as he led me into the woods to hide.

That evening eight Italian underground men working with the Yugoslavian Partisans came after dark and put antiseptic on my arm and bandaged it. They hid me for 3 days in a camouflaged hole in the ground, just big enough to hold me and a guerrilla who has a gunshot leg. He has gangrene in his leg. The stench is overpowering. We have no food, only a little water.

Career Elsie ~ 1971 ~
Assassination is *Not* a Word in Protocol

One year when the alumni from Finlayson High School schedule their reunion for August, they decide to ask Elsie to share some of her memories as Protocol Officer. After describing the basic inner workings of the Office, she recounts Tito's visit:

"When President Tito of Yugoslavia visited the United States, we began the tour as usual with a trip to New York City. We had a very sensitive security problem...."

~ ~ ~

"Mrs. Nurmi, wake up." Someone bangs on her four-star hotel room. "WAKE UP!"

Instantly alert (Protocol Officers never fully fall asleep on the job), Elsie throws on her robe and hurries to the door. "What is it?" she peeks out at one of the State Department staff.

"Please get dressed. There's been an assassination attempt on Tito."

"What?" Elsie feels all the color draining from her face. Coming out of a fog of sleep, she asks, "Who?"

"I don't know, but they want you to get dressed and go to the presidential suite right away."

She throws on yesterday's clothes. When she enters the room, it is filled with thick smoke, and body-to-body people including the chief of police of New York City. Sitting on the sofa is a dark-haired young man in handcuffs ... the would-be assassin.

She spends the next few hours taking notes for the State Department. Meanwhile a movie star tries to get off the elevator. Security shoves him back. "Get off on ANY floor but THIS one."

The next morning the delegation heads for Tuxedo Park, New York. Elsie goes to the underground garage. The driver warns her, "We're hitting the exit ramp hard. Hold on." (Security wants a tight formation around Tito's motorcade.) They take off. Elsie hears a piercing siren and hits the deck on all fours.

Looking up from her speech, she admits to the Finlayson alumni, "I have a strong instinct for survival."

The security officer turns around from the front seat, laughing. "That's the New York City police, Elsie. You can get up off the floor."

~ ~ ~

Tuxedo Park, one hour northwest of New York City, probably gets its name for the simplest of reasons—you have to be wealthy enough to own a tux. Living in this enclosed enclave of Colgates, Morgans, and Astors, Emily Post actually wrote her *Blue Book of Etiquette* based on manners within its stone gates.

Beleaguered by death threats, *this* delegation is rapidly adding gray hairs beneath Elsie's perfectly coiffed wig. But the climax to the trip makes everything else seem easy. Aboard Air Force Two, and asleep in one of the berths, once again she is rudely awakened.

"Mrs. Nurmi," the steward knocks on her door. "Wake up."

Shrugging herself awake, she opens the door, not even bothering to put on a bathrobe. Life has definitely gotten casual. "Yes?"

"The rest of President Tito's trip has been canceled. You're to give a press conference right now."

"I can't do *that*," Elsie protests. "I've never given a press conference."

"You're the top-ranking officer here. The White House is going to read it to you over the phone. You don't have any time to dress. We're taking off in 10 minutes. Grab your bathrobe."

So once again, Elsie picks up her notepad and shivering almost uncontrollably with nervousness, takes down verbatim what she is to tell the press corps, which had been asked to assemble beneath the wing of Air Force Two. It is so dark she can't see what she has written.

Someone (she never knows who) turns on a flashlight and holds it over her notebook. Steeling her voice, she begins to read her shorthand, "I must inform you ..."

It is Elsie's first, and happily her last, press conference. Ten minutes later they are in the air en route to Andrews Air Force Base where President Tito and his delegation will be transferred to another plane to return to Yugoslavia. The United States has accomplished the first and most important rule of protocol—never allow your guest to be assassinated.

~ ~ ~

Decades have passed. Records have been unsealed. According to Serbian Nicola Kavaja (later imprisoned for hijacking a plane), the CIA funded several attempts to assassinate President Tito. While the Waldorf attempt appears to have been an angry amateur, Kavaja was hired to assassinate Tito while he walked the grounds of Camp David when meeting with President Nixon. Fortunately for Tito, he never stepped outside.

Caregiver Barbara ~ 2000 ~ Making Final Plans

"I think everything's set, Sandra," I tell her on our now-daily telephone calls. "I've talked to Barbara Reddick. She's going to cut back on Mom's food the day before she travels. She'll be about 10 hours in the same incontinence diaper."

"Jeez, I didn't even think of that."

"Me neither." In spite of myself I laugh. I'm envisioning the people who've paid enormous money to not be with the riffraff. Here comes Elsie with her stinky diaper. "Well, the group home promised they'd use the thickest one and put it on pretty tight."

"I'm glad Hawa is going with you," Sandra admits. "You'd freak out."

True. I could easily envision countless disasters. *What if she struggles against the seatbelt? What if she does stink?* I am glad Hawa agreed to go. *Let all those first-class passengers glare at Mom* (I am, at this moment, a heartless caregiver.) I've booked two first-class tickets for Mom and Hawa, and a coach seat for myself.

"I'm picking out the clothes that will be useful in Seattle," I tell Sandra.

I feel a sadness wash over me but don't share that. I cannot believe, after all these years, I won't be the one taking care of Mom.

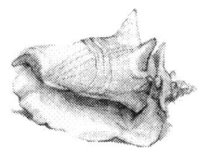

Elsie and Kenna ~ 2000 ~ Takeoff Time!

<u>Kenna</u>: Do you know what's going to be happening, Elsie?

<u>Elsie</u>: *Of course I know. Does Barbara think I am an old fuddy-duddy?*

<u>Kenna</u>: So you understand?

<u>Elsie</u>: *Yes, I'm going to see Sandra.*

<u>Kenna</u>: Yes, you're *flying* to see Sandra.

<u>Elsie</u>: *Ahhh, I always loved to fly, didn't I? Well, I'm ready!*

<u>Kenna</u>: Okay, you leave in about a week.

<u>Elsie</u>: *Are you coming?*

Kenna: No, but I will visit you there like I do now.

Elsie: *People will be coming to say good-bye, won't they?*

Kenna: Yes.

Elsie: *I don't like good-byes.*

Kenna: Well, just in case they don't see you again.

Elsie: *I understand.*

Caregiver Barbara ~ 1994 ~ Parking-Lot Striptease

In the early years of the disease, Mom and I often go out together. After our Finland trip, I trust Mom to stay put. One day I pull into the Barnes & Noble parking lot and ask her, "Do you want to go in?"

"No, you go. I'll stay here."

I roll down the window and leave her in the passenger seat. "I'll only be a few minutes, Mom," I tell her (and in my heart, I believe it).

Irresistibly drawn from shiny book cover to book cover, aisle to aisle, I am trying to hurry but the store has a magnetic grip on me. I don't exactly *lose* track of time; I expand it to meet my own idea of what 15 minutes *might* be.

Once in Seattle's Pike Place Market with my sister and our four kids in tow, I discovered a used bookstore. I totally forgot I even *had* a family.

"We've decided to charge you a nickel a minute," my sister interrupted my reverie.

"What?" I looked at her absent-mindedly, holding a hardback book on the history of South America.

"Starting now," she added, and my wicked sister of the west marched out with our munchkins.

How dare she! I thought. Then I realized it was a cheap price for my addiction. I emerged holding three books; they licked their loot in the form of ice cream cones.

Now in Barnes & Noble, after about 20 minutes, two books happily purchased, I guiltily run back to my mother.

She has opened the door to let the breeze in. I see her white cotton *bra* cupping her sagging breasts emerging as she unbuttons her blouse.

"MOM," I yell, running across the parking lot, "WHAT are you DOING?"

"I was getting hot, Barbara, so I decided to take this off."

In the driver's seat lies her blue cotton sweater, her checkered blouse about to become the next castoff.

If I'd stayed to buy a third book, the bra would have landed on the pile.

Eventually my rules for dining with Elsie change. I look for corner tables, seating Mom with her back to the wall. In Elsie's world, which includes frequent bouts of intestinal gas, her solution is to slide her elastic pants down.

After my initial horror, I decide it is a reasonable solution. Why hadn't I thought of that?

I learn to enjoy Mom's twists and turns, her astonishing creativity, her whacky solutions—so uncivilized, so unprotocol-like. So fun!

~ ~ ~

Other friends face similar situations. My neighbor Mary Jae's increasingly demented mother learned from Dr. Oz the Dollar Store had a paste that took years off aging skin. She demanded her daughter take her.

And what, precisely, was this paste? Pumpkin pie filling, generic lotion, exfoliating mitts, and ginseng tea. Did Dollar Store have the ingredients? No. Was the store mobbed, as her mother worried? No. They got "Dr. Vozzz's" stuff at Walmart.

And Mary Jae decided to take a contract out on the doctor.

August 12

Baby Sandra ~ 1945 ~ Radiant Birth

Sandra believes she was conceived on New Year's Eve. With Dad in the Merchant Marines, and World War II not yet over, her conception probably occurred between two sex-deprived, magnetically attracted adults. After all, how could they know the war was about to end. Yet 3 days after Sandra is born, Japan surrenders and World War II is over. So perhaps one could say that she is bookended by two very good events—*love* and *peace*.

At any rate, in the 1940s, fathers never attended deliveries. Mom had to face it alone. She had done that once before, with terrifying results.

~ ~ ~

"I think I'd better go home," Elsie hands her coffee cup to Mim and slowly stands up, very heavy with twins and near her delivery date.

"Let me walk you down the steps," Mim offers and they make their way to the door.

As Elsie starts down from the second-story apartment, she feels a horrible cramping. Had Mim not been holding her, she would have fallen. Mim eases her to the step.

"Elsie," Mim says, trying to sound calm, "I'm going to get Doris." Doris, a registered nurse, lives just a couple of houses up the street. In minutes, she is leaning over Elsie, taking her pulse, asking questions.

"You need to go to the hospital, Elsie. I'm calling an ambulance."

"Mim," Elsie looks scared. "Get to Herby. Let him know the babies are coming now."

"I promise," Mim reassures her and Elsie quickly tells her how to reach him. "He's stationed in upstate New York."

"We'll telegraph him right away Elsie," Mim promises.

ELSIE AT EBB TIDE

Fifteen minutes later, she disappears in an ambulance, sirens wailing. She is rushed to the nearby Seventh-Day Adventist Hospital. The babies, if born today, will be almost full term. They should be okay. But she's not feeling any movement....

Mim calls her husband Ed and together they send an emergency telegram to Herby. A few hours later they get one back—he's been given emergency leave and he's catching the next train. Ed plans to meet him at Union Station in D.C. Now they head for the hospital to be with Elsie.

When they enter her room, they are shocked by what they see. Elsie looks as pale as death. Mim rushes to her side. "What's the matter, Elsie? Are the babies okay?"

"They're dead."

An awful silence falls over the room. Tears run down Mim's face. Elsie seems in shock. The nurse walks in. "We have to get you ready, Mrs. Nurmi," she says as gently as she can. Mim and Ed, knowing the babies must be removed, sit in the waiting room. Mim wonders out loud, "I don't know how she'll handle this. Herby gone. The babies gone. I just don't know."

"I'll get Herby here as fast as I can," Ed promises and heads to D.C. to wait for the train. After Elsie gets out of surgery, Mim sits with her—unsure of what to say. Elsie says nothing at all.

~ ~ ~

Herby jumps off the train just as it stops. Ed stands in front of him. "They're gone," he tells him. "They died inside her."

Aghast, Herby says, "I've got to get to her."

"I know. Let's go. The car is outside."

Thirty minutes later, they arrive. The front door to the hospital is *locked*. Ed sees a security guard. "How are we supposed to get into the hospital?" The guard tells them, "Not until tomorrow morning. It's locked for the night."

"What the HELL?" Herby hollers.

"Come ON," Ed hisses—seeing Herby about to explode. "We'll find a way in." They leave the guard and begin casing it, window by window, door by door until they find one open. Ed tells him where to find Elsie. "I'll be here waiting."

"Go home, Eddie. I'm staying."

~ ~ ~

Sandra and I didn't even know Mom ever bore twins. My sister was well into adulthood when Mim told her the story, and then Sandra told me. "It was the only time I saw your mother depressed," Mim told her, "really depressed. She couldn't snap herself out of it."

When I asked Mom about it, she admitted it got to the point where she couldn't function.

Her typing desk faced a wall. It was like looking at a dead end, at nothing. Her friend Helmi, who once had seduced her to go to New York City, called. Listening to Elsie's monotone voice, she said, "Come to Florida."

She did. She bought a train ticket. Her seat passenger happened to be a minister. All the way down, Elsie cried. He listened. She spent a week with Helmi. When she returned, she picked up the pieces of her life and went on.

~ ~ ~

Now she is about to give birth again. Once again, she is alone. The nurse checks on her, then leaves.

"Please," Elsie pleads with her. "I need you to stay with me." But the nurse dismisses it, "Oh, you're doing *fine*, Mrs. Nurmi. And she leaves the room.

Elsie takes the side railing off the bed and throws it on the floor. It makes a horrendous crash—metal on linoleum. The nurse comes rushing in. "What have you DONE?"

"I'll keep doing it until you stay."

Never before (and probably rarely since) would Elsie be so obstreperous. The nurse gives up, pulls up a chair, and says, "Okay, here I am. I'm not going anywhere." Elsie grips her hand and begins to calm down.

And the *radiant one*—the sunny Sandra—enters the world at 8:34 a.m. Although not allowed in during delivery, this time Herby paces the waiting room. When he finally leaves Elsie and their newborn at Garfield Hospital, it's 2 a.m. The J-6 Takoma bus driver basically has no customers, so, what the heck, he drives the bus to a bar. They go in for a celebratory drink. He asks around, finds a cigar and hands it to Herby. As they leave, he asks, "So where do you live?" Then he drives Herby home.

When Elsie holds Sandra in those beginning months of life, even the photographs capture the love pouring out of her into this little sunbeam. Sandra soaks it up. From the very beginning, she *adores* this mother. And she wants to be adored.

Elsie's only regret (and given the magnitude of things, it constitutes a minor one) is the fact she misses the spontaneous block party celebrating Japan's surrender.

She will stay in the hospital for a full 10 days. She's already decided to bottle-feed Sandra, the *preferred* way of the day. While she recovers, the nurses feed her daughter. Only occasionally will she cradle her newborn. After all, she must get her rest.

So while she lies, somewhat bored, in the hospital bed, Herby embarks on making potato salad. He can't find a container large enough. Then he spies the wringer washing machine and peers inside. *Looks big enough*, he decides, and begins boiling dozens of potatoes.

Maybe the guests find eating potato salad out of a wringer washer (which after all laundered stinky socks, dirty underwear, carpenter-grimed clothing) a bit unnerving. At any rate, a great deal of the salad remains.

Herby calls his favorite seafood restaurant, Fred & Harry's. "Hey," he asks, "do you want some potato salad?" "Sure," they answer—and in the days before FDA, food regulation, kitchen sanitary standards, laws to imprison you—he drives the potato salad over in his pick-up truck.

Soon, unsuspecting restaurant customers are gobbling down Herby's *potato-a-la-wringer salad*.

~ ~ ~

Birthdays after Sandra's birth stick to a routine: favorite meal, presents, cake.

Sandra always chooses spaghetti made by a Portuguese cook on Dad's Merchant Marine vessel. Typical gifts include baseball bats, balls, mitts, badminton rackets, crochet sets, skates—anything outdoor. And a cake.

One year, when Sandra is 4 and I am 2, inventive Mom decides to have a two-for-one birthday. She neatly counts the days between July 6 and August 12, and creates a *new* day—July 24—to be *shared* by Sandra and me.

The two-layer cake has a chocolate half for me and a vanilla half for Sandra. Even the icing is divided. It has two candles (so we wouldn't argue over who has the most), and it sits on our play table in the yard.

ELSIE AT EBB TIDE

There's even a photo of us standing proudly in front of our cake, too dumb to know we've each received a half-birthday.

Confused Elsie ~ 2000 ~ Seattle, First Class

I feel my skin crawling with anxiety. Hawa and I are at the Reddick Group Home. Mom, unaware she's about to fly across country, lays contentedly in her bed. Barbara Reddick's prepared her, internally and externally, as best she can. Now we're waiting for the private ambulance to arrive. Ten o'clock has come and gone. *What if they don't get here in time? What if they're lost?* My mind is going crazy.

"Relax," Hawa tells me. "They'll be here." Distrustful, I call the company. It turns out the crew thinks they're to arrive at 10:30. They're sitting in a parking lot a couple of miles away, doing nothing. "Get them HERE NOW!" I scream into the phone.

At 10:15 a.m. they pull up to the door. They deftly maneuver Mom onto the ambulance stretcher and wheel her out the door. Her adventure is about to begin.

Hawa, Barbara Reddick, and I jump into my car. We know the shortest route to the Baltimore–Washington International Airport and assume the ambulance does too. As I speed down the road, I look in my rearview mirror. "My god," I holler with anger. "They're going the wrong way! That's the slowest route. It's filled with traffic lights."

We're going to miss the flight, I inwardly panic. We're already running late; we timed everything so there'd be no wait time at the airport; now the ambulance will be at least an additional 15 minutes late. *This won't work,* I am thinking, feeling absolutely hopeless.

We arrive at the airport. I throw the keys to Barbara Reddick who will take the car back.

"Good luck, girls," she shifts into drive. "Barbara, relax. They'll get here." To Hawa she whispers, "Call me if you miss the flight."

Hawa and I position ourselves in front of the Northwest Airlines entrance. Ten minutes later, the ambulance pulls to the curb. Now furious at the delays, I glare at the driver. "We may miss the flight."

Finally realizing they are in trouble, the crew yanks Elsie out and all of us are flying down the corridor toward Gate 28. "How do we get through security?" the ambulance driver hollers. "They'll wand her," I yell over my shoulder.

Grateful I had driven to the airport a week earlier to make sure our plan would work, Mom, the ambulance staff, Hawa, and I are all quickly wand-checked. We set off at a run again. I look at my watch and begin to slow down. We've got 20 minutes. We're going to make the flight.

Now I begin to see the craziness of what we're doing. I imagine myself—not as the daughter taking her advanced Alzheimer's mother to the airplane—but as another passenger in the airport.

They are not watching this diminutive woman being whisked *out* of the airport because of a medical emergency, but rolled *into* it. At Gate 28, what will fellow travelers think? *Well,* I tell myself, *I won't ask.*

Early boarding has already started. The crew rolls Mom onto the boarding ramp. They get the stretcher as close to her first-class seat as possible, and gently lift and lower her into 4A. Hawa settles down in the aisle seat. Elsie looks around in wide-eyed excitement. I walk back to coach. Thirty minutes later we are cleared for takeoff and make our steep ascent. I wonder if Mom is enjoying her last ride.

Sleep deprived and anxious, at last I start to relax.

Hawa and the first-class stewardess can take care of Elsie. Soon breakfast is served. I look at the brownish hash-and-egg mash. The stewardess whispers, "What do you think it is?" "Glop," I decide. We laugh. After they've cleared the trays, I walk into first class to check on Mom.

Elsie still looks wide awake. She's babbling away, but not loudly. The other passengers politely ignore what is happening. "How's it going, Hawa?" I ask. "Okey dokey," she replies with a huge grin. "We had eggs Benedict for breakfast, orange juice, and Belgian waffles with strawberries and whipped cream. They even asked if we wanted champagne." Then Hawa lifts up Elsie's empty Ensure can and I laugh.

"Well, I had glop. Nobody knew what to call it." The stewardess, who has charitably looked the other way, finally intercedes and ushers me back to my cramped coach seat with its non-amenities. We have 4 hours to go.

~ ~ ~

Two hours from arrival, Sandra, Ed, Kier, Mitch, and Chad pile into two cars. Ed and Sandra drive the Elsie-ready van with a mattress laid out in the back complete with blankets and pillows. They live over an hour away from Sea-Tac Airport. Everyone figures Mom will be exhausted. Now they wait at the gate for our arrival. There'll be no ambulance, stretcher, or crew to get her out of the plane. Inventively, Ed brings some extra blankets he and the boys can use to carry her off.

After everyone else deboards, only Hawa, a still-excited Elsie, and I remain with the cockpit crew and stewardesses. We all stare a bit dubiously at Elsie. Will she submit to "the blanket"? Ed and Chad walk down the aisle. "Elsie," Ed begins in his quiet matter-of-fact voice, "We're going to lift you onto this blanket so you can get off the airplane."

She grins, her hands doing their usual flapping, and says, "Okay."

They unbuckle her seatbelt, hoist her onto the blanket-bed, and quickly maneuver her off the plane onto the wheelchair. And out she rolls—queen of the airlines—into a sea of family faces, helium balloons, and a stuffed bear.

"Well," I hug Sandra, "happy birthday to *you*. Here's your birthday present." And Elsie obligingly grins.

It seems a miracle. Somehow Mom has made one last flight, and Hawa and I feel she knows it. "She kept looking out the window. I think she knew we were flying," Hawa tells Sandra and me. Of course, we'll never know.

Soon Elsie lies on her temporary bed as we drive to Stephanie's group home, a couple of miles from Sandra's work. She settles in—and sleeps for 2 days.

August 18

Wartime Elsie ~ 1944 ~ Swante Missing in Action

"Have you gotten any information from the Air Force about Swante?" Elsie asks Mayme over the phone.

"The other bombers say they saw some parachutes—not enough for the whole crew, but some bailed out in time."

"Swante's quick and smart. He'd have gotten out if he could."

~ ~ ~

I developed a high fever. My ears would roar. I'd pass out sometimes and come to wringing wet with sweat.

A Partisan came over one day with moonshine (they called it rakkia), and made me drink a glass. He dug out two pieces of shrapnel. He decided to try to set my arm and gave it a hard jerk. The bone did go back in place but it healed crooked.

I'm not getting enough food, so I am losing weight pretty fast. I turned 21 years old yesterday and, I feel pretty blue. I'm missing my wife and daughter and family.

The Partisans told me they planned to finally start me on the way back to Italy. I've been insisting I'm well enough to travel but the first night's travel was rough. I've been lying around too long. My muscles stiffened up, so they put a guy on each side of me and half dragged me until they picked up a small donkey and put me on it.

Angelita[1] and Elsie ~ 2008 ~
Conversations on the Other Side

After first popping in to my reading with Angelita in 2003, Mom continues to show up. I never ask her for advice. I assume that Angelita connects to special guides, angels, whatever entities she uses for psychic information—and that doesn't include deceased mothers. So I enjoy the visits but never ask her any questions. Now that's about to change. ...

"Angelita," I begin a bit hesitantly over the telephone, "you know I want to write a book about Mom."

"Yeah, are you getting ready to start?"

"No, not yet. I can't even figure out *how* to write it. But I think Mom could help."

"How?"

"I want you to interview her."

"You're kidding!" Angelita exclaims.

"Well, she's popping in anyway. Why can't we ask her some questions—see what we get. We just have no idea what was happening *to her* while she was going through the disease. What was it like? What would she want caregivers to know? It could really be helpful. And if it's just gibberish, well no harm done."

Angelita excitedly answers, "Well, I've never been asked to do something like this. I don't know what will happen but I'm willing to try."

"If this works, I plan to ask four other psychics," I admit.

"Why?" she asks.

"I guess it's the scientist in me. I want to see if she says the same kind of things. I know every psychic receives information differently, so I'm not expecting to hear the exact same words. But I want to see if she describes the experience in a basically consistent way."

---

[1] Angelita can be contacted via email: angelitarae@yahoo.com

The telephone line goes silent while Angelita thinks about this. Finally she admits, "That makes sense. Every psychic tunes in a different way, based on their gifts."

"That's my point. If the information is all over the place and doesn't match up at all, then ..." I pause.

"I know," Angelita finishes my sentence. "You'd doubt it was real."

"Exactly," I admit. "But all of that aside, I'm really curious. I want to know what she has to say. People with Alzheimer's ... it's like they live in a locked box with a secret key. Nobody can get inside their heads—and then they die and whatever they experienced dies with them. I really think Mom was crossing over *a lot* while she was still alive. I want to know if I was right."

"Well, let's ask her," Angelita suggests. "Do you want to do it now?" I answer excitedly, "Let me get my shorthand pad." Angelita replies, "Let me light a candle."

We are about to open a door to the other side. Will Elsie come through? Will she participate?

It's Like You're in an Apartment with Glass Doors

<u>Angelita</u>: Elsie tends to be very intelligent and in her head. At the same time, she's also really connected to nature. She's grounded. [Angelita sees Elsie sitting at the beach.]

She's too practical to oooh and aaah over nature. She's very analytical at times. Rational.

That's how she dealt with her emotions. If she could understand them on an intelligent level, then she wouldn't get carried away too much.

Elsie: *Barbara totally embraced her emotions. She was very comfortable that way, so she didn't feel out of control. I was afraid to be out of control. I loved to watch her. It was how she looked at life. I could experience it through her, without actually having to experience it. Barbara was like a sponge soaking up experiences whereas mine was an intellectual curiosity.*

Angelita: Can you tell us what it was like to have Alzheimer's?

Elsie: *It was like being locked in my body—but at the same time I wasn't in my body most of the time. I would watch myself. It was very frustrating because I knew there was no way to retrieve bits of information. I was an observer and I was observing but I was not able to change anything.*

Angelita: Was it gradual?

Elsie: *For me, it was like one day I was okay. But then it was kind of like someone hands you a piece of paper but your mind can't grasp that this is a piece of paper and this is what you do with it. It's not exactly memory.*

It's about discernment—*taking the impulses or actions and being able to put the mind at the right category. It was almost like one day I was there and one day I wasn't ... but there were times when I would have flashes of clarity.*

Angelita: What did you enjoy while on earth?

Elsie: I liked to dance. [Angelita sees pictures of Elsie dancing, like scenes from a movie covering her life. It was the one time she did not have to be on guard. It was the closest thing to flying.]

Angelita: Can you give us an example of what it was like to have Alzheimer's?

Elsie: It's like you're in an apartment with sliding glass doors. I'm on one side and knocking, but people on the other side don't see me. [She gives another example.] *It is like a room filled with objects. I pick up a dress and don't know what it is or what it is for. I go through the room looking for something. When I get to what I need, I'll know it. But I won't know how I know it. I can't rationalize, but I'm going through each of those little pieces. Eventually I will get to what I really want.*

Angelita: How did it feel?

Elsie: Before, I dealt with everything on a physical level and denied anything spiritual— but then I had to be in the spiritual state. Basically, a place as well as a state of being. I learned to enjoy it. But at first it scared the hell out of me.

~ ~ ~

We both remain silent. I think about Mom's words, *I was an observer and I was observing but I was not able to change anything.* I break the silence. "You know, it's like her soul was not affected by the disease, but was watching it."

"Yeah," Angelita agrees, "as if she could see it all happen but was helpless to fix it."

"I'm also intrigued by what she says about discernment, that it's not exactly memory. By the time she reached advanced Alzheimer's, if I held a pencil up to her, she might try to eat it. If I forget a name or an event—I still know it's a name or event. Losing your discernment is much worse. You can't figure things out; you can't use logic; you can't guess. Mom had no way to discern, for example, what a pencil was, or how it was used. It wasn't forgetting the *word* pencil—it was losing the *function* of it."

"I guess we always think in simplistic terms. We just figure Alzheimer's is about forgetting things," Angelita muses. "It's interesting how determined she was to remember. She showed me that room filled with stuff. She couldn't *think* of what she wanted, but said she'd know it when she saw it."

"I remember the time I visited her in Florida. She cupped her hands in the shape of a ball and said, 'You pull things off of it.' Somehow I figured out she wanted scotch tape. When I handed it to her she said, 'Oh, *that's* what I wanted. How did you know?'"

"She lived in a world separated by glass doors."

"I never thought about Mom being afraid to be out of control," I admit as I put my notepad down. "I just assumed it was a natural trait, like her good memory. I still see this image of her at her desk in the State Department. I remember visiting her one day. She stood talking on the phone, flipping through a 3 x 5 card index. Apparently that's how she controlled delegations. She had three card files on her desk, and she looked like a whirling dervish working at high speed. I had to wait as she made two more phone calls and pulled more color-coded cards. I remember thinking I could never move that fast, let alone think that fast."

"Oh, your mother wanted to control *everything*. That's what she showed me. It's like I saw her in this bubble and as long as she was there, nobody else's energy could get through. Her protection was up when she was alive."

I gaze out the living room window at the Mississippi River and watch a loaded barge slowly go by. "I guess dancing was her way of letting go."

"We are spiritual beings living temporarily in a physical body," Angelita reminds me. "That spiritual side needs nourishment but your mother resisted it so much. Let me tune into that to see if I can say more." Even when a reading seems to end, Angelita remains in an open state, keeping her psychic door open for any additional messages.

Silence falls over the telephone line. Holding the receiver in my hand, I pace between the kitchen, dining, and living room—my way of focusing. It's hard to think of Mom suffering yet she's admitting the disease *scared the hell* out of her. Just as I'm pondering this, I hear Angelita's voice.

"I'm getting the image of the first half of her life was about living one way and the second about healing from that. She resisted the psychic and spiritual. She needed to be in control and needed to be rational. So what did she get to experience? Irrational. No control. No mental level. She's resisting putting a medical label on it. She's showing that in fact, it was a process. She needed to learn how to deal with things on a spiritual level."

"All her life," I explain to Angelita, "Mom cut her losses. She didn't look back. She never had time to be open to her spiritual nature—and it probably scared her. But I guess, strange as it seems, the Alzheimer's became a doorway for her."

"That makes sense," Angelita admits. "She's showing me that fear, that wanting to be in control—but then showing me how she became peaceful in the spiritual realm.

"I guess you didn't know how much Mom loved music. But she rarely had time to play the piano. Months and years would go by and I'd never hear her play. She loved dancing too, but the Finns only got together once a month and eventually even that fell apart. She *loved* music—but didn't take time for it. *Just like me,* I think a bit nervously.

"Well, she got a message from a very young age that anything to do with spiritual or psychic was taboo—it was bad, the devil. In a way, music might have been considered frivolous," Angelita continues. "Anyway, that's where her fear originated. That's why she had to reject it so totally."

"Oh Angelita," I stop her. "I really get that." I pause, remembering the Askelin grandmother who shoved her off her lap, who tossed Elsie's handmade playing cards into the woodburning stove because they were evil, who couldn't even communicate with her husband and used Elsie as a go-between. I thought of Mom's emotional losses. She had little proof of a loving Source.

"You know," I go on, "her father died when she was 9. Her mother fell into a deep depression and Mom had to step up and run the household. I guess that's when she decided that the only way to be safe was to control her world as much as she could." I contemplated the tragedy of it: "Mom happened to be particularly good at it. Her amazing memory, her acute attention to details, her ability to multitask—all those traits reinforced her dependence upon her brain."

I feel as though I understand Mom better. *I would have reacted the same way,* I realize.

"What I find interesting," Angelita comments, "is that she felt she could experience emotions through you without having to experience them herself."

I burst out laughing. So many memories flood back—sobbing inconsolably over the unhatched wren's egg, the tantrum over the broken Elvis record, the rage over injustice, whether it was the Appalachian poor or racial discrimination. "I can't believe Mom enjoyed that," I admit.

"She's coming through again," Angelita pauses. "She wants to say one more thing, Barbara. She sees this issue of Alzheimer's around you—your fear of getting it. She is telling me that your path is not the same as hers, and the jury is still out whether the disease is hereditary. You know, Barbara, we can create from our own fear. You don't have to go there."

On that disconcerting note, we end our conversation. Holding the dead receiver in my hand, I feel a quick flash of anger. I get so *tired* of having New Age theology thrown at me: thoughts are things; we create our reality; fear attracts disease. Maybe it's true—but how do you stop thinking? *By getting Alzheimer's,* I decide fatalistically.

I seriously doubt Mom created her Alzheimer's by fear—but then again, she certainly refused to ever have the word spoken in her presence. She lived under the cloud of ancestry—her mother and favorite uncle succumbed to it.

But she's saying the jury is still out. I remember talking to my neighbor Vince just 2 weeks ago. He told me he knew identical twin brothers. They both worked in the same factory. They both owned farms. One got Alzheimer's; the other didn't. I couldn't figure that out.

Am I fearful? Could I attract this disease because of negative thoughts? It seems unimaginable to me. *Surely we are more complex than that.* But then I think about the identical twins.

~ ~ ~

"Thoughts are things," my friend Candace keeps telling me. For a long time, I considered her words strange. After all, thoughts are invisible. I prefer provable facts. But now Mom's words slowly filter down into my reluctant consciousness. I begin to consider them.

What about chronic anger? I ask myself.

All of us experience bouts of anger. It ties us up in knots: sour stomach, back pain, ulcers, sleeplessness. Hopefully we work through it but what if we don't? Slowly, people avoid us. Eventually angry thoughts lead to lost jobs, broken relationships, illness. Thought by angry thought, a negative worldview attracts a negative reality and concrete consequences. In such an extreme case, thoughts clearly seem to create things.

~ ~ ~

When I moved to Missouri, I transported possessions from both sides of the country—Seattle and Baltimore. I had no built-in Midwest network of friends.

As I faced daily exhaustion of moving and settling in, I often muttered, "I need a *break*!"

One cold winter evening, I saw a feral cat slinking beneath my van outside and decided to put some dry food under the chassis for him. I dashed out, slipped on the ice, crashed to the ground, and broke my wrist. My left wrist. My writing wrist. I was grounded.

Whimpering with pain, I got to the phone, called my new friend Michelene, and sank to the kitchen floor cradling my hand. In spite of all that pain, I started to laugh. "Oh," I said out loud, "you got your *break*."

Certainly I'm not convinced and most people would not believe I caused this fall by my thoughts. But then Louis Zamperini's story floats into my mind.

I just finished the book *Unbroken*, by Laura Hillenbrand, for our book club. In it, Louis and two other men shot down in World War II end up in a raft on the Pacific Ocean. They have no food, no water, and will be in that raft, constantly circled by sharks, for 47 days floating 2,000 miles before being captured by the Japanese. While in the raft, Louis and Phil begin to describe elaborate meals their mothers fixed.

Three times a day, they carefully narrate every aspect—the ingredients, preparation, how good it tasted. The third man, depressed and fatalistic, does not participate. Indeed, he thinks it absurd. But Louis and Phil strangely feel *as though* they have eaten.

Now, in those 47 days, the men caught an occasional albatross, used it for bait, learned how to collect rainwater. The third man gets his equal share of that scant bounty, but he diminishes day by day, and eventually dies. The other two men not only survive the raft, they live through daily torture as prisoners of war, return home, marry, and raise families.

Mom had a *determined* attitude about her Alzheimer's. She refused to succumb to it. For quite a long time, she used her remaining synapses to do battle against the dead and dying ones. She *assumed* her brain was the absolute and only center of her *Elsieness*. I can only imagine her surprise when the brain died, and she was still there—in some strange way. The eternal soul-of-Elsie beat on. As Mom neared the end of her battle, her younger sister Lucy began it. Unlike Mom, Lucy did little to fight it. A quiet person by nature, it seemed as though she inhaled the disease and shortly thereafter exhaled her last breath. Visited daily by her son Gary, and seen often by her near-by daughter Nancy, she certainly didn't die from emotional neglect or lack of love. Perhaps her way of facing life was not to fight it, or fight for it. So when the disease came, she simply assumed she'd die from it—and she did.

How much are thoughts "things"? I just don't know, no matter how many anecdotal stories. But now I feel such a strong connection with my mother—as though we are having a serious and important conversation.

Career Elsie ~ 1975 ~ How to Travel

A decapitated Styrofoam head resides in our Takoma Park home, perkily sitting atop Mom's dresser. If it is bald, Mom is traveling. Otherwise, it holds a medium blonde softly curled wig, sometimes in rollers.

As Elsie experienced the rigors of travel, she soon learned that keeping your hair coiffed fell into the dustbin of life. One overseas trip proved enough. Mom headed for the classiest wig shop she could find and purchased a high-quality human-hair wig.

Apparently, according to her friend Mim, she also bought an inexpensive Afro. "Elsie," Mim remembers asking, "Why on earth did you buy *that*?"

"Well," practical Elsie tells her, "I work late a lot. I go through some rough neighborhoods on my way home. They'll think I'm one of them."

Incredulous, Mim states the obvious. "But Elsie, you're *white*. You're as white as a Scandinavian Finn can get."

"Yes, but when I leave, nobody can tell that. It's pitch black outside," Elsie answers.

~ ~ ~

Now, I never saw this wig. But it is true that Mom took the craziest route through the inner city to avoid fast-moving traffic. Highways scared her. Once when retired and heading home after shopping, she found the road to her house blocked, all traffic being routed onto an interstate.

Confident in her cause, Elsie rolled down her window. "I live right over there. I don't do interstates," she explained to the policeman, expecting to be flagged through.

"LADY," the officer replied, "MOVE IT," and Elsie *shot* up the ramp like a terrified bunny.

But back to the wig. Consider this: Any self-respecting African American looking at this Afro-wigged Finn would rightly think, *This woman is way past crazy. No way am I tangling with that.*

So, in a way, I suppose it worked (if she even had it, which I doubted). Mom *couldn't* have been *that* crazy. Right?

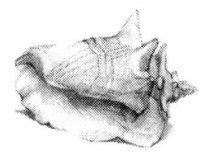

Kenna and Elsie ~ 2000 ~ I'm Just Fine!

<u>Kenna</u>: So how was it, Elsie?

<u>Elsie</u>: *I had FUN!* [She is laughing.] *It was like the good ole days, but I was the Commander-in-Chief.*

<u>Kenna</u>: Are you okay at the new place?

<u>Elsie</u>: *Well, I don't get very hungry any more. But I have no reason to die as long as I am having fun. I have no fear. I really feel good. I have always kept my heart to myself, haven't I? Anyway, now I am content and I hope my children are as well.*

<u>Kenna</u>: What else is on your mind?

<u>Elsie</u>: *I have been busy thinking about Barbara and Sandra. How is Hawa? I hope she had a good time.*

<u>Kenna</u>: Is there anything you want to tell them?

<u>Elsie</u>: *YES! Get me out of here! No, I am just joking. Just let them know I am fine.*

August 27

Career Elsie ~ 1958 ~ Elsie's Law

President Eisenhower signed Elsie's hand-typed hand-delivered Congressional bill into law, thereby releasing hundreds of gifts held captive in the State Department vault. As mentioned earlier, the U.S. Constitution refuses to allow U.S. citizens to receive foreign gifts while on national business without congressional approval and presidential signature.

But now, medals from almost every country in the world: Iran, Peru, Netherlands, Finland, Greece, Panama, even San Marino, that landlocked country in the middle of Italy, were to be released.

Among the items liberated by P.L. 85-704 were Master Sergeant Anthony P. Garcia's "Order of the Condor of the Andes" from Bolivia, Aubrey Hutchison's "Order of the White Elephant, 3rd Class" from Thailand, and Roscoe Good's "Order of the Double Rays of the Rising Sun" from Japan.

Elsie meticulously and laboriously documented over 1,200 gifts moldering in the vault. I can only imagine the surprise on Garcia's, Hutchison's, and Good's face when they found condors, white elephants, and rising suns in their mailboxes.

Unfortunately Elsie received no medal. In the secretarial world, all she received was a photocopy of her bill.

Retired Elsie ~ 1982 ~ Florida Diary

Two avocados fell this morning. Season is here! Took Herby to pick up MORE ham equipment. (Helen warned me.) Planted aloe plants around the avocado tree. Hope they grow.

September

Life is Measured by Family

September 7

Child Sandra ~ 1950 ~ I Gave School a Try

"Wear the plaid dress, Sandra," Mom helps her button it up. Already Sandra doesn't think school is such a good idea. She hates dresses and has been informed she has to wear one *every* day.

Now as Mom braids Sandra's hair for her first day, she hears Mom muttering, *Ainakin puhut Englanti*. "What did you say?" Sandra squirms around to stare.

"I said, at least you speak English," Mom answers, twisting another rubber band around her tightly braided hair. "I stood in a corner on *my* first day because the teacher thought I was sassing her for not speaking English. But I didn't know how."

School looks even *less* appealing to Sandra. Kids get punished for stupid things.

"Get your lunch box," Mom instructs as she finishes dressing for work. Sandra picks up her Roy Roger metal box with the heavy thermos inside. It is small comfort that it's brand new and Roy Roger is rearing up on his horse. It seems to weigh a ton but there isn't any time to snap it open and peek inside. "Come on," Mom opens the front door. "Let's go."

A mile later, Mom pulls into the school parking lot. "Okay, Sandra, here you are."

"Aren't you going to go to class with me?" Sandra asks incredulously.

"No. See the adults at the door? They assign you to your classroom. They don't want the parents to stay."

Since Finns don't kiss or hug, Sandra heaves her lunch box off the seat and, without enthusiasm, starts up the school steps. Near the top, she trips. The loaded lunch box goes flying, launching her milk-filled Dale Evans thermos, apple, crackers, raisins, and sandwich in the air. Dale Evans starts bouncing down the stairs—crash, crash—before she can grab it.

The apple suffers fatal bruising. The crackers lie, cracked, on the cement step. The sandwich has survived. The cookies are in crumbles. *How does she DO it?* Sandra wonders. *How can any mother get so much stuff into one lunch box?*

She tries, unsuccessfully, to put everything back. Dragging it in one hand, and the apple and munched crackers in the other, she gets to the top of the steps. Suddenly she knows with a certainty—she does not belong here.

She sees teachers holding rosters at the school entrance. Children are obediently giving their names and being directed to their class. "What is your name?" the woman asks.

Sandra doesn't bother with niceties. She *knows* she's not staying. "Look, school's really not for me," Sandra patiently explains to the adult. "So ... just carry on without me." She turns to go. Hands land on her shoulders. She is forcibly rotated in her brand new saddle shoes and marched to her room.

As she glumly sits in class, she wonders what they didn't understand. She'd been pretty clear. Even decades later, she remembers her exact words. After all, it made a searing impression on her juvenile (soon to be delinquent) consciousness.

At any rate, her first day at school finally ends. She trudges home, alongside our housekeeper Mary and tag-along me (deliriously thrilled to go to school to pick her up). Perhaps things might have gone better for her if she had spoken Finnish. Imagine the teacher's amazement at having a bilingual child muttering, *Mitä hittoa minä täällä teen*? "What the heck am I doing here?"

As the years passed, she played hooky, wondering *Mitä HELVETTIÄ minä täällä teen*—"What the HELL am I here for?"

Occasionally she actually has an answer, such as the day her biology teacher Mr. Wistort asks for some students to raise mice. Sandra immediately volunteers and arrives home with one very pregnant rodent. Since it's in the name of science, (which Dad heartily believes in), the mouse settles into a cage in Sandra's bedroom and soon has copious mice-ettes. She even teaches Mama Mouse not to poop on you when you hold her. I spend countless hours enjoying her. Meanwhile I start to notice that the baby population keeps shrinking.

"Sandra, where are the other mice going?"

"To the snake," she answers matter of factly.

"WHAT?" I scream. You're KILLING the MICE?"

"Yeah," Sandra answers uninterestedly.

Now I am reluctant to go into the bedroom, knowing their fate. But one day Sandra enlists me. "A mouse is loose in the house somewhere." We go on a determined search, but fruitless days go by, mouse-less. At last I decide to go into the attic, and to my amazement see a very dust-bally mouse scurry across. Together we capture him but he is filthy.

"Let's wash him," I suggest.

"He'll get too cold," Sandra believes.

"We'll put the oven on warm and dry him off there," I head downstairs.

And that's exactly what we do. We wash and dry-roast the mouse.

"He still doesn't look too good," I admit to Sandra. Just then Dad walks into the kitchen, wearing his paint-splattered carpenter overalls.

"Dad," Sandra holds up one very tired looking mouse. "We found him, but he was filthy so we gave him a bath and warmed him in the oven. He's still not looking good." The mouse lies in a flat heap on her hand.

Now comes the *Finnish* solution to all problems. "He needs vodka," Dad says pulling a pint bottle out of the cabinet. "But not much. He's only a mouse."

Somewhere in the kitchen debris we find an eyedropper. Sandra holds the mouse; I pry open its mouth with a toothpick; Dad squirts two or three drops of vodka down its throat.

The inebriated wash-and-dry mouse undergoes a complete resurrection and lives.

About a year goes by. I still come in to play with Mama Mouse. Then one day I go in and the cage is *empty*.

Alarmed, I ask, "Where is she?"

"Oh, I got tired of raising mice so I fed her to the snake."

Obviously, there are NO WORDS to express my outrage. Sisterly love does *not* flourish in the upstairs kingdom for some time. But then, how long can you mourn an 8-ounce mouse. Not that long.

And then, after all, there was Sandra's graduation to think of. As she flipped her tassel, never again would she have to say, *Mitä helvettiä minä täällä teen.*

Career Elsie ~ 1966 ~
Looking Up the White House in the White Pages

"Elsie," Alice calls her sister. "You're in *Life* magazine. I was flipping through the pages looking at the article about LBJ's summit in the Philippines, and there you were! I'd recognize you anywhere even though your back's to the camera."

She was referring, of course, to the "brilliantly lighted palace" party given by President and Mrs. Marcos. The wide-angle photo *shows* all 3,000 guests, everyone dressed in white. But it was the way Elsie stood—a sort of ballet pose where her right foot stands firm and straight, and her left foot, slightly ahead of her right, turns outward. Alice recognized *her feet*....

~ ~ ~

It is Elsie's longest trip away from home. She joins the Protocol team preparing for President Lyndon Johnson's seven-country summit about Vietnam. Australia, New Zealand, South Korea, the Philippines, Thailand, South Vietnam, and the United States plan to sign a *Declaration of Intent* to stand in solidarity with Vietnam's quest for freedom.

We get our first airmail letter from Mom:

"Well, here I am," she begins, "thrill, thrill. I unloaded a cargo plane singlehandedly 2 days ago. Today I took a 2-hour launch trip across Manila Bay to go to the commissary. We still need a lot of supplies. We went between big ships at anchor (waiting to go to Saigon to unload).

"You have never seen road traffic like they have here—D.C. is a cow pasture in comparison. Everybody here has an old jeep and every block, two or three are broken down.

"I have to cross the expressway to get to work. One embassy girl said, 'Just hold up your hand and they will stop.' NUTS—I'm not taking any chances."

"The White House advance team (Bill Moyers, military aides, president's secretary, secret service, communications) arrived last night. Girls, in an emergency, you can call the White House. Their number is in the white pages of the D.C. telephone book. Ask for the Action Line. When they answer, request Extension 1268. That line connects to our Manila office. Then ask for me."

Meanwhile, as Elsie helps prepare for the U.S. hosted summit, the Filipinos go utterly wild getting Manila ready. According to *Life*'s article, the whole country prepares. Buses with names like *Lolita* and *Carmelita* accessorize themselves even more garishly, adding psychedelic color and distinguishing touches such as Rolls Royce radiator caps and hood ornaments to bump celebratorily down potholed roads.

Unfortunately the very festive homosexuals are told to vamoose for a few days. First Lady Imelda (of the thousand-shoe fame) sends her minions, the "blue ladies," to spruce up town. They get lawns tidied up by verbal coercion, arrange for whitewashed fences to camouflage shantytowns, and discourage the Filipinos from carrying loaded guns around town. Temporarily.

A few days later, Mom writes, "I left home without *any* summer cottons. You really need them here. Lucky for me, you can go to a store, point at some fabric, get measured in all directions—and the next day your dress is ready. They even made an extra bulge for my stomach (not really, but it sure fits well).

"I am getting braver about traffic. I still expect to get hit, but at least I approach the expressway more calmly. I no longer expect to freeze if someone tries to plow me over. At first, I thought I'd have a heart attack and fall conveniently right into their path."

Finally Elsie weighs herself: "ALORS! ALORS! ALORS! Ten pounds overweight ... woe is me. I don't want to stop eating and get worn out and sick. Well, it's a good thing they have cheap dressmakers here!"

In this smoldering climate three degrees above the equator, Elsie, much to her amazement, finds the hotel offers a sauna service for $2. Well, you can take the sauna away from the Finn but you cannot take away Finnish determination to have a sauna. On a particularly grueling workday, she decides to unwind in one. "I understand you have a sauna service. I would like to order it."

"Yes, Mrs. Nurmi. We will bring it to your room. When would you like to reserve it?"

"Six o'clock this evening would be nice. Thank you."

At the appointed hour, two girls in white uniforms and one strong Filipino man muscle the portable sauna into the bathroom, position it in the center of the room and hook it up. One female attendant remains. A very delighted Elsie strips and pops into the plastic-bubble shaped sauna. She looks like a lollipop. Only her head sticks out.

The attendant explains, "Señora, you are the very first person to ever request a sauna," as she seals her in and turns a few knobs. The heat begins to go up and up and up. In 10 minutes, it's blasting at full 220-degree strength.

Soon sweat pours from Elsie's brow. The attendant helpfully mops it from her face. After about 30 minutes, Elsie is done. Surely her pores are cleansed. She hates to admit it, but she is *really, really* hot.

The attendant turns off the knobs and opens the door. Elsie staggers out followed by a gush of sweaty sauna air. She looks like a boiled lobster.

Now is the time for the cold shower to cool her back to her normal body temperature. "Señora," the concerned attendant asks, "are you all right?"

"Let me just cool down in the shower," Elsie explains as she hurries into the stall. She turns the cold faucet. Tepid water cascades out.

She unscrews the knob further. More warm water. She opens it full bore, waiting for the icy cold water to pour out the showerhead. Nothing.

She yells out of the shower, "There's no cold water!"

"Sí señora, I know," the attendant replies. "We don't have cold water in the Philippines."

A bit alarmed, a pink Elsie gives up on the shower. She throws on the white hotel-supplied bathrobe while the Filipino man and woman bundle up the sauna and take it from the room. The attendant remains to see if Elsie needs any other assistance (such as CPR).

Stoic Elsie tips the sauna team and hurries the female attendant out the door, muttering *muchas gracia* in her best Span-lish. As soon as the door closes, the naked Finnish Protocol Officer starts flapping like a crazed chicken in front of a fan.

Then she calls room service and orders a beer. Ice cold.

~ ~ ~

Meanwhile Dad arrives home with a bushel of apples telling Sandra and me, "We're going to make pies."

"Where did you get them?" we ask.

"From a customer. Okay, you two peel."

"Do you have a recipe?" (After all, I've *never* seen Dad bake anything.)

"No, we don't need that." He grabs the flour tin and Crisco from the cabinet. Soon we see him hurling flour, salt, and globs of white greasy Crisco into one bowl, and handfuls of sugar into the other containing apples.

To our utter amazement, pies (good-tasting ones) emerge from the oven.

Today I wonder how he did it. *Did his mother teach him on her days off? Was it the Portuguese cook in the Merchant Marines?* At any rate, the warm pies, excepting one, disappear. Dad delivered them to neighbors and friends.

Children Sandra and Barbara ~ 1955 ~ Arguing Parents

We never hear arguments in our home. So imagine our anxiety when one day we hear lowered intense voices coming from our parent's closed bedroom. At last the door opens.

Dad storms out of the house in stony silence to sit on the back porch. Mom shuts the bedroom door and refuses to leave despite our pleas. Sandra and I look frantically at each other. Nothing like this has ever happened in the Nurmi home. For such a thing to happen can only mean … divorce!

"What do we do?" I ask Sandra.

Sandra goes outside to talk to Dad. I hover near Mom pleading, *"What's wrong, Mom? Are you okay?"* Continued silence.

"What did you say, Sandra?" I ask.

"I asked if they are getting a divorce."

We look at each other glumly and go upstairs to wait it out. About two hours later, Dad calls upstairs. "Come on down, kids. We're going to Fred and Harry's for dinner."

Greatly relieved, we believe that *we*—single-handedly—have saved the marriage, though we know not from what.

If we experience minimal friction between our parents, the same is not true between parent and child. Usually Sandra and I plaster ourselves to the white refrigerator, frozen by Mom's icy anger and Dad's absolute (if silent) support.

I only remember one disciplinary trip to the den for a whipping. Dad solemnly walked me into the room, shut the door, slowly removed his belt, looked at it, and said, "Well, don't do that again."

What still strikes Sandra and me as remarkable is how indifferent Dad was to the cultural norm of his day. In the fifties, the fathers we encountered seemed like the *Father Knows Best* parents—they ruled the house and held the power. The women seemed submissive, the children unadventurous.

Everything in our house was upside down. Mom had the guaranteed income; Sandra and I babysat each other; and Dad sustained a whole house full of females by convincing us *we* could be whatever we wanted to be. Even the neighborhood children and our female cousins remember him with awe: "He *listened* to us as though we mattered."

Yet I never felt he *sacrificed* himself for us. In some remarkable way, this self-made highly intelligent man lived by his own rules and had absolute inner integrity.

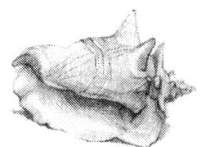

Kenna and Elsie ~ 2000 ~
I've Lived My Life the Way I Wanted

<u>Kenna</u>: So how are you, Elsie?

<u>Elsie</u>: *I'm feeling fine. I'm happy. I know Barbara was worried but everything is fine. I'm so happy to see so many of my family. In the end, they are all you have left, you know. There's more activity here so I'm not so bored. I'm something of a spectator although it's not so much seeing as sensing and knowing. It's a different way and quite useful. Actually it can be cunning and fun. People can't be sure what I see or don't see. Only I know. In a way, I like that! Like being a spy without an eye. Of course, I've got no one to give information to. That's the other part of the joke, you see.*

<u>Kenna</u>: Do you have any messages for Barbara?

<u>Elsie</u>: *I know Barbara wants to know about Sandra. Well, we're all fine. I know Barbara will be back.*

<u>Kenna</u>: She's traveling and coming to see you soon.

<u>Elsie</u>: *Good. We'll dance. I've always liked the change of scenery. New place, new people. Of course, I miss people but I'm not so attached as many are. Live and let live, I always say.*

<u>Kenna</u>: How did you get like this? [get Alzheimer's]

Elsie: When I broke my hip, I got very depressed and didn't want to be alive. My brain was getting weaker and weaker which was depressing too. Yet the brain reaches a point where depression becomes an unknown. [Kenna interprets this to mean you don't realize you are depressed.]

Kenna: Well, that is your *mental* level.

Elsie: This is where I'm a goner!

Kenna: Elsie, what do you want?

Elsie: I think I want to think straight and stay focused.

Kenna: [sensed a fear in Elsie that if she didn't have Alzheimer's, she would be very depressed and that was the more unbearable option.]

Kenna: What's in your heart, Elsie?

Elsie: I'm content. I like it here. It's good to have family. I lived my life the way I wanted.

~ ~ ~

Just as Sandra and I witnessed, Mom became quite animated at Stacy's group home once she recovered from her travel fatigue. *I've always liked the change of scenery. New place, new people*. Certainly a trademark Elsie comment. But then the *full-monty* Elsie unexpectedly pops into view: *I'm something of a spectator. It can be cunning and fun ... like being a spy without an eye.*

Our mother-whisperer reveals her secret—how much she used invisibility in a visible world. She silently listened as Sandra rattled the lunch money jar. At work, she overheard, and then silently *beamed* her best secretarial smile to get promoted. At Mrs. Cooper's Group Home, she sat in a tiny portico just outside the living room. In this part/apart way, she became a spy: *People can't be sure what I see or don't see.*

But *without an eye* (a working mind), she has *no one to give information to*. And that is the *other part of the joke.*

As I listen to Kenna describe Mom's depression, I remember the moment in rehab after her hip surgery and my certainty she was *not* ready to die. Yet she tells Kenna that she *did* want to die.

But which "she"?—the depressed ego-of-Elsie who wanted to control her world—or the essence-of-Elsie whose soul I felt connecting to me in that room? Or perhaps my felt connection was no more than my own need to keep her alive. Such is the caregiver's dilemma who makes decisions for those who cannot make them. Our best path is to follow love wherever it leads.

However the route, our family had no clinical history of depression and Mom in the end offers Kenna an intriguing insight: *The brain reaches a point where depression becomes an unknown.*

Confused Elsie ~ 1995 ~ Mall and Meals

"Mom," I suggest, "Let's go to Boynton Beach Mall." It's renewal-of-wardrobe season. Sandra and I find shopping a total nuisance so we put it off till ... well, forever.

Mom on the other hand used to come into her full acquisitive power when she walked past racks of clothing. Her diaries are filled with bargains and buys: "Stopped @ thrift shop & a pretty green dress jumped off the rack & followed me home." A week later, "Got a blouse 25¢." Even though her memory diminishes by the day, Sandra and I figure she'll have fun. It'll be good.

Off we go to Boynton Beach. We're happy. We're all together. It's a warped Nurmi tradition.

Soon, we are cruising through the stores, aisles of stores, racks in the aisles, hangers on the racks—this awful tedious process we both loath. Content to simply be with her daughters, Mom trails after us in her white canvas sneakers and white ankle socks, her blue polyester pants and white blouse, with her white vinyl shoulder bag.

To my shock, I find I am becoming like my mother when she was my age.

She rarely carried a purse, preferring to put a wallet in her pocket. I do the same. She never bought pants or skirts without pockets. Ditto. She swept her hand along the fabrics on the clothing racks, looking for softness. So do I.

Anyway, Sandra and I buy clothing with little regard to sales, bargains, or beauty. Now it is time to eat. With Elsie in tow, we head to the food court where crowds, menus, eateries, bright lights, and just the whole mess of a mall confuse Mom. Sandra and I consult. We try to think of what she would enjoy and come up with pizza and Pepsi.

We get in line, order our array of pizza slices, pick up our iced Pepsis and head to an empty table islanded among masses of hungry shoppers. Mom always has a good, if small, appetite. Now she sinks her tiny teeth into the greasy cheese pizza.

"Oh, this is SOOO DELICIOUS," she exclaims. "I'VE NEVER HAD THIS BEFORE. What is it?"

Whoa. Sandra and I look at each other, disheartened. All those years when Mom brought home frozen stacks of crappy pizza shells; all those tons of cheap tomato sauce and grated cheese ... utterly lost as though they never existed. And she hadn't even tried the Pepsi yet. Now we watch as she takes a sip.

"Oh, this tastes so good. I really like it. I've never tasted this." And there goes the soda pop of our youth—not that we ever got very many, none of them being a brand name like Pepsi. But still, it looks as though carbonated beverages have slipped off the memory grid along with the pizza.

At the time, I look at this like any daughter losing her mother—with fear and sadness and a sense of hopelessness about what the future might hold for us. But today, being much older I see it differently.

Think of it as an Eckhart Tolle *being-in-the-present* moment. This best-selling author tells us in every way possible, in book after book, to live in the *now*. *The Power of Now* drums it in chapter after chapter—God can only be found in the present moment.

Sandra and I are eating pizza too. We definitely are not in the *now*. We're chattering about what we just bought and where we'll go after lunch. For us, the present moment means nothing. We mindlessly stuff down the pizza and slurp our Pepsi, not really tasting any of it.

But Mom ... she has no place else to go. All exit routes blocked, her mind reduced to retaining *only* the present moment, she can sit there eating pizza and drinking Pepsi in a rapturous *now*. If we have pizza tomorrow or two days from now, she will still be in the present moment and eat pizza for the first time. She lives in an Eckhart Tolle universe whereas we can only peek in momentarily. We haven't a clue how to live this way.

Wouldn't any one of us love to take a bite of pizza as though we had never crunched through a crispy crust with sweet rich tomato sauce and salty cheese with oil running down our chin? Or sip a drink that we'd consumed gallons of—not remembering how fizzy bubbles tickled our mouth—not even knowing these foods were "not good for you"?

Without memory loss, we'll never get another experience of that type of awe and innocence. Our culture defines Alzheimer's as a disease. The thought of memory loss, of losing our identity, unsettles us so much we fail to see any hidden gifts. We assume—absolutely—there are none. Yet here is Elsie on this sunny afternoon in this ordinary mall on this ordinary day eating ordinary food—and to her, it is an amazing and unforgettable experience.

The mother we knew is so different from this diminutive woman munching on pizza. Mom, if she knew it, would *hate* the fact that her memory is disappearing like water running down a drain.

But I wish on that day that I could have chosen awe over dismay.

September 12

Wartime Elsie ~ 1944 ~ Swante Missing in Action

Elsie writes to Herby, "Still no word about Swante. Mayme is coping as best she can. One piece of hopeful news: other bombers on that run saw parachutes—so some made it at least to the ground."

~ ~ ~

I almost always travel at night with a six- to eight-man patrol. I am only with the same patrol about two nights as each has its own territory. We hide out in the woods or farmhouses during the day.

The Partisans are mostly Slovenians led by Marshall Tito, who is a Communist.

There are also the Croatian fighters called Chetniks. The two groups fight each other. There are Slovenians, Croatians, Nationalists, Ustaschi, and Serbian groups in the country. It seems they are all fighting each other.

Even though the Chetniks and Partisans fight each other, they both help Allied flyers get back to Italy. The U.S. Army O.S.S. airdrops a lot of supplies to underground. They have radio communication.

Two days ago, we toiled up a large mountain range. Just as we got to the edge, we spotted a German patrol—about a hundred Germans shooting at us. I could hear a few bullets whizzing over my head.

Nobody got hit. But by the time we got to the bottom, I was falling behind not only because I was weak with hunger, but the blanket I was carrying kept getting caught in the brush so I threw it away.

We eluded the Germans and hid in a barn. That's when the leader noticed I had lost my blanket.

He started screaming at me and put a submachine gun to my chest.

I was sure he was going to shoot me but another patrol member came and knocked the gun down. There was a big argument but the leader finally cooled off and walked away.

Needless to say, I would have hated to get killed over a lousy blanket.

Retired Elsie ~ 1982 ~ Florida Diary

Made avocado pie—pretty good. Took avocados to the Karjalainens and to the Tommenins.

ELSIE AT EBB TIDE

RVing Barbara ~ 2000 ~ "Gracious Living"

It started with a conversation. "You're turning 70?" I exclaim to my Key West friend, Rosemary.

"I'm trying to be optimistic about it," she answers over the phone.

"What are your plans?" I persist.

"Well, the kids want me to come to New York so we can celebrate."

I'm not sensing enthusiasm. She'll love the celebration but not the *reason* for it. "Well hey, why don't you come with me on my RV trip?" I immediately realize this borders on brilliance. Rosemary drives like a New York cabbie. I love to read maps. If she drove through cities while I navigated ...

She doesn't miss a beat. "Sure! Let's go."

No one could use the phrase "ambling through America" for this trip. In 2 months, we will see the Badlands—Minneapolis—Duluth—Yellowstone—Glacier—Waterton, Canada—Seattle—Oregon's ocean drive—the Sequoias—San Francisco—Yosemite—Zion—Las Vegas (at which point Rosemary will wonder *how much of the United States does she really need to see*)—the Grand Canyon—Mesa Verde—the Oklahoma City memorial (she almost refuses to get out of the RV)—and Hot Springs, Arkansas.

~ ~ ~

"Barbara," Rosemary peers into the Winnebago Warrior parked in front of my house, "There's not a lot of storage here." She walks down the aisle and discovers that her allotment is one drawer and half of one overhead compartment. "There's NO storage," she states, shocked.

I hadn't considered it: clothing for 2 months in temperatures ranging from freezing to torrid, camping gear for my Colorado vision quest, pots and pans, food for two, personal toiletries.

We sit in the RV, our knees inches apart in the narrow aisle, pondering the problem.

"What about the shower stall?" I suggest. "We can use campground showers."

Rosemary looks a bit wilted at this thought. Her home bathroom borders on magnificent luxury. Now her choice of cleanliness will be a 3' x 3' ABS plastic stall or *public* showers of questionable cleanliness. (I don't tell her about the coin-feed component.)

"Okay," she agrees. "Make it storage." The next morning, we snug *two* stackable three-drawer plastic units atop one another. We shove the last loaded drawer shut. I pop into the driver's seat ready to go. I am about to turn the ignition on; I glance back one last time, and suddenly envision disaster. "Rosemary, those units will go flying out of the shower stall and crash into the refrigerator if we turn any faster than 0 mph!"

We bungee them in place.

With the refrigerator humming, drawers brimming, and AAA maps unfurled, we head out for our grand adventure into togetherness.

"We can have a dining table, or convert it permanently to a second bed," I explain to Rosemary, my guest ... "or we can switch it back and forth every day." The latter doesn't appeal to me. I have to park the rig, level it, and hook us up to water, electric, and sewer.

"We can eat on our laps," Rosemary concludes. The dining table disappears.

~ ~ ~

"Wow," I say one day, "We're going through Sturgis while the Harley motorcyclists are here. That's about one million of them. They do an annual bike-in and we'll get there the last day."

Unfortunately, most of the bikers have left. We see an overweight farm boy in overalls pumping gas into an aged Suzuki—hardly the biker jock we expect to see. We learn that Wall Street–bikers, doctors, and dentists trailer their gleaming machines to Sturgis, then stand around swapping stories, before towing them back.

This works well for most people, but not for one. ...

"Is that smoke?" Rosemary asks. We look at the trailer on the shoulder ahead of us. A man and woman are frantically throwing things out the side door of the trailer. We slow down and stop.

I get out and walk over to a spectator. "What's going on?" I ask.

"They've got a $40,000 Harley burning up in that trailer."

"Whoa!" I say, awestruck.

"They say the Harley was hot going in; there was a gasoline can ... they don't know what sparked but it's too late to get it out."

Now the middle-aged man and his wife are holding each other in their arms watching the smoke billow out. Others have stopped behind us. I go back to the RV. We hear sirens in the distance.

"Let's pull around it now before the emergency equipment gets here," I suggest to Rosemary, "otherwise we'll be stuck for hours."

"It could EXPLODE," Rosemary stares at me dumbfounded. I sheepishly realize *she* would become the closest incendiary object ... so we wait it out. Pretty soon a convention of bikers loiters on the tarmac. We hang out while the trailered Harley turns to a charred wreck. Though not a biker, I can understand $40K. I go over to extend my sympathy to the couple watching the cremation of their beloved motorcycle.

We're particularly charmed by the tattooed, bikini-topped, sunburned girl and her leather vest-clad muscled guy sitting on the Harley behind us. "Where are you from?" I ask, staring at the colored dragons on her arms.

They name a Wyoming town of 87 people. It is impossible for Rosemary and me to believe these star-studded bikers could come from a one-silo town. We take their picture and promise to mail it to them.

~ ~ ~

Life in an RV is all about downsizing. Your wardrobe becomes crap not rescued by any form of laundering. You definitely eat to live, not live to eat. Clearly, you become intimate since two adults cannot inhabit one RV aisle at the same time. Private campground owners (men) do not believe women can back up an RV without decimating their electrical or water hook-ups, or taking out a tree or two.

Then there are the humbling moments of owning a rat-tattered RV with its once jazzy Winnebago stripes peeling off. In AAA-rated campgrounds, RV owners driving $100,000 rigs large enough to stow their own below-deck golf carts glide into pull-through sites, push a button to electronically level them, and watch their living room, kitchen, and bedroom unfurl into a ranch-style home.

They have marble counters, double-door refrigerators, wood floors, chandeliers, and satellite TV. When Rosemary and I need a washing machine, we search such a campground and park with the glitterati.

On one such day, Rosemary walks down our 18-inch aisle to the bathroom. The plastic storage units in the shower have become un-bungeed. All six cords dangle like colored snakes. Then she sees the label on our three-drawer plastic units of crap. It says "Gracious Living." She lets out a howl of laughter. She laughs so hard she can't even tell me—but just looking at her gets me going. Here we are duct taping and bungee cording stuff to keep it from falling off (or out of) our rig while other RVers nestle in their swiveling La-Z-Boys, watching flat-screen TVs, and sipping martinis.

Despite such RVing differences, we at last drive my rig onto the Seattle ferry to make the Bremerton crossing. After weeks apart, I will see my mother.

Mother Barbara ~ 1982 ~ Adjusting to Parenthood

"Six months," another adoptive mother promises. "It takes that long for things to settle down." I am not so sure. In the first weeks, I become so concerned about their adjustment that I totally ignore my own.

I stop eating. My monthly cycle goes from a steady 28 days to 21 days. My sleep is anything but sound. Bill, on the other hand, handles everything with Buddha-like calm.

"Six months is a long time," I admit. I was unprepared for the change in energy levels. They have lots; I have little. Then there is the communication problem. We have two walking, talking children.

~ ~ ~

Initially, Kendra assumed we'd speak Korean. She patiently named things and in a perfect world, I'd have relished learning a new language. But, with the exception of mama, papa, and rice, I remained linguistically ignorant.

One day I sat outside relaxing while the children played. Suddenly Kendra ran indoors and came out carrying a picture dictionary I had bought. She jumped into my lap, opened the page, and pointed. I said, "apple," "bed," "cookie."

Lisa faced a different set of problems. On the verge of speaking Korean, she suddenly found herself in a phonetic sea of English sounds. She had to backtrack, learn different linguistic tones, and *then* start speaking. The only word that threw her was squirrel which came out *kwerl* for a few months.

Meanwhile, I decided to go to my doctor....

~ ~ ~

"I'm losing a lot of weight," I admit.

"What are you eating?"

"Brown rice."

"What else?" he asks, looking astonished.

"That's about it. I don't have any appetite. I choke that down as best I can and just keep going. I'm so overwhelmed by parenting."

A father himself, he now gives me a prescription I never expected. He explains, "It's as though you've jumped into the deep end of a swimming pool, the water is ice cold, and you don't know how to swim."

A pretty apt analogy, I think as tears well up in my eyes. *I can't even parent.*

"So I want you to eat *all* your meals by yourself. And you need to put your daughters into day care at least 2 days a week."

I start to cry. All I can think of is the trauma to the kids. They can't speak English. *They won't understand. They'll think they're being abandoned again.* "I can't *do* that to the kids," I blubber through my full storm weeping.

The doctor pats my knee. "It's just too much too fast. Do what I say. Everything will be fine."

That evening I sit in Bill's office, alone with a magazine, with the door closed. I can hear Bill dealing with our daughters, who were chattering like magpies in the kitchen. I open the magazine and begin to read. I take my first bite.

The next week, I drop them at day care. As I leave, I hear their sobbing, their screams. I open my car door, sit down, and close it. Never again will I hit a point so low. Yet I inhale silence like a drowning person finding air. I turn on the engine and drive away ... for 3 hours.

Retired Elsie ~ 1981 ~ Selling an Explosive House

[What happens when a petroleum tanker dumps its fuel into the sewer line at a gas station? Elsie opens her diary, penning ... her last entry?]

9:30 Movers finally come to pick up furniture for Florida. Doing well until 11:30 Police riding around telling people to evacuate all houses. Eight have *blown up!!!* in Takoma Park from a gas leak. 11:45 Our movers are leaving! Herby turns off gas in house. 11:57 Termite inspector arrives. What a time to come!

12:00 Noon Officials are "sniffing" the sewer with instruments. Two fire trucks. Police walking away. Don't seem alarmed. Oops—firemen checking sewer across street. One has axe. 12:04 Photographer arrives. 12:08 They're right in front of me lifting up the sewer lid. Whew! OK. 12:20 Herby comes out. There are a few minor repairs. He goes back. 12:27 Helicopter circling. Police cruising.

12:30 Chillum Adelphi fire truck arrives. Another warning: "LEAVE AREA!"

Ambulance arrives. 12:40 Termite man leaving. Police blocking all intersections.

12:42 We're leaving! ...

PS: Hope we sell the house before it blows up.

Daughter Barbara ~ 2000 ~ Last Meeting with Mom

As Rosemary and I drive across Washington State, I cannot believe how much I *miss* my mother, this woman who virtually has *nothing* to offer me. No recognition. No conversation. No intelligence.

Before we moved her to Seattle, I recruited a friend whose photography I admired. "Can you help me take some pictures of Mom before she leaves," I ask. "I want to capture her beauty."

On the designated day, my friend shows up with her professional camera. I use my Canon Rebel.

We wheel Mom outside onto the front steps. The sun is shining. We begin a photo shoot. We photograph Mom's hands, her feet, her eyes, her head, angles of her body.

We treat her with all the reverence one accords the truly beautiful.

I still have those photos: All of them. And they look appalling. I see no beauty. I see the ravages of disease. I don't see my mother anywhere in these images. And I wonder what was I thinking? That I could find beauty in this physical devastation?

My sister, when she first saw Mom debarking from the plane on August 12, burst into tears. I never knew. She turned away from Mom, Hawa, and me. Then she quickly composed herself, and with a beaming face walked over to Mom and hugged her.

I still wonder—what do we *see*? What does a camera capture?

It occurs to me that when the person no longer connects with this world, as is true with Alzheimer's, a camera can no longer capture the person. We know cameras capture emotion—a child's smile, the raw ravages of war, a lover's kiss. The image is *filled* with *presence*. But the emotion for the mentally ravaged is gone.

Perhaps when I was with my mother, I saw past all the veils of the disease. Somehow I stayed connected to the essence of Elsie. I simply didn't *see* the disease.

Nevertheless, I clearly remember that when I first saw my friend's photos, I could not find even one image to match how I *felt* about Mom. Nothing to record the *relationship* I still experienced in her presence. Perhaps it was just too subtle at that point to be captured by a mechanical object—a camera.

Now, as I see Mom in Stephanie's group home, I burst into tears of joy not sadness. I really missed her. I missed her wildly flapping hands, her babble, her strangely vacant-present eyes.

Mom's eyes used to twinkle mischievously. She'd trick you with her sneaky blue-irised eyes: demanding attention, magnetizing you until you were roped into her agenda. On the other hand, you could be frozen mid-stride with one unblinking arctic-blue ice-cold gaze.

Now her eyes no longer beguile or chill me. Things have changed. The end-of-life gaze is still different from the mischievous eyes, the icy eyes, the lights-out eyes, or even the eyes-of-light.

~ ~ ~

It is 10 a.m. The RV is packed. Rosemary waits outside. I go in. Mom is dressed in khaki pants and a blue-striped blouse. She sits in a wheelchair near a window, motionless. She has finished breakfast. A can of Ensure. A barely touched bowl of oatmeal and applesauce.

Time quietly seems to stop.

I feel tears welling up. She seems so fragile, so near the end of life—and I am leaving her. It feels almost unbearable and I wonder why.

ELSIE AT EBB TIDE

I tell myself Alzheimer platitudes—she's already gone. She lives in a world nobody can reach. Yet I realize that every step she has descended into this disease has been a step deeper into my heart. Somehow, beneath the proud determined mother who once was a Protocol Officer rests this amazing, sturdy, happy, earth-loving person—resilient and very much alive even in the final stages.

I walk over to her and kneel down. Tears spill down my cheeks. I can't help it. I don't know when or even if I'll see her again alive.

Suddenly she grasps my forearms in her tight bony grip and gazes directly into my eyes with startling clarity. The fog is gone. She stares intently at me.

Suddenly I am seeing something I have never seen before—not in her eyes or any eyes.

It is as though pure consciousness is pouring through her. She is allowing me to see what *she* now sees. I am looking right into *Spirit*—pure *Love* unfettered by a human body.

She is allowing me to see the whole cosmos of Love pouring *through* her.

I gaze back in utter astonishment. I feel as though the last barrier between life and death has been exposed. And the Love pouring through her is unlike any human love she ever gave to me or Sandra. It is so clear, so powerful, so transcendent. I am literally knocked out of my senses.

I tear my eyes from her gaze. I—the living—must go. She—the dying—must stay. I kiss her on the forehead. Tears pour out of my eyes. I turn my back and walk away.

I do not know this.

But I will never see her again.

Retired Elsie ~ 1982 ~ Florida Diary

Quiet day to read and watch birds & listen to the avocados drop.

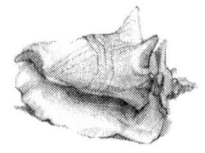

Kenna and Elsie ~ 2000 ~
Having Your Own "Mental Travel Agent"

<u>Kenna</u>: Did you enjoy Barbara's visit?

<u>Elsie</u>: Yes, but I don't remember when she's coming back. I'd like to go on a trip like that.

<u>Kenna</u>: Like Barbara's?

<u>Elsie</u>: Yes. I love to travel.

<u>Kenna</u>: You can travel in your mind. Just say where you want to go.

<u>Elsie</u>: You're right. I can. All I need is to go to a Mental Travel Agent. [She laughs.]

<u>Kenna</u>: What's in your heart today?

<u>Elsie</u>: I like it when my grandchildren visit.

<u>Kenna</u>: What about when the angels visit?

<u>Elsie</u>: Yes, but I like to see my family more.

<u>Kenna</u>: Angels are family too. You have your own family of angels.

<u>Elsie</u>: I never thought about it like that.

<u>Kenna</u>: It's true. You have your own angels and I have mine. Of course, some angels visit everybody. So you can have your angels visit any time. Just call on them.

~ ~ ~

While in earlier sessions with Elsie, Kenna mentions angels in passing, now she begins to be very focused on connecting Mom to her angels. She helps her to see them.

My sense is that Kenna knows the end is nearing and wants Mom to have a safe and easy passage to the other world. Kenna is taking the lead here.

For the first time, she is not just listening to Mom but guiding and instructing her.

September 18

Rebellious Barbara ~ 1989 ~
The Florida Cardboard-Box War

"Okay, Sandra," I holler down the hall. "We'd better get packed. We leave for the airport in 2 hours."

We've done our annual clothes shopping. I know my suitcase won't hold all my new purchases. "Mom, have you got a paper bag I can use? I can't get everything into my luggage." Mom pokes her head in the guest bedroom and looks in horror at the mound of clothes.

"You need a box," she advises.

"No, a bag will work."

"A box is sturdier, Barbara."

"I'd rather carry a bag onboard."

"What if it breaks?"

"It won't. I'll be careful."

"I'll get the box for you."

"I don't want a box."

"I'll pack it for you."

"No. It's too bulky. It's hard to carry."

"I'll make a handle for you."

"Mom, I don't want a box."

I get my reputation for stubbornness honestly. By now, our voices are ratcheting up. Sandra watches in horror. It seems as though Mom and I are actually having a *fight*—unheard of in our Finnish upbringing.

I am not backing down. I am not yielding. I am not going to give way on this box. I *don't want a box.* I am facing Elsie-the-Titanic in an all-out war over a *cardboard box*. How ridiculous is that. I could have at least made my Custer-like stand on world peace or saving Biafra.

At last, in stony silence, Mom leaves the room, returns, and silently hands me a paper bag. I, victorious but oddly unnerved, pack my paper bag.

~ ~ ~

I look back on that moment—the cardboard-box war—as the point when I moved from childhood to adulthood. Our relationship shifted on its axis.

Mom no longer tried to force her way on me. Eventually I would have to learn not to force *my* way on *her*.

I remember our having a conversation one afternoon a year or so after that. Just Mom and me. I bucked up my courage and talked about things I felt had badly affected me growing up.

I thought a lot about what Sandra had said—the effect on us from their nightly cocktails. Were we invisible children? Had they been emotionally remote because of *that*? To my surprise, Mom admitted twice in that conversation that they had been alcoholics. It was a shocking admission, one I never remotely expected.

If she and Dad were alcoholics, they hid it pretty well. We had our Sundays at the beach, our vacations, our nightly dinner table conversations, their intense interest in our grades, regular full-blown Thanksgiving and Christmas events. It didn't sound like alcoholism to me.

Whatever it was, it came to a stone-cold halt in one day. Stubborn as a board—which Finns call *sisu*—they did stop drinking. I wonder if addicted alcoholics could simply stop. Eventually I will decide that it is impossible to separate vodka and beer from the Finnish-American culture of that time.

I always wondered about their first post-alcohol party. In a BYOB Finnish world (bring beer or vodka), how did Elsie and Herby change it to BYOG—ginger ale? Yet the next time I saw the gang together, at least half the Finns were drinking soda pop. They morphed into BYO whatever-you-want.

I never needed another heart-to-heart conversation with Mom. She *listened*. I felt we made our final shift from a mother-daughter relationship to a woman-woman one.

It turned out to be critically important in order for me to eventually step into a caregiving role later. We needed to respect and trust each other. In a way, it was *my* turn to listen ... and I would be enormously slow in learning.

Retired Elsie ~ 1982 ~ Florida Diary

Avocados falling like rain—have about 12 on hand. They woke me up.

September 21

Wartime Elsie ~ 1944 ~ Swante Missing in Action

"No," Elsie writes Herby, "still no news of Swante. I try to call Mayme once a week."

~ ~ ~

One morning I noticed bites on my ankles that itched a lot. Then I felt something crawling on my chest. I reached down and caught a large gray bug which I found out was body lice. Now I pick and kill lice with everybody else.

When traveling, I pick a few hazelnuts, split and eat them. The food I get is sparse. I weighed about 165 pounds when I got shot down. Don't know what I am now but everything hangs on me. One day all I got was weak soup made of rutabaga peelings. Occasionally I get some hard dark bread. Now and then they give me mutton which I don't like but of course I eat.

Today I arrived in a small village. I met nine American flyers who bailed out of different planes. For the first time, I'm getting enough to eat.

~ ~ ~

"Elsie," they *found* him! He's *safe!*" Mayme weeps over the phone. "He's SAFE! He's with the Partisans but he's been found. They say his arm is broken."

Elsie holds the receiver as relief swamps her. "Oh, Mayme..." she says, unable to go on.

Career Elsie ~ 1962 ~ White House Flower Girl

"Mrs. Nurmi," the formidable Mr. Spruks stops by his new secretary's desk. "Come with me. I need you to hand Mrs. Kennedy flowers for Mrs. Selassie."

"But I'm not dressed to see Mrs. Kennedy," Elsie weakly protests. Thankfully he is already out the door or she might have been fired on the spot.

Eventually she'll learn there's really only one rule of protocol, even for the secretarial help, which is—now. It seems everything has a deadline and the deadline is the same minute you're standing in.

Well, I need my job more than my dignity, she decides and meets him at the elevator. Down they go to the basement to pick up a government car. Fifteen minutes later, they're parked at Union Station.

Elsie knows Emperor Haile Selassie is arriving from New York City after his U.N. meeting for a state visit at the White House. But knowing, from the safety of your secretarial desk, is a far cry from handing flowers to the first lady for the emperor's wife.

Like every other female federal employee, Elsie is wowed by Jacqueline Kennedy's style. Sheepishly as they walk through the train station, Elsie considers her own wardrobe. *Here I am, wearing a lime green sheath dress like Jackie; my hair in her bouffant style.* She hates to admit it. *I am a blonde blue-eyed Finnish farm girl version of Jackie from head to toe.* But, Elsie decides, *I think I carry it off rather well.*

Now she trembles. It is one thing to dress like Mrs. Kennedy. It's another to walk up to her representing the United States Department of State Protocol Office.

"Okay, Mrs. Nurmi," Mr. Spruks advises Elsie while they stand in the cavernous train station waiting. "Make sure you stay near Mrs. Kennedy so you can hand her the roses when she needs them." Then he strolls off to talk to some of the other State Department staff.

Elsie hears a faint horn announcing the train will soon be approaching the station.

She watches the empty track mesmerized. Mrs. Kennedy stands chatting quietly with her staff. Elsie casually gazes around the terminal. She used to work for the Atlantic Coast Line Railroad. Her glass-windowed office lay between two train tracks.

She loved trains, loved watching people hurry to catch them—going somewhere, anywhere.

She looks back towards Mrs. Kennedy. *Where is she?* Elsie panics. Far away from her, she sees Jacqueline striding gracefully toward the slowly arriving train.

Paralyzed with indecision, Elsie wonders, *Is she going to walk back?* Just then, she hears a booming voice hollering at her.

"MRS. NURMI," Spruks roars, "NOW!"

Elsie begins to run. She can hear her black-heeled shoes hitting the station platform like staccato notes on her piano. She runs faster and faster. She is closing in. The train groans to a stop. Mrs. Selassie is descending. Jackie stands at the foot of the metal steps. She turns to her left; Elsie throws the flowers into her hands; the first lady graciously turns and places the extravagant bouquet of long-stemmed red roses into Mrs. Selassie's arms.

Elsie manages to stagger discreetly behind a pillar, double over, and pant for breath. *This is no way to run a business*, she thinks to herself. *I may have a very short career here.* She worriedly glances back at her boss. She tries to walk back to him with dignity—what little is left in her disheveled state.

"Next time, Mrs. Nurmi," Mr. Spruks admonishes, "Try not to make so much noise running."

Being a White House flower girl sometimes leaves Elsie holding the bag when diplomatic disaster strikes. ...

On this particular day, she holds the bouquet to be given by Lady Bird Johnson. The helicopter flies into sight on a beautiful blue Washington day with fluffy cumulus clouds floating overhead. The flowers she carries are once again long-stemmed red roses. The helicopter starts to descend. Lady Bird Johnson stands nearby waiting. Elsie is ready.

Then the air begins to swirl around them as the copter blades roar overhead until the sound is deafening. She feels like she is in a tornado, the wind plastering her navy Brooks Brother suit against her, her hair being torn to pieces. Finally the copter touches ground and the rotor blades slow to a quiet slapping sound against the air. As the visiting dignitaries are escorted onto the grass, Elsie relaxes, ready to transfer the flowers. She steps toward Mrs. Johnson, giving the roses one last glance to make sure they weren't disturbed by the wind.

"Where are they? she stares in stunned silence. All she has in her hands are a bunch of green stems. She turns back to where she was standing. Hundreds of bright red rose petals are fluttering across the grass like brightly colored Easter eggs.

"What to do? as Herby would say. Well, there really was nothing *to* do. She walks up to the First Lady, whispers an apology, and hands her the bouquet of stems.

September 24

Wartime Elsie ~ 1944 ~ Swante, Almost Rescued ...

"Have you gotten any more news, Mayme?" Elsie asks on her weekly call.

"Nothing," Mayme replies glumly. "I know he's alive. I've been told they're trying to fly him to Italy with some other rescued fliers. But," she pauses, "he has a broken arm. At least that's the message they got from the Partisans."

~ ~ ~

Three C-47 cargo planes landed in a field near the village. They're flown by South Africans. The first took off empty to see if they could make it, and it got up. The second was loaded with six wounded Partisans and it got up. The last plane loaded us ten Americans plus some Partisan wives and kids. The seats were full. As it turned out, the plane was overloaded. I got the last seat but my seat belt was broken.

The plane took off and used up all the field but couldn't gain enough altitude. I saw a wingtip knock off the top of a tree. We came down and crashed in a river bank.

With no seat belt to stop me, I rolled down the aisle as the plane hit and slammed up against the door of the cockpit. When the plane stopped, I saw a flash of fire outside.

I shot back down the aisle and jumped out the rear door. People were jumping on my back but I managed to crawl away from the plane.

Retired Elsie ~ 1982 ~ Florida Diary

Have 30 avocados to get rid of—2 avocados to Chuck, 2 avocados to Harold. Sold 9 avocados at the Lake Worth Republican Club today (after they introduced the candidates).

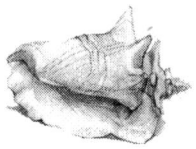

Kenna and Elsie ~ 2000 ~ Why So Quiet, Elsie?

<u>Kenna</u>: So what are you thinking about?

<u>Elsie</u>: *I'm thinking I like it here. Where's Barbara?*

<u>Kenna</u>: On a trip. In Colorado.

<u>Elsie</u>: *Will she be coming back soon?*

<u>Kenna</u>: I'm not sure. I think so. Do you want to say anything to her?

<u>Elsie</u>: *I miss her.*

<u>Kenna</u>: Is your family visiting more often?

<u>Elsie</u>: *Yes, and they brought fruit.*

<u>Kenna</u>: But Elsie, you don't eat fruit.

<u>Elsie</u>: *No, but my mind does.*

<u>Kenna</u>: Elsie, you seem quiet. [This is the most quiet Kenna has ever seen her. She's not talkative.]

<u>Elsie</u>: *I've settled down here. I'm ready for another adventure.*

<u>Kenna</u>: You can go on adventures in your mind. Look to your left, Elsie. See the angel?

<u>Elsie</u>: *Yes.*

<u>Kenna</u>: She can take you wherever you want to go.

<u>Elsie</u>: *Angels are light and fluffy. I like much more substance!*

ELSIE AT EBB TIDE

~ ~ ~

Later, as Kenna shares this conversation with me, she asks, "Does your mother tend to be indirect? She's not acting like herself."

It's a strange question but I try to answer it. "Oh, Mom was the master of indirectness," I admit, thinking back to her child-whisperer skills. "But really, I think it's a generational thing. You know, women of that era grew up in an unequal world. How were they supposed to get their way? Sometimes she drove Sandra and me crazy."

"How did she do that?" Kenna asked curiously.

"Well, one time she was worried about Dad's health. Sandra and I were both married, but she called us to give us our part in a 'script' she had put together." I started laughing.

"It was kind of … 'Okay, Sandra you say this, then Barbara, you stop by the house later in the week and say this'—and Mom gave us our speeches. It sounded absolutely insane to me. 'Why don't you just tell him what you want?' I asked. But I already knew the answer—they never had direct conversations about Dad's health."

"Did it work?"

"I think so—I honestly don't remember. But he *did* go to the doctor a few times in his later years. So maybe…."

"My mother is the same way. Maybe you're right. Anyway, I keep sensing your mother wanted to tell me about something bothering her. She was just too quiet. That's where I got this feeling of indirectness."

"I guess we'll just have to wait and see," I tell Kenna, a bit worried.

September 30

Wartime Elsie ~ 1944 ~ Swante Safe in Italy

No, Mayme," Swante tells her, "none of the passengers were injured. But that crash broke the pilot's back.

"You're okay, though?" she asks anxiously.

"I'm eating like a pig. Another C-47 arrived a few days later. We took off with no problem and got to Bari. I'm in this beautiful hospital with white marble floors and walls. All the cigarettes I want. They sprayed me with DDT to kill the lice and burned my clothes. I lost a hell of a lot of weight—55 pounds."

He raced on with his news, thrilled to be over his ordeal and actually talking to his wife. "I'm going to get an operation tomorrow to remove bone splinters. The doctor told me what I already know. My arm was set crooked. He thinks I'll get some sort of disability payment for the rest of my life because I'll never get full use of it.

"All I want to do is come home, Mayme. You know, they actually asked if we'd want to reenlist. Even gave us inducements. Hell no! Hug Patty for me. I'm coming home!"

Retired Elsie ~ 1982 ~ Florida Diary

Got 2 avocados from "old" tree. Lamp shade fell down & broke. Box fell on my head. Sweet potato can leaked all over the pantry. Read the wrong minutes at the Republican Club. I must be bewitched.

October

Letting Go

October 1

Retired Elsie ~ 1990 ~ Robert Adam's Misfortune

I honestly didn't know Mom (like many seniors) goes straight to the obit page in the newspaper to see who's died. It must be a coming-of-age thing. I've recently begun to read them, and I hardly know anyone in Hannibal.

When I visited Mom recently, it seems that Robert Adam, the brother of the second cousin of my father on his mother's side, died. Weeks earlier, Robert started acting crazy and ended up in a nursing home. Mom went to see him. Sure enough he sounded seemed pretty nuts. But a few days later, he returned to normal and even knew his doctor's name.

So imagine Mom's surprise when doing her daily obit scan over morning coffee, she sees Robert Adams *dead!* She rushes to the phone and calls the National Crematorium Society.

"Is this the Robert Adams who was at Lakeside Rest Home?" she asks.

I hear the loud (obviously for elder ears) response, "We can't give out that information. We're only the answering service."

"But I need to know so I can call his relatives in Colorado."

"I'm sorry. You'll have to wait until Monday. The offices open at 10 a.m."

Elsie, understandably distressed, loudly mutters into the receiver, "What the hell kind of answers *do* you give?"

I suppress a giggle.

"I'm sorry. We're just the answering service."

"Well, let me tell you this! I will NEVER go to YOU to be cremated!" Elsie angrily slams down the receiver.

"Why don't you call his room, Mom? If he answers, he's alive."

"I can't do that," Mom tries to explain to me. "If he answers, what will I say? "Hello Robert, I heard you were dead …?" We both start laughing.

"Well, call the nursing home," I suggest.

Knowing she's not family, she decides to grease the wheels by making them understand she *intimately* knows him.

Mom launches into a long story about visiting Robert, half-crazed, then Robert, seemingly sane. Finally she talks about the obituary.

"I saw his obituary in the paper today. Robert is the brother of my deceased husband's second cousin. I'll have to notify family in Colorado but I want to make sure it's the *same* Robert Adams."

"Oh, let me see," the receptionist puts Mom on hold. When she returns, she says, "Nobody's died here for 2 weeks."

"Whew!" Mom says as she hangs up. "There must be two Robert Adams. I'm sure glad I checked."

Now, most of us would probably have called Robert's room. If Robert answered, we'd probably say, "Hi, how are you." But that's not the Finnish way, which is naturally circuitously incomprehensible.

For example, if you are visiting a traditional Finnish-American home the hostess will offer you coffee, which of course you refuse.

After a bit of polite intercourse, she will ask again, and of course you say no. After all, you've only been asked *two* times.

More time passes during which you experience severe caffeine deprivation.

Finally when she asks a third time, you reluctantly agree, and the hostess pours coffee so weak you can see through it.

ELSIE AT EBB TIDE

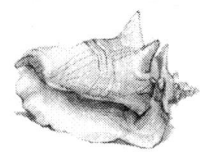

Kenna and Elsie ~ 2000 ~ Dancing with the Angels

When Kenna connects, she continues to be concerned that Elsie was so unnaturally quiet and not talkative the last time. It was the worst she had seen her.

~ ~ ~

Elsie: I'm not feeling well.

Kenna: How so?

Elsie: I've been thinking about the meaning of my life. Was I a good mother? Did I make the right decisions?

[Kenna senses something has happened at the group home that has depressed Elsie.]

Kenna: I'm here to cheer you up. Depression is an option you don't need. What is going on? What happened?

Elsie: I don't know.

[Kenna continues the energy-healing work on Elsie.]

Elsie: I feel better already.

Kenna: Let's remove all this heaviness from your heart.

Elsie: I'd like to dance now.

Kenna: Have you been talking to the angels?

Elsie: No.

Kenna: Why not?

Elsie: Oh, I don't know what to say.

Kenna: Just talk to them like you talk to me. They're here to be your friends and to help you. Just tell them what you would like.

Elsie: Okay.

Kenna: Think of the angels as a delegation from another country.

[Kenna finishes her energy work by filling Elsie with Light.]

Elsie: *It feels like sunshine.*

~ ~ ~

"Kenna," I ask, "what happens when you are filling Mom with Light? What does that mean?"

"Well," Kenna pauses, searching for words to explain something that can't be seen, "we're all connected to an eternal Source. Even in the Bible, it says, 'Let there be Light.'

"We have ways of expressing it, like saying, she lit up the room. The Light within us can be expanded until it kind of overflows. When I allow that, it starts pouring out of me in all directions. It's like I'm being filled with Divine Essence and then I channel it into your mother so she too can experience it."

"Like sunshine," I answer, remembering my own experiences with Kenna. I feel as though my whole body is *saturated* with Light, as though it cannot hold one more molecule of it.

But Kenna's effort to focus Mom on angels fails to work. Mom sidesteps, saying *Oh, I don't know what to say.* From my perspective, this is vintage Elsie—she isn't interested. I am left wondering why Kenna talks with Mom so much about angels. Is she preparing Elsie to go? Does she see the end nearing? She doesn't tell me.

After listening to Kenna, I call Sandra who tells me, "Remember the woman in the other bedroom?" I vaguely recall a bedridden woman so small and frail as to be barely noticeable. "She died a couple weeks ago."

I call Kenna back. "I wonder if Mom got depressed because, in some way, she sensed that death and knew that her time was coming?" Neither of us has an answer.

Mother Barbara ~ 1983 ~ Losing Lisa in a Haystack

I hear Kendra outside yelling to her best friend Julie who lives next door, "Let's put Lisa in the wagon. She can be the baby. You're the Daddy; I'll be the Mommy."

I look out the kitchen window and see Lisa unceremoniously dumped into the red racer wagon. "Let's take her for a ride," Kendra dictatorially decides. I watch them wheel the wagon toward the woods and go back to washing dishes.

Suddenly I hear a tiny knock on the door. It opens. Julie stands before me, white with shock. "Mrs. Taylor, Lisa rolled down the hill. The wagon turned over!"

I drop the wet sponge and fly out the door. Julie points toward the steep grassed hill that ends in the woods. I see the red racer upside down, the wheels still spinning. I tear down the hill. Just as I get there, I see this little head poking its way out of a pile of brown leaves and start to laugh. With leaves sticking to her hair helter-skelter all over her, all I know is that she's safe.

I give the mandatory lecture to Kendra: "*Never ever* let go of the wagon with Lisa in it." Kendra contritely agrees. I go back to washing dishes.

"Let's take Lisa to the sandbox," suggests Kendra, dragging her toddler sister by the hand. "She can be baby bear. You be daddy bear...."

October 8

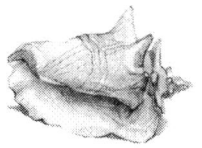

Kenna and Elsie ~ 2000 ~ I See Clearly Now
[Kenna sees Elsie's heart beating very slowly. But that is just the way it is at that moment. The guides tell her the issue is not her physical health, but a kind of nervous agitation—the death of the other woman has triggered a lot of issues for her.]

<u>Kenna</u>: What's going on, Elsie?

<u>Elsie</u>: *I don't know.*

[Kenna begins working on her telepathically.]

Elsie: You know my brain got clearer and I began to see myself more clearly.

[Kenna senses that she sees her true situation.]

Elsie: Tell Barbara I love her. I'm sorry I didn't show it much.

Kenna: So what do you want now, Elsie?

Elsie: Oh, I'm tired now. I just want to rest. Tell my family not to worry. I'm okay.

~ ~ ~

"Barbara," Kenna tries to explain what's happening, "all her life, your mother has been unable to let her real thoughts out. This is the way her body reacts to the fact that the woman's death has upset her."

"I don't understand."

"If we don't release our emotions, then our body holds onto them and releases them some other way—like an illness. Your mother had the opportunity to talk to me last Sunday but she didn't take it. That's not her way. It's not her personality. So she had to release it some other way. In a way, she is calling attention to herself. I get a strong sense that she needs more attention when something like this happens."

"So that death really affected her," I reply wondering how it can be avoided in a home for the elderly.

"This is definitely a reaction to what has happened there." Kenna explains. "It is on her mind, and heavy in her heart."

I realize once again—I just cannot make death go away.

Child Elsie ~ 1920 ~ Thief!

"Elsie," her mother calls into the bedroom, "come here so I can comb your hair."

Three-year-old Elsie dutifully goes in. Her mother uses the hairbrush to untangle her thick, straight, bowl-cut hair. "Are you ready for the party?" her mother asks.

Elsie isn't quite sure what a party is. She wanders into the living room while her mother and father finish dressing. On a round table right in the middle sits the plant that normally resides in the corner of the dining room. One white blossom shows. Elsie decides it's pretty, so she picks it.

Thinking her mother will be very pleased, she takes it into the bedroom. "Mom," she begins, "I picked this flower for you." Her mother turns around from the vanity. In Elsie's hand is the *century-old flower*—the one that blooms only once every 100 years. The *reason* for the party.

"ELSIE!" she screams. "YOU PUT THAT DOWN RIGHT NOW! That's our HUNDRED YEAR FLOWER!" Sooner than her mother can get up from her seat, Elsie turns and begins to run as fast as her plump legs will take her, up the stairs, under the bed—still clutching the now-mangled flower. She hears thunderous feet crashing up the stairs.

She sees her father's hands reaching under the bed to grab her. She sees her mother's heels and stocking legs on the other side.

She has no idea what a hundred years is. It must be the name of the flower. As she crouches under the bed, she promises herself—as her parents scream at her—she'll never pick a century flower again. It's too dangerous. She's too young to know she'll probably never live long enough to attempt it.

October 13

Confused Elsie ~ 2000 ~ The Emergency Room

"Your mother is having difficulty breathing. She seems to be in pain," Stephanie alerts Sandra.

"I'll be there in 10 minutes," Sandra hangs up the phone, grabs her keys, and yells to a coworker. "Something's wrong with my mother. Tell the boss," and she flies out the door.

Stephanie greets her at the door. "I've called 911."

Sandra walks into Mom's room. She's struggling to breathe, her skin is pallid. She looks frightened. Sandra grabs her wrist, feeling for the pulse. It's shallow and rapid. Sandra begins to croon to her while they wait. "Mom," she leans over whispering, "they're on the way. You need to go to the hospital."

Elsie looks lost and confused. She grips Sandra's hand. Watching her struggle to breathe totally unnerves Sandra. She can hear the siren coming down the road, growing louder as it turns onto the gravel driveway. She hears the door opening, the sound of heavy feet walking rapidly to the room.

The paramedics move her aside and start taking vitals. Their voices seem so loud. "Is there a 'Do-Not-Resuscitate' order?" the lead medic raises his voice. Sandra jumps. Stephanie says "yes," and heads out the door. It's supposed to be posted by the entrance, but it's not.

"We need it *now*," he orders. "Otherwise I need to put a trache in—she can't breathe."

The place is in an uproar. Stephanie is ripping through files. It's nowhere.

He turns to Sandra and starts yelling. "We NEED to get a trache in right now or she'll suffocate! Sandra is screaming "NO! There IS a 'Do-Not-Resuscitate' order."

"We can't wait." He starts ripping stuff out of his medic bag. Sandra, furious and unable to stop anything, collapses in a chair.

Then to everyone's surprise, he can't do it. Something isn't working. Neither Sandra nor Stephanie have any idea—they've never seen one done—but whatever he needs, he's missing it.

"Okay," he gives up. "Let's get her in the ambulance." Minutes later the siren is screaming down the driveway. They are 20 minutes from the hospital. Sandra calls Ed. "You've *got* to get me to the hospital right now. Mom's having an emergency. I *need* you!"

"Stay there. I'll pick you up in 15 minutes. I don't want you driving."

Sandra calls me from the group home. "Barbara, Mom's having trouble breathing. We called 911. The ambulance has just taken her to the hospital. Ed's picking me up. I called Kier. He'll meet us there. I can't get through to the other boys. It looks bad."

Emotions start colliding inside me. I am 3,000 miles away from Mom. I can't take charge; I can't take care of her. All I can do is ask questions. "What happened?"

"Stephanie thinks it may be pneumonia. I'll call when I know something."

We hang up. It is 7 p.m.

What is going to happen? I walk around the living room. I sit down and try to pray. I can't. I go to the phone. *I need to get there.* Then I realize there *is* one way I *can* be with Mom....

"Kenna," I talk rapidly into the receiver. "Mom's been taken to the emergency room. Sandra says she's having trouble breathing. Can you connect with her?

"Okay, Barbara. I'll check to see what's going on."

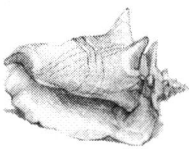

Kenna and Elsie ~ 2000 ~ I Want to Rest

<u>Kenna</u>: I'm here, Elsie.

<u>Kenna</u>: Are things going to be okay, Elsie?

<u>Elsie</u>: *I don't know.* [She seems scared and confused.]

<u>Kenna</u>: Well, let's try to hold on for Barbara to get here. You're giving them a good scare."

<u>Elsie</u>: *Yeah, well I'm good for something.*

<u>Kenna</u>: Who is with you now?

<u>Elsie</u>: *Just the usual crew.*

<u>Kenna</u>: Barbara is coming.

<u>Elsie</u>: *I'd like to see her.*

[Kenna sees that she can go either way. It seems that Elsie has vomited. Whatever is wrong, Kenna sees that she will have a recurrence. At this moment, Elsie does not know what she is going to do.]

~ ~ ~

"The doctor needs to talk to you, Barbara. You have the medical power of attorney."

"Give me an update, Sandra," I hear my voice sounding strangely tinny and high.

"She's not going to make it," Sandra answers in a choppy, heavy voice as unnatural as mine. "Here's Dr. Fisher."

"Is this Barbara Taylor?" I hear Dr. Fisher identify himself over the phone.

"Yes," I answer tensely, gripping the receiver.

"You have medical power of attorney, is that correct?"

"Yes."

"Her lungs are about 70 percent filled with fluid. She's too weak to cough. She's in septic shock."

"What does that mean?"

"It means all her organs are shutting down. She's experiencing severe abdominal pain. We can do heroic measures to keep her alive or palliative care to make her comfortable. What do you want us to do?"

"Can you keep her alive until I get there? I'm getting the next flight out."

"Then we'd have to start heroic measures for her."

I silently hold the receiver thinking of Mom. *I always promised you no pain—oh happy death.* The silence drags on.

"Are you there?" Dr. Fisher asks. "What do you want us to do?"

I start to cry. "I swore I'd do everything in my power to protect her from pain—that's what I've tried to do for her all these years." I had a hard time going on.

He waited. I could feel anger rising up in me—anger at *death*. I'd never see her alive again. I'd never get there in time.

"Oh happy death," I say in a defeated quiet voice. "No heroic measures."

"Okay, Ms. Taylor. I promise you, we'll make her comfortable."

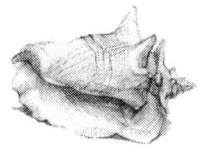

Kenna and Elsie ~ 2000 ~ No Wonder People Die

<u>Kenna</u>: What do you want, Elsie?

<u>Elsie</u>: *I sure am not going to hang around in a lot of pain. I will tell you that! I won't put up with this nonsense. All this coming and going. I want to rest. No wonder people die. To get some rest!*

[Kenna clears the energy between Mom, Sandra, and me. Whatever happens will be okay. Angels are with her. Kenna tells her what to do and how. All of that is set. Kenna gives her benediction.]

~ ~ ~

Kenna calls me as soon as she disconnects from Elsie. "Sandra needs to stay as calm as possible. Your mother is scared and confused. It's not her intention to die. She may recover but it could happen again.

Tell Sandra if she thinks your mother is dying, tell her to go to the Light. She is confused and she needs to stay focused."

I burst out crying. "The doctor called me. They can't save her without heroic measures. I can't get there in time. Kenna," I feel a sorrow so deep I cannot find the bottom of it, "I'm going to lose her. I can't even say good-bye."

"You can talk to her, Barbara. Tell her what's in your heart. "

"I know." *But really I don't. I'm not a psychic. I'm a daughter.*

~ ~ ~

Elsie is now slipping away so fast there's not even time to admit her to a hospital room. The emergency-room staff rolls her to a quiet, curtained area. Sandra, Ed, and Kier are with her.

I call Sandra. "Kenna says for you to tell Mom to head toward the Light."

"Okay," Sandra promises.

Departing Elsie ~ 2000 ~ Saying Good-Bye

"We're going to start an intravenous morphine drip to make her comfortable," Dr. Fisher explains to Sandra. "She's in septic shock and in abdominal pain."

Sandra now knows too. Mom will die.

All her phobia about hospitals and death surges up. She is remembering Dad's death—how she sat in the waiting room till she was sure he was dead, only to walk in and find him still dying.

Now once again, she is watching death. She watches Mom struggle for breath slowly ease. It's been 2 hours since they arrived. The nurse comes in periodically. She matter-of-factly explains Mom can no longer see or hear. It seems the only thing they can do is watch as her breathing gets slower and slower. Her dominating, controlling mother looks so diminished, so small.

Sandra frequently leaves her chair at the foot of the bed, takes her mother's unresponsive hand, and leans over to tell her, "Go to the Light; go toward the Light; go to the Light." The minutes tick by in timeless slowness.

After 2 hours, Sandra turns to Ed, tears filling her eyes. "I can't stay," she tells him. "I need to eat. I'm going to tell Barbara I just can't do this."

Ed, knowing the intricacies of Sandra, and loving all of her, says, "We'll go to the Chinese place and feed you. It'll be okay."

Sandra calls me.

"Barbara, I'm going to leave. I've got to eat. I've got to get some sleep."

I now know Mom will die alone and there's absolutely nothing I can do about it. I also know and love my sister. She doesn't do death vigils. It's just the way it is.

"Mom will understand. Just tell her you've got to eat and get some rest and you'll be back as soon as you can. Then she'll know. It'll be okay. You've got to take care of yourself."

We hang up.

~ ~ ~

"I can get you some food from The Keg," Kier offers.

Sandra stares at him undecided.

"Look, you can eat something and then decide what to do next," he adds.

"Okay," Sandra agrees. "But don't mess around. If you're not back in 15 minutes, I'm leaving."

Kier throws his sweatshirt hood over his overgrown thatch of hair, and shoots out the door, his long legs down the corridor, into the rain. Soon he's storming into the sports bar two blocks away. "You've got to give me a sandwich—any kind—to go right away," he tells the bartender, not even bothering to look at the menu. "My mom's got to eat. Her mother's dying *right now!*"

In 4 minutes flat, the cook hands Kier a roast beef sandwich with chips; Kier throws a twenty on the counter and doesn't wait for change. He heads off at a run with the food. Five minutes later he bursts into the cubicle. He's done the whole food run in 13 minutes flat.

Sandra eats. Kier sits back down by Ed at the foot of the bed. They are going to stay as long as it takes.

Elsie will not die alone.

~ ~ ~

I'm trying to pack and getting nowhere. I stand in the middle of the bedroom and say to Lisa, "I can't think." I feel myself going hysterical.

"Mom, where's your suitcase?" Lisa starts pulling clothes out of my closet to pack me. Never have I been so glad to have my daughter staying with me. She's taking over. She finds airline numbers, calls, locates a 10 a.m. nonstop flight to Seattle. Now she's choosing clothes. I can only wonder what a 21-year-old, high-style daughter will pack for her 53-year-old grieving mother.

I sit numbly in my mother's Queen Anne chair. Hours are passing. I cannot sleep. I pace in nervous agitation. Lisa keeps vigil with me. I turn to her. "I'm starving! I need to eat."

"Double-T Diner is open," she tells me.

"But it's after midnight."

"They're open all night. I'll drive."

As I hand her my car keys and we walk out the door, I mentally connect with my mother. I tell her matter-of-factly: *Let me know if you're passing over.* I don't say it with any adamancy. Not in a demanding way but in a bereft way. I am heartbroken my mother is dying and I will not be able to be with her. I never imagined such a thing. Always, always, I felt that I would be by her side to see her off. As Lisa whips the car down darkened roads past neon signs of closed businesses, all I can think is this: I am 3,000 miles and an airplane flight away.

~ ~ ~

Lisa and I arrive at the all-night diner. I am surprised at how *busy* a diner can be at 2 o'clock in the morning. I see lots of young couples, kids sleeping on vinyl booth benches while parents socialize at Formica-topped tables with old-fashioned juke boxes perched on them.

We sit down at our table, open our laminated menus, and are talking when someone taps me on the shoulder. I look up. I see two college-aged couples. They are laughing. One of them asks if I will sing for them. Just at that moment, I notice there's no restaurant table for them. Instead, three chairs have been placed, two backed against one. "What?" I ask, perplexed.

Then Lisa pipes in. "Mom, they want to play musical chairs."

"Oh," I hear myself saying. It makes absolutely *no* sense to me, but nothing makes sense. My mother is dying. I can't get to her. I'm sitting in a restaurant at some god-awful hour. The place is hopping alive and I can't figure that out either. Why *not* sing?

"Okay," I answer, and start a pretty loud version of "Coming 'Round the Mountain." That eliminates one guy. I move into "I've Been Working on the Railroad." A girl goes down. Now only one chair remains. "I'll have to close my eyes," I tell the remaining boy and girl. "If I watch, I'll make sure the girl wins." I shut my eyes and begin to sing one of Mom's favorite songs, "You are My Sunshine." As I sing, I feel all the sadness falling from me. *This is the strangest thing,* I think as I continue to sing. *I'm so happy. I almost feel like I'm flying,* and overcome with ecstasy. I yell "STOP," and look to see who won. The boy sits triumphantly on the chair, doubled over with laughter.

It is over. I turn back to Lisa. "What time is it?" I ask.

She glances at the restaurant clock. "It's 2:30 in the morning, Mom." All my anxiety is gone, completely gone. I don't know what to make of it. All I had wanted, with every particle of my being, was to be in Seattle. Now I feel my body letting go of trying.

When we return home, I feel peaceful, quiet. I go to my jewelry box to get Mom's bracelet—the one with the enamel pins identifying all the delegations she had been in charge of while a Protocol Officer. I have worn it to every major family event once Mom could no longer attend—weddings, graduations, birthdays.

The next morning, at 7 a.m. the phone rings. *Did Mom make it through the night?* I wonder, assuming she has because I've gotten no calls from my sister.

"Barbara, Mom died last night at 11:30 p.m."

"What?" I say in disbelief. I sink into a chair. "Why didn't you call me?"

"It wouldn't change anything. I knew you'd need your sleep before traveling today."

I hold the phone in my hand, my sister on the other side. The silence goes on and on as I feel my mind go absolutely blank, my body numb. Finally I shake myself and say, "Sandra, I've got to go. I've got to get to the airport. I've got to leave." And I hang up.

Lisa comes to my side. "Mom died at 11:30 last night," I tell her.

She stares at me quizzically as though thinking about something. "Mom, that's when you were singing for those kids in the restaurant."

I stare her uncomprehending. Then I realize ... 2:30 a.m. in Maryland would be 11:30 p.m. in Seattle.

I return in my mind to the moment I began singing "You are My Sunshine"—how ecstasy filled me, how I felt so happy, as though *joy* rushed through my body. *She was passing over*, I thought to myself, absolutely awestruck.

I have been told that when people talk to us from the spirit-side, they identify themselves so that we'll know who they are. Mom *loved* music and dancing. It was in her bones.

I had asked her to tell me if she passed over. She used *music* as the way I would know ... absolutely.

She didn't need her chair anymore.

ELSIE AT EBB TIDE

Career Elsie ~ 1969-1974 ~ Thank You, Mrs. Nurmi

"My secretary informed me of your close attention to many details, including arrangements for rental of attire. Thank you."

—Congressman Guy Vander Jagt, 1974

"Our trip to Ecuador was a most stimulating experience. I do want you to know of our appreciation."

—Herbert Singer, founder of one of the largest over-the-counter brokerage firms on Wall Street: Singer, Bean & Mackie, 1968

"I have been back from Panama a few days. I received such great courtesy and hospitality that I am afraid it has spoiled me for all future travel."

—Edward Marcus of Neiman-Marcus, 1968

"It was recently my good fortune to attend the Sesquicentennial celebration of Liberia as the personal envoy of President Nixon. I was very fortunate to have had the superlative service of Mrs. Elsie Nurmi."

—E. Frederic Morrow, Vice President, Bank of America, 1972

"As I told President Nixon, I was very glad to have the opportunity of paying my final respects [at King Frederik IX's funeral]. I want to commend Mrs. Nurmi for all the arrangements she made down to the last detail, especially since mine was complicated by missing connections in Washington on the way back."

—Guilford Dudley, Jr., Chairman of the Board, Life and Casualty Insurance Company, 1972

"Not only do you make excellent arrangements for difficult trips, I marvel at your patience, your persistence, and your efficiency."

—Admiral Arleigh Burke, 1973

"It was mighty nice running into you and Astronaut Borman almost at every stop in Europe. You did a remarkable protocol job."

—Ret. Col. Jack Gertz, U.S. Marines; Public Affairs, AT&T, 1969

October 14

Bereaved Barbara ~ 2000 ~ What's Wrong?

Lisa drops me off at Baltimore's BWI airport. I should be calm. It's all over. Mom has died. There is no longer any rush. I put my check-in bag through security and walk to the last gate, farthest away from security. I sit down and start to cry.

The grandparent-aged couple next to me watches sympathetically. Finally the woman touches my knee. "What's wrong?"

ELSIE AT EBB TIDE

I turn my tear-stained face to her, new tears falling over old. "My mother just died. I couldn't get there in time."

I suddenly look down. "Where's my pocketbook?" I shoot out of my seat. "Oh my god, I left it at security." We're about to board. I feel myself going hysterical. "I can't make it. I can't drag this suitcase all the way back. I can't leave it unattended!"

The woman puts her hand firmly on the bag. "We'll watch it. Run!"

"You can't," I wail through my tears. The airport doesn't allow it!"

"GO. It's okay. Run!"

And I take off.

I look a wreck—like someone released too soon from a mental institution. No matter whom I see, I sob, "My mother just died." I weep to the security officer—"My mother died"—he gives me my pocket book. At the gate, I hand in my boarding pass, abjectly weeping, "My mother died." I know I sound insane, but bucketfuls of grief—13 years of it are pouring out.

But once I'm buckled in my seat and finally on my way to Mom, I stop crying. My role as caretaker is *finally* over. The baby monitor to my heart has turned itself off. I am strangely free—and not used to the feeling. Yet.

~ ~ ~

"Do you want to go to the funeral home first, or go home?" Sandra anxiously asks. She's not sure what she'll be dealing with. Hysterical sister. Demanding sister. Weeping sister. What she actually gets is tired, calm sister.

"I'd like to see her first."

Sandra and Ed wait outside on the plush mute-colored sofa in the reception area. I am ushered into a small sterile room with cream-colored walls, no art, no furniture—just one straight-backed chair to sit on, and a stainless steel gurney holding my mother.

I am completely indifferent to the stark setting, my eyes riveted on Mom.

She lies on the stretcher-like bed with a white cover up to her chin. She looks ... dead. Soft and dead. Relaxed and dead. Old and dead. I kiss her forehead. It's cool and dead. I find no *Elsie* here at all. No *essence-of-Elsie*. Nothing. Now it's hard to cry. I poured all my tears out on the way. I sit with her for a while. Nothing happens. All I am left with are my memories.

After 30 minutes, I get up and leave. I feel ... I don't know what I feel.

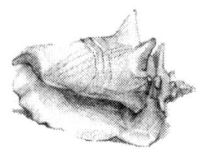

Elsie to Kenna ~ 2000 ~ I Feel Great!

I DID IT! You were right. A lot of people met me and I have been busy. But I have come off by myself to talk to you. I feel great!

Everything works! My brain! My legs! Of course, it is not that I have them [she has a body of light], *but you know what I mean.*
I told *you I was ready for another adventure. Tell Barbara and Sandra I am happy. I wasn't expecting things to go like this. All so quick. But I am happy and I feel great.* [Under her breath,] *I should have done this sooner.*

It all worked out fine. I got extra time with Sandra. Tell Barbara not to worry. I really didn't die alone.
You [Kenna] *have been with me as Barbara's representative, and all the angels were there. It was a big send-off. And now I can* really *fly! But I am just spending time with old friends right now. BYE!*

And she disappears.

October 18

Bereaved Barbara ~ 2000 ~ Hands of Light

I take Sandra's car and return alone the next morning to hold vigil with Mom. I can stay as long as I want. I don't worry about Sandra and Ed sitting, waiting. The funeral home is ready for me. The undertaker ushers me into another room, equally empty. Mom rests in the center, again on a stretcher bed. He closes the door behind him. I am alone.

I walk over to Mom. She has been frozen overnight. Her facial skin sags downward, pulled by gravity, making the skull outline more pronounced. She looks ghastly unnatural. Since she has no friends in the Seattle area, we won't be having a viewing. This is it. The last time I will be able to touch my mother.

I look at her and state the obvious out loud. "You are *really* dead."

I don't like seeing her this way—as a frozen corpse with skin stretched unnaturally over her body. This isn't Mom.

I stay with her, perhaps an hour. I cry. But they're soft quiet tears that trickle and dry before they've even fallen. I really cannot make *any* connection between the living Elsie and the dead Elsie.

So I leave. I'll never see Mom again. Two days later, she will be cremated. Her death certificate will read the immediate cause of death was septic shock: interval between onset and death—6 hours, due to, or as a consequence of pneumonia: interval between onset and death—24 hours. But the real reason, the significant *other* condition, is severe Alzheimer's disease. Dr. Fisher signed the certificate. Hour of death. 23:30 hr. Friday the 13th. 2000.

~ ~ ~

Sitting in the kitchen, Sandra and I throw ourselves into discussing our version of a family memorial service. As we sip coffee, we wonder where in Sandra's house to place Mom's ashes. I take a quick mental tour.

Ed designed and built the home virtually single-handed. Sandra made only one request—no 90-degree walls. As a result, every corner lacks a certain corner-ness. Then there's the turret that, in theory, *should* have given Sandrella a view of her kingdom but in reality only shows her the very tall pine, cedar, and spruce trees surrounding her castle. Then there is the lack of a living room in preference for a maroon-walled entertainment center.

Lastly, there is the "useless" room. Everyone should have one. It is the room that has absolutely no corners because it is as circular as possible. It is not wide enough for a bed or any furniture, so a carpet-upholstered bench becomes the built-in seating. The windows mimic the narrow slits in a castle to be used by son-archers to defend their queen mother. In the center hangs a punching bag, and barbells rest on the red carpet floor.

The useless room actually serves many uses—mostly, escape. Her four teen-aged boys take their girlfriends there. They sprawl, hang out—knowing that the adults have forgotten the room even exists. Stray kids sleep there. It serves a vital purpose—that of no purpose.

There is no doubt in either of our minds. *This* is the room for Elsie's memorial!

Sandra and the boys began to clear it out. They drag in a pedestal and place it in the center. "Kier," Sandra enthusiastically suggests, "put your hands in there." She's referring to the plaster-of-paris hands he just completed for his high school art project, modeled after his own. The fingers stretch up toward the heaven from the cupped palms. When I see it, I agree. It has a surreal between-world feel.

We buy white lilies and place them in a red vase.

Lastly we place Elsie in her maroon ceramic container on the pedestal. We turn it so the brass plaque identifying her as Elsie Nurmi shines near the flowers. Leaving Mom, we head to the kitchen to fix lunch. After eating, I wander into the room just to sit quietly with her. As I step in, light seems to bend itself in an impossible angle through the archer's windows directly into the cupped hands.

ELSIE AT EBB TIDE

It looks as though the light is *coming* from them, pouring out of them, making the fingertips incandescent. I scream to Sandra, "COME HERE!"

As Sandra runs in, I run out. *Where is my camera?* I realize I don't have one. I left home too quickly. I didn't pack it.

The light will be gone, I know. The turret windows are so narrow, the sun moves so fast. It'll disappear in a second.

Sandra's second-born, Donovan, hears me screaming. He grabs his Canon Rebel and thrusts it into my hands. To my amazement, I am holding the exact same camera I own. I know every button, switch, option like my own skin. I race back. With the light still exploding out of the hands, I begin shooting pictures.

It's as though Mom has shown up for her own memorial ... her way.

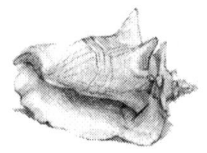

Kenna and Elsie ~ 2000 ~ It's All Right Now

<u>Kenna</u>: Your mother just appeared and said, "I'm here."

<u>Kenna</u>: How are you?

<u>Elsie</u>: *I'm just fine. I'm still having a good time but things have calmed down a bit—like after a cocktail party.*

<u>Kenna</u>: Well Barbara wants you to know that she's at peace and she's delighted you had a good crossing. She says to say hi to these people for her. She would like to visit too.

<u>Elsie</u>: *Oh, she will. Her time will come. Tell her I want her to be happy. We loved her. We always did. We just lacked understanding, didn't we? It's all right now. Barbara understands. Tell Barbara I am nearby and I will see her Saturday. Can you imagine that all that is left are those ashes?* [Kenna sees a twinkle in her eye] *I got the better deal, didn't I?!*

~ ~ ~

What makes this reading particularly interesting is that I have not told Kenna we plan to hold the memorial service on Saturday, nor have I mentioned that Mom was cremated.

There was no reason to tell her.

Mom becomes the messenger.

Retired Elsie ~ 1989 ~ Doorstep Surprises

I woke up about 9 a.m. and went to my neighbor's house to pick up the paper as I had promised to do while they were on vacation. Alors! There was a cat in front of the door with its feet sticking straight up, dead as a doornail.

I called the friend I was supposed to call in an emergency. Surely this was an emergency....

He answered the phone, "Yes, yes, yes."

"This is Elsie, Clem's neighbor."

"Yes, yes, yes!"

"Who are you?" I asked, unsure. "Are you Mr. Wilson?"

"Yes, yes, yes."

"Well there's a dead cat with its feet sticking up at Clementine's."

"Yes, yes, yes," he said. "I'll come and throw it in the alley."

I thanked him, thinking ... *yes, yes, yes*!

October 23

Bereaved Barbara ~ 2000 ~ A Carry-On Mom

In the days before the Saturday memorial service, Sandra and I decide to create a photo album of Elsie's life that we can give to the grandchildren and remaining living relatives.

Sandra pulls out boxes of archived photos and we begin. Soon the floor is strewn with pictures as we sift through them. We are repeatedly awestruck by her beauty.

"She got the looks," Sandra admits.

"Yeah," I agree. (Though I suspected that if our search turned up any photos of Elsie dwarfed in her A-shaped SCAN dresses, Sandra would revise her opinion.)

Eventually we winnow the hundreds of photos down to about fifty—the earliest ones often the most entertaining. Elsie as tow-headed, bowl-cut, bow-tied girl. Elsie as valedictorian in floor-length slinky satin dress. Elsie as butler's girl. Motorcyclist. Guitarist. Photographer. Sun goddess. Elsie in love. Elsie as Mom. Elsie the Air Force Two frequent flier. Elsie with pearls. Elsie with minks chewing on each other's tails. Elsie playing the piano. Elsie aging.

Elsie not remembering.

I carry the photos to the nearby copying store, and make twenty bound copies. I had already written an abridged history of Mom's life, having scoured birth certificates, job applications, letters of gratitude, diaries, protocol memorabilia, published articles.

We sit in a circle surrounding Elsie, the white lilies, the urn, the cupped hands. Once again, the erratic unpredictable Washington sun emerges at precisely the hour we gather, this time shooting a beam of light right onto the gold-plated plaque attached to the cremation vessel making the name, Elsie Nurmi, glow incandescently. Remembering Kenna's words, I imagine this is Mom's way of letting us know she still rules the oceans and the waves or at least manipulates the sunbeams. It is a nice thought.

We each take time to share stories, none spectacular, all memorable. We've told them countless times. None are new to us, but they are comforting. Sandra and I now step across a threshold. We—the next generation—are next in line to step across the portal from life to death. Though hopefully decades away, still, it is a lonely thought. We no longer have living parents to hold our hands.

Two days later, I fly home. I have purchased a rolling backpack to transport my mother's remains to Maryland where a more elaborate memorial service will be held. Then I'll fly to Minnesota where she will be buried in the Finlayson cemetery.

~ ~ ~

"Have you got the death certificate?" Sandra asks.

"Yes. And the transit permit." The funeral director had been very explicit about that: "In order to get your mother through security, you *have* to have a burial transit permit."

Obviously I guarded this piece of paper with my life.

Ed plans to drive me to the airport, so Sandra and I say our teary good-byes. It is hard to leave Sandra. Somehow each step we take makes the death more real. Now Ed hoists the heavy urn encased in its rolling backpack into the car and we head to SeaTac Airport.

At the departure entrance, Ed helps me strap the pack with Mom's ashes on my back.

Once I check my bag, I'll take the backpack off and roll it. He gives me a big hug. I turn toward the entrance feeling, for the first time in days, alone.

Check-in goes easy. I watch my tagged suitcase disappear from sight. Clutching my boarding pass, Mom's death certificate, and her burial transit permit, I head for the dreaded security. I heave the backpack onto the conveyor belt. Mom disappears into the X-ray machine. Just as quickly she zips out. Nobody has asked for my papers!

"Don't you need to see these?" I unfurl the tightly clutched permit and death certificate.

"Oh no," the female security officer answers me. "Some people don't want their loved ones X-rayed. So then we need to see them. You're fine."

I think, *Oh jeez!* I look down at the backpack. *I just processed my mother like she was a carry-on.* I take the now-desecrated mother off the conveyor belt and heave her onto the floor. I have failed Protocol 101: Proper Handling of the Deceased. She bounces down the corridor behind me as I head toward my departure gate thinking, *How bizarre is this?*

Eventually we board. I attempt to lift the backpack into the overhead storage. I immediately realize my upper body strength is no match for urned Elsie. "Excuse me," I turn to the gentleman behind me. "Would you mind putting my mother into the overhead compartment?"

Yes, I actually say that. Realizing adding anything to *that* would border on ultra-desecration, I sit down and shut up. I promise myself, *I will* not *say that on the next flight.*

We debark in Denver and I am starving. I head for the food court with Mom rolling along behind me. *Okay, Mom,* I admit, *this is weird but I have to eat, and you have to come with me.*

Death, I am finding out, has no relationship to life. Unlike any other opposite where shades of variance can be found—dark-dusk-dawn-light, hot-tepid-cold-ice, there is no *shade* between life and death.

Mom is dead.

BARBARA ERAKKO

November

Learning to Talk
in a
Different Way

November 1

Deceased Elsie ~ 2000 ~ One Last Dance

I mentally tick off the assets. *No steps. Large open living room. Everyone knows how to get here. People can stay and eat afterwards.* "It's large enough to handle the Forsbackas, Williames, Pellinens, Lehtanens, Smiths, Saarinens, and Chitwoods," I proclaim, grateful that my ex-husband Bill has offered his house for Mom's memorial service.

"Hey," Sandra puts her wine glass down with a thump, "Let's wear *purple*!"

Immediately stubborn (in the Finnish *sisu* way) I say, "I don't want to." Ed gives me a *look* (as in ... get a *life,* Barbara).

A good night's sleep brings me out of my crustacean mood. *Why* not? I decide. One last *purppurava* for Elsie—the one color she liked that Dad hated. Determined to purple myself, I buy the most god-awful dress I've ever owned. It looks like a purple tent beneath which we could have served canapés and cocktails.

Sandra on the other hand goes for the classy purple look—pants and a turtleneck.

After the service is finished, everyone breaks up for refreshments. Lisa, my daughter, walks over to me looking unnerved. "Mom," she whispers, "I saw them dancing."

"What?" I turn to her confused.

"Grandma and grandpa. They were dancing on the grass."

Lisa never really got to know Mom and Dad. We lived too far apart; Dad died when she was only 7 years old. She knew nothing, really, of their love of dancing and I never knew her to be psychic.

But now, she clearly was spooked and stayed close to my side.

Retired Elsie ~ 1989 ~ Writing Memoirs

Dear Sandra and Barbara,

I joined a class at the Palm Beach Junior College and promised myself I'd try to recollect some things that happened during my 31 years with the federal government. (Unfortunately, I'm being distracted by a gang of tree surgeons who are removing the almond and fichus trees. Our water line broke and turned the backyard into a small lake. Your father vowed to get rid of everything with roots and is now in charge of making the backyard into a prairie.)

But now, back to my literary efforts. Here are a few:

- How to get a new typewriter by 'losing your platen'
- Roses should not be presented under a helicopter rotor
- Never, never pick a blossom off a century plant
- If you need money, go to the Treasury Department
- The President died at 2 p.m.
- Mother's Day is lovely if you can overlook good wishes
- When asking directions, go to the top
- What? An assassin in our midst?
- Will it sell or will it burn?
- A press conference in your bathrobe is unnerving
- Crabs don't like to be boxed in
- A quick lesson on how to clear a cargo plane in less than an hour
- Give them to her NOW!

Mother Barbara ~ 1989 ~ My Little Angel's Quest for Perfection

"He is mean," Lisa stomps into the house, making a final irrevocable judgment on her school-bus driver. "The kids can't do anything. They can't even look over the seat to talk to someone behind them. You know what he does?! He *stops* the bus and walks down the aisle and makes the kid turn around."

"Oh," I answer, "Did he do that today?"

"Yes. He's so mean. I don't like him at all. He's the worst bus driver we've ever had. Ever," she adds for emphasis.

I make a small pitch for this unknown driver. "He may not like the job very much. Maybe he couldn't get the job he really wanted. Maybe it's the only money he can make to pay his bills." I decide not to add sick children, credit-card debt, or dying parents in my effort to elicit some sympathy from my third-grader's heart.

"He should have gotten a job as a clerk then."

"Maybe he couldn't stand up 8 hours a day."

"But he's just so mean. He stops the bus all the time.

"Who was the kid he stopped for today?" I asked. Dead silence. Then Lisa's eyes look at me through a thicket of hair.

"Me," she answered.

WHAT?! My irreproachable daughter—the one who reproaches us if we go one mile over the speed limit? The one who admonishes us to use sidewalks instead of grass? Who insists we should pick up everyone else's litter? Who wonders if it's legal to fish?

Oh the sheer joy of it—Lisa has finally joined the massive ranks of miscreants. At last we'll have peace whenever we go through a yellow traffic light. No longer will we have to be berated by a 9-year-old. No—we can simply say, "Remember the day the school-bus driver?"

Our littlest angel's wings have gotten a bit charred.

November 8

Retired Elsie ~ 1982 ~ The Importance of Lime

"Herby," Elsie yells out of the kitchen. "I'm going to make a Key lime pie."

This in itself is remarkable—Elsie *never* bakes—and it's a hot Florida day. Nevertheless, she lays out the ingredients on the kitchen counter—her enthusiasm undaunted by heat or inexperience.

Herby enthusiastically endorses her efforts. "Chef Boy-Ar-Dee Elsie, Queen-of-the-Lime," he cheerily encourages from the family-room storage closet housing his ham radio.

Elsie dusts off the eggbeater, and gets out the bowl.

Soon she is cracking eggs, rolling the yolk back and forth between the eggshells letting the albumin slowly plop into the sink. Soon five yellow eyeballs look up at her. She doesn't own a whisk, so she turns the eggbeater on medium speed. The yolks go spattering all over. She scrapes them down, muttering, "Good enough."

Next she tackles the graham crackers with her rolling pin. They refuse to stay put, flying like brown confetti all over the counter. She pushes them into a pile, dumps them in a bowl, adds the softened butter, and squashes the mix into the pie pan.

Now comes the sweetened condensed milk. She pours it over the splattered egg yolks, beats it to a froth, pours it into the pie pan, tucks it in the oven, and sets the timer—completely satisfied with her efforts. Forty-five minutes pass. She walks into the kitchen to retrieve the zesty Key lime pie only to notice the cup of lime juice still sitting on the counter.

A shocked Elsie reports the culinary disaster to Herby. "What will Saarinens and Forsbackas think when they come for dessert?" she laments.

Not being a Protocol Officer for nothing, she immediately goes into crisis mode. *What to do?* she wonders as she looks at the lime-less pie cooling on top the stove.

She stares at the congealed filling. She stares at the lime juice. *No problem,* she decides. Out comes the hot filling, on goes the eggbeater, in goes the lime juice. WHIRRRRR. The blended mess goes back into the graham-crackered pie pan eventually to be buried under a mountain of whipped cream—better to hide the churned up, now-limed pie.

"Oh Elsie," admits Millie, "*such* a good pie! You sure can't take the lime out of a lime pie."

Elsie thinks, *Oh yes you can,* but remains silent.

Millie adds, "Can I have the recipe?"

Elsie beams. Once again, she has safely navigated the shoals of protocol. But never, she decides, will she make a start-from-scratch Key lime pie again.

Bereaved Barbara ~ 2000 ~
May They All Rest in Peace … or Party

I meet Alice in the Duluth airport. We've scheduled our arrivals to coincide so we can share car rental. Now we're heading to Doris's home (Alice's high school friend) who offered to put us up.

I am still maneuvering the Elsie-urn-on-wheels, but no longer make loony comments. I realize that our final separation will soon be complete. This is my last caregiver task—to place her remains in the ground.

I check with the Finlayson Funeral Home. They have opened the ground for Mom's ashes. Her tombstone has now been in place for over a year. Realizing I'd be utterly unable to leave Mom under an empty mound of dirt, I had taken her sketch of what she wanted written on it with me to Minnesota on an earlier trip.

Very specifically, she wanted it to read:

It troubled Mom that no marker existed for her husband, hence the wording. Her only instruction on size was a handwritten note on the back suggesting that her stone be "a *little* bigger" than her mother's.

"Why don't we add PROTOCOL OFFICER beneath her name?" Sandra suggests, not having seen Mom's drawing. Years later, when Sandra and I visit the cemetery and she sees the stone for the first time, she points to it. "See," she says, "It's missing."

"What?" I ask.

"Wife and *Mother*."

"Well," I consider this, "at least we had a solid third place in her life."

"Maybe second," Sandra offers. "I think protocol and Dad shared first place."

~ ~ ~

At any rate, when Alice and I drive to the tiny Lutheran Church adjacent to the cemetery, I mention to the minister in passing that several people coming to the memorial service don't attend church.

He stares at me with sudden intentness. "It's *important* for them to *know* Jesus Christ as their savior."

WHAT? I feel anger rising up. *This isn't an evangelization moment. It's a* memorial *service.* But how do you put a cork in a minister? I just insist that the service end with me playing two of Mom's favorite songs on the piano.

When Alice and I get back to Doris's, I explode. "He's going to ruin the service," I wail, bursting into tears. Alice and Doris thoughtfully consider this, staring at me in silence, no doubt wondering how to tame the enraged, bereft daughter. Finally Alice says, "It doesn't *matter,* Barbara, what he says. Nobody cares."

Somehow this logic breaks through, and I start to laugh. Alice, a pillar in her Lutheran community, is just pointing out the obvious. Nobody will remember what the minister says. The weight of his words will be held only as long as the service. The memory of Mom will last as long as we remember.

~ ~ ~

The gathering is small. Her brother Swante and his wife are dead; her sister Lucy lives in a nursing home with advanced Alzheimer's. The nieces and nephews, Alice, a few scattered Finlayson residents who knew her, and I attend on this cold sunny November morning. The minister provides a safely anemic service. I nervously play the piano, missing chords and notes. It doesn't really matter. I played just as badly when Mom was alive.

Now we walk to the Finlayson cemetery across the country road passing under the aging wrought iron arch with the words **Finnish Lutheran Cemetery** engraved upon it, over to the grassy site where Mom is to be buried. I glance around. Like farms scattered across a prairie, the tombstones of families are clustered comfortably apart from one another. Her mother rests two stones up; her mother's parents are nearby in the same row.

I see a 3-foot square hole deeply scooped out in front of Mom's memorial stone. I plan to place her urn into the ground myself. The cemetery attendant stands by.

"Where is the shovel?" I ask. "I want to put the dirt over her."

"By the shed," he answers, turning to get it. We stand in a small silent group waiting. I don't know my cousins all that well. They don't know Elsie or me that well. And Minnesota Finns aren't that much given to talking anyway.

He returns with the shovel. I get on my knees and hold Mom one last time. *This reminds me so much of Dad's burial at sea.* The sadness of it hits me, but there's nothing I can do.

I lean over and try to reverently lower Elsie into the hole. I lean over more. And more. And more. My red-panted bottom sticks straight up in the air in front of my relatives. *Where the hell is the bottom of this hole?* I start to panic. Will I have to drop her in—THUNK? Will the urn land straight up?

Just at that moment, it touches the bottom. I pat it one last time on the top, stand up, take the shovel, and scoop dirt over Mom.

I ask if anyone else would like to place a shovel of dirt over her. Movie scenes notwithstanding, nobody comes forth. I keep shoveling with a certain determined madness. The silence of my Minnesota relatives might be just patience or incredulity—I have no way of knowing. At last, the urn is covered. I give up. The cemetery can do the rest. It's over.

We leave the graves of her toweringly tall paternal grandfather Marcus Norlund who once did carpentry and dug wells by hand; her maternal grandparents: Liisa Askelin (who burned Elsie's cards) and her husband, Henry, who doted on the tow-headed girl; and her mother Jennie and father Hjalmar whom she loved so much. Such was the crowd Mom now joined. May they all rest in peace ... or party.

November 11

Career Elsie ~ 1967 ~
Funeral Delegations, Protocol-Style

1. Information is received at the State Department of a VIP death abroad ...

2. If a delegation is expected, a memorandum is immediately prepared and submitted to the White House ... recommending who should go—based on (a) importance of the deceased, (b) level of attendance expected from other countries, (c) our political relations with the country, and (d) previous high-level U.S. contacts with the deceased.

3. The White House informs Protocol [i.e. Elsie] of the names selected.

4. If the White House does not extend the invitation, Protocol [Elsie] calls the persons named ...

5. As soon as the composition of the delegation is firm, an Elsie-cable is sent with White House clearance to the Embassy concerned ...

6. Arrangements are made with the White House to issue a press release ...

7. Each delegate is contacted personally [by Elsie] ... arrangements being made for their travel are given.

8. The Office-of-Elsie contacts the administrative officer regarding funding the trip; arranges for special USAF aircraft (or makes reservations on U.S. airlines); contacts the aircraft commander with flight details; gives the chief steward the manifest, food and beverage requirements; contacts the Medical Division for inoculation requirements and has someone stand by during off-duty hours to administer the shots; contacts the Passport Division and arranges for necessary visas; if necessary, makes arrangements for renting formal attire; prepares information packets; arranges individual transportation; makes sure each delegate has ticket, passport, health card, and other necessary material. (This may require Elsie to go to the airport where group will depart as a presidential delegation.)

Author Barbara ~ 2009 ~
Arguing with a Dead Mother

I have foisted a myth upon my dead mother—now that she is on the other side, she is always nice, enlightened, a superior being. *Gone* is the mother who manipulated and controlled us.

Imagine my shock when my psychic friend Angelita connects with Mom and she tells me Elsie wants to be remembered as *funny*—not *diseased!* My friend Julie on the other coast and months earlier, had received the exact same message from Mom.

"I don't think there's much of a market for a book about a funny mother," I abruptly tell my spirit-mother. "I can't even remember all your stories."

When I calm down I realize, *All she wants is not to be shown solely as a sick elderly person, for god's sake.* And I admit, she *is* a funny character. But the book, I continue to tell myself, is about how to look at this disease differently. *Why can't you read my brain and know that?* I mentally ask her.

By now I am completely frustrated. Mom died 9 years ago. Over the years, I slowly realized that one day I'd want to tell her story but didn't know how. Books I'd seen thus far tackled the story in a chronological way, from onset to death—whether from a caregiver, spiritual, medical, or biographical perspective. I wanted the reader to have an *experiential* sense of dementia. Yet as I watched the years trickle by, I sometimes wondered if a book would ever be written. Then I'd say, *Maybe it doesn't matter.*

And I kept waiting.

Curious Barbara ~ 2011 ~ 11.11.11

For perhaps the last 20 years, I have noticed an unnatural frequency of 11:11s. Initially I paid little attention—thinking no more about it than it was kind of attractive to see all these 1's—sort of like a little picket fence.

Then one day while in West Virginia, I bought gas for $11.11. I glanced at my watch. 11:11 a.m. I walked into the grocery store and bought $11.11 worth of groceries. All in 15 minutes. *WHAT is it with these 11:11s?* I mentally hollered.

Over the next few years, I tried to find out the "meaning" of 11:11. Since I knew absolutely nothing about New Age, numerology, psychic readings, or anything else, I didn't have much in the way of resources.

One day, while visiting a small New England town, I saw a bookstore. Of course, I walked in. I gazed at bookcases filled with books on angels, tarot, the occult, alternative healing, meditation techniques, Far Eastern religions. I was in a New Age store. As I browsed, I saw books on numerology. *Numbers,* I thought to myself. *Maybe I'll find something here.* But while various books talked about elevens, there was nothing about 11:11s. More time passed.

On a visit to my sister, we decided to trek up to Port Townsend, Washington—a beautiful waterside artisan town. Once again, I was sucked into a major New Age bookstore. I immediately began to browse the titles, bending sideways to read the spines. There, to my amazement, was a white book with silver lettering on the spine, 11:11.

I grabbed it off the shelf, sure to find my answer. I sat on a bench and began to read. It made absolutely *no* sense. Written by someone called *Solara*, she was anchoring new energy into vortexes all around the earth. People who frequently saw 11:11 had a special connection to this new consciousness vibration being birthed on earth.

I put the book back on the shelf, mostly because I couldn't understand anything about what she wrote. I kept browsing and soon it was time to leave. On the point of exiting the store I asked myself, *How many books do you think you're going to* find *on 11:11?*

I walked back in and grabbed the book. It didn't cost that much.

Now I'd like to say the book had a shattering impact on me—but it never did. I didn't buy airplane tickets to join Solara on volcanic mountains, ancient ruins, or pyramids. Nor did I wear white clothes or do prescribed mantras. I tried to read the book as best I could, and then I put it on the shelf—passing it on to other people who mentioned they saw a lot of 11:11s.

Regardless of whether I am an 11:11 dropout or a wannabe 11:11 believer, I still enjoy seeing them. I always say *thank you*—probably for the same reason I enjoyed them when I first saw them. They look like a nice picket fence.

As I write this manuscript, our calendar has crossed 11.11.11. It turns out November 11, 2011 would have been the very day I would have written about my mother's death. I decided *not* to write that day. So, in manuscript terms, she was alive on 11.10.11. The next day 11.11.11 became a passage. And I wrote of her death on 11.12.11.

How is it that a manuscript over 11 years in the making would dovetail into the nexus between life and death on the very number that had become such a focal point in my life? 11.11.11

November 22

Career Elsie ~ 1963 ~ Death of a President

We all know where we were that day. I was sitting in my tenth-grade English class. My mother was in a taxi heading back to the State Department after picking up an altered dress from Garfinkel's. Later, we would see the images again and again, seared into our consciousness. The president smiling and waving, the elegant Jackie at his side. The shot. The slump. The first lady atop the motorcade car reaching for ... what? The sirens. The silent vigil. The announcement, "The president of the United States has died...."

While the country was emotionally paralyzed, the Protocol Office had no time for shock or grief.

Within minutes of his death, Elsie would be sending telegrams around the world to every American Embassy: "The President of the United States died at 2:00 p.m. on November 22, 1963."

The next days fell into a blur of nonsleep. The men in Protocol never went home. The women were ordered home for rest. Mom caught 3, maybe 4 hours of sleep, then she'd return.

Because of the enormous popularity of the president, and because the United States was a superpower, every nation wanted to send a representative. From a protocol perspective, all the usual respect shown a foreign nation had to be given during this time of intense grief.

At a state funeral, how would a world of nations be accommodated—in what order? In which limousine? At what reception table? All these details had to be coordinated—immediately—by the Office of Protocol. Elsie was on the front line in a way she never experienced, and never would again. Those 3 days seared themselves into her memory, almost *never* to be erased...

~ ~ ~

As the years passed, she told everyone she rode *two* cars behind him when he was struck. Later, "I was in the car *right behind him* when he got killed. It was terrible."

The very last memories she lost were the favorite two songs she played on the piano ... and JFK's death.

Curious Barbara ~ 2008 ~ Pushing the Pocket

I pick up the phone and dial Kenna. I now live in Missouri, so we stay in touch by telephone. I hear her birdlike voice saying, "Hello?" into my telephone receiver.

"Hi there," I answer back. We catch up for awhile on weather, shared friendships, books we're enjoying. Then I move the conversation to the reason for my call. "You know," I begin, "I seriously want to have a few psychics interview Mom and I really want to include you because you connected with her so many times while she was alive."

"Why would you want to do that?"

I pause for a moment trying to figure out—and say coherently—exactly why. "Because nobody could really see inside her head while she was going through the disease. We have no idea what it *felt* like to be experiencing it." I rush on. "Since you were connecting with her while she was alive, and you connected with her right after she died, I see no reason why we can't interview her for this book."

Kenna laughs. "Well, I'm sure she'd have something to say!" Whenever Kenna works on me with energy healing, Mom often pops in, just as she has with Angelita, usually to say hi and that she loves me.

"I just finished reading this book by John Edward called *One Last Time.*"

"Oh yes," Kenna interjects, "he has that TV show—connecting with loved ones on the other side."

"Yeah," I race on. "He said in his book that spirit-energy vibrates at very high rates while ours, encased in physical bodies, work at a much lower rate. A spirit must slow their vibrations down, and the psychic must raise his or hers in order for a connection to be made."

"Yes, that's the way it seems to work," Kenna agrees.

"He wrote that since the spirits have no vocal cords, they must use telepathic means—that it's not like having a conversation. So for example, the spirit impresses thoughts upon Edward but it is his own voice he hears. Or he receives images—like how they once looked in the physical world, or a smell—like a cigar or perfume. And sometimes, if they had physical pain or strong emotions, he feels *that* in his body." I *finally* pause. "So I was wondering how *you* receive information? Do you actually *see* Mom?"

"Well, kind of the same way. Once I saw a man and he kept pointing to his nose and then to a spot on his cheek. When I told the woman, she said, 'Oh yeah, his nose was large and he had a scar on his face.' Now she hadn't asked to connect with him; he just showed up. But it convinced her it was real."

Kenna continues, "I see your mother sometimes. Other times I just hear her. With her, I haven't gotten physical sensations but I often do when I am working with clients. I have to be careful to properly cleanse those energies off of me, in order for me to continue doing this level of healing.

"You know," she admits, "It really is remarkable. I know I've told you this, but when I think about light and radio waves traveling through space—most of us don't understand how that happens. Even telephones. You hear my voice; I hear yours. It's amazing."

"Edward gave this poignant example of how complicated it can be," I tell Kenna. "He said that all those sensations come in simultaneously. Sometimes he stumbles around because he can't put the message together. Once he kept getting the picture of a bell. He started making suggestions—Liberty Bell, Philadelphia, Ben Franklin, Betsy Ross, colonial America. Finally he gave up and admitted to the client, 'He's showing me a *bell*.' She burst into tears. Her husband brought a souvenir bell home from a business trip but forgot to give it to her that night. The following morning he was killed in an accident on the way to work."

"Ohh," Kenna sighs, "her husband really wanted to comfort her. It's true, it's like we're translating but it's coming through *us*—our backgrounds, our minds, our language. It was easier with your mother because we connected regularly so I got to know her."

"So," I pause, "would you mind interviewing Mom? I want to ask her two questions. How did she experience the disease and what would she want caregivers to know?"

"Well, I'd be interested to hear what she has to say. I can connect with her later on today."

Interior Communicators are Needed

<u>Kenna</u>: Barbara wants me to ask what the experience of Alzheimer's was like for you, Elsie. You know she's writing this book, and she wants your help.

Elsie: It was like entering a fog. [Kenna is actually seeing what Elsie describes.] *Sometimes there are patches of fog and you can see around you but sometimes it's so dense you have no idea where you are. You know everything must be there but you have no connection [to it]. You try to rely on your memory, but in the fog you lose your place. Everything may still be there, but you're lost because you've ventured too far. Then you enter into confusion and fear and feel so lost and forlorn. None of your senses—sight, touch, etc.—can help you. You are just dangling, wishing you could go home. That's why Alzheimer's patients go out roaming—they are looking for home where they feel safe.*

Alzheimer's is a nowhere land. In the early stages you are aware of this but as it progresses you lose even this awareness.

[While Elsie is saying this, Kenna is seeing something like two big panes of glass, one to the left, one to the right. What they want to do is overlay, but there is a distance between them. Almost like patio doors that normally slide over one another when open so they look like one door. But these doors have space between them so they never touch.]

It is losing touch, so you go from, for example, recognizing someone but not knowing their name to seeing a complete stranger. Think about your TV. When it's turned on, you see and hear and are connected. But if it's off, you are just looking at a box.

Caregivers really need to use their brain, their intuition to know what is going on. They need to use all their senses to maintain connection and communication. Alzheimer's patients are often like this box. They're there, but the information cannot come out. Sometimes it will and sometimes it won't.

That's why someone like you, Kenna, was so nice. Because the Alzheimer's patient has gone into an interior world, "interior communicators" are needed. Life goes on in this "other world."

It was a relief to know I had someone to "talk" to, someone who could really communicate with me. It is nobody's fault: the Alzheimer's patients or the caregivers—it's a new language that needs to be learned because really, it's like two people from different countries.

In a real sense, this is the gift of Alzheimer's. [It is an opportunity] for both patient and caregiver to put away all that is familiar and get down to the basics of caring, giving, helping, kindness, love. One person is offering another person an opportunity to become a true human be-ing, someone who is no longer do-ing anything. The ideal in all of this is to reach a balance, to even out one's life between do-ing and be-ing.

The Alzheimer's patient is teaching so much in this stillness; even actually inviting the caregiver into it. It is no secret that that is where you find God—in the stillness.

The Alzheimer's experience is an inter—reality experience—being in a place between the two realities—of this world and the other world. It is actually a <u>long</u> journey between the two. We know where we have been and we're in no hurry to get where we are going—until finally the time is right, the opportunity is there, the door flies open, and you know you'd better run fast to catch that train! Otherwise, misery awaits you.

I never was one who enjoyed pain. It all went very well, I think. It was like going to a BIG party and you know how I love parties. [She smiles a big smile and her eyes are twinkling.]

~ ~ ~

Kenna calls me afterwards and reads the notes she'd written as she listened to Mom. "She really went into a lot of detail," Kenna tells me. "I was surprised."

"Remember when you connected with her just after she died?"

"Oh yes. She said she didn't plan to hang around if she was going to be in a lot of pain."

"It's like she's describing that moment once again—*the time is right.* You know, Sandra and I always felt she'd leave fast. She'd make up her mind—and poof, she'd be gone. And that's how it happened.

I go on. "Some of it you could almost guess—the fog, the confusion, the fear. I guess I'd pretty much expect that—feeling out of control and afraid. But I never thought much about how she was learning to go from do-ing to be-ing."

"Well, when you think about it," Kenna reflects, "it really *does* help two people ... if they're open to it." She pauses. "You were open, and so was Hawa."

"I think I really changed a lot as I took care of Mom, though I didn't realize it at the time. I *had* to listen to my intuition even if it wasn't very developed. I just slowed down. It was a *totally* different way of being with her—kind of relaxing—as though I could slip into this quiet, safe, comfortable space of just *being.* After all," I laughed, "we had nothing we could *say* to each other!"

"You distrust your intuition too much, Barbara," Kenna suggests.

"I don't think so," I insist. "I just don't know *what* I'm listening to—myself or my higher self or my angels or my guides. In the end, I go with what feels right in my heart. What else can I do?"

"And that's the best," Kenna answers.

November 28

Holiday Elsie and Herby ~ 1982 ~ Let Us Give Thanks

It all started with a goose.

"Sandra," her spelunking friend Barry from the University of Maryland calls her in late October, "the geese in one Ag Lab experiment are going to be put down. They finished the project. Do you want me to bring your parents a Thanksgiving goose?"

"They weren't feeding them arsenic or anything, were they?"

"Naw. Just some weight and food study. They're safe."

"Well, sure," Sandra enthusiastically agrees. "I'll be hiking then, but Dad will love it. Just drop it off."

A couple of days later, Barry shows up with a wildly squawking box and tells Herby, "I grabbed the biggest one I could get."

Together they take it out to the aged paint-peeling garage. Herby unlocks the door, flips the latch, and drags the door open. They decide to take the bird to the back of the garage hoping they can get out before the bird flies away.

"Okay," Herby plans. "I'll stand by the door while you release it. If the bird starts to fly, I'll slam the door shut till you get here then I'll let you out."

They agree. Barry busts open the box, and the bird, startled, sits there. Barry runs out the door; they slam it shut and lock it. It is a month before "turkey-time." Only this year, it'll be *goose* for Thanksgiving.

Now wed, Bill and I show up frequently to share a meal with my parents. I feel pretty sorry for the goose trapped in the dark garage with only three small windows that give light. I try to convince myself it's no worse than poultry farms raising thousands of birds for our dinner tables. But then I remember the story of Mom's chicken....

~ ~ ~

Elsie happened to be washing dishes during wartime when a chicken sauntered up the sidewalk looking remarkably like a free food-ration coupon. Farm girl Elsie ran out in her bathrobe, and made clucking noises dropping bread crumbs leading the bird to the garage. Once inside, the clueless chicken was left to his meager meal.

When Herby came home on leave, Elsie, with her glowing radiant young-wife smile, sprang the surprise: "Look in the garage window," she told Herby. There, happily perching on a beam, sat Emma-the-chicken.

Herby dispatched the bird; Elsie prepared the candlelight dinner. Herby dug in, exclaiming how good it was; Elsie stared at roasted Emma, ruefully thinking, *I should never have named her.* Emma lay safe, if dead, on her plate. Elsie picked up a carrot.

~ ~ ~

The garaged goose clearly hopes to have a better outcome than Emma.

The battle between Dad and the goose begins. Every day as he nears the garage with goose-fattening feed, he can hear the goose's wing-flapping body rev up like a helicopter getting ready to take off.

He unlocks the door, flips the latch. The bird swoops across the garage like a dive bomber. Dad swings the door open, throws the food down, slams the door shut. He hears goose wings wildly flapping up into the rafters, just seconds before a bird-on collision with the door.

Anyway, Thanksgiving Thursday. Bill and I show up. It is the goose's last hour. Bill and Dad shoulder their way into the garage and use all their masculine ingenuity to capture the goose.

I tell myself, *you ought to watch. After all you are going to eat it. You need to know how your food gets to the table.* I want to be like cousin Pat who milked cows and ate *mojakka* for dinner—a country girl capable of wrenching necks off chickens.

I stare at the goose. Suddenly my courage deserts me. "Tell me when it's over," I say over my shoulder as I head to the kitchen. *Next time, maybe …*

Now, Herby sketchily remembers the plucking technique from childhood. That involves scalding soapy water. So in the bird goes, and the next few hours they pluck the mighty fowl, reducing it to a much diminished goose.

By the time they hand it to Mom, there isn't much to be thankful for—the hour of eating has come and long gone. We sit down to hungrily devour all the fixin's—mashed potatoes, gravy, green beans, cranberry sauce sans goose, and pie.

"Come back tomorrow," Mom suggests.

After all, the goose has specifically been feted and fattened for a month. The next night we try again, waiting for the much anticipated goose to be cooked. The timer dings; Mom opens the oven; heavenly fragrances waft out … then we see this shriveled-looking thing the size of a Cornish hen on steroids.

"I followed the directions exactly," she says leaning over to pull out the drip pan. We stare in shock. Two-thirds of the bird was *fat*.

The goose won.

Reflective Barbara ~ 2011 ~
Dr. Jill Taylor's *Stroke* of Insight

In 1996, a 37-year-old brain scientist suffered an extremely rare form of stroke. In a matter of hours, she experienced the loss of sight, sound, touch, smell, taste, and even fear as blood hemorrhaged over the neurons in the left side of her brain. She lost her ability to speak, to understand words, and she could not even define where her body ended and the rest of the world began. Unable to sustain any aspect of her memory-based life, she experienced a profoundly spiritual "letting go."

In a very real way, she experienced Alzheimer's *on the fast track*. What makes her journey utterly amazing is that, as a scientist, she *observed* her disintegration—and remembered it.

Through her eyes, we catch a glimpse of what Alzheimer's *might* look like ... from the inside.

~ ~ ~

On the day of her stroke, Dr. Jill explains in her book, *Stroke of Insight,* she awakens with a splitting headache and finds herself off-kilter in the shower, when she hears her left brain giving step-by-step instructions on how to bathe. We might be wondering why her brain isn't screaming *STROKE! STROKE!*—but her neuron connections are already breaking down. It's like she's in a maze without a map.

Now let's observe Elsie. When she finds *herself* increasingly lost in a maze, she also gives sequential cue cards. She remembers the word *Olympic* by dragging one leg behind herself muttering o-limp-along. She knows scotch tape is like a ball and you pull things off of it.

Dr. Jill's brain chatter becomes erratic, interrupted by silence. "Even though my thoughts were no longer a constant stream of chatter about the external world and my relationship to it, I was conscious and constantly present within my mind."

Likewise, Elsie is *watching* her mind disintegrate—and *knows* it is happening. She tells me, "Something is wrong with my brain, Barbara. Can't you take me to a doctor to fix it?"

As Jill experiences the actual disintegration of herself as an ego-based being, we see her essential *Jillness* peeking out.

"*Okay, well, I'm having a stroke.... But I'm a very busy woman! ... I'll do this for a week! I'll learn what I need to know ... and then I'll meet my schedule, next week.*" She doesn't yet know she will, for a period of time, lose everything she considers to be "Jill."

Elsie fights in every way possible to prevent the loss of her *Elsieness*. To her, that is the very *heart* of the disease. Yet we, as caregivers, finally *see* the essence of Elsie.

Gone are the masks, the protocol, the pretending, the politeness. Now we see the mischievous twinkle, the "NO," the anger—the *real* Elsie. Elsie's "Let's get *on* with it," is matched by Jill's *Okay, I'll do this for a week but I'm a very busy woman*.

Meanwhile for Jill, the blood rapidly sweeps over parts of her brain, stripping one precious cognitive ability after another. She explains that a normal brain works like filing cabinets. "When I am looking for a thought or an idea or a memory, I scan the cabinets and identify the right drawer." But now, she is finding the drawers rapidly slamming shut.

How does Elsie experience this?

She explains to Angelita that her world was like a room filled with objects. She'd go through this room looking for something (she can't remember what) but when she gets to what she wants, she'll know it.

She explains, "It's like someone handing her a piece of paper but her mind can't register that it's paper or what to do with it. It isn't exactly memory. It's *discernment*.

In the same way, Dr. Jill doesn't find information by memory, but by discerning where it's been filed. This seems a subtle but significant difference. Memories come in clumps— we recall the family reunion and all our senses are engaged. But paper (and its uses) is not memory. It's information.

Amazingly, Dr. Jill has instants of clear thinking that eventually saves her. "I vacillated between moments of being able to think clearly (I call these 'waves of clarity') and the lack of ability to think at all."

Likewise Elsie tells Angelita, *There were times when I could come in—like flashes of lucidity.*

Throughout this devolvement, Dr. Jill's brain chatter disintegrates and then stops entirely. She feels a "growing sense of peace," as though "enfolded by a blanket of tranquil euphoria." She is detached from the memories of her life. She can "no longer clearly discern the physical boundaries of where she began and ended."

She writes, "In the wisdom of my dementia ... it was clear to me that this body functioned like a portal through which the energy of who I am can be beamed into a three-dimensional external space. This cellular mass of my body had provided me with a marvelous temporary home."

She begins to experience that movement from body to spirit while still firmly anchored in her body. She experiences, in some metaphorical way, the miracle of the caterpillar and butterfly. Her body, like the caterpillar, is literally turning to mush. Yet in the moment and at the depth of disintegration, she begins to see this marvelous butterfly, this soaring spirit. "In this void of higher cognition and details pertaining to my life, I am comforted by an expanding sense of grace ... my consciousness soared into an all-knowingness, a 'being at *one*' with the universe."

Elsie, her brain being slowly wrapped like a caterpillar into a chrysalis, tells each psychic the same. She explains to Angelita that before Alzheimer's, she dealt with everything on a physical level. She needed to be in control. She denied anything spiritual. But because of the Alzheimer's, she had to be in a spiritual state, and she learned to enjoy it, though at first it "scared the hell out of her."

To Kenna, she explains, "We have gone into an interior world. Life goes on in this 'other world.' It's sort of like we're all in the same house but we're in different rooms."

Even though Dr. Jill is rescued in 5 hours, from the time her alarm clock went off to hospital admission, she has gone from a fully functioning brain scientist to one whose cognitive brain has almost shut down. What takes an Alzheimer's patient years to experience, she undergoes in rapid motion.

As the hospital staff begin to aggressively work to save her life, she finds herself saying, *I'm not supposed to be here anymore! I let go! My energy shifted and the essence of my being escaped. This is not right. I don't belong here anymore!*

But she has traveled as far as she will be allowed to (at this time) on her journey from body to spirit. Elsie would go further. As she told Kenna, *Finally the time is right, the opportunity is there, the door flies open, and you know you'd better run fast to catch that train! Otherwise, misery awaits you.*

Homeowner Barbara ~ 1989 ~ Everyone Loves a Tree (Not)

While on vacation, Bill and I decide to take Kendra and Lisa to a hands-on science museum in San Francisco. Near closing time and near the exit stands a tall metal tree filled with crevasses and holes where objects are hidden. Kendra and Lisa quickly thrust their tiny hands into the holes, just as quickly get bored, and leave me alone with the tree. I begin to explore, from one touch to another, totally intoxicated with the experience. Brushes. Carpet strips. Nails. Icy-cold coils.

The guards begin sweeping the museum, "Closing time. Please move toward the exits. Closing time." The kids and Bill are bunched by the door waiting for me to leave the tree. But I keep circling it, thrusting my hands addictively into its hidden spaces. Finally Kendra comes and grabs my hand, tugging me. "Come ON, Mom," she says, dragging me away.

In that one singular instance, I realize I am a *tactile* person. Of all my senses, this oddly ignored one—compared to sight, sound, and taste—enraptures me. I think back to majestic mountain vistas. They overwhelm me. I consider music. I become so enraptured I can hardly think. But touch. It seems tiny. Accessible. My brain can wrap its delight around things I can touch.

I learn much about myself because of a metal tree. But *that* tree causes no homeowner problems. My tactile relationship with the swamp maple in my front yard is a different story.

~ ~ ~

"I have to cut you down tomorrow," I say, wrapping my arms around the silver maple, also called swamp maple. "You're cracking my sewer line. You've got to go," I tell its rough bark. "I've called the tree company. I am really sorry." I feel tears welling up. I turn to go inside the house, as sobs start to erupt. I close the front door, bawling, "I'm KILLING a tree!". My sane self watches in utter dismay. *Are you NUTS? That tree is a weed tree. It's destroying your sewer line. It's got to go.*

I call the tree company. "Can you just cut it back, like really trim it, so its roots will stop growing into the sewer?"

"No, lady. No amount of trimming will keep roots from growing."

By now, I have become a full-fledged tree-hugging, weed-tree savior. "Well, that's what I want—just trim it back a lot. I want to give the tree a chance."

"Okay. We'll be there at 8 o'clock and we'll do whatever you want."

The next day, the crew appears and radically trims not only that tree but also the overgrown silver maple in the back. That evening, shocked by the savage severing of limbs, I go to both trees to apologize.

"I'm sorry." I touch each one, imagining their cells screaming. I run my hands along the trunk of the silver maple in the backyard where one particularly large limb has been severed off. To my amazement, I see a perfect image of a silver maple leaf—due to some strange sort of cellular discoloration—imprinted into the growth circles. The base of the stem perfectly overlays the first ring of the amputated limb; the edge of the perfect leaf image ends in the last circles of the limb's life. I run to get my camera and take a photo—never understanding then or now why or how such a thing could happen.

Curious Barbara ~ 2008 ~ The Search Continues

"Why do you want to have so many psychics interview your mother?" my friend Ann in Maryland asks me as we catch up over the telephone. "Don't you believe what Kenna and Angelita told you?"

I take a sip of tea. "Yeah, *I* believe it—but I've had years of slowly getting to that point. In the beginning, I was scared." Even as I say the words, I find myself grateful that Ann pushes me on things. I can see her, slender as a willow, probably standing in her kitchen doing chores while she talks, her short blonde hair framing her oval face, dressed in slim-leg pants and a chenille top, with huge silver earrings dangling from her lobes.

"Scared of what?" Ann prods me.

"I don't know. I guess I worried a psychic would peer into my secret thoughts. You know, the stuff we wish we didn't think or feel—but do. I'd be embarrassed."

"So were you?"

"Oh no. Absolutely the opposite happened. That's when I think I really began to understand the difference between the soul and the ego." I walk to the kitchen to pour more tea still wearing my bathrobe—it's an hour earlier than in Maryland.

"I don't understand. How did working with Angelita or Kenna do that?" Ann asks skeptically.

"Well, there was such a kindness that they channeled—such love and generosity. The messages they received untangled the crazy thoughts my ego would get me tangled up in. Well, okay, let me give you an example. I was getting tied up in knots about trying to market this book about Mom. Here's where I got stuck. When I wove sacred shawls, it was always for someone else—their spiritual journey, their needs. When I created peace jewelry, it was always so the person buying the necklace or bracelet could connect with peace in their own way. But with this book, it's *my* thoughts, *my ideas*—I have no place to hide. And I don't feel comfortable being in public like that. I thought a psychic connecting with my guides could help me."

"But you do your own channeled writing, don't you? Why didn't you just ask your guides yourself—why pay a psychic?"

I think of the notebooks where I keep my channeled messages beside the chair where I meditate in the darkest, quietest room in my home.

"Sometimes you just want someone else to double-check what you're receiving. Yes, I trust the messages I get. But it's still being filtered through my ego, no matter what. The psychic won't be snared by that so the message might be clearer, or nuanced differently—or it might be information I unconsciously keep blocking."

"Okay, I get it. So how are you going to find these other psychics?" Ann persists. "Are you going to go for really famous ones? Or newspaper ads? Or Dial-a-Psychic?" she asks, laughing.

"Well, I can't afford the famous ones—and I wouldn't want to go that route. I want to use everyday psychics with solid reputations that anyone could afford.

A friend in Hannibal has been using a woman in New Mexico for years. Kay Wagner. And Bill suggested I try Donna Edwards who has been doing psychic work in the Baltimore area for a long time. She lives in Florida now. I've already had a personal session with each of them to see how I feel about their work.

"So how'd it go?"

"Oh, real well. But one thing I've learned ... every psychic has a unique style. For example, Kay goes so deeply into a trance that you can't interject questions while she's in that state. And she talks *really* fast—like the information is literally *flooding* through her and she wants to get it all out so you won't miss any messages. I tried asking questions—sometimes she'd say something that would instantly trigger that in me—but she literally didn't hear me. It was pretty funny.

So I just wrote them down, knowing we could go back—which we did.

"Working with Donna was more paced, but there was still a lot of information coming through. She writes all your questions down. Because, once she connects, she is really in that altered space and can't flip back into mental consciousness easily. She gets a lot of information but speaks a bit slower." I laugh. "Maybe her guides talk slower! Anyway, I can insert questions when she pauses."

"So did you prefer one over the other?"

"Oh no. Both readings were really good. It's just different personality styles."

"Have you asked them to interview your mother?"

"Yeah. I have appointments set up for next week. And this really touches me—both of them refused to take any payment. They just want to help."

"Well, let me know how it all works out," Ann says before hanging up.

December

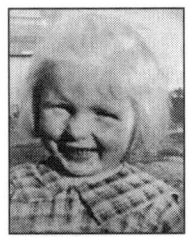

When Saints Go Marching In

December 8

Retired Elsie ~ 1982 ~ Florida Diary

Last avocado *still* hanging on the old tree. Smith Photo made 100 copies of my Christmas letter. Also cut them to size. Total cost? $2.50. Hard to believe.

Went with Helena Himankka to First Baptist for "Singing Christmas Tree." WOW! What a show. The Christmas ball decorations changed to *live* singing faces in the tree that was three stories high. We were there from 7 to 11 p.m.

Plaid Sandra and Barbara ~ 1957 ~ The McIver Finns

When Sandra finally gets around to going through Mom's belongings, she notices an abundance of plaid and calls me on the phone, laughing. "She *died* with plaid," Sandra yodels as I answer the phone. "There are plaid blouses, a plaid bathrobe, even a plaid beret."

"Yeah, well, we *bought* her those things," I remind her.

"Not all of them," Sandra triumphantly answers, refusing to budge on the point of plaid. "Some of this stuff dates back to Florida."

That's all it took for us to go back in time to the emergence of the Nurmi plaid girls....

~ ~ ~

By 1958 Sandra and I have been underpaid maids for the better part of 2 years. Usually as soon as the cash hits the hand, I am on my bicycle heading for the stores. Over time, my bedroom becomes a shrine to cheap merchandise—yo-yos, stuffed animals, Cracker Jack prizes. Nothing is too cheesy for my dime. But I remember the era of austerity—the quarter-a-week allowance. *Then* we actually *wanted* to go shopping with Mom.

~ ~ ~

"Come on, girls," Mom picks up her purse and car keys, "you need some new winter clothes." I envision a poodle skirt. Clothes-phobic Sandra even has faint hopes of landing a pair of jeans. We leave a happy Dad drinking coffee in the kitchen and run to get into our pink-and-gray Travelall. I wrench open the door and plop onto the short middle bench. Sandra sprawls on the full-length back bench. I resent this. After all, even though younger, I am *taller*. By rights, I should have the bigger seat.

"So," Sandra asks, "where are we going?"

"The beauty parlor," Mom answers, throwing the car into reverse.

Okay, I think to myself, *it's going to be a long day.*

We sit on brown vinyl chairs watching as Mom's hair slowly disappears into tiny metal rollers. Our stick-straight hair, perfunctorily cut by a junior beautician, lies in a blonde heap on the floor.

So we sit. We stare at these strange ladies. We leaf through stupid magazines. We sit some more. And then, stupefied beyond measure, we sit ... some more.

Finally when Mom looks like a metallic poodle, we wonder what will happen next. To Sandra's and my astonishment, the beautician hooks Mom up to a pole with electrical cords sprouting out of it, each one being snapped onto one of the metal rollers encasing her head. Then the stench begins—an acrid all-consuming odor of ammonia. There is no place to hide. It is a very ugly moment to see your mother tethered to an octopus-looking pole with round black tentacles slithering out of its body onto her head.

Now this takes our concept of shopping to a whole new level. Here our mother is paying good money to become a fried Finn. I can see no good coming from this. Sandra and I retreat to the farthest corner, hoping for air, and wait while the minutes tick by. The timer dings; the current stops; curious, we creep from our corner as the beautician de-metals our mother.

Unfortunately, her hair really does get fried. Too much ammonia; too much electricity? We'll never know—but she becomes a brittle blonde, with hair breaking off at the slightest touch, leaving her with a much shorter "do" than she envisioned.

A somewhat deflated mother herds us back into the car. "Well," she stoically decides, "my hair grows fast." We, her loyal child troops, assure her she looks *beautiful* in short hair.

"What's next?" I ask.

"We're going to Penney's," Mom decides. Unlike the Penney's of today, the 1950s Penney's were moderately sumptuous department stores.

"Why didn't we bring our gloves, Mom?"

"That's only for going downtown, Barbara." When shopping in the nation's capital, Mom insists we wear gloves. Somehow, going from climbing trees, biking, running through poison ivy, and playing softball to wearing ladies' gloves fails any version of a Nurmi fashion statement. We always return like cinder girls, our gloves grimed with candy wrappers, pencil marks, and general pocketbook debris. Anyway gloves will soon be as obsolete as the city's last streetcar.

Mom, being a practical budget-minded mother, steers us to the plaid racks every single year. Plaid jumpers. Plaid skirts. Plaid jackets. If it is plaid, it is okay. It can be blue plaid, green plaid, or red plaid. I can be a Scottish McIver Finn or a McGregor Finn—it makes no difference to my mother.

Reading Christmas Cards

Sandra and I dutifully stand in our new plaids while Mom checks hems and waistbands, our initial glee in shopping slowly turning to sullen gloom. Sandra, being the smarter, savvier one, probably knows all along that we are doomed the minute we get into the car. I, being the naïve perennial optimist, hope year after year I'll get a poodle skirt.

Probably any mother on earth can quickly explain why we always get plaid. "It goes with anything," my mother promises. All those blouses and shirts will look very nice—with plaid.

Decades later when my daughters *run* to the plaid racks of clothing, thrilled with their brilliant beauty, I stand in numb shock. They haven't grown up in plaid prison.

I try to explain that plaids are really awful clothing. But they'll have none of it. So, as penance (for I don't know what) I am forced to watch my children cheerfully trot off to school, dressed in plaid.

But that saga lies decades ahead. In the meantime, we continue to try on excruciatingly large amounts of *un*-purchased clothes. "Why are you making me try on boots? I *have* boots," I whine.

"Well, your feet might grow. I'm just thinking ahead." (*These* are the very boots that end up under the Christmas tree—along with socks, on-sale winter coats, and larger-sized pajamas—not the puppy-in-a-wrapped-box I really want.)

Our winter-clothing purchases completed, Mom now moves to the women's-clothing racks that she dearly loves. At this point we are warned to behave if we want any ice cream later on.

Sandra and I slump dejectedly beneath the aluminum poles supporting the dresses, sitting on the floor in the worst boredom known to children.

Watching a mother select armloads of clothing, try on each garment, look at herself from every angle in the three-way mirror, take each garment off, and put it carefully back on the hanger—is a form of torture only amplified when she *returns* to the dress racks looking for *more* dresses and suits and jackets and skirts and blouses.

I really think children should be paid a living wage for this. If Sandra and I had a child-labor-union shopping representative, I'd have a poodle skirt by now; the school principal would allow Sandra to wear jeans. We would be happy.

Instead, we return home. Dad, not knowing the disaster that has befallen his children, opens the door, helps us carry in the boxes and bags, and asks (thinking we have enjoyed ourselves), "So, how did your day go? What did you get?"

We dutifully model our McGregor and McIver plaids.

Psychic Conversations from the Other Side

My next psychic interview with Mom is through Kay Wagner, who lives in New Mexico. When I ask how she receives messages, she admits, "I don't connect as though I'm having a conversation. I see visual images and get impressions. It feels like instantaneous *thought* and it comes in clumps rather than verbatim conversations. It literally *leaps* through me. I don't have time to think about it, let alone judge or edit it. I also get emotional information," she adds. "I *feel* it in my body. I will laugh or giggle or be filled with sadness—and see gestures, like the wave of a hand."

Of all the psychics I've worked with thus far, Kay receives information extremely rapidly.

As a result, once she starts getting messages, she goes nonstop like a flash flood until the information stops. From my personal session with her, I learned to write down any questions that came up *during* the reading, so we could go back to them. But initially, I give her all my questions (I now have more than two), and have my pen and notebook ready. Kay begins by asking that all information being received be for the highest good. Then she begins ...

Kay[1] and Elsie ~ 2008 ~ An Easy Way Out

Kay: Elsie, Barbara wants to ask what Alzheimer's was like for you.

Elsie: It's kind of an easy way out of the body. The mind seems lost and confused to others, but we have found another avenue of expression. It's not so bad.

Kay: Do you think Barbara understood?

Elsie: Barbara treated my mind, even though it seemed diseased, with respect. I am so grateful. She understood—even though she was uncertain. She simply allowed it to be.

Kay: What were your fears?

Elsie: As time went on, few. As I got further along, the communication on the other side was easier. I was listening and talking more with those there than with you here; though I was communicating with you somewhat. The rest didn't matter—just the quality of the energy around me—voice, touch. Some sounds can make you cringe.

Kay: What were the beginnings of Alzheimer's like for you?

Elsie: Very frustrating, aggravating, frightening. The transition is the worst. How we hate change! [She sees Elsie putting the brakes on.] *Ohh ... I didn't want to go there. But then you get further, and go back and forth. It is an easy way out.*

Kay: How did you feel about being tested for Alzheimer's by the doctors?

---

[1] Kay can be contacted via email: kaylynnwagner@q.com

Elsie: [Kay sees her as really angry, really negative.] *Forget the doctors! There is little compassion there. Loving kindness is important for anyone—especially with this disease. There is no surgical procedure.*

That's what Barbara needed for herself—and that gave her the right—but it wasn't in agreement for me. I had real resistance. But for those who depend on doctors and tests, that might be exactly what they need. You can't put everyone into one basket.

Kay: What about the way you were cared for?

Elsie: Barbara made it so natural and normal. That is the most important. She didn't try to change or stop the process.

Other things can be done for the body. Communication is key even though we feel lost. To hear the tonal vibration of a voice is nice though we may seem out of sync with what you are saying. And touch, for those who are willing to allow that.

There is a different way to respond emotionally to each individual. You would not do the exact same thing for every person, but go with your gut. How you are receiving their energy at that moment.

Kay: Barbara thinks you needed to see Sandra.

Elsie: Yes and I am very grateful. It was a quick resolve. It can be as simple as two hearts together. [Kay sees Elsie putting her hands over her heart and then opening them several times.]

Kay: How was it for you when you passed over?

Elsie: I had abdominal pain. That was really *painful too. But I felt very completed. No need to finish up business. I didn't need to go on.*

Kay: So the actual death ...?

Elsie: Whoosh! A quick flow out. Pop! Not like a firecracker— well like it but without aggravation. But remember that I was already there. I had practiced this run many times. Many do not have that experience. They have to go through detachment from home, family, friends, grandchildren, loved ones. Sometimes there is such a pull from some family members for a person to stay, such grief—it makes it more difficult for a person to just freely go.

Kay: Barbara says your eyes were different—the way you looked at her the last time she saw you.

Elsie: *She was seeing pure consciousness, clear consciousness. It was a blessing, a gift, for her to see it—the soul from the other side. The presence of that energy.*

~ ~ ~

"You know," I tell Kay, "Mom describes her death the same every time. Quick. Fast. But I've never asked her specifically about the testing for Alzheimer's."

"She sure had strong emotion around that issue. I could feel a surge of anger running through me."

"It's very painful for me to remember," I admit, feeling my own heart shutting down with pain. "You see," I explain to Kay, "the one thing Mom insisted on before agreeing to be tested was that she would *not* be told she had Alzheimer's. We warned the team. Then in the end, they utterly ignored us and told Mom when she was all alone."

I vividly flash back to that awful ride home in the car. "I bore the brunt of her anger and she ordered me to leave her Florida house."

I force myself to continue. "She has a point and I am guessing she wants to make it strong. Some doctors—not all doctors, but some—probably see a person with clinical-level Alzheimer's as dismissible. They forget the patient is still human. She's saying kindness is what is needed."

I thank Kay. Later, when asked about caregiving, she will tell other psychics the same thing: love, kindness, touch, gentle voices are needed—the rest doesn't matter.

Confused Elsie ~ 1998 ~
When the Saints Go Marching In

We begin singing in the car, a favorite pastime of my mother and myself. I am amazed at how Mom holds onto tunes, even as she advances ever deeper into Alzheimer's. Today, we're going to yet another doctor. It seems that our outings these days are no longer to restaurants but to repair minor damage due to her confusion.

She hurt her foot a week ago. The severely bruised foot was swollen like a balloon. Yet she walked to the car, and all she said was, "The sidewalk feels funny."

I thought perhaps she felt no pain because Alzheimer's suppressed the nervous system's ability to transmit messages.

Now we've set out for a follow-up visit to her family doctor. The foot is less swollen, and we are singing. As I walk her down the sidewalk, our tune matches a marching cadence. Mom begins to stomp her feet with her red sneakers going up and down in her tiny mincing steps.

We near the doctor's office. I know that when I open the door, she won't know to stop singing—or marching. I feel embarrassment mounting.

~ ~ ~

It is as though my rational world is slipping away along with its rules of good behavior, politeness, and manners. She is teaching me the wisdom of humor and simplicity because in Elsie's world ...

Whenever I arrive to visit her, her eyes beam with delight. She has a smile that could enkindle hope in the most discouraged person.

When I play the piano, missing half the notes, she stomps her feet and claps her hands. And when I inevitably stumble, she looks me square in the eye and says, "Don't give up."

When I suggest we go anywhere at all, even the post office, she springs out of her chair, makes a dashing motion, and says, "Let's GO!"

I feel I live in a parallel universe—one where the whole world says it's an awful tragedy—and the one where my mother lives. I keep liking *her* world....

Anyway, it doesn't seem right to let her sing alone.

I yank open the door to the doctor's office, still singing at the top of my lungs. Mom marches in, a mischievous grin on her face as though she knows *exactly* what she is doing. She stomps her small red-shoed feet.

Suddenly an office where everyone comes to talk about pain and sickness turns to laughter. People smile. Chuckle. It's a grand performance.

When the saints go marching in.

December 18

Mother Elsie ~ 1965 ~ Shorthanded!

Hungry, I abandon my chemistry textbook and head into the kitchen. As I'm scrounging through the cabinets in hopes of finding some cookies, I glance at the blackboard. The White House has its "situation room"—my mother has her blackboard. Her *life* becomes organized, week by week, in some fashion known only to her.

Curiously, I look at notes she's written in shorthand in the upper-right portion. I begin to translate out loud. *Christmas.* Beneath it, I see two columns. Emboldened by my ability, I keep going. *Sandra. Barbara.*

"WOW!" I scream—"I can read your shorthand, Mom! I can read what you're buying us for Christmas!" *Finally,* I crow to myself, *being forced to take shorthand has paid off.*

Needless to say, Mom whips into the kitchen, grabs the eraser and in 2 seconds, it is expunged. As I watch, I wonder, *How DUMB can I get? What rock was I born under?*

The next day I come into the kitchen, ever hopeful the magical list will have rematerialized. To my amazement, it has. I stand in front of it, thrilled beyond reason, prepared to translate: Yo-Lu-A

What's that? I wonder. "Hey, Mom," I holler, "why can't I read this shorthand?"

She doesn't miss a beat. She doesn't lift her head up from addressing Christmas cards. "It's in Finnish, Barbara."

And I was *so* close.

Mother Barbara ~ 1989 ~
Celebrating Christmas Early

We celebrated Christmas one week early this year so we could spend time with both sets of grandparents in Florida. Bill's folks live near St. Petersburg. Their planned community is so planned, it's pet segregated.

Bonnie and Kanardy live in a poop-free world. That means I must *carry* runt-sized "Pookie" six blocks to a poop-tolerant neighborhood. Then there are the pool rules....

"Let's go SWIMMING," Kendra and Lisa beg Grandpa, who obligingly hands me three white ankle tags.

"But there's four of us, including Bill," I tell him.

"Well, one of you will have to wait. We're only allowed three tags. And there's no diving, no jumping, no roughhousing." He points to my daughters. "They have to be out by 2 o'clock."

Kendra looks up at me. "Can we swim?"

"Well," I answer, brushing my hand through her long hair, "I'm absolutely sure you can *stand* in the water."

"Oh, I forgot. You have to tie her hair up," Grandpa adds.

Ten minutes later, we leap into a pool of screaming, non-ankle-tagged, loose-haired kids, stealthily adding the anklet-free Bill.

~ ~ ~

Two days later we drive across Florida to Mom's Lake Worth home. There, instead of taking quiet evening strolls in a protected community, Mom unbolts the front door, turns off the alarm system, and unlocks the metal grill covering the sliding doors to the porch before sighing, "It's so good to be home."

But on a positive note, Pookie can poop anywhere.

We can purchase *nisua* at the Finnish bakery. And we can go to Africa ... or the *Lion Safari* version of it. Yes, ostriches stick their bony heads into your car windows as you frantically try to close them; sheep graze on your bumper; and lions hold up traffic. But things are too quiet in the back of the van. I glance back. Lisa's lying on the floor.

"Don't you want to see all these animals?" I ask, perplexed.

"I'm bored."

I go into a lengthy litany about *why* we came—because she loved animals; it was better than a zoo; we had *paid* for it. Finally we park the car. Lisa gets out and throws up.

Oh.

Retired Elsie ~ 1972 ~ The Year of Discontent

Mom keeps a massive Christmas Rolodex, numbering nearly three hundred people at its peak. So the Christmas letter becomes something of a production. Every year, we feel like our home turns into the little Nurmi post office. Sandra and I seal envelops, lick stamps, tote stacks of cards to the corner mailbox. Usually Mom writes an interesting missive, often about her work adventures. But once retired, she has to dig deeper—and reaches for a Tennessee Ernie Ford moment to tell the tale of '72....

>CAMPER VACATION BLUES
>(sung to the tune of *Sixteen Tons*, accompanied by a dulcimer)
>
>~
>
>The campaign year for president
>Was the year of our discontent
>Nineteen hundred and seventy two
>Was the year we really blew.
>
>~
>
>The water pump leaked, the sink trap froze,
>We'd forgotten to drain it—oh such woes!
>The transmission stopped—just at the Co-Op
>And as it was towed, the rear tire popped.

ELSIE AT EBB TIDE

~

For sixteen days and seven long weeks
The man at the shop, he tried to feex;
It cost us dough; the thing wouldn't go—
We owe our soul to the company store.

~

Life seemed so peaceful under the sun
But it wasn't yet over; there was more to come—
I cracked my rib; he lost his teeth
That in itself was a remarkable feat.

~

We are paying our bills, counting days,
Hoping somehow to get out of this daze;
St. Pete don't call us because we can't go
We want to go and travel some more.

~

My favorite word is *feex*. I see Desi Arnaz attempting to help Tennessee Ernie Ford *fix* this song … somehow. At best, it couples Mom's valedictorian love of rhyming poems with an offbeat polka.

Mom, ever the one for procedure, copyrighted it.

Author Barbara ~ 2011 ~
Finding an Finnish Radio Interview of Elsie

Among Mom's possessions when we cleaned her house was a cassette labeled, *Unto Kaartinen Interviews Elsie Nurmi.*

We vaguely remembered her talking about it—someone in Finland wanted to interview Mom about her life as a Protocol Officer. Neither Sandra nor I wanted to play it. We couldn't bear to hear her voice. We packed it with her things and stored it. There it sat for 18 years.

~ ~ ~

As I begin to write her story, I buck up my courage, retrieve the cassette, and put it into my dated CD/radio/cassette player.

The first thing I hear is Mom playing the piano in that indescribable offbeat rhythm I can never mimic. A Finnish dance song. Her soft nuanced use of the piano keys. I feel happy and sad. Any time I want I can go home. But in reality I can never go back.

Then I hear the voice I hadn't heard in 10 years. I have forgotten how soft she sounds—like water gently lapping a shore. Not understanding the Finnish words, I just listen and wonder, grateful I don't understand. To hear my mother speak to me in English would make the loss too great. I turn it off.

Weeks later, as I continue sifting through her papers stored in box after box, I stumble across a typed Finnish transcript of the interview. All I need is someone who might understand archaic Finnish—the Finnish of immigrants arriving in America in the late 1800s. Margaret Kangas, an American of Finnish descent, offers to help me. As she translates, I hear old well-worn stories, but occasionally something new.

~ ~ ~

Elsie recalls her childhood, "The school bus was made of gray boards. There was one door and two benches to sit on. In the summer, there were large wheels under it and in the winter, runners. It was always pulled by two horses the 5 kilometers to school."

After graduating, "I had just turned 19 years old. During the day I would work in some places as a *biikapaikassa*—a maid. With my wages, I paid for evening business classes."

Remembering her protocol years, "Foreign visitors almost always wanted to go to New York, Los Angeles, Disneyland, Hawaii, New Orleans, Cape Kennedy, Seattle—and then places where their country's people lived.

"I went to Guatemala, Iceland, Columbia, Ecuador, England, France, Belgium, Holland, West Berlin, Germany, Italy, Japan, Portugal, and also to Sweden for King Gustaf VI Adolph's funeral."

And what did she think of using the presidential aircraft? "That was the only way. It was wonderful to travel on them.

ELSIE AT EBB TIDE

There was lots of room, excellent service, good drinks and food, and excellent areas where you sleep. I loved to travel. Everything was free—food, drinks, theater, plays, concerts, hotels. I only had to get my travel wardrobe."

"For State of the Union addresses, I took the diplomats and invited guests to their right places. Once I noticed the wife of Vice President Agnew was lost so I quickly brought her to her reserved seat. I always sat close to the president's wife.

"The King of Saudi Arabia purchased so many things (such as hair dryers, expensive cars, even a little log cabin for his kids) that another airplane had to be used. I had to make our guests understand that a log cabin the size of a sauna would not fit into a hotel elevator."

And she ended, "If I feel lonely, wonderful memories fill me—and I also love music. My father often played the polka with the violin that was leaned against his shoulder and his left foot kept the rhythm. The floor shook."

"I still play that polka on the piano too."

The cassette ends. As Margaret falls silent, I tell her, "I play that polka."

Psychic Conversations from the Other Side

My fourth and last psychic interview is with Donna Edwards. Finally the scheduled day arrives.

I enter a small room beautifully decorated in soft, rich colors. A Tiffany-style lamp with low lighting glows, though the afternoon sun also sends rays of light into the room. A small table between two purple-cushioned wicker chairs holds a large amethyst and a quartz crystal.

This will be the only reading where I will actually meet—and sit across from the psychic.

As always, I ask Donna, "How do you receive information?"

I am struck by the gentle, inviting quality of her voice. "Well, I connect with several levels of spirit guides. When connected with very highly evolved spirit guides, I will feel stronger energy coming though my body as though I'm being pulled into a higher vibration."

"You know," I admit, "I don't know if I'd feel all that comfortable being yanked into higher vibrations."

Donna laughs, "Well, you get used to it. Once I'm connected to the spirit guides, I open my mouth and the information just comes through. If I sense the answer is too general, I will stop and wait for more. Then sometimes I may hear something very specific."

"Let me write your questions down," she suggests, taking notes as I talk.

The we quiet ourselves. She lights a white candle and offers a blessing for this reading that it may be for the good of all and the benefit and merit of all.

Then she silently opens up the channel to my first question. As she listens, she begins to speak. She lets me know what question she is asking, and then gives Mom's response.

Donna[2] and Elsie ~ 2008 ~ Peace of Mind

<u>Donna</u>: What was it like going through Alzheimer's for you, Elsie?

---

[2] Donna can be contacted at: www.donnaedwards.com

Elsie: It was like I was going into an unknown place that made me fearful, a bit of darkness—not being able to see clearly or navigate through it—like stepping into a void. But in many ways there was a gentleness about it, as though I was being eased out of one world and into another—a world of peace, escaping from thoughts.

Donna: Did it frustrate you?

Elsie: Yes, especially initially. I felt my identity lessening. It's like thoughts floated in my head but I didn't know which ones were mine—part of my physical reality and what was just imagination.

Donna: So what happened?

Elsie: At some point, I surrendered. I didn't totally resolve the fear until the end, but I more and more almost welcomed the retreat into another plane of reality. I reached a point where it was like flipping a switch between human reality and this other reality. Like I had one foot here and one foot there.

My reality started to shift. I felt more comfortable in the other reality. The attempts to bring my attention back to [earth] reality were almost intrusive to me. I had landed safely in the other world. As that became familiar to me, I felt a bit less safe when jarred out of that because someone was speaking to me or taking care of my physical needs.

And the glimpses of Light were beautiful. I felt as though I was being lifted to a high place, a much gentler energy than the human consciousness.

Donna: Can you tell me more about the Light?

Elsie: I could see lights dancing as though they had their own rhythm to them, and they were beckoning me to get into their rhythm. It was a beautiful rhythm—I hadn't experienced it while on earth. I saw beautiful lights and glimpses of people I had known.

I felt I was having conversations with people, loved ones, and I could communicate better on that level. I had lost touch with communicating on the earth plane. I could feel the love and peace as I got closer to the other side.

Donna: Did Kenna help you?

Elsie: I was very happy to be able to communicate with Kenna. She was, for me, a bridge between the two realities because she was on earth and in human form—but she was communicating where I was vibrationally. She calmed me down a lot and let me know everything was okay. She really helped me to accept where I was instead of having to struggle to be more in the physicality.

Donna: What about physical pain? Did you experience any?

Elsie: The body almost becomes a place where you feel you are trapped. There is some detachment to physical pain because there is a desire to be out of the body. You aren't fully in physicality and aren't connecting the brain to your physicality, so as the brain detaches it also is detaching from the nerve endings associated with the physicality. In that way, the pain is almost transparent and you are not paying attention to it. *If I had my full focus of my mind on the pain, I would have felt it more but I was almost in a place where I could not recognize that as pain.*

~ ~ ~

"Do you have any more questions for your mother?" Donna asks.

"No," I answer quietly putting my pen down. I wait for Donna to separate from her guides.

"Did what she say help you?" Donna asked, curious.

"Well, what's most meaningful to me is the fact that she describes her experience the same way every time, but here a bit more poignantly. For example (and I flip back through my notes), she says *there was a gentleness about it as though I was being eased out of one world and into another*. She's clearer this time too about how she began to prefer the other side and found returning to her physical reality jarring."

I pause for a moment. "There were a couple of new things, too: that she didn't know which thoughts were hers and which might be coming from someplace else." I laughed. "Sometimes when I've had a very realistic dream, I have to reorient myself—did it actually happen?"

I go on. "Her comments about pain and the detachment; that's very interesting. It explains why she could walk on an injured foot."

"What did she say?" Donna asks. "When I'm channeling I'm not reacting to or remembering. I just let everything flow through me."

"Well," I pause to flip to the end of my notes, "apparently she found she could detach from her physicality and the pain would become almost transparent. That would explain," I add, "why she *should* have felt pain in her foot when it was swollen but she didn't."

I gather up my notepad and pocketbook and stand up to leave. "Oh," I turn back to Donna, "she said one other thing that was new to me—that the glimpses of Light were beautiful, that she felt as though she was being lifted to a high place" (I glance at my notes), "*a much gentler energy than the human consciousness.*"

"Sounds like she had a nice journey," Donna admits.

"Yeah, strange as it sounds, in some ways I have to agree," I admit.

When I get home, I file my notes away feeling my psychic-interview process is complete. True, I had wanted one final psychic, and I thought it should be a man. But it hadn't happened. Little did I know that 2 years later I would be having quite an unusual conversation with a medium in his eighties, residing in London.

December 25

Nurmi Christmas Traditions

In our home, it begins with the tree. Like any child, I remember Dad taking Sandra and me to the tree-distribution centers. Certain parental rules prevailed. *No* long-needled trees. (I suspect those trees do not exist in Finland.)

Anyway Sandra and I ranged up and down the needle-scented aisles looking for a spruce, especially a silvery blue one. We agreeably debated the merits of the final selection. We didn't argue because it's hard to get too emotionally involved with a 6-foot tree.

We tied it to the roof of the Travelall, and went victoriously home. Dad stabilized it; Mom watered it; Dad strung the lights. Then they disappeared into the den with their beer or vodka, leaving Sandra and me to trim it.

We both lacked profound curiosity—where did the ornaments come from? Were they family heirlooms or dime-store specials? We never asked. Now they're in my house, on my tree, 60 years later.

At any rate, the last task generated the most enthusiasm. We grabbed fistfuls of tinsel and hurtled it onto the tree in globby messes. Then Dad and Mom magically returned, and we all stood around as Dad plugged the lights in and voila, Christmas began.

Now, *those* were the normal-tree years.

~ ~ ~

Somewhere along the line, Dad eyes the overgrown, needing-to-be-pruned holly trees in the side yard off the kitchen. Suddenly, to *him*, they appear to be the perfect Christmas tree.

He disappears into the basement and some hours later emerges with what can only be called a pole-with-holes. Ingenuity has prevailed, however, for the holes are drilled diagonally into the post, and one hole crowns the top. Anchored to a wooden base, he sticks it in the living room and marches outdoors with his clippers.

Now remember, hollies are not the friendliest of shrubs. In come endless red-berried boughs. Before our bemused eyes, Dad begins to assemble a tree. It has the rough (very rough) shape of a Christmas tree. But its great advantage is that no one else in the world has one like it.

He gingerly casts strings of lights on it and leaves us to prick ourselves endlessly in our feeble attempts to decorate it. No one suggests that we hand-lay the tinsel. We *all* hurl it onto the chopped holly limbs.

It becomes the *Nurmi* tradition. Decades later, I inherit this pole. I too have a holly tree in my yard. I too go outdoors on an icy-cold day and lop off branches. I march indoors filled with enthusiasm. I plan to make a tree-in-memory of good ole Dad. But there is *nothing* in my brain that apparently matches my father in actually succeeding. The tree crashes to the left, tilts to the right, looks bloody awful. The pole-tree has a life of one year in my house. When I move, I sadly but resolutely throw it in the dump.

But okay, back to the Nurmi Christmas. The tree is up. We dance around it. The stockings are hung. Santa should come—we haven't been *that* bad (and we did clean our dresser drawers for Mom). We go to sleep in our merchant-marine handmade bunks, the drawers beneath us clean and tidy awaiting new toys and treasures. I, of course, am the last to give up Santa. Too restless to sleep, I peer into the living room and ... well ... there's my parents stuffing the bare underside of the tree.

The next snowy morning, Dad drags us—pajama clad with boots—outside and says, "Look up there!" We gaze at the snow-topped roof and what do we see?

SANTA'S footprints!

What father actually gets on a roof on December 24 in the SNOW to stomp around the chimney—and what mother lets him? Where is the "DEATH? You'll *die*. You'll fall off the roof. The children will be ORPHANS!"

Mom probably held the flashlight.

So now comes the big moment: Christmas morning. The base of the tree is stacked with gifts, the stockings full. Well, we know from history that the stockings are worthless. Junk. Apples, boxes of raisins, Cracker Jacks, a ball maybe. But that's *all* we can touch till they wake up from natural sleep. We make every effort to make it as unnatural as possible until they drag themselves out.

Every year I want a puppy. I am very constant about this. But no box ever appears with pee dripping from the bottom. I always want a doll. Nope. That never materializes. Ditto for the stuffed animals.

I slowly realize that the Penney's boot, bathrobe, pajama, winter coat I dutifully tried on 2 weeks earlier now lies beneath the tree wrapped in bright Christmas paper. After that 80 percent of the haul is dispensed with, Sandra and I find the baseball mitts, the badminton rackets, the bike (now *that* was good), roller skates—basically, any object designed to keep us *out* of the house. No dolls. No dollhouse. No art projects. No books. I am an alien in an alien land.

My sister is ecstatic.

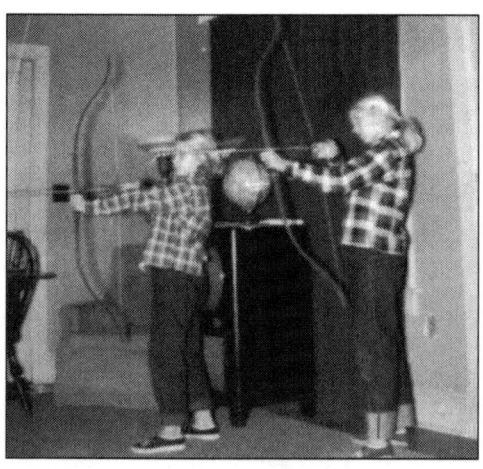

Then there's the year when Mom simply does not have time to wrap the endless boxes. I apparently have total amnesia about this one, but Sandra tells me we awoke, eager as usual, and ran into the living room.

There, before our startled eyes, were two pyramid-piled stacks of white boxes, one for Sandra and one for me, each held together by a large red ribbon. *That* was it.

We finished Christmas that year with a flick of the wrist—we untied the ribbon, popped the box lids, and in 5 minutes Christmas was over. Very disappointing, which is, no doubt, the reason why I forgot it.

Now the last Nurmi tradition unfolds.

Tired Elsie disappears into the kitchen, (after being a mother I definitely know what post-present tiredness feels like), and proceeds to make Finnish pancakes.

We love these things.

Mom has a special Finnish pancake pan—cast iron with several 2-inch circular depressions in it. The batter (technically it could be called *Swedish* batter) is very thin and watery.

The first few pancakes look anemic but eventually the pan gets with the sizzle, and they pop out with crispy brown edges. We dump lingonberries over them.

Once the last mouthful is swallowed ... Christmas is over.

Caregiver Barbara ~ 1998 ~
I Don't Need a Christmas Tree

Mom arrived months ago in my home by private ambulance. My sister watched with anxiety as I tore my house apart getting ready for her. I herded my precious solitude out the door, and welcomed a nursing home complete with mother and live-in caregiver.

I put on hold my plans to write in a western Maryland farmhouse overlooking 150 acres and entered the murky incomprehensible world of health care, Medicare, hospital supplies, and pureed food.

Yesterday, Bernadette (an acquaintance from church) stopped by. Mom sat in her wheelchair watching Hawa fry shrimp. Bernadette sat beside Mom listening to her soft endless babble. Occasionally Mom waved her hand at the ceiling, perhaps seeing angels, deceased friends, or just as likely, nothing at all.

Later, as I walked Bernadette to her car, she turned to me sympathetically. "It must be so hard for you to see your mother like this."

I paused, thinking about the past several months. After all, no one thus far had consoled me.

I know everyone's experience of Alzheimer's is different. Sometimes the person, once gentle, becomes abusive or even violent. I thought about that. But finally I turned to her and said, "I hate to tell you this, but we're having a great time."

For the first time, I realized how much I was being steeped in love. Mom opened up like a flower under Hawa's care. She became mischievous, stubborn as a toddler, her eyes twinkling. We were all being bathed in the strange glow of love, much of it emanating from my mother. Her inner light—the essence of Elsie—was getting stronger and stronger.

I couldn't have put words to it if Bernadette hadn't offered sympathy.

Perhaps Mom is experiencing a better childhood than the harsh one where her father died when she was 10. A Depression childhood where she had to tend her younger siblings and worry about a grieving mother. A time when she stopped crying because it did no good.

Now after eight decades, she is Queen Elsie. Occasionally she'll stop babbling to issue an order to Hawa or me such as, "No, I'm sick!" which means, "I refuse to do this."

But the story is not so much about Elsie as about her transforming effect on others.

She is like an onion, now peeled down to the last layer—and that layer is about a woman who *loved* life. And now when she no longer has to be responsible in the world—or even reasonable in her demands of it—she eats all that is left of life with autocratic childlike enthusiasm.

In amazed wonderment, I laughingly tell friends, "She's *never* going to leave. She has no intention whatsoever of dying."

But of course she will. One day she will actively begin to die and I do not look forward to that day.

But dying is not a tragedy. I do not see Alzheimer's as dehumanizing but as humanizing. I am in awe of my mother—much more so than when she could give me wisdom and advice. For now I see her as she is and always was: A woman with an immense love for life. A woman who reaches out and grabs it with both hands. And a woman who laughs, even now, with indecipherable knowing in her eyes.

I don't know when I've been happier than now. I really don't need a Christmas tree, or tinsel, or lights, or even the manger scene.

I have my mother-child in my home.

December 28

Friend Barbara ~ 2002 ~ Where's the Brooklyn Bridge?

I manage to find the cordless phone and grab it just before it goes to answer-machine land. "Barbara," the matter-of-fact voice I know so well comes through the receiver, "I'm back in Maryland. I just landed. Let's get together."

"Why are you here and not Peru?" I ask Pam, worried. After over a decade of close friendship, we cherish time together. These are in very rare supply now that her husband works on a cholera research project in South America.

"I've got to get my mother out of her Brooklyn apartment. Her friends called me. She's getting too confused to be on her own. I've only got 3 days to do it but at least I've found a group home here in Columbia. I plan to drive up to get her tomorrow. She doesn't know a thing."

"I'll go with you," I irrationally promise, throwing schedules to the wind.

"Oh Barbara, I can't ask you to do that."

"Well, look at it this way—we'll get to catch up on the drive there. And you're going to need an extra pair of hands for this."

The next morning we zoom up I-95 to Brooklyn to rescue her mom. Pam ticks off the things she has to do—close out the bank accounts, arrange for all her furnishings to be removed and sold, notify her friends of her new address and telephone number, contact her doctor and get her medical records, verify all her prescriptions, pack her mother's clothing, hand the keys to the apartment to the manager, and, most importantly, get her mother voluntarily into the car.

Flabbergasted just listening to her, I ask, "How do you plan to get your mother into the car?"

"Oh, I'll just suggest we go out to lunch."

"She'll refuse," I flatly promise. "She'll say, 'Oh, you two just go ahead. I'm not hungry.'"

"How do you know that, Barbara? She always likes to eat out."

"Trust me. I guarantee you she'll say no. I don't know why. Maybe it's because she only feels safe in her apartment now. She's too confused. You can try it, but you'd better have a backup plan."

"I don't have one."

"Well," I turn to her, "Tell her she has a *doctor's* appointment. That'll work."

"Why?"

"I don't know. It's an authority thing. It's about that generation. Whatever it is, I really think it'll be the only way you'll get her into the car."

~ ~ ~

A couple hours later, we are standing in Loreine's tiny Brooklyn apartment. She's happy to see Pam. I mentally begin my checklist—she recognizes her daughter ... good. Pam whisks off to the banks to close accounts and empty the safe deposit box.

"So, Loreine," I turn to her. "That's a wonderful view you have out of your window. What's that big bridge out there?" I ask, pointing to the Brooklyn Bridge.

"Oh, it's just some bridge. I can't remember the name of it."

Okay, I think to myself, *Pam's made the right decision.*

That evening we relax. Pam's gotten the medical, legal, and financial transactions accomplished. Her whirlwind efficiency is paying off in spades.

"What about the apartment stuff, and all her clothing," I whisper after Loreine has gone to bed.

"I talked to her friend. She's going to take care of everything. She'll ship her clothes to Maryland. She'll make sure the apartment is clean—I've given her enough money to cover that and her time. She'll give the keys back to the manager."

While Loreine soundly sleeps through the night, Pam packs a week's worth of clothing into an overnight bag, and stashes it in the trunk of the car. We are ready.

I crash on the sofa; Pam stretches out in a sleeping bag on the floor; and we all fall asleep until d-day … departure day.

~ ~ ~

"Hey, Mom," Pam enthusiastically turns to her mother, "let's go out to lunch!"

"Oh, you two go. I'm not hungry."

"But Mom," Pam persists, "we can go to your favorite deli."

"No, you go and have a good time."

Pam glances at me. I almost burst out laughing. I wait to see what's next up Pam's sleeve.

"Well, you have a doctor's appointment today."

"I dooo?" Loreine looks up.

"Oh yes," Pam confidently continues. "I'll take you but we'll have to leave soon."

"Okay," Loreine agrees, looking up from her chair.

~ ~ ~

"Are you comfortable?" Pam swivels her head to look at her mother, seat-belted in the rear seat.

"Oh, yes," chirps her mother.

Pam deftly pulls into traffic and I watch through the side mirror as Loreine's life in Brooklyn recedes into forgotten memory. Soon we are whizzing down I-95, mother in tow. About an hour passes. Pam and I have re-engaged in our catching-up conversation—our lives, our children, our writing. Suddenly this voice pops up from the back seat. ...

"HEY, where are we GOING???"

Our heads whip around in unison to stare at the suddenly verbal Loreine.

I have no answer for this in my mini lesson on how-to-handle Alzheimer's patients. I wait to see what Pam comes up with.

After a long pause, Pam says, "We're heading down the road, Mom."

"Oh," says Loreine, and falls silent once again.

Another journey has begun.

Epilogue

Barbara, Elsie, Sandra (1994)

When my mother died, except for gut-wrenching tears at the airport, my grief settled into quiet sadness. Even in the end stages when no Elsie seemed left, I always felt her *presence*. Then even that disappeared.

As that door closed, however, new horizons opened. The years rolled by. I sold my Maryland house in 2004, moved to Hannibal, Missouri and ramped up my weaving and jewelry business. In the endless stretches of quiet required to weave, sometimes my mind wandered back to Mom. Friends whose parents got Alzheimer's admitted they looked at it differently because of my experience with her, and I realized working with Kenna had opened unusual doors.

During this post-Elsie period, I knew I *wanted* to tell Mom's story, and I wanted to use psychics to interview her from the other side. How many? Five, I immediately decided but wondered, *Why five? Why not four or six?*

I knew Mom's and my experience was unusual. After all, psychic communication isn't exactly like chatting up someone in the grocery store aisle between the potatoes and canned coffee. Also, I was curious. Would Elsie tell the same story to random people who didn't know each other? But why five? I guess like the story of Goldilocks trying different bowls of porridge, four seemed too few, and six too many.

I quickly decided to include Kenna, who worked with Mom while she was alive, and Angelita, because Mom popped so frequently into our sessions.

For the others, I talked to friends and acquaintances seeking psychics with solid reputations.

I checked each referral out with a personal reading. In this way, I added Kay Wagner of New Mexico and Donna Edwards in Florida to my list. Now I had four of my five. The last eluded me.

I wanted a man. I wondered how a man, whose entire life perception is obviously quite different from a woman, would receive Elsie—and how she would express herself. Unfortunately, my network yielded nothing and eventually I forgot.

Then one day, my ex-husband showed me a website he had designed for a London-based medium, Ronald Hearn.[1] Immediately I felt an inner *click* and emailed him. He became my fifth interviewer.

My connection to Ronald was unusually "clean" in the sense that we had absolutely no contact. All he received from me were two emailed questions I wanted him to ask.

With the other psychics, I could at least talk on the phone or be with them in person, and interject information during the interview.

Some might suggest that in this way I could tip off unscrupulous charlatans. But since each psychic voluntarily refused payment, one could hardly find a self-serving motive. I even searched the Internet to see if family information existed online, but found nothing other than a gravesite photo.

As psychics interviewed Elsie, I slowly noticed Mom used certain identifying characteristics.

She came through *strongly* which, I am told, is somewhat uncommon. She often spoke in a pithy way quite like in real life. She invariably mentioned how she loved dancing and the piano. Lastly, the information cross-correlated very well between the psychics, making it credible that one person, Elsie, was indeed connecting to us.

---

[1] Ronald can be reached at: www.ronaldhearn.com

I also learned subtle differences exist between psychics and mediums—not in their innate ability but in the way they refine it.

A psychic, generally speaking, sees their role as message transmitter. Often the person coming for a reading has concerns about *this* life so the psychic focuses on that. A medium on the other hand *specializes* in connecting you with loved ones on the other side. They hone their ability to pick up concrete details about that person's *life* so the person receiving the message can decide if a connection has indeed been made. Not unsurprisingly, Ronald Hearn as a medium provides extraordinary proof of a connection to Elsie.

He doesn't literally *see* persons who have passed on or hear them speaking, but receives impressions. "I find myself able to describe people and situations which I could not normally know about," he explains and goes on to say, "I would never expect to get a hundred percent success. In many ways, [this work] is like looking for gold dust, and before the prospector can find a few grains of gold, he must first wash away all the dirt and unnecessary things from his pan."

Of course the proof lies not in the technique but in the information. In culling through the five transcripts, I find six basic categories of information coming through:

- Her personality: in various ways, Mom says or shows herself in distinct ways unique to her.

- Dying Process: in four separate accounts, she gives remarkably similar descriptions.

- Alzheimer's Experience: all accounts have a strongly similar emotional feel but each psychic receives different metaphors to describe the experience.

- Advise for Caregivers: all accounts have strong similarity.

- Alzheimer's from a Medical Perspective: remarkably, while I never once asked the psychics to question Mom about this, she interjected her comments about it in several places.

- Life Contract: did Mom *choose* this disease as a life lesson, even before she took on a physical body? Some psychics say yes. Is this even remotely credible? *Why would she choose such a terrible disease?*

Some of the material presented below has already been covered in the book, but here it is cross-correlated with similar information from other interviews thereby adding to its relevance.

While I had the unique and graced opportunity to work with Kenna while Mom was alive, I now believe that many psychics could have provided a telepathic bridge of communication between my diseased mother and myself. But let the reader decide.

Personality

As mentioned earlier, the psychics I used tended to concentrate on the *messages* that Mom gave and only coincidentally gave concrete details about her persona.

For example, Angelita notes, "Your mother tends to be very intelligent. She's very analytical at times—that's how she dealt with her emotions. If she could *understand* them she wouldn't get carried away too much." Later Angelita adds, "She liked to dance. It was the one time she didn't have to be on guard. It was the closest thing to flying—letting her defenses down, being free and spontaneous."

Unknown to Angelita, Mom told Kenna almost precisely the same thing when still alive: "Dancing is not just exercise for the body; it is a way to clear the mind too."

Kay provides identifying information of an emotional nature. When asked about the testing for Alzheimer's, Mom didn't mince words. "I was totally disgusted with it."

Kenna provided numerous pieces of information in the year she worked with Mom—her love of music and the piano, the fact that she loved flying while Dad preferred boats, and so on.

Ronald on the other hand emphasizes identifying characteristics. Like Angelita, he sees that, "Your Mom is quite an intelligent lady." He goes on: "She was always ready for things."

I immediately remember seeing Mom jumping out of her seat, saying, "Let's *go!*'

"She has sparkling eyes.

I think she could look at people and through people somewhat." He adds, "She was not a person to feel sorry for herself. She would make the most of it and get *on* with it."

I remember when Dad died. She resolutely buried his ashes at sea within days of his death, and got rid of everything—his clothing, his tools, his ham equipment—except his battered leather wallet which we found hidden among her belongings.

Ronald, recording his sensations of her onto the CD he sent me sometimes presents his information as questions. "Did she play the piano? She seems to come through with what I call lovely piano music. Happy memories of piano playing."

Then he offers the single most startling identification of any of the five psychics: "She says Herbert is here watching on—her husband, of course."

This takes me by complete surprise. *Could he have learned this some other way?*

But then, I look at the facts: He's in his eighties. He's done this work for decades. He's written three books on the subject. He's had hundreds of clients—and he's doing this reading for *free.*

He turns to Mom's feet. "Before she passed over, she had difficulty with her feet and shoes—some difficulty with getting the right shoes."

Mom, suffering from bunions and hammertoes, bought so many shoes Dad nicknamed her Imelda Elsie after the Philippine First Lady Imelda Marcos who owned nearly a thousand pairs.

When Ronald tells me, "She is giving me a strong message about flowers—something funny she did with them," Sandra reminds me of the petal-less bouquet Mom handed Lady Bird Johnson.

I delight in these concrete details but am clueless when he sees something funny about umbrellas. Then I recall he explained that spirits do not operate in *our* time. A message may refer to the past, present ... or *future*!

Lastly he notes that "she tends to wave her hands around a lot when she is speaking." I don't remember that—until, months later, I read an entry in *my own journal* about her flapping hands!

I feel Mom has worked hard to identify herself so as to establish her credentials. She adds one more extremely important detail—how she died.

Dying

I wasn't by Mom's side when she died. I only know that from calling 911 to death took about four hours. And of course, she had *no* way of communicating with the family—Sandra, Ed, Kier—who were beside her. Yet to four psychics, she describes the experience almost exactly the same way.

First, we have Kenna who connected with her hours after her death. Mom exclaims, *I wasn't expecting things to go like this—all so quick! But I am happy and I feel great.* [Under her breath,] *I should have done this sooner.*

While I hadn't specifically asked psychics to query Mom about her dying, she naturally discusses it as part of her experience of the disease.

When Angelita talks with Elsie about it, she says, "Your mother just lit up saying, *I was ready to go!* Angelita gets this a-ha feeling from Elsie of completion—and that the moment she got that, she knew she was ready. Very easy.

Kay picks up the acute abdominal pain Elsie experienced. *Boy,* Elsie says, *that was REALLY painful.* Then she shows Kay how the death occurred: *Whoosh! Similar to a bird. Quick. Pop! Without aggravation.*

Ronald simply explains, "Your mother was happy to be released. She said it was a wonderful experience to wake up and find oneself in another dimension, another world, but without pain, without problem, with only clear thinking, and to meet up with loved ones."

Eight years later, when asked to interview Mom for this book, Kenna returns to this topic and Mom shows her:

> *Finally the time is right, the opportunity is there, the door flies open, and you know you'd better run fast to catch that train!*

Alzheimer's Experience

If, having reached this point, we are convinced we are actually talking to Elsie—and I am—then what she has to say about Alzheimer's and caregiving takes on significance. We can peek behind a locked door—for who can communicate with a living person whose mind has literally been wiped clean?

In virtually every instance, Mom vividly describes her fear, frustration, and anger as she entered the downhill slide into Alzheimer's.

She tells Angelita, *It scared the hell out of me.* To Donna, she admits, "*It was frightening*; to Kay, *very frustrating, aggravating, and frightening.*

To Ronald, she explains, *It is like a feeling of wanting to escape from an unhappy situation. Sometimes people with Alzheimer's get very angry and unhappy—as though one is trying to get out of prison. Anything to get away from this disease!*

I well remember Mom's anger that ranged from frustration to all-out fury.

These might be defined as the beginning stages of the disease, when she could observe her own diminishment with frustration, anxiety, and fear. None of what she says here surprises me. I also observed these stages.

She shows several examples of how it felt to her.

Angelita sees Mom in a room filled with objects looking for something she can't remember but will know when she gets to it. Mom explains she won't know *how* she knows but by going through each of those little pieces, she'll get to what she really wants.

It's like when you know that you know a word or a person's name but you can't retrieve it at the moment you want it.

Then you reach the point where you can no longer search because you no longer remember that you once knew the word. It's like someone hands me a piece of paper but my mind can't grasp what it is and what you do with it.

It's not exactly memory; it's discernment. It was as though I had thoughts floating in my head and I couldn't understand which thoughts were mine and which might be coming from some place else.

I clearly remember the day I brought in a photo of Mom to show Hawa. She exclaimed, "Oh Elsie, you were really *HOT!*" and held it close to Mom's eyes but the link was broken—the image, the paper, the memory itself all severed from Mom's memory.

The beginning stages of Alzheimer's are filled with trauma both to the one experiencing it and the caregiver. Fear, frustration, anxiety, and loss overwhelm everyone.

At this stage, anyone would unanimously agree—it is the most wretched awful unbearable disease imaginable.

I remember *wanting* Mom to "progress" to the next stage of the disease where caregiving would be easier. But once she arrives there, I no longer have any way to communicate with her. A door between us closes.

But now, that locked door opens...

It was like entering a fog, she explains to Kenna. To Donna she says it was like *stepping into a void and I didn't know if I would fall deeply into it.* She uses different phrases: *A bit of darkness, lack of clarity, unfamiliar territory, not being able to see clearly or navigate through it.*

This reminds me of a time when I was working quietly in the basement and my husband thinking no one downstairs, turned off the light.

Sure I could navigate because of my memory, I didn't say anything. I walked to where I thought the stairs would be and immediately began crashing into objects.

Soon I was completely disoriented. Without a single point of reference, my world suddenly became meaningless, my memory useless. Unlike Mom, I could yell for help. She could not.

Kenna sees two big panes of glass—almost like patio doors that slide over one another when open so they look like one door, but these have a distance between them and will never touch.

Angelita also sees sliding glass doors—Elsie on one side and knocking but the people inside don't see her.

Eventually Mom leaves the anger and frustration behind. Why? Because emotions need a cause, and cause needs memory. Without memory, the link between cause and emotion dissapears. She also leaves the caregivers, Hawa and me, behind. We can continue to care for her physically, but the emotional link is broken. Now she begins to cross over.

At first, I was puzzled. Mom's eyes would focus on the wall or ceiling, gesturing and talking. When I asked, "Who are you talking to?" she always gave me the name of a deceased friend, family member, co-worker.

I was having conversations with people, with loved ones, Elsie now explains to Donna, *and I could communicate better on that level. I lost touch with communication on the earth plane, but on the other side, all could be understood without the use of vocal cords. There was a language, so language was used, but so much understood at a high level, it felt as though language was not necessary.*

From Mom's perspective, she saw herself drifting from the shore of her remembered life. *In many ways there was a gentleness about it,* she says, *as though I was being eased out of one world and into another without fear. It was a world of peace, serenity, escape from the thought process, escape from a human reality one does not want to face. It became more and more welcome to retreat into another plane of reality,* she explains to Donna. *I reached a point where it was almost like flipping a switch. One moment I would be in human reality and then the switch would go off and I'd be in the other reality. It was like having one foot in one plane and the other in quite a different place.*

Over time, she preferred the other reality: *I saw glimpses of Light that were beautiful. I felt I was being lifted into a higher place with much gentler energy than human consciousness. I saw glimpses of people I had known before. It was as though the real world was becoming muted.*

My escape from the real world became more and more pleasurable. The more I wasn't present in my human body, the more I experienced living heaven on earth.

Eventually it got to the point that being forced back into human consciousness jolted her.

She tells Donna, *I felt more comfortable in the other reality. Those around me, in their well-intentioned attempts to bring me back to the present—that was intrusive. I had landed in the other reality very safely and that became* more *familiar to me. I felt a bit less safe when jarred out of that—perhaps by someone speaking to me or taking care of my needs.*

She tells Kay precisely the same things. *I was communicating with the other side and was further and further into the other dimension. It was quite natural. The rest didn't matter—just the quality of energy around me.* [Loud] *voices,* [harsh] *touch—just as some sounds turn you off—it could make me cringe.*

Elsie takes a different tack with Ronald. She spends more time explaining how it *feels* to be in a blocked crippled mind.

"Your Mom wants to make it clear that the soul or the spirit, the life force, is a thing of clear thinking. There is no deterioration. She says to Ronald, *The soul knows it cannot get out of the physical body. It is blocked off. Therefore it tends to cross over. Of course it does not cross over completely, but it is trying to escape from something it knows it cannot fight, it cannot cure. So there is a natural pulling over.* Later she repeats herself, *The soul is* fine, *but it is being blocked off.*

The idea of "lights out" doesn't really portray the true reality of the disease. On some level, the soul sees and observes—but can no longer speak through the diseased mind.

In my understanding, when the mind is healthy, the soul uses it as a conduit for self expression and all is well. But as the mind slowly diseases, the soul's energy becomes trapped, imprisoned—yet the *urge* to be connected remains strong, healthy, and utterly unchanged.

This blockage forces the soul's energy to find another outlet for expression. Although the spiritual side was always accessible when her mind was healthy, Mom had little interest in connecting to it—life itself was much more exciting and interesting. Only when trapped does she finally quiet down and allow the always present spiritual energies to interface with her soul-self.

Angelita explains the blockage using a different image. In her healthy life, Elsie made choices: "It's like she's in this bubble and as long as she's there, no one else's energy can penetrate—and none of her energy goes out.

Your mother worked hard to control her world. Alzheimer's 'scared the hell' out of her. It's like the first half of her life was about living one way; the second, about healing from that. She needed to be in control and be rational. So what does she experience? Irrational. No control. No mental level to deal with that. She ends up learning how to be with things on a spiritual level."

As Elsie herself said to Kenna, *The Alzheimer's experience is an inter-reality experience—being in a place between two realities—this world and the "other world." It is actually a l o n g journey between the two worlds. We know where we have been and we're in no hurry to get where we are going!*

Caregiving

In the beginning stages of Alzheimer's, much advice exists for the caregiver. The first recurring frustration between caregiver and afflicted concerns forgetfulness. "I just told you that." "Don't you remember, we can't take the escalator." "You just ate!"

In ordinary circumstances, in *healthy* circumstances, the one being addressed would re-direct, recall, and somehow the situation would resolve itself.

Not so with Alzheimer's. The afflicted one has no *way* of recalling, and often angrily, with toddler-like determination, insists that he or she is right.

Eventually caregivers learn tricks. They stop saying, "I just told you," because it never works. They redirect. "Well, we'll take the escalator in a couple of minutes. I need to look for a sweater." "Oh, you're hungry. How about a snack?"

What works for the two-year-old now works as well with the beginning stages of Alzheimer's.

Once the dementia really sets in, the caregiver loses all the cues and clues. That brings on a completely different set of worries, guilt, and anxieties.

Here Elsie offers a great deal of compassionate advice, based on her own experience. She affirms for the first time the value of Kenna's telepathic presence.

I was very happy to communicate with Kenna, she tells Donna. *Kenna was a bridge between the two realities because she was on earth but she could communicate with me. She calmed me down, and let me know everything was okay. It really helped me to accept where I was instead of struggling. It gave me tremendous peace. It became exciting to be able to communicate at a higher level what I was feeling.*

When Kenna reconnected with her eight years later, Elsie comments, *That is why someone like you is so nice because the Alzheimer's patient has gone into an interior world and "interior communicators" are needed. Life goes on in this "other world." It's sort of like we're all in the same house but in different rooms.*

She adds later on, *It was a relief to know I had someone to talk to, someone who could really communicate with me. It's nobody's fault—Alzheimer's patients or caregivers—it's a new language that needs to be learned because really, it's like two people from different countries.*

She expressed gratitude for Kenna similarly to Kay: *Kenna—her way of being present—was helpful in freeing me.*

But Elsie still remained tethered to the physical world. *People carrying this illness,* she explains, *become more sensitized to what is happening around them vibrationally. They sense who feels they are a burden.*

To Donna, Elsie goes into detail concerning why it is so valuable for caregivers to keep talking to those with Alzheimer's—even in advanced stages.

It is *not to elicit a response,* Elsie explains, *but to allow the caregivers to express what they are feeling towards the person. It may be an apology—I am sorry if you are picking up on my feeling burdened but I have a lot of stress right now. I'm having a hard time coping with losing you.*

Elsie suggests caregivers *speak from the heart because people often don't do that. Families that have never touched each other's hearts find that there is so much anger and resentment left unsaid.*

This is a good opportunity to fully communicate from their heart, their emotions, frustrations, disappointments. Allow everything to be communicated and released while the person is still on earth, and then when the person has parted there are no regrets. Everything is said when the afflicted one is in a semiconscious state where it will not be hurtful but fully understood.

Mom herself realized this.

When I asked Kay if I had been right in thinking Mom needed to see Sandra one last time before she could pass over, Mom said yes. Kay saw her patting her heart as though her heart were opening several times, saying it was a *quick resolve.* Sandra admits she grew fonder of Mom even though lingering issues remained.

I also had my own experience when I told Mom that she would be moving out of my home. I talked to her as though she comprehended everything—and I was miserable with grief, and yet also relieved.

It seems that once Elsie began to live more in the spirit world, she could see the human condition more clearly, with more compassion. She adds that caregivers should not feel guilty around seeking other care, be it a nursing home or hiring help.

In the advanced stages, she explains, *the person cannot distinguish family from people anyway. You reach a place of peace. You just want to be on the other side anyway and are not in a place of judgment or even awareness of who is giving you the care.*

But she does emphasize to Kay *one* aspect of caregiving that remains powerful even in advanced stages — touch and sound. *Touch is important,* she explains, *and the tonal vibration of the voice.*

She also comments that *Kenna's way of being present was helpful in freeing her to go when she was ready.*

Kenna did, in fact, prepare the way. She told Mom telepathically how to navigate in this quasi-spiritual realm. As Kenna connected with Elsie each month, she observed changes.

Very near the end, she saw Mom reach a moment of clarity—after another resident died—about the true reality of her condition. Before, Mom always enjoyed Kenna's visits. Now Kenna saw her quiet and reflective. Later she told me, "It seemed as though your mother had made a decision."

Now Mom acknowledges Kenna *was helpful in freeing me to go."* All the preparation, showing Elsie her angels, clearing worries and concerns about this life, prepared Mom to depart. It was an unusual form of caregiving, but important nevertheless.

With Ronald, Mom becomes quite specific. *Caregivers have got to act or react to the people in their care with love and caring. They are called carers and that is what they must be doing. It is very very important—the attitude with most nurses, carers, doctors, all sorts of people—is that when people develop Alzheimer's, it is deterioration—but they don't think about the soul, the spirit, the life force within. They treat the physical.*

Elsie asks Kenna, *Who is helping who in the end? One person is offering another an opportunity to serve, to become a true human* be-*ing while helping someone who is no longer do-ing anything. That is hard work.*

She continues, *The Alzheimer's patient is teaching so much in this stillness, actually even inviting the caregiver into it. It is no secret that that is where you find God—in the stillness.*

But she reserves the most inspiring message for Ronald. *Love is the greatest thing. It has to be the sort of love that will understand people's conditions, people's situations. Barbara has a lot of love in her. She is very loving and caring. The more love you have, the stronger you will be—and if you do things with absolute love you cannot fail.* She tells Kay, *Barbara's understanding and her freedom allowed me to be. There is such a pull from some family members to stay—such grief—it makes it more difficult for a person to just freely go.*

She also seems to imply that love is an important ingredient in addressing this disease. *Things can happen and go ahead, but with love, they can really go ahead, and that can really have a breakthrough. You know, love conquers everything.*

Personally I don't see how love could have healed or minimized Mom's Alzheimer's. I just felt I bought her time. My intuitive sense kept telling me, *she's not ready yet*—so my caregiver job was to support an extension of her life until *she* decided it was time to leave. Otherwise it would have been abrupt, like a premature birth into the other world.

What I wanted was a *natural* birth into the next world. So in that sense, I suppose, love *was* an important factor. It *did* allow things to go forward.

Alzheimer's as a Disease

Here, Elsie takes us across yet another portal. Personally, I didn't ask—or expect—Mom to talk about this, which means *she* is going "off-script." I had my agenda, but apparently she had one too and they didn't entirely mesh. More specifically, I only thought to ask questions that I already had some opinions about—how she experienced Alzheimer's and her caregiving recommendations.

Consider the humor in this. Stubborn daughter that I am, I stay completely fixated on *my* questions. It never occurs to me that *Mom* might have some other topics she'd like to discuss. I never ask, "Is there anything else you'd like to add?" So I go through psychic one, psychic two, psychic three, psychic four—and still she can't crowbar her way into these tightly scripted, Barbara-directed interviews.

After two years of waiting, one last opportunity arises ... Ronald Hearn. And what does she do?

"I was watching television trying to relax," he later tells me, "and suddenly, it was like the TV was turned off. I could feel someone bringing through a whole lot of things about the other world."

Mom comes in with such force that Ronald has to stop what he's doing and write down her messages, even though his scheduled time to connect with her isn't until the next day.

Of course I know nothing of this for the next several days, as Ronald burns a CD with the information from his reading and mails it to Hannibal from his London residence.

Every day, I check the mail anxiously awaiting its delivery until one day the reinforced padded envelope arrives. I immediately tear it open, put the CD into my player and press PLAY.

Right away he describes the strange events in front of his TV. Then he diverts and takes time to describe Elsie so I can be sure it is my mother giving the information that follows. I delight in all the detail he gives, laughing at some images and being awed by others.

At last he goes back to the message, and it begins with her words, *Alzheimer's is <u>NOT</u> a disease.*

I slam my thumb on the pause button, stunned, and mutter irately and loudly so Mom would be sure to hear me, *Then what the HELL is it?*

I feel my whole book whooshing down the toilet bowl of wrong ideas. A major premise of my writing has been that we should consider telepathic communication with loved ones suffering from any mental impairment. But what if the information seems insane, crazy, and unbelievable. How could Alzheimer's NOT be a disease? Feeling a bit tremulous, I push the PLAY button and continue listening.

To my amazement, she repeats this exact precise declaration not one or two times, but SEVEN times. So it's important, I reluctantly decide, to try to understand her point of view. For the next several months I turn her message over in my head, replaying the CD several times. The other messages fit nicely with the psychic information I've already received, but this one remains enigmatic until I *really* listen.

Ronald relays Elsie's words: *The soul or spirit is normal and remains normal. It is the deterioration of the body and things that affect the blood. Things are out of balance, but the soul or life force is strong. It doesn't get older in the same sense as the body. It is the deterioration of the body in old age creating an imbalance.*

So that is Elsie's first salvo.

A couple of clues emerge. First, the brain *is* bathed in blood. If that blood is no longer as healthy, as nourishing to the brain—if it has *imbalances* in it—certainly, it seems, the brain *will* suffer.

Imagine the brain bathed in blood nurtured every day by fast food, sugary snacks, alcohol, lack of water, no exercise? The human brain, though only two percent of the body mass, receives 15-20 percent of the blood supply.

Secondly, she continues to see the soul as utterly healthy. This appears to be very important to her—the *essence* of Elsie cannot be destroyed by this disease.

She continues, *Things are bound to deteriorate with age. Life has to run its course. But there are so many wrong diets.* She gives Ronald the sense telepathically that diet, vitamins—that sort of thing—make a difference. In particular, Ronald relays, "I keep getting the feeling of *green*. A lot of greens connected with it. She doesn't seem to be saying people should eat a lot of greens but that something taken from greens will be very important."

Ironically, shortly thereafter I stumble across an article in the June 2012 issue of *Mind, Mood & Memory,* published by Massachusetts General Hospital, entitled "Green Tea May Help Conserve Cognition, Cup by Cup." *Well,* I decide, *it's green.*

In one of the innumerable studies now going on about Alzheimer's, this one finds that polyphenols called catechins in green tea are a potent antioxidant. It helps retard brain aging. Using words like "in some research," "suggests," and "may" to add cautionary notes, it reports reduced risk, slowed progression, reversed age-related loss, and repaired neuronal injury associated with aging.

Mom explains to Ronald, *The whole physical body has to carry you through life and it needs to be strong. But it deteriorates and that deterioration causes untold problems. Therefore Alzheimer's is not a disease—it is an aging process that has to be dealt with and the only way is by building up the system.*

It seems as though she is giving the word *disease* a make-over. But then the medical establishment itself has done a similar turn-around with regard to cancer, heart disease, diabetes, and obesity. In every case, evidence mounts concerning how strongly diet, exercise, and lifestyle affect these *disease* statistics unlike the AIDS *virus,* for example, which seems more intractable.

This is not to discount genetics or Mom's earlier comments that things are bound to deteriorate. It just suggests we can do certain things to slow, or possibly eliminate, the *causes* of it. But currently, virtually all medical thinking seeks a cure for Alzheimer's in much the same way pharmaceutical solutions are sought in the war on cancer.

Elsie comments, *They are not really working on the right thing in the right way. But they will get there. Alzheimer's is not a disease and the sooner it is put into the right category—that it is something quite normal in its way in so far as aging goes—the big question is how to slow the aging process.*

If Elsie had made insights about the disease only to Ronald, it might have been easy to dismiss. But she also commented—without being asked—on the disease question with both Angelita and Donna.

She shows Angelita her resistance to putting a medical label on it and then tells her, *The jury is still out on whether this disease is even hereditary.*

To Donna she explains, *Alzheimer's is a disease of the times. It is physically caused by the erosion of the brain both with over-chattering of the mind, and not taking care of the body. It is of these times because people are learning to live from the higher mind and to take care of their bodies. When that is accomplished, then people will be able to live heaven on earth without having to do it through the illness.*

I sometimes think how frustrating it must have been for Mom, on the spirit-side, to get the attention of her stubborn truculent daughter.

I hadn't asked the *one* question she desperately wanted to answer. Even when she gives clues to Angelita and Donna, I ignore them.

Given one last chance, she blasts into Ronald's peaceful evening trumpeting, *Alzheimer's is NOT a disease.*

At last she gets my attention.

Life Contract?

I don't know if I believe in life contracts, though I've heard about them often enough, especially from psychics and intuitives. First of all, what *is* a life contract? It assumes a belief in reincarnation.

It accepts that the soul comes to earth to learn lessons, and because of free will, those lessons can be chosen. Parents can be chosen, along with life tasks, special skills, difficulties, and even the mode of dying. I like to believe that if contracts and reincarnation exist, it's because the soul instinctively seeks to become more loving—it *stretches* itself towards love. I also like to believe it can take "recreational breaks"—an easy life. Perhaps that's a cosmic-level of free will.

Some souls on a fast track to soul evolution may pick particularly challenging lives so as to learn many lessons. Also reincarnation implies that if lessons have *not* been learned and the soul has misused its sacredness in past lives, it may face specific difficulties relating to those issues.

So do I believe all of this? I will say I'm a fairly practical person. Personally, I find the idea of contracts limiting—but perhaps we have some over-arching contract goals. I have noticed that my personal astrology/numerology/palmistry always identify the same basic traits—and problems—about this life. I find that strangely comforting because it makes me feel that I am cosmically noticed, recognized, recorded.

Do I believe in reincarnation? Until 2010, I would have said I liked the *idea* of it but never personally had a past life flashback. That all changed when I stepped into the Great Mosque in Cordoba, Spain in the spring of 2010.

My friend Ann and I walked in and sat down among the 500 striped pillars. Suddenly I said—completely without reason—"I've been here before." It was almost as though another voice was speaking through me.

Firmly and with absolute conviction, I continued, "But this was not my favorite spot. My favorite place was ... and here I gestured to the right. We could see nothing but more pillars.

I rose up and walked in that direction and came to the *Mihrab*—the most sacred part of any mosque because it points east to Mecca. I said, "I was a young man. I don't know if I was married or not. I don't know anything else about this life."

And for the next thirty minutes, I was not myself—but completely overcome by this past life. Nothing like that had ever happened to me before, or since, the Cordoba episode.

In the end, each of us has to decide where we stand on the mystery of life and whether contracts and reincarnation play into it at all—or are sheer nonsense.

It would have been easy to simply ignore or delete Mom's references to her own contract.

I could have said that these are the psychics overlaying information coming from Mom with their own interpretations. But in the end, I decided that *all* the information coming from Elsie had to be treated on an equal footing. I couldn't cherry pick. It's up to the reader to shift and sort—not me.

When Angelita connected with Elsie, she literally saw that Elsie had tried to completely control her situation in the first half of her life, so she experienced having no control in the second.

Here she adds, "Nothing is ever chosen *for* us—we are always the ones choosing. Alzheimer's was a byproduct of the lessons Elsie needed to learn. It was a choice."

When Donna asked Elsie why she had gotten Alzheimer's, she replied, *It was of my own choosing. Make no mistake about that. You hear talk about contracts—it was part of the contract. There was a past life when I was quite disagreeable—always negative and complaining and criticizing. I realized at some point a chemical dependence contributed to that.*

I wanted to come into this lifetime with some of the same challenges. I chose Alzheimer's because I wanted to see what it would be like to have peace of mind—to not have my mind tormented in each and every moment.

I wanted a way to be in the world but not of the world which I didn't have before when my entire life was caught up in drama and the inability to escape. I wanted a way of escaping without turning off the volume and the reality. I wanted to see what it would be like to have peace of mind. In that past life I didn't have one moment of peace of mind.

In this life, I just wanted to be able to feel there was a place I could escape to in what could be termed a good way, where I could find peace and be elevated to a higher state. I longed for that peace and disconnection from other people—but I also didn't want to be intrusive or disagreeable in this lifetime.

She concluded, *It's a different way of living peace on earth, and I understand that with the transition the earth is going through, people are going to be able to reach that peace in a different way.*

She wanted caregivers to know that, *For all persons carrying this illness, they were called to experience it at a soul level. Each and every one of them undertook it as part of what they are saying is a mission atonement lesson, or for growth, or simply the desire to have the experience. In the progression of the soul, the soul yearns to have as many experiences as possible while it is still in some form of physical life so it can feel it has lived a wealth of experiences.*

At this point she shows Donna a platter being held out where souls say, "Well, I'll do a little bit of this or that." *It is just the soul choosing the experience of Alzheimer's for whatever particular reason they have.*

There are myriad reasons but what is important is it is always the choice of the soul prior to coming into a given earth existence. She hopes that helps the caregiver to work toward a deeper understanding and degree of acceptance.

I sometimes think there are very few things we can actually control in this life—hence my questions about contracts. But perhaps death is an exception. After all, we must die of something.

Certainly programming the physical body with certain weaknesses gets things off to a start. Given a specific culture, family, belief systems, dietary lifestyle—all of these could nudge one's predestined choice along.

Yet perhaps the contract can be derailed. What if the soul learned all the lessons it could have been culled from a particular death to the point it no longer offers the soul much of a new experience? Can contracts be changed?

And in the end, all we are left with is belief. We *believe* in contracts—or not. We believe in reincarnation—or not. Beliefs are just that—beliefs. They get us through the day. Something in our psyche aligns with them or rejects them.

Personally, the only bedrock belief I hold onto is love.

Two years before I commited to writing this book, I connected with my own spirit guides, uncertain about the whole project. I pointedly asked, What do people <u>really</u> need to hear? The answer came swiftly: *It is really a tale, a story, of love, Barbara.* I shot back, Love?! I thought it was about her disease, and how we witnessed her transformation from body to spirit.

No, they replied, *it's about love because everything that happened came out of that energy.*

<u>Why</u> is it a story about love? I asked, still unconvinced.

Because, they answered, *the reader will see it growing in every direction. Your growing love for this diseased helpless person. Her love being cracked open by the illness. Hawa's love pouring into your house. And finally, all of you seeing Divine Love at work, and that death is not really death.*

That is contract enough.

BARBARA ERAKKO

Book Discussion Questions

Chronology of Elsie's Life

Acknowledgements

Website Information

Author Bio

BOOK CLUB QUESTIONS

1. Before reading *Elsie at Ebb Tide*, how would you react if you or someone you loved received a diagnosis of Alzheimer's?
2. Why do you think Barbara viewed her mother's Alzheimer's so differently?
3. Have you ever had similar thoughts or experiences with someone who has had Alzheimer's?
4. Which person in the book would you most like to meet, if you could?
5. Have you ever known about, or experienced, any form of energy healing? Would you consider trying it as a result of reading this book?
6. What do you think made Elsie so successful? What character traits did she have?
7. Do you believe psychic connection is possible with mentally compromised people? Have you ever had an intuitive sense of that with someone yourself?
8. If you or a loved one got a diagnosis of Alzheimer's, what might you do differently as a result of this book?
9. Do you think everyone's experience of Alzheimer's is the same, or were Elsie's and Barbara's experiences unique?
10. What would be one thing you'd want to take away and remember after reading *Elsie at Ebb Tide*?

Elsie Julia Elizabeth Norlund Nurmi
Life Events

July 7, 1917	Born in Duluth, Minnesota to Jennie and Hjalmar Norlund
September 1923	Starts school, Finlayson, Minnesota, unable to speak English. She lives with her Finnish grandparents on their farm.
1927	Her father Hjalmar dies in a grainery accident. Her mother is pregnant with their fourth child, Alice.
May 31, 1935	Graduates with class of 17 as valedictorian.
September, 1935	Duluth. Becomes nanny and attends Duluth Business University.
March 1936	Duluth. Works for Great Northern Candy Co; acquires stenography.
September 1936	Oyster Bay, Long Island. Works at butler's girl for Howard Caswell Smith and attends NYC Business School.
September 1937	Wall Street. Works as Mr. Smith's substitute secretary.
October 1937	Lexington Manufacturing Co. Clerical. $5/week.
February 1938	North American Accident Insurance Co. $12/week.
October 1938	Kieckhefer Container Co. $16.25/week.
August 1939	U.S. Census Bureau. $26/week.
February 12, 1940	Marries Herbert Nurmi at Warrenton, Virginia courthouse.

August 1940	Social Security Board, Bureau of Old Age. Elmira, NY $25/week.
September 1941	Panama Canal, Washington, DC. $2,430/year.
October 1942	USDA Graduate School. Course in Government Contracts.
December 8, 1942	Takoma Park, Md. Buy home. $5,850.00
August 12, 1945	First Daughter, Sandra, born. Unemployed.
July 6, 1947	Second Daughter, Barbara, born. Unemployed.
September 1949	Atlantic Coast Line Railroad Co. $3,114/year.
December 1950	U.S. State Department. Office of the Chief of Protocol, Gifts and Decorations Office. Secretary. $3,275/year
1958 - 1966	U.S. State Department. Office of the Chief of Protocol, Protocol Assistant.
1966 – 1974	U.S. State Department. Office of the Chief of Protocol, Protocol Officer in charge of delegations to: Swaziland, Iceland, Paraguay, Mauritius, Tonga, Guatemala, Philippines, Berlin, Canada, Ecuador, England, France, Brussels, Netherlands, Germany, Italy, Spain, Portugal, Colombia, Brazil, Nicaragua (among others)

January 1975	Retired after 25 years at the U.S. State Department.
January 1980	Lake Worth, FL. Move permanently. Sell Takoma Park house.
April 15, 1987	Husband Herbert dies of complications from a stroke.
July 1992	Finland. Elsie, her sister Alice, and Barbara travel throughout country.
March 31, 1994	Finnish-American Rest Home. Elsie moves into assisted living.
December 1, 1995	Alzheimer's Facility, Maryland. Elsie moves to Maryland assisted care.
August 9, 1996	Cooper Group Home. Elsie moves to three-3-bedroom assisted care unit.
October 1998	Barbara Taylor's Home. Elsie moves in with daughter.
November 1999	Barbara Riddick Group Home. Elsie moves to assisted care.
July 2000	Washington State. Elsie moves to assisted care near daughter Sandra.
October 13, 2000	Elsie dies.

Acknowledgements

Throughout the process of creating this book, I continually gave thanks to my family for being interesting. It helps the writer's craft enormously if your sister skins animals; your mother flies around on presidential aircraft, and your father believes women can achieve anything. It also helps to be both a daughter and a mother—to be accountable to the past and the future.

I never realized I lived in a unique family until I spent two solid years with them ... at my keyboard.

No matter how many articles, columns, books you have written, without good editing you can easily find yourself in a ditch. Carolyn Males, current editor of Coastal Isles magazine, has nurtured a whole cadre of women aspiring to be writers. I well remember two decades ago my transformation from amateur to serious writer. It happened when my writing was torn to pieces and I *was grateful* for the criticism. This book met its share of writing myself into a ditch, which Carolyn with good humor pointed out.

I actually can claim two editors. Pam Taylor, a member of our writing group, but also a former AP photojournalist currently working on social issue documentaries, also agreed to edit my manuscript. Neatly bookended by these two women, the manuscript had a much greater chance of success. And no manuscript should see print without a good copy editor. Deb Nicols, an avid bird watcher, turns the same keen eye on *current* uses of grammar and punctuation. I quickly learned that I could not create an entire manuscript based on em-dashes, ellipses, and commas.

This book owes a great deal of its strength to Hawa Kargbo who stepped across the threshold of my mother's and my heart. It owes its psychic integrity to Donna Edward, Ronald Hearn, Angelita Rae, Kay Wagner, and Kenna. All of them, voluntarily and of their own accord, refused payment. I always offered it. They always refused. I am humbly grateful because without them, both the reader and I would have been deprived of a tremendous source of information from my mother.

Deciding on a title very likely drove an entire circle of friends into despair. Perhaps two hundred possibilities were floated to not only Carolyn and Pam, but my dear friends Ann Strader, Anne von Lossberg, Karen Fredette, and virtually anyone having a cup of coffee with me at the wrong time. Ditto for the cover.

Brenda Beck Fischer, one of our finest Midwest artists, took a sepia-aged photo of my mother and turned it into the watercolor used on the cover for this book. In fact, this photograph always served as the goad to finding a title. The final graphic design owes its birth to many people, including Joan Atkins, Caroll Williams, and Pam Taylor. J. Barry Wright put the many ideas together.

Finding photos sent me to the basement and my aunt Alice, cousin Patty Norlund, and sister Sandy into closets, boxes, and albums. I pored over hundreds of images, many for the first time. Some were in wretched condition, but Dennis Evan of Copy Cat Photo Restoration reconstructed them.

It actually *does* take a village to make a book. A drive from Hannibal to Philadelphia with potter/artist/musician Fred Carelli allowed me to meet his daughter Lauren Dreier, who just happens to be a font specialist. She recommended PoynterGothicLight as highly readable for older eyes (mine included). Retired art teacher Pat Kern, adept in multiple mediums and techniques, created a wave image used in the dedication.

My Hannibal and Maryland friends listened endlessly to where I was in the manuscript, how it was coming, when I lost hope, when I regained it—often with a glass of wine. This includes Betty Atkins, Bob and Mary Ann Buchmeier, Sherry Bukstein, Candace and John Klemann, Michelene Mankowski, Karen Martino, Ann Nagy, and Toto Rendlen. Karen Fredette in Hot Springs, North Carolina truly became my writing buddy. As we both worked on manuscripts at the same time. I recommend her book, *Where God Is Ever Found: From Cloister to Couple, A Woman's Autumn Journey.*

Sometimes, it was the unexpected help that came one's way. I thank Candace for the word "tundra." Whenever we're in St. Louis, and someone asks where we're from, she always answers, "The tundra"—Hannibal.

Writing is a lonely task, yet also an exhilarating one. I felt as though I lived in dual worlds—one emerging from my keyboard, and the real calendar and-chore life. One writer said it's hardest to show up at the computer in the beginning because a vast wordless plain lies ahead of you. True. Until the first draft is complete, you remain unsure a book will ever emerge. After that, however, a love affair begins—one of nurturing and nudging, chopping and rewriting.

But now I am actually writing the final word—acknowledgements are the final amen of an author. So I thank each of you, those mentioned and unmentioned, who nurtured and supported me as I accompanied my mother, once again, on her journey from body to spirit.

www.ElsieAtEbbTide.com

order additional copies
discounts for book clubs
interview with author
audible portions of book available

profiles and contact information
for psychics at
www.ElsieAtEbbTide.com

and also directly as follows:

Donna Edwards: www.donnaedwards.com
Ronald Hearn: www.ronaldhearn.com
Angelita Rae: angelitarae@yahoo.com
Kay Wagner: kaylynnwagner@q.com
Kenna: www.ElsieAtEbbTide.com

Barbara Erakko

began her writing career accidentally—creating "interesting" budget requests for her library at Computer Sciences Corporation. She felt it should be compelling reading in order to keep a viable budget.

Once she left the workplace to raise her daughters, she began writing in earnest. She became a weekly columnist for *Catholic Review* published by the Catholic Diocese of Baltimore. While there, she received a National Catholic Press Association award for an article she wrote after traveling to Central America for Catholic Relief Services. Three years later, she became the columnist for *Laurel Leader*, a Maryland suburban newspaper.

Her first book, *The Lost Cord: A Storyteller's History of the Electric Car,* published by Greyden Press in 1995, chronicled the story of Bob Beaumont who mass produced a modern all-electric CitiCar in the 1970s.

Drawn to exploring the nature of silence—and America's fear of it—she entered a modern-day quiet lifestyle, exploring how one could silence one's world. *Silence: Making the Journey to Inner Quiet*, was published by Innisfree Press in 1997. Receiving positive reviews, essays were excerpted for *Utne* and *Yoga Journal*. This book focused on the different sounds and feels of silence: welcoming and terrifying, nurturing and humorous.

Reader-generated interest led to writing *Silent Dwellers: Embracing the Solitary Life*, published by Continuum Publishing Company in 1999. Answering the question of how one enters into, and sanely lives, a quiet lifestyle provided hard-earned wisdom and humor about what to do (and not do) when alone.

www.ElsieAtEbbTide.com

Made in the USA
Charleston, SC
05 December 2012